H. P. BLAVATSKY,
TIBET AND TULKU

H. P. BLAVATSKY, TIBET AND TULKU

BY

GEOFFREY A. BARBORKA

1974

THE THEOSOPHICAL PUBLISHING HOUSE

ADYAR, MADRAS 600020, INDIA

Wheaton, Illinois 60187, U.S.A.

68, Great Russell St., London W.C.I., England

© The Theosophical Publishing House, 1966

First Edition   *1966*
Reprinted   *1969*
Third Printing *1974*

ISBN   0-8356-7159-3

PRINTED IN INDIA
———————————————————————
At the Vasanta Press
The Theosophical Society, Adyar, Madras 600020

PREFACE

This work is not offered as a biography of Helena Petrovna Blavatsky. It is not intended to be one. Here is the reason: the usual procedure in a biography is to show the background, growth, development, aims and purposes which enable an individual to reach the position that is eventually shown to the world. These factors cannot be shown in the case of H. P. Blavatsky, for the simple reason that she consistently refrained from giving them. In other words, there is a hiatus between the years following her marriage (July 7, 1849) up to the date of her coming to America to commence her work in the world (July 7, 1873). It is known, of course, that she was travelling, and very extensively, too, during that period. In fact, an account may be given of where she went, even though it is doubtful, at times, and perhaps not consecutive. All the same, the explanation of why she did so is lacking. Obviously she had a purpose, and her quest was successful, for when she arrived at New York she was equipped in a remarkable way for the task which she accomplished. Furthermore, she was able to demonstrate some of the faculties which she had acquired.

Rather than make any attempt to show the causes which led her to follow her chosen career, instead, H. P. Blavatsky is presented in a manner which is in keeping with what she accomplished. As there is no single English word to describe the status she had attained, a Tibetan term is chosen—the word " Tulku ". Thus, it is the purpose of this work to show that H. P. Blavatsky demonstrated certain qualifications, or attainments, which are best described by the Tibetan term. So, naturally, the term is fully described and the reason for its use is given in the Introductory chapter (consequently there is no need to describe it in the Preface).

Because of the hiatus that has been mentioned, it may be truthfully remarked that it is not possible to provide a complete biography. Anyone who has attempted to follow H. P. Blavatsky's career from a biographical point of view will sooner or later come to the conclusion that the attempt to do so is not feasible. In spite of this situation, it was deemed advisable to supply a biographical survey, using the material that is available. This has been provided in the first chapter.

The writer realizes that he is laboring under a distinct disadvantage, in that he is not able to give any personal testimony in support of his declared object. Nor can any personal account be given of the land which is referred to in the title. Therefore, it becomes necessary to rely upon the words of others. While personal observation does give weight to the narrative, nevertheless, such testimony is not altogether conclusive when other facts are to be considered. In this instance there are the writings of H. P. Blavatsky herself to turn to, and these are utilized to the greatest extent. Hence citations are necessary, and these are copiously supplied. Yet, in this type of work it should not be a drawback; instead, it may be regarded as the most satisfactory method of achieving the purpose intended. For it may be determined by means of H. P. Blavatsky's own words whether or not the writer has achieved his objective, namely, that of placing her in a status meriting consideration as an exponent of Tulku. However, this idea is not one that can be judged hastily. It is suggested that judgment be reserved until the full testimony is evaluated, as provided by the sequence that is presented.

Albeit, a definite stand is taken: that a new presentation of H. P. Blavatsky is a long needed requisite. It is especially necessary in view of the calumnies that are circulated in the public press from time to time. Altogether too many attacks have been made against H. P. Blavatsky, villifying her personally. The reason for this is so obvious: besmirch the name of the person who brought the teachings of the Ancient Wisdom to the western world and people will not xeamine the message that she brought. By creating clamor and confusion, people will not know which way to turn. Where there is sufficient smoke, the flame of Truth will be obscured. People who are confused cannot reason clearly. They are unable to judge between what is true and what is false. It is the old story: truth can never overtake a falsehood which has been deliberately circulated.

Instead of striving to counteract misrepresentation, it is preferred to present H. P. Blavatsky in an unsullied role: as a Torchbearer; as a member of a noble band; as belonging to a Brotherhood of dedicated Helpers, pledged to serve selflessly and without thought of recompense. Their reward (if it may be so regarded, although it certainly is not so looked upon by those who have earned the right to display their knowledge) is that they are equipped with capabilities which enable them to demonstrate a knowledge of the use of hidden laws in Nature. Yet, that very fact caused a most harmful repercussion upon H. P. Blavatsky. For although she demonstrated the ability to use "powers"—which were considered impossible of achievement by men reared in the West— her utilization of them seemed but to incite the observers the more to denigrate her achievement.

Indeed, it is high time that H. P. Blavatsky should be placed before the world in a manner befitting her capabilities. Therefore, by declaring that she manifested the characteristics of a Tulku, she is at once portrayed in a superior status—for the reason that the performance of Tulku requires the use of the higher Siddhis. Moreover, this does not nullify the fact that she was likewise able to utilize lower Siddhis in the demonstration of her phenomena, so often mentioned in connection with her.

But, it may be asked, why place H. P. Blavatsky in this category? Why not regard her in the manner that other biographers have described her? For the simple reason: they have not been able to portray her befittingly, or even designate a proper status for her. Realizing their inability, they left the matter unsolved by declaring that she was a "mystery"—and let it go at that. To illustrate the point by an instance. Colonel Olcott, H. P. Blavatsky's closest associate, sought to portray her in a befitting role, and came close to describing her in the status here employed. However, because of submitting alternative speculations, which were incompatible, and by falling back on the "mystery", he only confused the issue and thus defeated his own efforts.

It is understandable, of course, that a comment such as this one may be made: Who in the West will understand the statement that H. P. Blavatsky was a Tulku? The term is practically unknown. Why bring forward something which is foreign to the Western mode of thought?

In answer: while Western thought may be baffled by the ideas which are associated with Tulku, such is not the case in the Orient, where the idea is a familiar one, especially in Tibet. Hence, by including Tibet in the title of the work, an immediate clue is given where one's thought should be directed, in order to gain an understanding of the term and all that is associated with it. By gaining an understanding of what the term Tulku means in Tibet, assistance will be given in the exposition of the word—which, it should be taken for granted, is also the purpose of this work.

In a work of this nature, where the testimony must be gathered from whatever sources that are available, a great deal of research is involved. The process is both laborious and tedious. Examination of passages requires patience. Search must be made even when there is little likelihood of finding desired data. As well as being arduos, it becomes very frustrating at times. All the same the writer is not hesitant in acknowledging his indebtedness to the sources from which his information has been gathered, and deems it a privilege to mention the books which have been consulted in this quest.

Before doing so, however, mention must be made of a singular situation. Heretofore, anyone desiring to write an account of H. P. Blavatsky's life has had to rely upon the information passed on to posterity by means of A. P. Sinnett—principally through his book entitled *Incidents in* *the Life of Madame Blavatsky.* He mentions the fact that " The first edition of this book published in 1886, was issued during Madame Blavatsky's lifetime as an indirect protest against the cruel and slanderous attack on her embodied in the Report to the Committee of the Psychical Research Society appointed to investigate the phenomena connected with the Theosophical Society." * Since Mr. Sinnett obtained his information for his biography from H. P. Blavatsky herself, it has been customary to regard his account as authoritative. However, nowadays we may examine the letters which formed the basis for his book and evaluate them. That is to say, a good portion of the material which he used may be found recorded in the volume entitled *Letters of H. P. Blavatsky to A. P. Sinnett.* Many of these letters were written forty or more years after the events had taken place, when H. P. Blavatsky was undergoing severe trials and tribulations. She even wrote to Mr. Sinnett—in the very letter which gave most information to him:

" To tell you about America! Why goodness me I may as well try to tell you about a series of dreams I had in my childhood. Ask me to tell you now, under danger and peril of being immediately hung if I gave incorrect information—what I was doing and where I went from 1873 July when I arrived in America, to the moment we formed T.S., and I am sure to forget the half and tell you wrong the other half. What's the use asking or expecting anything like that from a brain like mine! Everything is hazy, everything confused and mixed. . . ." (*The Letters of H. P. Blavatsky to A. P. Sinnett,* p. 150).

In addition to the Letters contained in this volume (just cited), new material is available. It is stated to be " new " here, since no one in the West (at least so it would seem) has had access to it. It is material in book

---

* Author's Preface to the Second Edition, p. 5, published 1913 by the Theosophical Publishing Society.

form recorded by members of H. P. Blavatsky's family, which gives details about her which have not been published in any biographical account of her. This material consists of two books: (1) the personal account of H. P. Blavatsky's maternal grand-father, Andrey Mihailovich de Fadeyev, written in Russian, under the title *Vospominaniya*—1790-1867, signifying "Reminiscences" (for the years mentioned), in which an account of the doings of his family was recorded; likewise the various official positions which he held were duly noted. (2) An account written by H. P. Blavatsky's younger sister, Vera de Zhelihovsky, entitled *Moya otrochestvo*. This may be rendered "My Adolescence". In it Vera gives a month to month account of the events occurring to her and to her family in that period of her life. It is, of course, full of references to her elder sister, Helena.

This material has been carefully scrutinized by Boris de Zirkoff—known in Theosophical circles for his splendid work in connection with the publication of his great-aunt's writings, first under the title of *The Complete Works of H. P. Blavatsky*, recorded in Volumes I to IV respectively of the series, and continued in the volumes *H. P. Blavatsky: Collected Writings* (Volumes V—X), Volumes VII, VIII, IX and X having been produced by the publishers of the present work, namely The Theosophical Publishing House, Adyar, Madras, India. On learning of the endeavours of the author in the preparation of this work, the compiler of H. P. B.'s works graciously made his translated memoranda available to the author for inclusion herein.

This "new material" uncovers evidence that some of the data concerning H. P. Blavatsky given in *Incidents in the Life of Madame Blavatsky*, and repeated in all subsequent biographical accounts, could not have taken place in the years assigned to them by Mr. Sinnett. Two instances stand out pre-eminently; the first one especially giving a wrong impression regarding H. P. Blavatsky from the worldly point of view. Following the lead which she jotted down for him, Mr. Sinnett published the information about her marriage, that it was in the nature of a mismatch—because she was wedded to an " old man ". In addition, a wrong date was given.

As a matter of fact, State Official Nikifor Blavatsky was only forty years of age—which certainly does not entitle him to be dubbed " old " (which in ordinary language signifies a doddering and aged individual). Then, in regard to the date of the marriage it took place in 1849, not 1848. This would make her almost eighteen, instead of almost seventeen, and the age of eighteen is usually regarded as the coming of age of a maiden.

The second instance is of particular interest to Theosophists, concerning, as it does, the date on which she first met her Teacher, and her journeys to England. In the same letter to Mr. Sinnett which was cited, there occurs this rather emphatic statement: " I was in London and France with Father in '44 not 1851 " (L.B.S. p. 150). But a few lines later on, in the same letter, H.P.B. wrote: " In 1845 father brought me to London to take a few lessons of music " (L.B.S. p. 150).

Already a change in the year! However, according to her sister, Vera, the sisters were living with their grand-parents in Saratov in 1844 and 1845. Furthermore, Vera writes that in her eleventh year—which would be 1845-46—their father paid them a long postponed visit. As they had not seen him for three years he was con-sidereably altered in appearance. The conclusive proof that the journey to London *did* occur in 1851 (not 1844) is brought to light by a written note made by Helena herself at the time of its actual occurrence, in 1851, when (as she wrote) she was twenty years old. (This is fully covered in the Biographical Survey in Chapter I.)

Is it not more logical to accept a written document made at the time that it happened that a statement made from memory some thirty-odd years after the event had taken place?

This factor, too, should be taken into consideration. After commencing public work in connection with The Theosophical Society, H. P. Blavatsky was subjected to vilification and calumny. She was loath, therefore, to give out any precise information about herself. When prodded by the former editorial writer to give him information so that he might publish it in her defence she finally jotted down some items about herself. These were gathered together and used by Mr. Sinnett in his biographical account. Because of H.P.B.'s overwrought condition prevailing at the time the memoranda were written, some of the incidents were inaccurate and consequently tended to give a wrong impression.

The question is bound to be raised: Well, then, how are we going to judge the accuracy of any of the biographical dates in connection with H. P. Blavatsky? The answer: By comparing the items with other known factors, such as historical events, as well as by data provided by members of her family, and further by information supplied by individuals who were closely connected with H. P. Blavatsky. When this is done a far more accurate record is available than that which is supplied from one's memory alone. Everyone knows how the memory can play tricks upon a person. Ask a voter on what date he first voted in an election. It is not likely that a man of sixty can remember such an event, unless it was written down at the time of its occurrence. Of course a person may respond: " When I was twenty-one." But that is not a reliable record. Especially if it should be determined that there was no election in the year when the individual attained majority.

It is because of the assistance provided by Boris de Zirkoff, as already intimated, that a better and clearer understanding was obtained of the complex situation to be met with in following the career of H. P. Blavatsky. Since words of acknowledgment are fitting in a Preface, therefore the writer takes the opportunity of expressing his thanks and indebtedness to the one who gave him assistance. In the first place, interest and enthusiasm was shown in this work when it was in its formative stages. Then, the *Collected Writings* series proved to be invaluable, not only as source material, but in a saving of time and labor. Furthermore, aid was provided in locating obscure data, which alone could be provided by one who

had worked along similar lines of endeavour, in addition
to research and probing for material.

Concerning the material that has been consulted, the
writer expresses his indebtedness to the literary works
which will be enumerated. Due credit is given to all
passages which have been cited. That more works on
Tibet are not mentioned is simply because books on that
country are not plentiful. It is understandable that a
great deal more could have been included with regard to
the land of Tibet. Yet, because of the changes which
are taking place in that country it was deemed advisable
not to devote too much space to conditions as they had
existed prior to the changed status—for the obvious reason
that it would no longer be applicable. Although that
which is supplied with reference to Tulku necessarily
must apply to the historical period, that is to say, from
the period commencing with the passing of Tsong-Kha-pa
(1419 A.D.) to 1940 (the date of the enthronement of the
present Dalai Lama of Tibet).

Of great importance in this work are the citations
employed from the volumes entitled *The Mahatma Letters
to A. P. Sinnett* and *The Letters of H. P. Blavatsky to A. P.
Sinnett*. The owners of the copyright to these volumes—
the trustees of the Mahatma Letters Trust—graciously
granted the writer permission to quote from these books.
They wish it understood that the citations are made from
the Section Edition of the first named work, in view of the
fact that a new revision has been published—the third
edition—under their supervision, by the publishers of the
present work, namely The Theosophical Publishing
House, Adyar, Madras, India.

In the enumeration of works consulted, prior consider-
ation is given to those wirtten by H. P. Blavatsky herself:
*Isis Unveiled; The Secret Doctrine; The Key to Theosophy;
The Voice of the Silence;* and her posthumous publications:
*The Complete Works of H. P. Blavatsky; The Collected Writings
of H. P. Blavatsky; From The Caves and Jungles of
Hindostan* (translated by Vera Johnston).

Works on or about H. P. Blavatsky: *Incidents in the Life
of Madame Blavatsky*, by A. P. Sinnett; *The Occult World,*

by A. P. Sinnett; *Old Diary Leaves,* by Colonel Henry S. Olcott; *Personal Memoirs of H. P. Blavatsky,* by Mary K. Neff; *Reminiscences of H. P. Blavatsky and The Secret Doctrine,* by the Countess Constance Wachtmeister; *The Real H. P. Blavatsky,* by William Kingsland; *H. P. Blavatsky and the Theosophical Movement,* by Charles J. Ryan; *Some Unpublished Letters of Helena Petrovna Blavatsky,* by Eugene Rollin Corson; *How Theosophy Came to Australia and New Zealand,* by Mary K. Neff; *H. P. Blavatsky Speaks,* and *Letters of the Masters of Wisdom*—both prepared by C. Jinarājadāsa; *The Path* Magazine, edited by William Q. Judge.

Works on Tibet were consulted as follows: *Lamaism,* by L. A. Waddell; *The Buddhism of Tibet,* by L. A. Waddell; *Tibet, Past and Present,* by Sir Charles Bell; *The People of Tibet,* by Sir Charles Bell; *The Religion of Tibet,* by Sir Charles Bell; *An Account of an Embassy to the Court of the Teshoo Lama in Tibet,* by Captain Samuel Turner; *Peaks and Lamas,* by Marco Pallis; *Beyond the High Himalayas,* by William O. Douglas; *Seven Years in Tibet,* by Heinrich Harrar; *Tibet's Great Yogi Milarepa,* by W. Y. Evans-Wentz; *Tibetan Yoga and Secret Doctrines,* by W. Y. Evans-Wentz.

Whereas search was made in these works for corroborative material on Tulku, as well as for information, this does not necessarily imply that material has been used from all these volumes. When citations are used their source is always indicated.

Finally, the authority for Tibetan orthography: *A Tibetan-English Dictionary,* by H. A. Jäschke; and *Tibetan Grammar,* by H. A. Jäschke. In a work of this nature the two volumes just mentioned are indispensable, and the writer does not hesitate to acknowledge his indebtedness to them, inasmuch as information on Tibetan orthography is very infrequently referred to; and a great many difficulties are encountered when laboring in this field.

Special mention should be made and thanks given to those who rendered assistance in providing specific items requested: to Mr. and Mrs. Iverson L. Harris, Joy Mills, and Mary Stanley.

At this time, too, an expression of thanks is tendered to N. Sri Ram, president of The Theosophical Society, for accepting this work for publication, and for granting the use of facsimile reproductions of caligraphy from Theosophical publications. This has added greatly to the documentary evidence, as well as to the historical value. And, finally, a message of appreciation to the publishers, The Theosophical Publishing House, Adyar; especially to the manager, K. N. Ramanathan, for his assistance and co-operation in producing this work, along with his corps of workers.

In concluding this Preface it is fitting that some words should be included in the nature of a tribute to H. P. Blavatsky herself, especially so because of the author's association at Point Loma, California, with those at the Theosophical Centre there who knew H. P. Blavatsky personally, as well as contacting many Theosophists there and at the American Theosophical Headquarters at Wheaton, who reverenced her because of what she has meant to them because of having come in contact with the teachings which she brought to the western world. For that matter there are Theosophists all over the world who yearly celebrate White Lotus Day in tribute to her.

Those who study the teachings which have been written by H. P. Blavatsky cannot refrain from being impressed by the magnificent heritage which the human race has received, because of her determination to pen her message —as outlined herein—in spite of the trials and tribulations which confronted her as she continued writing her manuscripts. In our day and age we are surrounded with comforts; she was without these, having only the barest necessities. Today one has access to dictaphones, tape-recorders, and reproductive equipment of various kinds—all of which may be used to pass on the labor of copying to secretarial assistants. H. P. Blavatsky had none of these. The modern generation has little idea of the laborious task involved in the writing of all her manuscripts, amounting to thousands of pages, in pen and ink by hand. Such was H. P. B.'s task, and she toiled on alone when writing *The Secret Doctrine*, in spite of acute physical pain. Her sacrifice, devotion and suffering are an unparalleled example of achievement in her field. Yes, the word "suffering" was used; for she labored on in spite of physical pain and mental anguish bordering on torture.

The author cannot refrain from expressing the gratitude that wells within a person's heart when contemplating the heroic endeavour made by H. P. Blavatsky, amounting to sacrifice of all personal concerns, in order to act in the capacity of a transmitter of the message of the Ancient Wisdom to the western world under the name of Theosophy. Her superb devotion to her inspirers, whom she regarded as her Teachers, was maintained throughout her career. Hers was a splendid example for all who would seek to attain the status she achieved: Chelaship — the path of selfless service to humanity. Well may H. P. Blavatsky be classed among the benefactors of the human race.

Ojai, California   GEOFFREY A. BARBORKA
March, 1965

CONTENTS

2

ILLUSTRATIONS

FACSIMILES

CHAPTER I

INTRODUCTORY

One of the purposes of the present work is to call attention to the great heritage which was left to the world by H. P. Blavatsky in her writings. It is not the amount of her listed books that is the chief concern, but rather their content. Likewise, how and why they were written. Moreover, it is asserted that her writings demonstrate the fact that she had the ability to use powers which are at present latent in man.

If there is any doubt as to the authenticity of the last statement, one need only turn to her major works. It will be observed that they are studded with references to works of varied character, displaying knowledge not easily obtainable. It is not only the profusion of citations, but the manner in which they are used that is such a striking feature. Where did H. P. Blavatsky acquire the knowledge of the mere existence of the books quoted? She had only half a dozen or so books on her writing desk, no encyclopedias, was far from any university, and had no access to a library. A lifetime of study would be required to obtain the ability to evaluate and utilize the citations that are provided in her volumes—that is if one but had access to the source of this knowledge. Just imagine the time that it would require to hunt through the pages of the hundreds of books cited!

It will soon be made apparent, too, by glancing through her published works, that Mme. Blavatsky had the ability to obtain information of conditions existing in far out-of-the-way places, and this without access to any books. As an example, the description of Bamian may be used to illustrate the point. This is an isolated spot, if there ever was one. It is not on any travel route and there are no ordinary means of getting there. For information about such a remote spot in the world, a writer normally will turn to an encyclopedia. If no adequate description is available, search will be continued at a Public Library, or a specialized library perhaps, turning first to the catalog index to find whether there is such a listing in the files. If not, one may be obliged to purchase a book, hoping to find the information desired. Then the search goes on in the book itself and the taking of notes. A rather matter-of-fact proceeding, but time consuming and very exhausting. Did H. P. Blavatsky resort to such detailed research? Not at all. Without moving from her chair, she was able to describe Bamian's one-time splendor, as well as its decay. She supplied the period when the famous Chinese traveller, Hiuen-Tsang, visited the spot—in the seventh century. She cited his description of what he saw without even having a copy of his book in her hand. Amazing! Truly so, even if it were but an isolated instance. But when not one, but hundreds of citations are produced demonstrating this ability, it borders on the miraculous. It is positively fantastic— viewed from the standpoint of a writer who must diligently search for every single fact required, spending hours in running down a single item, and finding very often that his labour has been fruitless!

How did H. P. Blavatsky learn to do such a feat? She gives the clue when she states that she was taught how to do this. She contacted those who were able to demonstrate this ability, as well as far superior powers (or Siddhis, to use the Sanskrit term for such abilities). (This will be elaborated upon in a later chapter, telling how she met her teachers in Tibet and studied with them.)

However, not only is it a matter of contacting such persons and being instructed by them, one must have in addition the ability to become an exponent of the powers that are being taught—the instrument must be ready. This may be well illustrated by reference to the proficiency exhibited in the art of performing musical works on an instrument. How we marvel at the skill of a concert artist! Exhibited is not only talent, but the result of concentration, of diligent application, of study, of practice, in order to become proficient upon the instrument. Also represented is the ability of a teacher to pass on to a student the means of performing capably.

When a pupil contacts a teacher, it will not take long for the instructor to judge whether or not he will be able to impart his method to the learner. If the aspirant does not have the talent nor the willingness to study, the teacher will find it difficult to pass on his proficiency in the art of performing music, try as he may, and he does not hesitate to tell his pupil so. On the other hand, when the tutor succeeds in imparting his knowledge to his student, he will be the first one to acknowledge that his protégé already had the talent and the necessary ability within him. It only required stimulation and instruction in the art of performing.

So, it is maintained that H. P. Blavatsky had attained the ability to become an exponent of the powers which she later manifested, as well as skill in employing them. Furthermore, that she had a vehicle, or instrument, suitable for carrying out what is demanded in demonstrating the Siddhis. It is important that these factors should be borne in mind. It immediately places Mme. Blavatsky in a superior status. Moreover, it indicates that she had achieved this status through her efforts along these lines.

The powers produced by means of the use of spiritual faculties may be termed Siddhis, whereas those manifested by means of psychic faculties are designated as the lower Iddhis. Although Iddhi is the Pâli word which is equivalent to the Sanskrit Siddhi—a word derived from the verbal root *sidh*, meaning to attain—this is a definition which H. P. Blavatsky herself supplied:

" The Pâli word *Iddhis*, is the synonym of the Sanskrit *Siddhis*, or psychic faculties, the abnormal powers in man. There are two kinds of Siddhis. One group which embraces the lower, coarse, psychic and mental energies; the other is one which exacts the highest training of Spiritual powers." *

---

* *The Voice of the Silence*, page 73 (of ed. published in London, 1889).

The ability to demonstrate the employment of Tulku exemplifies the use of spiritual faculties in a highly conscious manner. Therefore, this in itself immediately places the exponent of Tulku in a superior status.

But why should H. P. Blavatsky's name be coupled with Tibet and Tulku? The reason for the inclusion of Tibet is easily explained. It is this. For centuries individuals who have been exponents of Tulku have been known in Tibet. The rulers of the land have been recognized as demonstrating the functioning of Tulku. While it might be possible to play upon the credulity of the populace, so that they would regard their king as a god-like ruler, possessing supra-normal attributes, this in reality has little bearing upon the matter, for this reason: the selection of the sovereign is made by a conclave of dignitaries of the religious hierarchy. The ruler is chosen because he is credited with being an exponent of Tulku. Then, too, at a certain stage, before final investiture, the one chosen for the office of supreme ruler is obliged to undergo a test in regard to his knowledge, ability and proficiency in expounding the canonical scriptures of Buddhism, by those versed in the Canon. Solely a person displaying superior intellectual as well as spiritual qualities would be able to qualify for the position. Moreover, the superior abbots of the hierarchy in Tibet are not deceived by claims of Tulku, for the reason that they themselves are credited with the ability of performing Tulku.

What then is Tulku? And why is it unknown in the West? Why is it associated only with Tibet?

Tulku is a Tibetan word and it describes one of the Siddhis. Its use is a closely guarded secret. For that matter Tibet itself has rigorously excluded all foreigners from entering its domain for centuries. Tulku has been employed in Tibet during past eras and there are exponents of it in present times. There is no single English word to describe it. "Transference", may be suggested as giving a meaning in a single word, but obviously that is inadequate. For the mind will immediately query: Transference of what?

In order to explain Tulku, then, it is necessary to bring forward ideas which are foreign to Western culture and civilization. Consequently a mist of disbelief will most likely arise in a mind reared in the West. This not only fogs the understanding, but it prevents new ideas from being accepted. Of necessity, then, one must turn to the Orient in order to point to an exposition of the functioning of Tulku. Moreover, the explanation of the subject, as well as its importance, concerns itself not so much with the actual meaning of the word, but rather with the significance of the demonstration of what the term implies. For this reason, again, Tibet must be included, as well as the supreme Lamas of the land. (The supreme Lamas are the Dalai Lama and the Tashi Lama.)

Of course, there is a popular idea current in Tibet regarding the word Tulku, and those who have been to the land repeat the belief without understanding what it means. Thus they declare that the Tibetans look upon the Dalai Lama as an Incarnation of a Living Buddha. In fact, they go on to say that the present Dalai Lama of Tibet is regarded as the fourteenth Incarnation. The basis for this popular belief will be duly considered in a following chapter, while the philosophical exposition will be reserved for the conclusion of this work.

H. P. Blavatsky's name is associated with Tulku, because it is asserted that she represented phases closely similar to Tulku, or that she demonstrated the qualifications of performing Tulku, or, again, that at times she exhibited the functioning of Tulku—all of which comes to the same thing as declaring that she represented a Tulku. By regarding H. P. Blavatsky in this manner, moreover, it establishes her in a status in keeping with her qualifications, and aids in forming a basis for understanding the mystery that seemed to swirl around her. Furthermore, because of this definition, it should be borne in mind that the association with Tulku does not have reference to other capabilities which she possessed, that is to say, such as the ability which she demonstrated of producing phenomena, usually referred to as the possession of psychic powers. Consequently, it would be entirely

erroneous even to suggest that anyone who displays
excellent psychic powers, or clairvoyance, or clairaudience,
would straightway be entitled to be regarded as a Tulku.
This should be made clear at the outset and stressed with
clarity and conviction. In other words, the ability to
perform phenomena and manifest psychic powers does
not represent the qualifications of Tulku.

An illustrative example will assist in making this statement clearer. In Tibet those who are classed as Tulkus
(that is to say, those who are regarded as exponents of
the art) are not associated with possessing what are termed
psychic powers. Nevertheless, this statement does not
imply that they do not possess the ability to utilize
Siddhis, or powers which are at present unknown to the
vast majority of people.

BIOGRAPHICAL SURVEY

It was deemed advisable to present a biographical
survey of Mme. Blavatsky in the opening chapter, even
though it is not the intention to follow the pattern usually
undertaken in a biography. Her career was so extraordinary that alone the recounting of it by means of a
summary of dates should be sufficient to capture the interest
of a person, and make one desirous of learning more about
this remarkable woman.

It will be seen that H. P. Blavatsky's travels were of
staggering proportions. No attempt has been made to
enlarge upon them or recount the incidents that must
have happened on these journeys. It should be borne
in mind that they were undertaken in an era in which
every journey was difficult of accomplishment. The
record makes no mention of the primitive conveyances
and hazardous nature of the trips, many embarked upon
without any accommodations arranged for, and landing
in out-of-the-way places, where conveniences for travellers
were unknown. Her childhood years were eventful
enough and full of journeyings, but no sooner had she
freed herself from marital ties than she set out travelling

in earnest, evidently moved by an adventurous spirit, having no thought of danger to herself; her enthusiasm carried everything before her.

A biography naturally commences with a birth-date, and, remarkable to relate, this was considered to be unique in Russia—occurring on the traditionally auspicious date of July 30-31. Immediately a controversy arises: are we to regard the birth-date in the manner that Russian folk-lore viewed the date (since Helena was born in Russia and the calendar then in use is now considered to be outmoded), or are we to use the date which the rest of the world was employing at the time, and also uses today? After weighing the pros and cons it is considered advantageous to give both dates.

1831—Helena Petrovna Blavatsky was born at Ekaterinoslav, Ukraine, Russia, on August 11-12, 1831, according to the present mode of reckoning the calendar—although in her day it was recorded as July 30-31 (since the old Russian style of calendar was then in vogue). Her father, a military man, Peter Alexeyevich von Hahn,* was a captain at the time of her birth and was later promoted to the rank of Colonel. Her mother, Helena Andreyevna,

---

* A captain in the horse-artillery of the Russian army, and absent in Poland in connection with the Russian-Polish War (lasting until September, 1831) at the time of Helena's birth. An epidemic of cholera had swept over Russia and it is believed that Helena was born prematurely. Capt. von Hahn (1798-1873) was the son of Lieutenant-General Alexis Gustavovich Hahn (pronounced *Gan* in Russian—since an initial " h " is seldom if ever used) and Countess Elizabeth Maksimovna von Pröbsen. Vera (Helena's younger sister) maintained that Helena inherited her vivaciousness from this grandmother along with her curly hair. One of Capt. von Hahn's brothers, Ivan Alexeyevich, was Postmaster-General at St. Petersburg. Lieut.-Gen. von Hahn was descended from an old Mecklenburg family, the Counts von Rottenstern-Hahn, one branch of which had emigrated from Germany to Russia about a century before his time.

nèe de Fadeyev, * was renowned in Russia as a novelist, but died in 1842. On her maternal side, Helena was the granddaughter of Privy Councillor Andrey Mihailovich de Fadeyev † and Princess Helena Pavlovna Dolgorukov. It was these grandparents who supervised Helena's education at Saratov and Tiflis in the Caucasus, following the death of her mother.

---

* Helena Andreyevna (1814-1842) born Jan. 23 (11 old style) near the village of Rzhishchevo (province of Kiev) was the eldest daughter of Andrey Mihailovich de Fadeyev (1789-1867) and Helena Pavlovna, née Princess Dolgorukova (1787-1860). This princess was a very talented woman. Among her accomplishments may be listed that she was an exceptional botanist, a linguist, an artist, well versed in natural sciences, history, archaeology and numismatics. She corresponded with Russian as well as foreign scientists of her day. Her daughter was reared in a highly cultural manner and was entirely unsuited to Capt. von Hahn, both in temperament and outlook as well as his mode of life as a military man. Helena Andreyevna found solace in her writing, her first book, a novel named *The Ideal*, was published when she was but 23 years of age, under the name of Zeneida R——va. This work was followed by: *Utballa; Jelalu'd-din; Theophania Abbiadjio; Medallion; Lubonka; Lozha v Odesskoy opere* (A Box at the Odessa Opera); *Sud svyeta* (The World's Judgment); and *Nap rasniy dar* (A Fruitless Gift). Her Complete Works were published in 4 volumes at St. Petersburg in 1843; a second edition was published by N. F. Mertz in 1905. Byelinsky (greatest Russian literary critic) called Zeneida a " Russian George Sand".

† His " Reminiscences " (in Russian, *Vospominaniya*—1790-1867) recall a culture no longer existent and include an account of his family and the various official positions he held. They also provided the information for this compilation concerning the occasions in which his granddaughter (Helena) and her parents sojourned at his domicile. The other children of the Fadeyevs, Helena's maternal uncle and aunts were: Rostislav Andreyevich (1824-1884), a Major-General in artillery, known as a writer on subjects of military strategy; also Joint Secretary of State at the Ministry of Interior. H.P.B. occasionally referred to this uncle as Uncle Rostislav. The beloved aunt of H.P.B. was Nadyezhda Andreyevna de Fadeyev (1828-1919) who was only three years her senior. This was the aunt who received the first known Mahatma letter: it was written in French and was received in November, 1870. She was visited three times by H.P.B.'s Teacher (Mahatma Morya). Nadyezhda never married; she acted in the capacity of a member of the Council of The Theosophical Society for some years. An elder daughter was born in 1819:

The first ten years of Helena's life already indicated symptoms of a hectic career, bearing out the notoriety associated with her birth-date. These years were spent in a continuous sequence of moves: every time her father was transferred, in connection with his command of a horse artillery post, his family moved with him. In addition, her mother was in poor health, and finally succumbed to tuberculosis.

1832, Summer—Helena's father returned from Poland and settled in Romankovo (a small community in the province of Ekaterinoslav).

1833-34—Moved to Oposhnya (a small place in the province of Kiev). After several moves the family returned to Romankovo.

1834—Andrey Mihailovich de Fadeyev (Helena's maternal grandfather) became a member of the Board of Trustees for the Colonisers and moved to Odessa. Helena, with her mother, joined him at that city. It was at Odessa that Helena's sister, Vera, was born: April 29 (April 17 old style), 1835.

1835—Travelled with her parents in the Ukraine and the provinces of Tula and Kursk.

1836, Spring—Accompanied her father and his command to St. Petersburg.

1836, May or early summer—Journeyed with her grandfather and aunt to Astrakhan, even though her father had been reassigned to the Ukraine. Her grandfather had received the appointment of trustee for the Kalmuk nomadic tribes of that region.

1837, May—Moved with her mother to Zheleznovodsk (in the Caucasus) for hot water baths, in the company of her grandparents.

Katherine Andreyevna. She married Yuliy F. de Witte and was the mother of Count Serguey Yulyevich de Witte, who became Prime Minister of Russia. Sad to relate, it was Count Witte, who in his published *Memoirs*, repeated unfounded gossip and mendacious slanders about his cousin, Helena. A fourth daughter, Eudoxia Andreyevna (born 1821) was married to Ivan de Zhelihovsky.

3

1837 (late in year)—Reunited with her father who had been transferred to Poltava, at which place Helena's mother met Miss Antonya Christianovna Kühlwein. The latter became the governess of the family.

1838, Spring—Moved to Odessa, so that Helena's mother might have the benefit of mineral water treatments (her health considerably worsened).

1839, June—Miss Augusta Sophia Jeffries was engaged as an additional governess. Taught Helena English with a Yorkshire accent. (H.P.B. never got over the discomfiture which was hers when she first spoke in England " with a Yorkshire accent".)

1839, December—A. M. de Fadeyev received the appointment of Governor of the province of Saratov (on the Volga river). Helena with her mother and sister accompanied her grandfather to Saratov.

1841, Spring—Reunited with her father in the Ukraine.

1842, Spring—Transferred to Odessa (with the two governesses and her mother's physician, Dr. Vassiliy Nikolayevich Benzengr).

1842, July 6 (June 24 old style)—Death of Helena's mother.

1842, Autumn—Helena and Vera took up residence with their grandparents at Saratov.

1845,* Summer—Col. von Hahn visited his daughters at Saratov (for about a month). According to Vera's statement, she was in her eleventh year and had not seen her father for three years. He had become considerably altered by age and was not at first recognized.

1845 (latter part of year)—Helena visited an uncle in the vicinity of the Ural mountains and Semipalatinsk (along the borders of Mongolian lands). Spent the winter in and around Saratov; also early spring of 1846.

---

* This is the period (1844-45) usually assigned to a trip to France and London (following A. P. Sinnett's *Incidents*, etc.). This would be very unlikely, according to the record made by Vera for this period. Probably the trip was made in 1851 ?

1846, January—A. M. de Fadeyev appointed by the Viceroy of the Caucasus to the post of Director of the Department of State Lands in Transcaucasia.

1846, August—Helena, Vera, Leonid (a younger brother) in the company of their married aunt (Katherine A. de Witte), her husband (Yuliy F. de Witte) and two children, together with the teachers, Mme. Pecqoeur and M. Tutardo, took up their residence at a country place near the village of Pokrovskoye (on the farther side of the Volga river), the grandparents going to Tiflis, in the Caucasus.

1846-47—Returned to Saratov.

1847, May—Rejoined their grandparents at Tiflis. The journey, with appropriate stops en route, was completed by the end of June.

1847, Summer—Travelled to Borzhom, a resort on the estate of Grand Duke Mihail Nikolayevich; then to Abbas-Turman for hot baths; and on to Ahaltzih. Returned to Tiflis by the end of August.

1847-48, Winter—At Tiflis—in the Sumbatov mansion.

1848, May—Journeyed with the Wittes to Pyatigorsk and Kislovodsk for water cures. It is recorded that Helena narrowly escaped an avalanche en route, between Koyshaur and Kobi.

1848, August—Left Pyatigorsk for Elizabethtal' (a German colony); then on to Ekaterinenfeld (another water resort).

1848-49, Winter of—Residing in Tiflis, in a mansion formerly belonging to the Princess Chavchavadze. Helena was betrothed to N. V. Blavatsky.

1849, June*—Moved to Gerger, in the vicinity of Yerivan, with the Wittes and also Uncle Rostislav.

---

* This date is important in that it establishes the correct year of H.P.B.'s marriage. A further check as to the date of this event is available. Vera records that her cousin Serguey was born just prior to Helena's marriage. Her cousin, Serguey Yulyevich de Witte, the future Prime Minister of Russia, was born June 29 (June 17 old style), 1849.

1849, July 7—Married at Dzhelalogli (Kamenka) to
Nikifor Vassilyevich Blavatsky,* a 40-year old State
Official, who was appointed to the post of Vice-
Governor of the newly formed Province of Erivan on
Nov. 27 (old style), 1849.

CONCERNING H.P.B.'s MARRIAGE

The biographical account is temporarily halted for the
purpose of considering one of the phases of H.P.B.'s
career, which although one of the most obvious in so far
as the world is concerned—in that the marriage of Helena

---

* Nikifor Vassilyevich Blavatsky was born in 1809 of parents who
were members of the landed gentry in the Province of Poltava in
the Ukraine of southwestern Russia. After attending the Poltava
Gymnasium for the Gentry, he became a clerk in the Office of the
Civil Governor of Poltava in 1823. He was transferred to Georgia,
Caucasus, in 1813, continuing service as a clerk. In 1830 he served
for some months on the Staff of the Commander in Chief, Field-
marshal Count Paskevich-Yerivansky, and until 1835 was Assistant
Journalist in that Office. From that post he entered the Office of
the Commissary of the Active Army, and in 1839 was transferred to
the Office of the Civil Government of Transcaucasia. In the following year he became Inspector of the Police at Shemaha. His next
assignment was Head of various *uyezds* in the Caucasus (1842-43).
After a short residence in Persia, Blavatsky was appointed Vice-
Governor of the new-formed Province of Yerivan' on November 27,
1849, governing it during the absence of the Military Governor.
In 1857 he was temporarily appointed on an International Committee
to investigate controversial issues concerning the frontiers. In the
summer of 1860 he was given a two months leave of absence and
went to Berlin for treatments, which he also continued during the
following summer.

Vice-Governor Blavatsky resigned his post on November 19, 1860;
nevertheless, he was assigned to the Central Administration Office
of the Viceroy. His resignation from all positions was accepted in
December of 1864, and he retired to a small estate in the Province
of Poltava. In a contemporary document he stated that he was
still married. (Cf. *Service Record* drawn up in 1864, in the Central
State Historical Archives of the U.S.S.R.) The date of his death
has not been ascertained.

von Hahn to Nikifor Vassilyevich Blavatsky was duly witnessed—is not at all intelligible in regard to the whys and wherefores of the event.

It is quite transparent that although the marital ceremony was accomplished on the date specified, the marriage was solely in name, in view of the fact that Helena vanished from the husband's home within three months of the formal event, and would have done so sooner except for the fact that she was prevented from doing so because of the armed guard which was placed about her by an irate husband. Even while the couple were travelling to the Blavatsky domicile, Helena endeavored to escape from her matrimonial ties, without success. Because of this her husband placed a strong guard about Helena, under the leadership of a Kurd tribal chief named Safar Ali Bek Ibrahim Bek Ogli. Helena used to go horseback riding with this Kurd chieftain. On one occasion the young horsewoman, who could ride bare-back, thought she had won the tribal chief over to her way of thinking, and they rode off together. But, to her dismay, she discovered that her bodyguard had forewarned his master and had foiled Helena's plan for making good her escape.

Strangely enough, there is some confusion in regard to the date of the marriage. Most biographies, following A. P. Sinnett's Memoirs—which he later entitled and published under the name *Incidents in the Life of Madame Blavatsky*—give the marriage as taking place in 1848. But this does not tally with her sister's month to month account of events as recorded in Vera's book, *Moyo otrochestvo* (rendered *My Adolescence*), which forms the basis for this record, along with her grandfather's *Reminiscences*. These are unquestionably the best accounts available. This would make Helena almost 18 at the time of her marriage—although still 17 (as mentioned by her Aunt Nadyezhda).

Then, too, the biographies repeat what Mr. Sinnett's *Incidents* relates regarding Helena's engagement and marriage to State Officer Blavatsky. Here is the story as there narrated. It was said that Helena had become engaged to " old Blavatsky " * (who was not really an old man—only 40) to prove to her governess that she was not so ill-tempered and mean-dispositioned as Miss Jeffries declared her to be, and that no man would have her as a wife. It is likely that there was no truth in the story. H.P.B. later hinted—in a letter to her friend Prince Dondukov-Korsakov—that there were other reasons, which, however, she did not fully divulge. Be that as it may, she probably also had formed the idea that she would have had more freedom by being married than by remaining single. This was quite likely true of Russian noblewomen in her day—after whom she patterned her life, perhaps unconsciously: as, for instance, she took up smoking, quite prevalent among the noblewomen of that era, although frowned upon in England and America. So, Helena immediately became freed from the restraints of her family circle and the over-seeing governesses, only to find an even more distasteful situation: she was guarded over by a watchful, if not jealous husband, who had doubtless been entranced by the attention that had been bestowed upon him by the young noblewoman.

However, there is another side to the story, as just hinted above. This is to be found in a biographical sketch of Mme. Blavatsky, written by Madame Helena Fyodorovna Pissarev for the Russian public, entitled

---

* William Kingsland in his biography *The Real H. P. Blavatsky* stretches the bridegroom's age to " at least three times her age ". As a matter of fact his age was just a little over twice that of the bride's. Civil Councillor (*Statskiy Sovetnik*) Blavatsky, writes Mr. Kingsland, " appears to have tried to get a divorce after she left him, on the ground that the marriage had never been consummated, but Russian law at that time was very strict in the matter and the attempt failed ". (*Op. cit.*, p. 38)

Incidentally, Mr. Kingsland, who knew Mme. Blavatsky well, relates this anecdote: " I well remember on one occasion, on a visit by her to my house in London in 1889, she sat down at the piano and played Schubert's *Erlkönig*, to my great surprise and delight, as I had never even heard that she had ever been a pianist." (*Op. cit.*, p. 38)   An extraordinary feat—as H.P.B. had probably not touched a piano for sixteen years!

*Yelena Petrovna Blavatskaya,** Biografichesky ocherk (Biographical Sketch). In this sketch an account is given concerning H. P. Blavatsky's marriage which is quite different from the version given in A. P. Sinnett's biographical work. It somewhat approximates the story told by H.P.B. herself, which may be found in the work entitled *H.P.B. Speaks.* †

Mme. Pissarev asserts that the account in her book was related to her by Mme. Yermolov,‡ who was the wife of the Governor of Tiflis between the years of 1840 and 1850. All the Yermolovs were intimate friends of H.P.B.'s family, especially with the de Fadeyevs, when they were stationed in Tiflis. In addition to information derived personally from Mme. Yermolov, Mme. Pissarev was unquestionably familiar with Mme. Yermolov's "Reminiscences," which, however, are no longer extant —evidently being destroyed during the twentieth century Russian revolution. According to Mme. Yermolov, Helena was a brilliant but very fantastic girl. The following is the high-light of her narrative.

Prince Galitzin was a Mason, who had a reputation of being a magician. He often used to visit the home of the de Fadeyevs, Helena's grandparents, who supervised their grand-daughter's education when they resided in Tiflis. Prince Galitzin used to have lengthy conversations with Helena. On one occasion, following the visit of the Prince to the de Fadeyevs, Helena disappeared from the house. Mme. Yermolov asserted that this was the cause of a scandal in the province. Upon the return

---

* First published in an anthology called "Theosophical Subjects" by the Russian Theosophical Society, about 1911. A second edition, revised, was published in 1937 by the Editorial Office of the Russian Theosophical Journal *Vestnik*, Geneva, Switzerland.

† Volume II. Published by the Theosophical Publishing House, Adyar, India, 1951. In a letter to Prince Dondukov-Korsakov.

‡ Madame Mariya Grigoryevna Yermolov was married to the elder son of the famous Russian General, A. P. Yermolov, who was indeed a great military leader in his era.

of Helena, her family made haste to arrange a marriage for her. The person selected for her was Nikifor Blavatsky, who was a functionary in the Chancellery of the Governor. According to Mme. Yermolov, Helena's family were prepared that she would oppose the marriage. Imagine their astonishment to find that Helena readily consented to go along with their plan.

Basing her conclusions upon this narration of Mme. Yermolov, Mme. Pissarev opines that Helena had accepted this arrangement of marriage to State Officer Blavatsky for the express purpose of being freed from family restraint and supervision, so that she might continue with the plans that she had formulated of devoting herself to Occultism. Helena Pissarev suggests that Prince Galitzin had introduced Helena to an Occultist, who tested her psychic capacities, and gave her an address of an Occultist in Egypt. Further, that the prince had arranged for her to travel in company with another Russian lady, after she had terminated her marital ties.*

Resuming the biographical narrative:

Following the marriage ceremony, the couple left the same day for Darachichag (a word meaning "Valley of the Flowers"). The marital status was terminated within three months. In October an extensive travel program was commenced.

1849-50—Travelling with Countess Kisselev in Turkey, Greece, Egypt, France. Late in 1850 toured Europe with Countess Bagration-Muhransky and was with her in London.

1851, Summer—In London, with her father. In August met her Teacher. The sequence of travels is now interrupted in order to tell the story of how the meeting between H. P. Blavatsky and her Teacher took place.

---

* Cf. *The Theosophist*, Adyar, Vol. XXXII, No. 8, May, 1911.

THE MEETING OF H. P. BLAVATSKY WITH HER TEACHER

Theosophists are especially interested in the account of how H. P. Blavatsky met her Teacher, who is known to them as the Master Morya, or again as the Mahatma M. The story was publicized by Countess Constance Wachtmeister in her *Reminiscences of H. P. Blavatsky and " The Secret Doctrine"*. As her book has long been out of print, instead of retelling the story, the Countess' narrative is repeated in full, as it carries an authenticity which could not be conveyed in any other manner, repeating as it does an incident which occurred between herself and H. P. Blavatsky. All subsequent accounts are either repetitions or elaborations of Countess Wachtmeister's story. The basis for her account is, as will be shown, a Memorandum written by H. P. Blavatsky herself at the time of its occurrence, as is easily determined by the words themselves, which were written in a moment of elation. The message itself conveys the enthusiasm and fervor which a young person would exhibit upon having such an unusual experience. But here are the words of the Countess:

" When she was in London, in 1851, with her father, Colonel Hahn, she was one day out walking when, to her astonishment, she saw a tall Hindu in the street with some Indian princes. She immediately recognised him as the same person that she had seen in the Astral.* Her first impulse was to rush forward to speak to him, but he made her a sign not to move, and she stood as if spellbound while he passed on. The next day she went into Hyde Park for a stroll,

---

* Countess Wachtmeister added this paragraph about H.P.B. in explanation: "During her childhood she had often seen near her an Astral form, that always seemed to come in any moment of danger, and save her just at the critical point. H.P.B. had learnt to look upon this Astral form as a guardian angel, and felt that she was under His care and guidance.—*Reminiscences, etc.*, p. 56.

that she might be alone and free to think over her extraordinary adventure. Looking up, she saw the same form approaching her, and then her Master told her that he had come to London with the Indian princes on an important mission, and he was desirous of meeting her personally, as he required her co-operation in a work which he was about to undertake. He then told her how the Theosophical Society was to be formed, and that he wished her to be the founder. He gave her a slight sketch of all the troubles she would have to undergo, and also told her that she would have to spend three years in Tibet to prepare her for the important task."

There is an interesting anecdote in connection with the portrait of H.P.B. in her youth which is reproduced on the opposite page. The portrait has come to be known as "the lovely maiden". This photographic reproduction is an enlargement made by means of a special process from a printed copy which was first published in A. P. Sinnett's book entitled *Incidents in the Life of Madame Blavatsky*. That print was made from a reproduction of a medallion painting—the first published reproduction clearly showed this—which had been sent to Mr. Sinnett by H.P.B.'s aunt, Nadyejda de Fadeyev.

That Mr. Sinnett had received this portrait reproduction from Mme. de Fadeyev is authenticated by means of a statement appearing in one of the letters which he received from the Mahatma M. This letter also establishes the fact that it was this Mahatma who first visited Mme. de Fadeyev on November 7, 1870—at the time that Mme. Blavatsky was in Tibet—and delivered the very first Mahatma letter in person, according to the written statement made by Mme. de Fadeyev. Here is a paragraph from Letter No. 39 of *The Mahatma Letters to A. P. Sinnett*:

"The Odessa Old Lady—the *Nadyejda*—is quite anxious for your autograph—that of ' a great and celebrated writer '; she says she was very undisposed

"THE LOVELY MAIDEN"

H. P. BLAVATSKY IN HER YOUNG WOMANHOOD
Reproduced from *Incidents in the Life of Madame Blavatsky,*
by A. P. Sinnett, 2nd ed., London.
Theosophical Publishing Society, 1913.

to part with your letter to the General * but had to
send you a proof of her own identity. Tell her I—the
' *Khosyayin* ' † (her niece's *Khosyayin* she called me as I
went to see her thrice) gossiped the thing to you
advising you to write to her furnishing her thus with
your autograph—also send back through H.P.B. her
portraits as soon as shown to your lady, for she at
Odessa is very anxious to have them back especially
the young face. . . . That's her, as I knew her first
' the lovely maiden '. " ‡

Resuming Countess Wachtmeister's account:

" After three days' serious consideration and consultation with her father, H.P.B. decided to accept the
offer made to her and shortly afterwards left London
for India.

" In Würzburg a curious incident occurred. Madame
Fadeyev—H.P.B.'s aunt—wrote to her that she was
sending a box to the Ludwigstrasse containing what
seemed to her a lot of rubbish. The box arrived, and
to me was deputed the task of unpacking it. As I took
out one thing after another and passed them to Madame
Blavatsky, I heard her give an exclamation of delight,
and she said, ' Come and look at this which I wrote
in the year 1851, the day I saw my blessed Master ';
and there in a scrap-book in faded writing, I saw a few
lines in which H.P.B. described the above interview.
This scrap-book we still have in our possession. I copy
the lines:

" ' Nuit mémorable. Certaine nuit par un clair de
lune qui se couchait à—Ramsgate, 12 Août, 1851—
lorsque je rencontrai le Maître de mes rêves.' "

---

* The General referred to is General Rostislav Andreyevich de
Fadeyev (1824-1884), H.P.B.'s uncle.

† *Khosyayin* is Russian for a master of the house, or host; also
rendered landlord, owner, as well as employer. It is the word by
which N. de Fadeyev designated H.P.B's Teacher. Nadyejda may
also be transliterated *Nadyezhda*.

‡ *The Mahatma Letters to A. P. Sinnett*, p. 250 (Letter No. 39).

"I was in England at the time of the visit of the Indians, and remember hearing that they and their suite were a fine set of men and one of them immensely tall." *

So much for Countess Wachtmeister's account of the meeting. What a pity that she did not add the date of the visit of the Hindus to London. It would have made her narrative still more valuable with regard to the time-factor of the event.† For while H.P.B.'s notation

---

* *Reminiscences of H. P. Blavatsky and " The Secret Doctrine "* by the Countess Constance Wachtmeister (published 1893), pp. 56-58. A note was added by H.P.B. in her sketch book, written in French, reading: "Le 12 Août—c'est Juillet 31 style russe—jour de ma naissance—*vingt ans!* " In translation: "The 12th of August—that is July 31st Russian style—the day of my birth—20 *years!* "

The translation of the first message in the sketch book reads: " A memorable night. A certain night by the light of the setting moon—at Ramsgate, 12th of August, 1851—when I met the Master of my dreams."

Countess Wachtmeister in her turn added a footnote to her narrative, explaining about Ramsgate—a seaside town in Kent, England, in this manner:

"On seeing the manuscript I asked why she had written ' Ramsgate ' instead of ' London ', and H.P.B. told me that it was a blind, so that anyone casually taking up her book would not know where she had met her Master, and that her first interview with him had been in London as she had previously told me." (*Op. cit.*, p. 58)

† Countess Wachtmeister (née de Bourbel—1838-1910) spent many years in England—from her childhood until her marriage in 1863. For that matter she could have added something more to her narrative. This may be supplied by citing a passage from a letter written by H.P.B. to Judge Khandalavala (dated July 12, 1888):

"Countess Wachtmeister joined the T.S. because she recognized in the portrait of *my Master her living Master* who had saved her on several occasions, whom she saw in his *physical body* years ago when he was in England, whom she saw in his astral body a number of times, and who wrote to her from the first in the same hand-writing He uses for our Society. When she assured herself of this, she joined the T.S. at *His advice*, and now for three years or more she lives with and takes care of me . . ."

in her sketchbook is clear enough, the date does not tally with the statement about her visit to London that she herself gave to A. P. Sinnett when he was preparing his biographical sketch, later published as *Incidents in the Life of Madame Blavatsky*. This will be considered presently.

First, however, some historical factors which bear directly upon certain aspects relating to the incident, as narrated, may be brought forward, in order to clarify the time-factor, inasmuch as every effort is made to authenticate each date that is placed in this historical survey. Referring, therefore, to the group of Hindus who were present in London: it is a matter of record that the Prime Minister of Nepal, Sri Jung Bahadur Koonvar Ranajee (1816-1877) and his party left Calcutta for London on April 7, 1850. Secondly, some of the accounts describing H.P.B.'s meeting with her Teacher have intimated that Prince Jung and his party were present in London in connection with the International Exhibition, which was held in London about that time. However, the Crystal Palace, which was built for the International Exhibition, was opened on May 1, 1851, and was closed to the public on October 11, 1851. Since the Prime Minister of Nepal and his retinue left Marseilles on December 19, 1850, they evidently were not present in the British metropolis during the Exhibition.

The situation becomes more complicated when H.P.B.'s statements to A. P. Sinnett are examined. She writes:

"Visit to London? I was in London and France with Father in '44 not 1851. This latter year I was alone and lived in Cecil St. in furnished rooms at one time, then at Mivart's Hotel, but as I was with old Countess Bagration, ..." *

But according to her sister's account, Vera and Helena were living at Saratov, and their father, Colonel von Hahn visited them there for a month during the summer

---

* *The Letters of H. P. Blavatsky to A. P. Sinnett*, p. 150.

of 1845; and they had not seen him for three years. A few lines lower in the same letter above cited we read:

"In 1845 father brought me to London to take a few lessons of music. Took a few later also—from old Moscheles." *

Regarding Ignaz Moscheles (1794-1870): the Bohemian pianist although living in London during the 1830's, made his home in Leipzig in 1846, by request of his friend Felix Mendelssohn, teaching in the Conservatory. So that the piano lessons must have been taken in Leipzig. Nevertheless, this statement from the same letter to A. P. Sinnett should be taken into consideration:

"Everything is hazy, everything confused and mixed. I can hardly remember where I have been or where I have not been in India since 1880. I saw Master in my visions ever since my childhood. In the year of the first Nepaul Embassy (when?) saw and recognised him. Saw him twice. Once he came out of the crowd, then He ordered me to meet Him in Hyde Park." †

Since the Prime Minister of Nepal and his party were in London in 1850, perhaps the sentence "Saw him twice" may signify two meetings: one in 1850 as well as one in 1851?

The next point for consideration in connection with H.P.B. and her meeting with her Teacher in her own statement made public in her book which is known in the West under the title *From the Caves and Jungles of Hindostan*, where he is described under the name of Gulâb-Singh. This work first appeared as a series of articles written for the *Moskovskiya Vedomosti* ("The Moscow Chronicle"), and the statement under consideration appeared in the issue of April 29, 1880, in this manner (in English translation):

---

* *Op. cit.*, p. 150.
† *Ibid.*

"A good while ago, more than twenty-seven years, I met him in the house of a stranger in England, whither he came in the company of a certain dethroned Indian prince. Then our acquaintance was limited to two conversations; their unexpectedness, their gravity, and even severity, produced a strong impression on me. . . ." *

Twenty-seven years prior to 1880 gives the approximate date of 1853. There is on record the visit of a dethroned Indian prince in England, namely the Mahârâjâ of Lahore, Prince Dhulip Singh. This visit should not be confused with that of the Prime Minister of Nepal and his retinue which took place in 1850. The date of the dethroned Indian Prince's arrival in England was Sunday, June 15, 1854, landing at Southampton. In company with his guardian, John Login, the Mahârâjâ sailed from India on April 19, 1854 on the *SS Colombo*. It is also recorded that Prince Dhulip Singh was presented to Queen Victoria on July 1, 1854.

Having established the date of the dethroned Indian Prince's visit to England, it would seem as though the biographer's task were solved, in so far as this meeting of H.P.B. with her Teacher is concerned. It is not as simple as it would seem. A difficulty arises in establishing H.P.B.'s presence in England in July of 1854. On April 23, 1854, Emperor Nicholas I issued his Manifesto declaring a state of war between Russia and England. H.P.B.'s presence in England from April to July, 1854, would have been very embarrassing for her. Furthermore, if the rest of the passage concerning Gulâb-Singh in *From Caves and Jungles of Hindostan* were to be analysed critically, it would be most embarrassing for the biographer! The biographical survey had better be continued without further probing for data!

---

* *From the Caves and Jungles of Hindostan*, p. 256 et. seq. (p. 263, 1908 ed.)

CONTINUATION OF THE BIOGRAPHICAL SURVEY

1851, Late summer or autumn. Left London for Canada,
bent on investigating the Red Indians. H.P.B. had
become interested in them because of having read
Fennimore Cooper's novels about the American
Indians. The novelist's descriptions had evidently
captured her fancy along with her imagination.
Meeting with a band of Indians near Quebec, she
hastened to gather information about the medicine-
men from the squaws. But her investigations came
to an abrupt ending when she found that her much-
admired "friends" had vanished from her sight,
and along with them a much-prized pair of boots—
which she had great difficulty in replacing in Quebec.

1851, Late autumn (?) Decision made to look into the
Mormon community. By the time she reached
Nauvoo, Illinois, she found that what had once been
a flourishing Mormon center was no longer there.
The Mormons had fled across the Rocky Mountains,
establishing themselves in Salt Lake City, Utah,
under the leadership of Brigham Young.

1851, Winter (?) Went to New Orleans, intending to
investigate Voodooism. Before becoming too much
involved in this dark aspect of witchcraft, she was
warned by her Guardian that she was meddling with
sinister forces which had better be left strictly alone,
whereupon she left Louisiana for Texas, aiming to
go into Central America by way of Mexico.

1851-52, Winter-Spring (?) In Texas with an old Canadian
whom she knew by the name of Père Jacques. From
Texas into Mexico. From Mexico into South America—especially in Peru. In *Isis Unveiled* some of her
wanderings amid strange surroundings are described.

1852, Summer-Winter (?)—In the West Indies, with an
Englishman whom she had met in Germany about
two years prior. She discovered that he was searching in the same manner that she was. Also met
with a Hindu Chela in Mexico. The party of three
set out together in a sailing vessel, rounding the

Cape and heading for Ceylon, which they reached toward the end of 1852.

1852-53—Made an attempt to enter into Tibet from India, but was stopped by British officials and brought back to India. Went to Southern India, Singapore and Java. From Java travelled to England.

1853, Autumn—Was in England at the time of the outbreak of the Crimean War. (Turkey declared war on Russia September 26—14, old style—1853, but it was not until April 23—11, old style—1854, that Emperor Nicholas I issued his Manifesto concerning a declaration of war against England and France.) Vera mentions the fact that her sister was detained in England because of some contract. Vera also states that at one time Helena was a member of the Philharmonic Society in London.

1854, Early Summer—Possible meeting with her Teacher again in London before leaving for America.

1854, Summer—Was in New York, then Chicago. In late summer joined a caravan of emigrants travelling west in covered wagons. Crossed the Rockies and was in California.* May have visited South America again.

---

* In *Isis Unveiled*, H.P.B. mentions a singular feature of the sands of California: " In Southern California there are certain places on the sea-shore where the sand when disturbed produces a loud musical ring. It is known as the ' musical sand '." (Vol. I, p. 605)

The phenomenon of the " musical sand " is explainable in this manner. During very high tides the upper reaches of sandy beaches are washed by the waves and become as smooth as cement walks. Then when the waves recede and the upper beach remains above normal tide-levels, the hot sun beats down upon the sand. The surface of the sand then forms into a crisp, dry crust-like coating. When this is struck, either by a stick, or by one's shoes in walking— especially when scuffing—it produces " a loud musical ring ". The writer can testify to the fact that in Southern California, on the sea-shore off Point Loma, there is such a particular area along the beach. After very high tides one may produce the musical ring from this stretch of sandy beach.

4

1855-56—Left the West for the Orient. Was in Japan, where she met certain members of the Yamabushi brotherhood. Went via the Straits to India, where she travelled extensively:* also in Kashmir, Ladakh, parts of Tibet and Burma.† In Java " on orders ".

1857—Returned to Europe.

1858—In France and Germany, eventually returning to Russia, arriving at Pskov on Christmas night, to the great surprise and delight of her sister, Vera. ‡

While en route across the continent wagon trains customarily stopped at Salt Lake City in Utah. Confirmation is available in a statement from the pen of Mrs. Wells that the covered wagons, in whose company H.P.B. travelled, did certainly make a stop-over at this haven of Mormonism. Emmeline Blanche (Woodward) Wells (1828-1921), editor and publisher of *The Woman's Exponent*, Salt Lake City, states that Mme. Blavatsky had made an overnight stop with her. The editor commented further that H.P.B. was wearing heavy men's shoes as she intended to travel over rugged country. Mrs. Wells was the author of a volume of poems, *Musings and Memories* (Salt Lake City: G. Q. Cannon & Sons Co., 1896, 2nd ed.; publ. by " The Desert News ", 1915).

* These travels in India were later written up into the series known as *From the Caves and Jungles of Hindostan*—later published in book form. One incident of her travels in India is mentioned in *Isis Unveiled*, II, 622.

† Here is an anecdote from her Burma travels: " A fearful fever contracted by the writer near Rangoon, after a flood of the Irrawaddy River, was cured in a few hours by the juice of a plant called, if we mistake not, *Kukushan*, . . ." (*Isis Unveiled*, II, 621)

‡ Vera was first married to Nikolay Nikolayevich de Yahontov, who was born in 1827 and died in February, 1858, leaving her with two infant sons—Feodor (1854-1920); Rostislav (1858-1922). After his death, Vera temporarily resided with her father-in-law, General N. A. de Yahontov, at Pskov. It is not mentioned how H.P.B. learned of this change in Vera's status, but she certainly surprised her widowed sister by bursting in upon her Christmas party. Later, Vera was married to Vladimir Ivanovich de Zhelihovsky. From this marriage there were four children, one of whom died in infancy, Valerian. The second child was named after her mother's aunt, Nadyezhda (1862-1932). She was married late in life to General A. A. de Brussilov, and had no children. She died in Prague, Czechoslovakia. The third child was named Vera (1864-1923),

1859, Spring—In St. Petersburg with her father * and half-sister, Lisa (at the Hotel de Paris). From there she went to her widowed sister's estate at Rugodevo (in the Novorzhevsky district, province of Pskov). Here occurred a serious illness, in which a singular wound near her heart appeared. This was cured in a remarkable manner.

1860, Spring or Summer—Left with Vera for Tiflis to visit her grandparents: travelling for three weeks in coach and post-horses. En route stopped to visit Isidore, Metropolitan of Kiev. Lived for about a year with grandparents at the Chavchavdze mansion. During this period her grandmother (Helena Pavlovna de Fadeyev) died—August 24 (12, old style).

1861 (?)—Lived with N. V. Blavatsky for about a year in Dobrzhansky.†

1863—Left Tiflis for Zugdidi and Kutais for a while. Then returned to her grandfather's home for about another year.

1864-65—In the Caucasian region. Travelled through and lived at one time or another in Imeretia, Guriya and Mingreliya, in the virgin forests of Abhasia, and along the Black Sea Coast. For a while was in the military settlement of Ozurgety, in Mingrelia, and even bought a house there. At Ozurgety experienced both physical and psychic crises. As an outcome of the latter, she acquired complete control over her occult powers which had been manifest in her since

---

after her mother, and married Charles Johnston. She translated some of her aunt Helena's writings from the Russian, notably *From the Caves and Jungles of Hindostan.* The fourth child was named after her aunt, Helena (1873-1949) remained unmarried and also died in Prague, Czechoslovakia.

* H.P.B.'s father married a second time. His second wife was Baroness von Lange, by whom he had a daughter, Elizabeth Petrovna (1850-1908). The latter is referred to by H.P.B. as sister Lisa.

† The authority for this statement is a letter written by H.P.B. to her friend Prince Dondukov-Korsakov. (*H. P. Blavatsky Speaks*, II, 152, 156)

childhood. She remarked that "between the Blavatsky of 1845-65 and the Blavatsky of the years 1865-82 there is an *unbridgeable gulf.*" *

1865—Travelled in the Balkan states. Also in Egypt, Syria, Italy.

1865, Summer—At Petrovsk, Dhagestan, region of Caucasus.†

1865 (Autumn?)—Was in Italy.

1865-67—In Tibet.

1867, Spring—Travelling in Balkan states, Transylvania and Hungary.‡

1867 (Autumn?)—In Bologna, Italy; made a short trip to Southern Russia and returned to Italy. Was present at the battle of Mentana (Italy) and was wounded (November 2, 1867).

1868 (beginning of year)--In Florence. Then went to Antivari and on towards Belgrade stopping in the mountains ("on orders") for a while, before proceeding to Constantinople—from there on to India.

1868 (late in year)—Went to India and Tibet with her Master.

1869-70—In Tibet.

1870, November 7—H.P.B.'s aunt, Mme. Fadeyev, received the first Mahatma letter; it was delivered to her in person.

---

* *H. P. Blavatsky Speaks*, II, 58.

† *Isis Unveiled*, II, 568.

‡ A small Notebook, now in the Archives of the T.S. at Adyar, contains some travel memoranda written in French. Although undated, H.P.B. mentions one or two historical facts which provide a key to the dating of these travels. She jotted down that she was at Belgrade at the time that the Turkish garrison yielded the Fort, and that the administrator, Riza Pasha, withdrew therefrom. This occurred in April, 1867. H.P.B. then travelled by boat on the Danube, and continued journeying by means of coach between various towns of Hungary and Transylvania, mentioning Brassó, Szeben, Fehérvár, Kolozsvár, Nagyvárad, Temesvár, Belgrade, Neusatz and Essek.

1870, December—In India. Returned to Europe via Suez Canal (which was opened November 17, 1869 —her steamer being the third one to cross it), going to Cyprus and Greece.

1871, Summer—Set out for Egypt from the port of Piraeus on *SS. Eunomia*, but was shipwrecked en route. The vessel was blown up, due to the fact that it was carrying gunpowder. This occurred between the islands of Doxos and Hydra within sight of Spezzia on July 4 (June 21 old style). The Greek government offered assistance to the survivors —giving them passage to their destination. Availing herself of this assistance, H.P.B. arrived at Alexandria, Egypt.

1871, (Autumn)—1872 (spring)—In Egypt. Formed a Société Spirite in Cairo (1871) for the purpose of investigating spiritualistic phenomena, but the venture was not successful. With its collapse she left Cairo (April, 1872), travelling in Syria and Palestine. Met Countess Lydia Alexandrovna de Pashkov; went with her to El Marsum, the Libanus and Anti-Libanus. Was with the Druzes on Mount Lebanon.*

1872, Summer—Arrived In Odessa, 18 moons after the letter which was received by her aunt (November 7, 1870) promised her return to Russia.

1 8 7 3

Early in year—Left Odessa for Bucharest, Rumania, visiting Mme. Popesco.

Spring—In Paris, France, staying with her cousin, Nikolay Gustavovich von Hahn, at Rue de l'Université 11. Left abruptly " on orders ". Made the trip to America by steamer, towards the end of June, travelling steerage in order to help a lady in distress.

---

* Cf. *Isis Unveiled*, Vol. II, pp. 308-15.

July 7—Landed in New York City. Because of leaving
Paris so hastily she had not arranged for the transference of her remittance from home. In fact, her
father (Col. von Hahn) died July 27 (15 old style),
but she did not receive the message of his death
from her sister Lisa until October.

July (middle of month)—Interviewed by Anna Ballard,
veteran journalist, on staff of the *New York Sun*.

August—At 222 Madison Street, New York City—a
tenement-house, where she was visited by Elizabeth
G. K. Holt, whose friend, Miss Parker, lived in a
room next to H.P.B. (The tenement-house was an
experiment in co-operative living entered into by
about forty women workers.)

August-September—Completed the unfinished novel
Edwin Drood, which had not been concluded when
Charles Dickens died in 1870 (according to Elizabeth
Holt). Also translated into Russian the work of a
medium (by the name of James). Later offered it
to the publisher Aksakoff (October 28, 1874).

September—Moved to Henry Street, New York City.
Lived with a French-Canadian, by the name of
Mme. Magnon.

October-November—Moved to the northeast corner of
14th Street and 4th Avenue, New York City.

1 8 7 4

June 22—Articles of co-partnership entered into with
Clementine Gerebko, for the purpose of working
certain farm-lands of Northport in the County of
Suffolk, Long Island, New York, to commence
July 1, 1874.

July—Moved to Long Island, New York.

August 15—" Complaint " against her partner signed by
her attorneys, Bergen, Jacobs & Ivins.

September 9—" Complaint " as drawn up by attorneys signed by H.P.B. and verified under oath
before a Notary Public in King's County, New
York.

October—Received intimation to go to the Eddy home at Chittenden, Vermont.

October 14—Met Colonel Henry Steele Olcott, at the Eddy farm-house, who was investigating Spiritualism.

October 27—Wrote first letter to a New York newspaper —from 124 East 16th Street, New York City.

October 30—The "letter" was published as an article in *The Daily Graphic*, New York, entitled "The Eddy Manifestations". This commenced her literary career.

November 10—Wrote second letter to a New York newspaper—from 23 Irving Place, New York City. This was published in *The Daily Graphic* under the title "About Spiritualism" (Nov. 13, 1874).

November 12—Interviewed at the office of *The Daily Graphic* by a reporter.

December 3—Letter to the *Spiritual Scientist* of Boston published. First of a series of articles published in this journal. Also supported this magazine until its collapse, in the spring of 1876.

December—In Hartford, Connecticut, with Col. Olcott in connection with the publication of his book *People from the Other World*.

1 8 7 5

January—Had a fall in New York, injuring her knee.

January 4—In Philadelphia, at Mrs. Martin's, 111 Girard Street. Col. Olcott joined her there. Investigating mediums—Holmes and Dr. Child—until January 25.

February 13—Wrote letter to General Lippitt informing him of an accident to herself: in trying to move her bed, the bedstead fell on her leg seriously injuring it.

March 16—Orders received to expose Dr. Child, the medium.

March 22—Living at 3420 Sansom Street, Philadelphia.

April 2—In Boston, in connection with E. G. Brown, editor of the *Spiritual Scientist*, to whom she had sent an article.

April 12—In Philadelphia. Wrote to Gen. Lippitt on the 17th that she must go to Riverhead, Long Island, in connection with a lawsuit regarding her farm.

April 17—Luxor circular entitled " Important to Spiritualists", published in the *Spiritual Scientist*.

April 26—At Riverhead, Long Island, in connection with her lawsuit. Judgment filed in her favor on June 15, 1875.

May 1—Writes to Gen. Lippitt that she is returning to Philadelphia.

May 21—Leg considerably worsened and paralysis of the limb set in. Amputation threatened.

May 27—Notice published in *Spiritual Scientist* that two or more great " Oriental Spiritualists " have passed through New York and Boston heading for California and Japan. Identified by H.P.B. as Hilarion and Atrya.

June 30—Writes to Gen. Lippitt that her health is poor but danger is over. Though lame she must go to Boston.

July 15— " A Few Questions to ' Hiraf ' " written in Boston and published in *Spiritual Scientist*. Called by H.P.B. " my first occult shot ". Guest of Mr. and Mrs. Houghton. With Col. Olcott investigates mediumship of Mrs. Thayer.

August—Back in New York City: first at 23 Irving Place; then at 46 Irving Place. Investigating mediumship of Mrs. Young.

September 7—Formation of The Theosophical Society proposed.

September 8—Founding of The Theosophical Society at 46 Irving Place, New York City, with Col. H. S. Olcott, William Q. Judge and 14 others.

September 13—Second meeting of The Theosophical Society.

September 17—Visited the Corsons at Ithaca, New York, site of Cornell University (for three to four weeks).

October 16—Meeting of The Theosophical Society: reading of By-laws and preamble; discussion on same.

October 30—Meeting of The Theosophical Society: By-laws read, discussed and adopted; followed by election of officers.

November 17—Meeting of The Theosophical Society, at which Col. Olcott delivered his inaugural presidential address. (The Colonel decided to record this date as the " formation date ".)

December 26—" A Story of the Mystical " published in the New York *Sun*. This was followed by a series of mystical stories.

1876—Engaged in the writing of *Isis Unveiled*.

1877, September 29—Publication of *Isis Unveiled* (by J. W. Bouton, N.Y.).

1878, July 8—Became a citizen of the United States of America.

1878, December 17—Left America for India on *SS Canada*, accompanied by Henry S. Olcott and Edward Wimbridge.

1 8 7 9

January 3—Arrived in London, en route to India.

January 18—Left Liverpool for India on *SS Speke Hall*, accompanied by Col. Olcott, Mr. Wimbridge and Rosa Bates.

February 16—Arrived at Bombay, India. Settled in the native quarter of the city, at 108 Girgaum Back Road.

February 25—Alfred Percy Sinnett, Editor of *The Pioneer* (most influential Anglo-Indian newspaper in India) writes to Col. Olcott desiring to meet him and H.P.B.

April—Made trip to northern India: visiting Karli Caves (April 4th); Rajputana (April 11th); Allahabad (April 13th); also Cawnpore, Jajmow (an ancient ruined city), Bhurtpore, Jeypore, Amber, Saharanpore, Meerut.

May 7—Return journey to Bombay commenced.

July 4—Decision made to establish a monthly journal: *The Theosophist*. (Prospectus prepared July 6th.)

October—First issue of *The Theosophist* published.

November 29—Celebration of the founding of The Theosophical Society, featuring three events: the Fourth Anniversary of the Society; the founding of *The Theosophist*; the opening of the Library.

December 4-30—Visiting Mr. and Mrs. A. P. Sinnett at Allahabad, India.

1880

January 4—First formal meeting of The Theosophical Society in India, held in the Library of the Bombay Headquarters.

January 15—Word received from Russia regarding the publication of H.P.B.'s first " letter " to the Russian newspaper. " Letters " continued serially entitled " From the Caves and Jungles of Hindostan."

April 25—Bombay Branch of T.S. formed.

May 7—Embarked for Ceylon on an extended Theosophical trip.

May 25—Took Pansil, along with Col. Olcott (by formally accepting the five chief Precepts of the Buddha) thus becoming Buddhists.

May 25—Galle Branch of The Theosophical Society formed; followed by Branches at Kandy, Panadure, Bentoba, and Welitara: all in Ceylon.

July 13—Left Galle, Ceylon, for Bombay.

August 27—Left Bombay for Simla, stopping en route at Meerut.

September-October—Visiting the Sinnetts and Alan O. Hume at Simla. Correspondence with the Mahatmas commenced resulting in the publication of *The Occult World* (1881) and *Esoteric Buddhism* (1883). After Sinnett's passing the correspondence was published as *The Mahatma Letters to A. P. Sinnett* (1923).

October 21—Left Simla for Amritsar; then on to Lahore.

November—At Lahore, until Nov. 25th; then on to Cawnpore, then Allahabad.

December 11—At Benares. Visiting the Maharaja. During this visit permission was received for the T.S.

to adopt the motto of the Maharaja of Benares: "There is no Religion higher than Truth." (Taken in a slightly transposed form from the *Mahâbhârata*, Santiparva, chap. 160, stanza 24.)

December 20—At Allahabad, visiting the Sinnetts.

December 28—Left Allahabad for Bombay, arriving the 30th, and occupying a new bungalow, named "The Crow's Nest", on the slope of Breach Candy (Bombay, India).

1 8 8 1

July—Went to Simla to stay with the Humes at Rothnay Castle.

August—Simla Anglo-Indian Branch formed; known later as Simla Eclectic T.S.

October—Journeyed to Umballa, Dehra Dun, Saharanpore, Meerut, Rohilcund and Bareilly (where a Branch was formed).

November—At Allahabad with Mr. Sinnett for a few days.

1 8 8 2

February—At Poona: Poona Branch formed.

March—Travelled to Allahabad to spend a few days with the Sinnetts.

April 6—Made a trip to Calcutta, meeting Col. Olcott there. Organized the Bengal T.S.

April 19—Left Calcutta for Madras, by boat.

April 23—Arrived at Madras—by invitation of T. Subba Row.

April 30—Took a party of 17 to Tiruvellum, returning same day to Madras.

May 3—Journeyed by house-boat with Col. Olcott down the Buckingham Canal to Muttukar, then by coach to Nellore—to found the Nellore Lodge (May 8). On to Mypaud; then to Padaganjam; then travelling three days by jampans to Guntur. Returning to Nellore, the journey therefrom to Madras was completed by train.

May 31—From Madras visited the Huddlestone Gardens at Adyar. Decision made to purchase the estate and make it their permanent headquarters.

June 8—Arrived at Bombay, returning from Madras.

June 16-24—Visiting Baroda.

September—Journeyed to Sikkim in order to be with the two Mahatmas (in their "natural bodies") with whom she had not been for two years.

October 9—At Darjiling: writes to Sinnett from there (LBS. 38) after having been in Tibet, 20 or 30 miles beyond Sikkim.

October-November—At Allahabad with Sinnetts.

November 25—Returned to Bombay T.S. Headquarters from Allahabad.

December 7—7th Anniversary of T.S. celebrated at Framji Cowasji Hall. 39 Branches represented on T.S. banner.

December 16—Farewell party given by Bombay T.S.— leaving Bombay December 17th.

December 19—Arrived at Adyar, Madras, to take up residence there; transferring T. S. Headquarters from Bombay.

1883

February 11—Special meeting at Headquarters (Adyar) welcoming members of the Madras Branch.

July 7—Left Adyar for Ootacamund, staying at Major-General H. R. Morgan's home about three months. Visited primitive tribes residing in the Nilgiri Hills. Wrote *The Enigmatical Tribes of the Blue Hills* for Russian papers (Preface dated July 9). Wrote "Replies to an English F.T.S." (F. W. H. Myers) on *Esoteric Buddhism*—a lengthy series of articles for *The Theosophist*.

July—Published in *The Theosophist* article "Chelas and Lay Chelas", followed by "Gurus and Chelas" in August.

September 16—Left Ootacamund for three days' visit at Coimbatore, with Col. Olcott.

September 20—Arrived at Pondichéry.   Reception held there.

September 23—Returned to Adyar, with Col. Olcott.

October 20—Departed for Bombay, staying there with the Flynns.

October 22—Left Bombay for Adyar, stopping en route at Poona and staying with Judge N. D. Khandalawala.

October 26-27—Arrived at Adyar.

December 27-29—8th T.S. Convention celebrated at Adyar Headquarters.

1 8 8 4

February 7—Left Adyar for Kathiawar, visiting H. H. Dajiraj.

February 10—At Varel, visiting Prince Harisinghji.

February 15—Left Wadhwan for Bombay—arrived there Feb. 18.

February 20—Left Bombay on *SS Chandernagore* for a trip to Europe, accompanied by Col. Olcott, Mohini, Babula and others.

March 12—Arrived at Marseilles, France.   Met by Baron J. Spedalieri and Capt. D. A. Courmes (of the French Navy).

March 15—Journeyed to Nice—visiting Lady Caithness, Duchesse de Pomar.

March 27—Left Nice for Paris; arrived at Marseilles 9: 30 p.m.

March 28—Arrived at Paris—staying at 46 rue Notre-Dame-des-Champs.   Plans for work on *The Secret Doctrine* outlined, W. Q. Judge assisting.

April 6—Left Paris for London " on orders "—staying with Sinnetts.

April 7—Attended meeting of London Lodge (although not expected).

April 15—Returned to Paris.   Visited H. G. Atkinson at Boulogne-sur-Mer.

May 4—Attended meeting of the Société Théosophique d'Orient et d'Occident.   Reorganized (June) as a Branch of the Parent Society.

May (second week)—Invited to Enghien—Château of
Count and Countess d'Adhémar—for three weeks'
stay. Visited there by W. Q. Judge and Countess
Wachtmeister.

May (middle of month) H.P.B.'s aunt and sister arrived
at Paris to visit her—staying until June 29th.

June 19—Hermann Schmiechen begins portraits of the
Mahatmas in London, finishing them July 9th.
H.P.B. present on one occasion, also at conclusion
of painting.

June 29—Left Paris for London; staying at the home of
the Arundales, 77 Elgin Crescent, Notting Hill until
Aug. 16.

June 30—Attended meeting of S. P. R. with Sinnetts and
Col. Olcott.

July (middle of month)—Visited Cambridge with F.
Arundale and Mohini.

July 21—Attended open meeting of London Lodge at
Prince's Hall.

August 9—Attended meeting of S. P. R. at Cambridge
with Mohini.

August 16—Left London for Elberfeld, Germany, accompanied by Mohini, B. Keightley, 3 Arundales and
Mrs. Holloway—staying with Gebhards.

September—Coulomb conspiracy erupted at Adyar.

September 15—H. Schmiechen arrived at Gebhards to
paint portrait of H.P.B.

October 4-5—Left Elberfeld for London via Flushing,
with R. Gebhard and Mrs. Holloway.

October 6—Arrived in London—staying with Cooper-
Oakleys.

October 31—Left London for Liverpool and boarded SS
Clan MacCarthy, accompanied by Cooper-Oakleys en
route to Adyar via Alexandria.

November (late)—At Cairo—dined with Egypt's Prime
Minister. Also visited Bulak Museum with G.
Maspero.

December 17—Arrived at Colombo, Ceylon, with Mrs.
Cooper-Oakley and C. W. Leadbeater. Met by Col.
Olcott and Dr. Franz Hartmann.

December 21—Arrived at Adyar, Madras. Greeted by students of the Pachiappa College at Madras.

December 22—Richard Hodgson visited Adyar.

December 27—T.S. Convention at Adyar.

December—The *Russkiy Vestnik* ("Russian Messenger"), Moscow, publishes first instalment of *Enigmatical Tribes of the Blue Hills*.

December—The S. P. R., London, issues its First (Confidential) Report on Phenomena and H.P.B.

1885

January 2—Richard Hodgson at Adyar, making investigations for The Society for Psychical Research.

January 9—Receives the plan for *The Secret Doctrine* from her Master.

February 5—Gravely ill—on the point of death. Revivified by her Master.

March 31—Left Adyar, India (never to return) on the *SS Tibre* with Babaji, Dr. Franz Hartmann and Mary Flynn, for Naples.

April 23—Arrived at Naples, Italy.

April 29—At Torre del Greco (not far from Naples) at Hôtel del Vesuvio.

June-July—Remains at Torre del Greco—suffering from rheumatism.

July—Engaged in writing Second Part of *From the Caves and Jungles of Hindostan*.

July (last week)—Left Torre del Greco.

August (first week) At Rome with Babaji and Mary Flynn—at Hôtel Anglo-Américain.

August (second week) At St. Cergues, Switzerland.

August (after 12th) Arrived at Würzburg, with Babaji—occupied apartment at 6 Ludwigstrasse. Stopped at Lucerne en route.

September 1—Visited by Nadyezhda A. de Fadeyev (her aunt); also by Miss F. Arundale and Mohini.

September (late)—At Würzburg, visited by Sinnetts.

September—*Five Years of Theosophy* published (London: Reeves & Turner).

October—At Würzburg, engaged in the writing of *The Secret Doctrine*.

November (late or early December)-Countess Wachtmeister joined H.P.B. at Würzburg, to live with her until the following spring.

December—Official (Second) S. P. R. Report published in the Society's *Proceedings* (Vol. III, Part IX). Copy sent to H.P.B. by Sellin; received Dec. 31.

1886

January-February—At Würzburg writing *The Secret Doctrine*. Visited by Sinnetts (stayed 3 weeks); also by her aunt and by the Soloviovs.

March 3—Some 300 pages of foolscap of *The Secret Doctrine* finished (letter to Sinnett, *LBS*. 194-95).

April—At Würzburg; visited by Dr. Hartmann; by Kislingbury; by Gebhards.

May 8—Left Würzburg with E. Kislingbury for Elberfeld; staying with the Gebhards.

May (middle of month)—At Elberfeld. Visited by her sister and niece.

July 8—Left Elberfeld for Ostend, Belgium, via Brussels, with her sister and niece. Her address for a while: Villa Nova, 10, Boulevard Van Isgham; later 17, rue d'Ouest (in August). Working on *The Secret Doctrine*.

July—At Ostend; visited by Sinnetts. Her sister and niece left on July 14th for Russia.

August—At Ostends; visited by Mohini; by Arthur Gebhard; by Miss Bates; by Marie Gebhard   Countess Wachtmeister rejoined H.P.B.

October 5-8—At Ostend; visited by Dr. Kingsford and Edw. Maitland (they stayed for two weeks).

November-December—*Incidents in the Life of Madame Blavatsky* by A. P. Sinnett published (London: George Redway, 324 pp.).

1887

January-February—Dr. Archibald and Bertram Keightley
visit H.P.B. at Ostend; they urge her to move to
London.

March (last week) Gravely ill—from kidney infection.
Revivified by her Master (who gave her the choice
of finishing *S.D.* or dying). Dr. Ashton Ellis from
London present; also Marie Gebhard.

May 1—Left Ostend for London; residing at Maycot,
Crownhill, Upper Norwood (Mabel Collins's home).

May 19—Blavatsky Lodge organized: inaugural meeting
held at Maycot. H.P.B. one of founding members;
President G. B. Finch.

September (early) Moved to 17 Lansdowne Road, Holland Park, London, by carriage (the move supervised
by the Countess Wachtmeister).

September—Establishment of *Lucifer*, her second Theosophical monthly; designed to bring light to " the
hidden things of darkness." (First issue Sept. 15.)

September—Founding of the Theosophical Publishing Co.

November-December—Publication of " The Esoteric
Character of the Gospels " in *Lucifer*. Also an Open
Letter to the Archbishop of Canterbury.

1888, October 9—Formation of the Esoteric Section of
the T.S. (for which the *Instructions* were written).

1888, October—Publication of *The Secret Doctrine* (two
volumes of the proposed four volumes): London and
New York. As the first English edition of 500 copies
was exhausted before the date of publication, a
second edition was published in 1889.

1889, July-August—In France, at Fontainebleau; then
at St. Héliers, Jersey Island. Returned to London
middle of August.

1889—Publication of *The Key to Theosophy*. Publication
of *The Voice of the Silence*.

1890—Established the European Headquarters of The
Theosophical Society at 19 Avenue Road, St. John's
Wood, London (NW.), England.

1891, May 8—Died at 19 Ave. Rd., London, England.

5

The Founding of the Theosophical Society

The story of the founding of The Theosophical Society was related in detail by Colonel Henry S. Olcott, one of the founders of the organization, and publicized by means of a series of articles in the Society's organ, *The Theosophist*, from March 1892 till September 1894. This series was later published in book form under the title of *Old Diary Leaves*.* However, certain factors were omitted in the Colonel's account, especially the aspect dealing with H.P.B. and her Teachers who sent her specifically for the very purpose of establishing the Society in America. Since documents may be brought forward demonstrating this to be so, it is fitting in a work that is dedicated to H.P.B. that the recording of it should be included.

It is to be noted, moreover, that Col. Olcott prided himself on his journalistic ability. He had in fact been on occasions a reporter for one of the New York dailies. His account, therefore, at times takes on the idiosyncrasies of a reporter, rather than the historical aspect pertaining to a Society. This may easily be shown, simply by referring to the manner in which the Colonel narrates how the two Founders of the Theosophical Society first met—as though it were but a chance occurrence:

> "It was a very prosaic incident: I said '*Permettez moi, Madame*,' and gave her a light for her cigarette; our acquaintance began in smoke, but it stirred up a great and permanent fire." †

Nevertheless, if Col. Olcott really entertained such an opinion at the time he was writing his memoirs, such was certainly not the view held by H. P. Blavatsky, as may be seen from her forthright declaration, penned in a letter addressed to Dr. Franz Hartmann:

---

* Volume I was published by G. P. Putnam's Sons, New York and London, in 1895.

† *Op. cit.*, I, page 1.

" I was sent to America on purpose, and sent to the Eddys. There I found Olcott in love with spirits, as he became in love with the Masters later on. I was ordered to let him know that spiritual phenomena without the philosophy of occultism were dangerous and misleading. I proved to him that all that mediums could do through spirits, others could do at will without any spirits at all; that bells and thought-reading, raps and physical phenomena, could be achieved by anyone who had a faculty of acting in his physical body through the organs of his astral body; and I had the faculty ever since I was four years old, as all my family know. I could make furniture move and objects fly apparently, and my astral arms that supported them remained invisible; all this before I knew even of Masters." *

" Being sent to the Eddys " signified that H.P.B. had " received orders " (as she was wont to express it) to go to Chittenden, Vermont, to the farmhouse known as the Eddy Homestead. The reference to Olcott being " in love with spirits " meant that the Colonel was able to see, touch and even converse with phantom forms of deceased relatives, which appeared at the Eddys and were termed " spirits " in those days. His meeting with Madame Blavatsky occurred on October 14, 1874. Following their meeting the materializations appearing at the Eddy farmhouse took on an entirely different character. So remarkable were the appearances that they were truly deserving of being written up for the New York dailies. At the time, however, Colonel Olcott was quite unaware of the fact that Mme. Blavatsky was responsible for the change in the character of the materializations.

When Col. Olcott had concluded his investigations of the spiritualistic phenomena at the Eddys, he decided to have his articles which had appeared in the New York

---

* The letter was dated April 13, 1886. Cited in *Personal Memoirs of H. P. Blavatsky*, by Mary K. Neff, p. 255. (Published by E. P. Dutton & Co., Inc., New York, 1937).

Daily Graphic published in book form, choosing as his title *People from the Other World.**

In her turn Mme. Blavatsky had commenced her literary career by writing to *The Daily Graphic* concerning the happenings at the Eddy farmhouse. Her first article appeared in the issue of October 30, 1874. †

In the Spring of 1875 Colonel Olcott was desirous of continuing further investigations with mediums, and for the purpose established what he called " The Miracle Club". Although he did find one or two genuine mediums for his Club, the majority who responded to his appeals resorted to fraudulent practices, so that what he had hoped to accomplish proved fruitless and he discontinued his Miracle Club. In later years Colonel Olcott looked upon this effort as an initial attempt to organize a society, or a nucleus of people along the lines of the Theosophical Society. However, H. P. Blavatsky wrote this memorandum in regard to the Miracle Club:

" An attempt in consequence of orders received from T.B. (a Master) through P. (an Elemental) personating John King. Ordered to begin telling the public the truth about the phenomena and their mediums. And now my martyrdom will begin! I shall have all the Spiritualists against me, in addition to the Christians and the Sceptics. Thy will, oh M., be done. H.P.B." ‡

Even though this very memorandum was cited by Col. Olcott in his book, nevertheless he gave the impression that the founding of The Theosophical Society was not specifically the result of definite orders, or in accordance with a plan, for he states:

---

* This procedure occupied the winter of 1874-5. The date of the publication of his book was March 11, 1875; it was illustrated by Alfred Kappes and T. W. Williams; published by the American Publishing Co., Hartford, Connecticut.

† See *The Complete Works of H. P. Blavatsky*, Vol. I, pp. 13-16.

‡ From the Theosophical *Scrap-book*, Vol. I, quoted in *Old Diary Leaves*, p. 25. T. B. stands for Tuitit Bey of the Egyptian Brotherhood.

"This wonderful organisation, which grew out of a commonplace parlour gathering in a New York house, in the year 1875. . . ." *

When he penned this passage for his preface in 1895, at Gulistan, Ootacamund, he must have overlooked this message which H.P.B. had written in the Theosophical *Scrapbook* (now on file in the archives at Adyar):

"*Orders* received from India direct to establish a philosophico-religious Society and choose a name for it,—also to choose Olcott. July 1875." †

It was in compliance with these orders that H. P. Blavatsky commenced holding gatherings in the parlor of her suite of rooms, inviting people who were interested in travels and in Spiritualism, as well as in subjects which would be called metaphysical today. There was no doubt that she was a fascinating raconteur, entertaining her listeners with anecdotes of exciting experiences which had befallen her in her many travels.

And so the summer of 1875 went by, until a certain Tuesday in September arrived. All was in readiness. One by one the members of a group of about twenty people called at 46 Irving Place—the suite of rooms that Mme. Blavatsky was occupying in New York City. What force was drawing them together so that they should be present on that particular evening? Unquestionably they were drawn together by a bond of interest, yet most of them were hardly aware of the significance attaching to that first Tuesday in September. The members of the group knew, of course, that they would be attending an interesting lecture that evening; they had been apprised of that fact. For that matter it had even been published in the *Liberal Christian* of September 4th—a newspaper under the direction of Rev. J. H. Wiggin, a Unitarian

---

* *Old Diary Leaves*, I, page vii.
† *The Theosophist*, Vol. LIV, p. 332, December 1932.

clergyman. The lecture to be delivered by George H. Felt on the 7th of September was upon the subject of " The Lost Canon of Proportion of the Egyptians " accompanied by diagrams which the lecturer had himself prepared.

Mr. Felt's lecture created quite an impression upon the gathering; so much so that a vote of thanks was tendered to the speaker. Whereupon an animated discussion followed. Keyed up by the spirit of enthusiasm that had been evoked, an idea occurred to Colonel Olcott, so he narrates. He drew a pencil from his pocket and wrote the following message upon a scrap of paper: " Would it not be a good thine to form a society for this kind of study? " * The Colonel handed the note to Mr. William Q. Judge, who in turn passed it on to H. P. Blavatsky. She nodded assent. Whereupon Col. Olcott rose and addressed the gathering, giving voice to this idea.

Being conversant with parliamentary procedure, since he was an attorney, Mr. Judge rose and proposed a motion that Col. Olcott be elected chairman for such a society. This was carried, and in turn Col. Olcott proposed that Mr. Judge be made secretary of the meeting. This proposition was also carried.

Little mention is made of any other deliberation that first evening, although it was definitely proposed and agreed that a gathering should be held on the very next evening, Wednesday, September the 8th, 1875.

No official record is extant of the first preliminary meeting of The Theosophical Society, as here outlined. Nevertheless, an account of this first gathering was recorded by means of an announcement which was published in one of the New York daily papers. This account was preserved because of having been published in a book written by Mrs. E. H. Britten,† who was present at the gathering. This account was further publicized by being printed in *The Spiritual Scientist*. The announcement runs thus:

---

* *Old Diary Leaves*, I, p. 118.
† *Nineteenth Century Miracles*, by Emma Hardinge Britten, p. 296,

" One movement of great importance has just been inaugurated in New York, under the lead of Colonel Henry S. Olcott, in the organization of a society, to be known as the Theosophical Society. The suggestion was entirely unpremeditated, and was made on the evening of the 7th inst. in the parlors of Madame Blavatsky, where a company of seventeen ladies and gentlemen had assembled to meet Mr. George Henry Felt, whose discovery of the geometrical figures of the Egyptian Cabbala may be regarded as among the most surprising feats of the human intellect. The company included several persons of great learning and some of wide personal influence. The Managing Editors of two religious papers; the co-editors of two literary magazines; an Oxford LL.D.; a venerable Jewish scholar and traveller of repute; an editorial writer of one of the New York morning dailies; the President of the New York Society of Spiritualists; Mr. C. C. Massey, an English visitor [barrister-at-law]; Mrs. Emma Hardinge Britten and Dr. Britten; two New York lawyers besides Colonel Olcott; a partner in a Philadelphia publishing house; a well-known physician; and, most notable of all, Madame Blavatsky herself, comprised Mr. Felt's audience. . . . During a convenient pause in the conversation, Colonel Olcott rose, and after briefly sketching the present condition of the spiritualistic movement, . . . he proposed to form a nucleus around which might gather all the enlightened and brave souls who are willing to work together for the collection and diffusion of knowledge. His plan was to organize a society of Occultists and begin at once to collect a library; and to diffuse information concerning those secret laws of Nature which were so familiar to the Chaldeans and Egyptians, but are totally unknown by our modern world of science." *

Very likely this announcement was prepared by W. L. Alden, one of the seventeen present, who was an editorial

---

* Quoted in *Old Diary Leaves*, I, 118-20.

contributor to the New York *Daily Graphic* and also an editorial writer for the New York *Times*. Later he held a consular position for the U.S.A. in Paris.

On the next evening, September the 8th, sixteen persons gathered in order to continue the formation of The Theosophical Society. A record of the meeting is preserved as an official document on the first page of the Minute-Book of The Theosophical Society. It is a handwritten account, made by John Storer Cobb of Boston, for the gathering was held in the era before the invention of the typewriter, and records were maintained in handwriting. A photographic copy of the minutes of this meeting was published in *The Path* magazine * reading as follows:

" Meeting held at No. 46 Irving Place on Wednesday Evening, September 8, 1875.

" In consequence of a proposal of Col. Henry S. Olcott, that a society be formed for the study and elucidation of Occultism, the Cabbala, etc., the ladies and gentlemen then and there present resolved themselves into a meeting, and upon motion of Mr. W. Q. Judge it was

" Resolved, that Col. H. S. Olcott take the chair.

" Upon motion it was also Resolved, that Mr. W. Q. Judge act as secretary. The Chair then called for the names of those persons present, who would agree to found and belong to a society such as had been mentioned. The following persons handed their names to the secretary:

" Col. Olcott, Mme. H. P. Blavatsky, Charles Sotheran, Dr. Charles E. Simmons, H. D. Monachesi, G. C. Massey of London, W. L. Alden, G. H. Felt, D. E. de Lara, Dr. W. Britten, Mrs. E. H. Britten, Henry J. Newton, John Storer Cobb, J. Hyslop, W. Q. Judge, H. M. Stevens.

" Upon Motion of Herbert D. Monachesi it was

" Resolved that a committee of three be appointed by the chair, to draft a constitution and by-laws and to report the same at the next meeting.

---

* Volume IX, No. 1, April, 1894.

"Upon motion it was Resolved, that the chair be added to the committee.

"The chair then appointed Messrs. H. J. Newton, H. M. Stevens and C. Sotheran to be such committee.

"Upon motion it was

"Resolved that we now adjourn until Monday, September 13 at the same place at 8: 00 p.m. "

The minutes of the meeting were signed by H. S. Olcott, Chairman; and William Q. Judge, Secretary.

The second leaf of the Minute-Book of The Theosophical Society contains the account of the third meeting, and occurred as scheduled, five days later, on Monday, September 13th, at H. P. Blavatsky's suite, 46 Irving Place at 8:00 p.m. The account was also published in *The Path* magazine, and reads in this manner:

"Mr. George H. Felt continued from the previous meeting, September 8th, the interesting description of his discoveries on the Cabbala, which were illustrated by a number of colored diagrams. After a discussion thereon, matters in reference to the proposed Society were made the order of the day. Col. H. S. Olcott presided and Mr. Charles Sotheran acted as Secretary.

"The Committee on Preamble and By-Laws reported progress, and Mr. D. E. de Lara read a paper which he had been requested to write for the Committee.

"At the suggestion of the Committee it was upon motion

"Resolved, that the name of the Society be 'The Theosophical Society'.

"Upon motion it was

"Resolved that a committee be appointed to select suitable rooms for the meetings of the Society and report at the next meeting.

"The chair appointed the Rev. J. H. Wiggin and Mr. Charles Sotheran, and upon motion the chair was added.

"Several persons then gave in their names or were proposed for membership, and upon motion it was

"Resolved, that these names be added to the list of founders.

" Upon motion it was Resolved, that we now adjourn, subject to the call of the chair."

Signed by H. S. Olcott, Chairman and John Storer Cobb for C. Sotheran, Secretary.

In response to a notification by the Chairman, Saturday, October 16th, was the day assigned for the next meeting. The minutes of this meeting record that eighteen people were present and that the principal business transacted was that of the reading of the Preamble and the By-Laws of the Society, by Col. Olcott and Charles Sotheran respectively. After considerable discussion it was decided to table the preamble and by-laws until the next meeting, which was held on October 30th. The by-laws were then read again at that meeting and after further discussion they were adopted with the stipulation that the preamble should be further revised and then printed. Voting for officers then ensued and the result of the election was announced:

President, Col. Henry S. Olcott; Vice-Presidents, Dr. S. Pancoast and George H. Felt; Corresponding Secretary, Mme. H. P. Blavatsky; Recording Secretary, John Storer Cobb; Treasurer, Henry J. Newton; Librarian, Charles Sotheran; Councillors, Rev. H. H. Wiggin, R. B. Westbrook, LL.D., Mrs. Emma Hardinge Britten, C. E. Simmons, M.D., Herbert D. Monachesi; Counsel to the Society, William Q. Judge.

Following the declaration of the officers, the meeting adjourned until the 17th of November, on which date the president, Col. Olcott, delivered his inaugural address.

Because of thus presenting his inaugural address on November 17, 1875, Col. Olcott regarded that date as the constitutionally organized date of the founding of The Theosophical Society, and for that reason November 17th has been considered as the anniversary date of the foundation of The Theosophical Society. Nevertheless, in order to complete the historical record it should be stated that the first publicly printed document, consisting of the Preamble and the By-Laws, carried the notation that The Theosophical Society was founded on October

30, 1875. Many diplomas issued before the turn of the century also bore October 30th as the founding date.

At this point it would be well to observe what H. P. Blavatsky wrote eleven years later concerning the founding of the Society:

"In order to leave no room for equivocation, the members of the T.S. have to be reminded of the origin of the Society in 1875. Sent to the U.S. of America in 1873 for the purpose of organizing a group of workers on a psychic plane, two years later the writer received orders from her Master and Teacher to form the nucleus of a regular Society whose objects were broadly stated as follows:

"1.   Universal Brotherhood.

"2.   No distinction to be made by the member between races, creeds, or social positions, but every member had to be judged and dealt by on his personal merits;

"3.   To study the philosophies of the East—those of India chiefly, presenting them gradually to the public in various works that would interpret exoteric religions in the light of esoteric teachings;

"4.   To oppose materialism and theological dogmatism in every possible way, by demonstrating the existence of occult forces unknown to science, in nature, and the presence of psychic and spiritual powers in man; trying, at the same time to enlarge the views of the Spiritualists by showing them that there are other, many other agencies at work in the production of phenomena besides the ' Spirits ' of the dead.   Superstition had to be exposed and avoided; and occult forces, *beneficent and maleficent*—ever surrounding us and manifesting their presence in various ways—demonstrated to the best of our ability.

"Such was the programme in its broad features . . . . " *

---

* *H. P. Blavatsky Collected Writings*, Vol. VII, pp. 145-6.

Thus far attention has been focused on the founding of The Theosophical Society and no consideration has been given to the most important factor concerning the formation of the Society itself—in fact, the principal reason for the existence of the organization. It was mentioned in the latter portion of numbered paragraph 3 in the citation above, namely, that The Theosophical Society was to be the channel through which a vast continent of thought would be made available to the western world.

Thus The Theosophical Society can definitely be regarded in two categories: (1) the aspect covering the physical framework of the organization, created for the purpose of calling the world's attention to its declared purpose for existence, as conveyed by means of its declared objects. (2) The aspect which has made The Theosophical Society the repository for the dissemination of the Ancient Wisdom—humanity's priceless heritage. Knowledge of this wisdom had been absent from the western world in any tangible form for two thousand years—ever since the destruction of the Alexandrian Library. It is because the Society has been the channel for this vital essence that it has been such a great source of inspiration.

In order to give direct evidence of this delineation, attention is directed to the first work written by H. P. Blavatsky, bearing this dedication:

" The author dedicates these volumes to The Theosophical Society, which was founded at New York, A.D. 1875, to study the subjects on which they treat." *

And the preface to *Isis Unveiled* opened with these words:

" The work now submitted to public judgment is the fruit of a somewhat intimate acquaintance with Eastern

---

* Dedicatory page to *Isis Unveiled.*

adepts and study of their science. It is offered to such
as are willing to accept truth wherever it may be found,
and to defend it, even looking popular prejudice straight
in the face. It is an attempt to aid the student to
detect the vital principles which underlie the philosophical systems of old." *

The work was actually begun before the Society was
founded. Col. Olcott narrates how it was commenced.

" One day in the Summer of 1875, H.P.B. showed
me some sheets of manuscript which she had written,
and said: ' I wrote this last night " by order", but
what the deuce it is to be I don't know. Perhaps it is
for a newspaper article, perhaps for a book, perhaps
for nothing: anyhow, I did as I was ordered.' And
she put it away in a drawer, and nothing more was
said about it for some time." †

Since the subject of H. P. Blavatsky's writings form
the major portion of this work, subsequent chapters carry
on this theme in full. That which should be brought
forward in this initial chapter is the fact that even though
one of the principal founders apparently seemed to be
unaware of the auspiciousness of the event that was
being inaugurated in America, some there were who
were fully aware of what was involved in that effort.
Witness this citation from an article which appeared in
The Theosophist, under the title " Coming Events Foretold ". In order to obtain the full significance of the
quotation it is necessary to cite as well the rather lengthy
introduction which was supplied by H.P.B. to the article,
in order that the explanation of that which follows it
should be understood. The author of *The Occult World*,
referred to in the first sentence of the introductory
citation, is A. P. Sinnett.

---

* Preface, page v.
† *Old Diary Leaves*, I, pp. 202-3.

" When, in answer to a direct challenge, the author of *The Occult World* wrote to the *Bombay Gazette* (April 4, 1882), he began his letter with the following profession of faith: ' I was already sure, when I wrote *The Occult World*, that the Theosophical Society was connected, through Madame Blavatsky, with the great Brotherhood of Adepts I described. I now know this to be the case, with much greater amplitude of knowledge.' Little did our loyal friend fancy, when he was penning these lines, that his assertion would one day be capable of corroboration by the testimony of thousands. But such is now the state of the case. Sceptics and prejudiced or interested witnesses in general may scoff as they like, the fact cannot be gainsaid. Our friends—and we have some who regard us neither as lunatics nor impostors—will at least be glad to read the statement which follows.

' While at Madras, we were told that a well-known Tamil scholar, a Pandit in the Presidency College, desired to have a private conversation with us. The interview occurred in the presence of Mr. Singaravelu, President of the Krishna Theosophical Society, and of another trustworthy Theosophist, Mr. C. Aravamudu Ayangar, a Sanskritist, of Nellore. We are no more at liberty to repeat here all the questions put to us by the interviewer than we are to divulge certain other facts which would still more strongly corroborate our repeated assertions that (1) our Society was founded at the direct suggestion of Indian and Tibetan Adepts; and (2) that in coming to this country we but obeyed their wishes. But we shall leave our friends to draw their own inferences from all the facts. We are glad to know that the learned Pandit is now engaged in writing, in the Tamil and Telugu languages, a more amplified narrative than he has given here; and that he is taking steps to obtain certificates of respectable living witnesses who heard his Guru prefigure the events which have had so complete a fulfilment.'

STATEMENT OF THOLUVORE VELAYUDHAM MUDELLAR, SECOND TAMIL PANDIT OF THE PRESIDENCY COLLEGE, MADRAS

" To the Author of *Hints on Esoteric Theosophy:*

" Sir,—I beg to inform you that I was a *Chela* of the late ' Arulprakasa Vallalare ', otherwise known as Chithumbaram Ramalinga Pillay Avergal, the celebrated Yogi of Southern India. Having come to know that the English community, as well as some Hindus, entertained doubts as to the existence of the *Mahatmas* (adepts), and, as to the fact of the Theosophical Society having been formed under their special orders; and having heard, moreover, of your recent work, in which much pains are taken to present the evidence about these Mahatmas *pro* and *con*—I wish to make public certain facts in connection with my late revered Guru. My belief is, that they ought effectually to remove all such doubts, and prove that Theosophy is no empty delusion, nor the Society in question founded on an insecure basis.

" Let me premise with a brief description of the personality of and the doctrines taught by the above-mentioned ascetic, Ramalingam Pillay.

" He was born at Maruthur, Chittambaram Taluq, South Arcot, Madras Presidency. He came to live at Madras at an early period of his career, and dwelt there for a long time. . . . In 1849, I became his disciple, and, though no one ever knew where he had been initiated, some years after, he gathered a number of disciples around him. He was a great Alchemist. . . . Among many other things he preached that:

" Though the Hindu people listened not to him, nor gave ear to his counsels, yet the esoteric meaning of the *Vedas* and other sacred books of the East would be revealed by the custodians of the secret—the Mahatmas—to foreigners, who would receive it with joy; . . .

" That the distinction between races and castes would eventually cease, and the principle of Universal

Brotherhood be eventually accepted, and a Universal Brotherhood be established in India. . . .

" In the year 1867, he founded a Society, under the name of ' Sumarasa Veda Sammarga Sungham', which means a society based on the principle of Universal Brotherhood, and for the propagation of the true Vedic doctrine. I need hardly remark that these principles are identically those of the Theosophical Society. Our Society was in existence but for five or six years, during which time a very large number of poor and infirm persons were fed at the expense of its members. . . . .

" His whole occupation was the preaching of the sublime moral doctrines contained in the Hindu *Shástras*, and the instilling into the masses of the principles of Universal Brotherhood, benevolence and charity. But to his great disappointment he found among his large congregations but few who could appreciate his lofty ethics. During the latter part of his visible earthly career, he often expressed his bitter sorrow for this sad state of things, and repeatedly exclaimed :

" ' You are not fit to become members of this Society of Universal Brotherhood. *The real members of that Brotherhood are living far away, towards the North of India.* You do not listen to me. You do not follow the principle of my teachings. You seem to be determined not to be convinced by me. *Yet the time is not far off, when persons from Russia, America* (these two countries were always named), *and other foreign lands will come to India and preach to you this same doctrine of Universal Brotherhood.* Then only, will you know and appreciate the grand truths that I am now vainly trying to make you accept. You will soon find that *the Brothers who live in the far North* will work a great many wonders in India, and thus confer incalculable benefits upon this our country.'

" This prophecy has, in my opinion, just been literally fulfilled. The fact that the Mahatmas in the North exist, is no new idea to us, Hindus; and the strange fact that the advent of Madame Blavatsky and

Colonel Olcott from Russia and America was foretold several years before they came to India, is an incontrovertible proof that my Guru was in communication with those Mahatmas under whose directions the Theosophical Society was subsequently founded."

THOLUVORE VELAYUDHAM MUDELLAR, F.T.S.

" This is one of those cases of previous foretelling of a coming event, which is least of all open to suspicion of bad faith. The honourable character of the witness, the wide publicity of his Guru's announcements, and the impossibility that he could have got from public rumour, or the journals of the day, any intimation that the Theosophical Society would be formed and would operate in India—all these conspire to support the inference that Ramalingam Yogi was verily in the counsels of those who ordered us to found the Society. In March, 1873, we were directed to proceed from Russia to Paris. In June, we were told to proceed to the United States, where we arrived July 6th. This was the very time when Ramalingam was most forcibly prefiguring the events which should happen. In October, 1874, we received an intimation to go to Chittenden, Vermont, where, at the famous homestead of the Eddy family, Colonel Olcott was engaged in making his investigations—now so celebrated in the annals of Spiritualism—of the so-called ' materialization of Spirits'. November, 1875, the Theosophical Society was founded, and it was not until 1878, that the correspondence begun with friends in India, which resulted in the transfer of the Society's Headquarters to Bombay in February, 1879." *

Concerning the members of the great Brotherhood to the north of India, who were referred to in the citation, there is direct testimony which may be brought forward, demonstrating their directive activity in the founding of

---

* *The Complete Works of H. P. Blavatsky*, Vol. IV, pp. 27-30.

The Theosophical Society, as well as the reason for their effort, and the manner in which their endeavor was inaugurated. The extract which follows is from a letter written by one of the members of that Brotherhood, with whom Mr. Sinnett had the inestimable privilege of corresponding.

"I will tell you something you should know, and may derive profit from. . . . . One or two of us hoped that the world had so far advanced intellectually, if not intuitionally, that the Occult doctrine might gain an intellectual acceptance, and the impulse given for a new cycle of occult research. Others—wiser as it would now seem—held differently, but consent was given for the trial. It was stipulated, however, that the experiment should be made independently of our personal management; that there should be no abnormal interference by ourselves. So casting about we found in America the man to stand as leader—a man of great moral courage, unselfish, and having other good qualities. He was far from being the best, but . . . he was the best one available. With him we associated a woman of most exceptional and wonderful endowments. Combined with them she had strong personal defects, but just as she was, there was no second to her living fit for this work. We sent her to America, brought them together—and the trial began. From the first both she and he were given to clearly understand that the issue lay entirely with themselves. And both offered themselves for the trial for certain remuneration in the far distant future as—as K.H. would say—soldiers volunteer for a Forlorn Hope. For the 6-1/2 years they have been struggling against such odds as would have driven off any one who was not working with the desperation of one who stakes life and all he prizes on some desperate supreme effort. Their success has not equalled the hopes of their original backers, phenomenal as it has been in certain directions." *

---

* *The Mahatma Letters to A. P. Sinnett*, p. 263.

In amplification of the phrase "there was no second to her living fit for this work" the following passage is appropriate:

"After nearly a century of fruitless search, our chiefs had to avail themselves of the only opportunity to send out a European *body* upon European soil to serve as a connecting link between that country and our own." *

An explanation is provided as to the meaning of "Forlorn Hope", and the passage also shows that Colonel Olcott and Mme. Blavatsky were definitely regarded as the agents for the work of the Brotherhood.

"What I meant by the 'Forlorn Hope' was that when one regards the magnitude of the task to be undertaken by our theosophical volunteers, and especially the multitudinous agencies arrayed, and to be arrayed, in opposition, we may well compare it, to one of those desperate efforts against overwhelming odds that the true soldier glories to attempt. You have done well to see the 'large purpose' in the small beginnings of the T.S. Of course, if we had undertaken to found and direct it *in propria persona* very likely it would have accomplished more and made fewer mistakes, but we could not do this, nor was it the plan: our two agents are given the task and left— as you now are—to do the best they could under the circumstances. And much has been wrought." †

"Then you will of course, aim to show that this Theosophy is no new candidate for the world's attention, but only the restatement of principles which have been recognised from the very infancy of mankind." ‡

---

* *The Mahatma Letters to A. P. Sinnett*, p. 203.
† *Op. cit.*, p. 35.
‡ *Op. cit.*, p. 34.

Along with the necessity for study and re-orientation
of ideas, the importance of the prime objective for the
formation of The Theosophical Society should not be
lost sight of. This objective was clearly enunciated:

" The *Chiefs* want a ' Brotherhood of Humanity', a
real Universal Fraternity started; an institution which
would make itself known throughout the world and
arrest the attention of the highest minds." *

In concluding the extracts which have been presented
from the letters of two of the members of the Brotherhood
—to the north of India—with regard to the founding of
The Theosophical Society, attention is directed to the
fact that the Society is but part of a larger undertaking
which has been referred to as the Theosophical Movement, in contradistinction to The Theosophical Society
itself—a distinction made by H.P.B. herself.

" Europe is a large place but the world is bigger yet.
The sun of Theosophy must shine for all, not for a part.
There is more of this movement than you have yet had
an inkling of, and the work of the T.S. is linked in
with similar work that is secretly going on in all parts
of the world. . . . . The cycle I spoke of refers to the
whole movement. Europe will not be overlooked,
never fear; but perhaps you even may not anticipate
how the light will be shed there. . . . You know K.H.
and me—buss! know you anything of the *whole* Brotherhood and its ramifications? " †

Having thus presented what may be termed the causative aspects of the founding of The Theosophical Society,
an insight may be gained in regard to the underlying
movives concerning its formation. At the same time it
enables one to obtain the true status of H. P. Blavatsky's
position in the endeavor.

---

* *The Mahatma Letters to A. P. Sinnett*, p. 24.
† *Op. cit.*, pp. 271-2.

A Celebrated Buddhist's Reaction to the Founding of The Theosophical Society

One more item may be included in this introductory chapter, showing as it does how an eminent Buddhist regarded H. P. Blavatsky. As the account is written biographically, it fits in admirably with the chronological theme. It is narrated by Anagarika Dharmapala (or as he was also known Dharmapâla, the Anâgârika, 1865-1933), the founder of the Maha Bodhi Society. Born in Ceylon, of the family of Hewavitarne, he adopted the cognomen Dharmapala—the name of the celebrated disciple of Gautama the Buddha—as well as the epithet Anagarika (signifying " the homeless wanderer ") at the time that he founded the Maha Bodhi Society in Calcutta, India, in 1891. Before this event he had already become a member of The Theosophical Society. As the principal purpose of the Maha Bodhi Society was to recover into Buddhist hands the Buddha Gaya—the site where Gautama attained enlightenment—Dharmapala worked unceasingly towards that end. In 1892 he founded the Maha Bodhi Journal, the monthly magazine of the Society, the largest magazine devoted to Buddhism (still in publication—1961). He attended the World's Parliament of Religions, which was held in Chicago in 1893, representing Buddhism.

The autobiographical account which follows is a portion of an illustrated article entitled " On the Eightfold Path", prepared by Dharmapala for *Asia* magazine:

" When I was ten years old, I attended a great debate in a temple pavilion sixteen miles from Ceylon [Colombo?], where the Christians on one side and Gunananda on the other argued out the truths of their respective religions . . . . thousands came from the most distant parts of the island to hear this famous debate. Mohotiwatta Guna anda supplied the oratory; and the Venerable Sumangala furnished him with the scholarly material and references. The debate lasted three entire days.

" Dr. J. M. Peebles, an American Spiritualist, who was visiting Colombo at the time, obtained an English report of the controversy between the Buddhists and Christians and, upon his return to the U.S., showed it to Colonel Henry S. Olcott and Madame H. P. Blavatsky, who had organized the Theosophical Society in New York in 1875. Deeply impressed, they wrote to Gunananda and Sumangala that, in the interest of universal brotherhood, they had just founded a society inspired by oriental philosophies and that they would come to Ceylon to help the Buddhists. The letters from Colonel Olcott and Madame Blavatsky were translated into Sinhalese and widely distributed. My heart warmed toward these two strangers, so far away and yet so sympathetic, and I made up my mind that, when they came to Ceylon, I would join them.

" They did come to Colombo a few years later, when I was sixteen. The Buddhists entertained them royally. I remember going up to greet them. The moment I touched their hands, I felt overjoyed. The desire for universal brotherhood, for all the things they wanted for humanity, struck a responsive chord in me. I began to read their magazine. I was at this time still attending school. I was self contained and independent and preferred solitude, flowers and beautiful scenery to the games and pastimes of the average school-boy. And, as I walked in the gardens overgrown with fragrant plants or along the shore shaded by teak and coco-palms, I pondered on the conversations I had had with the two Theosophists.

" My Buddhist training had early taught me to regard the world with its fantom pleasures as a transitory dwelling-place filled with every kind of disappointment and suffering. I was confirmed in this belief when I was seventeen. My baby sister, not yet two, bubbled over with health and playfulness. Suddenly, she became ill, and the next day she died. As a result my dear mother sank for a while into deep despondency. When I saw her quietly weeping over the loss of our previous baby, I looked at life with feelings of pity.

I, a boy of seventeen, decided that I would never be the cause of sorrow to a woman, and I made up my mind not to entangle myself in the net of worldly desires. I would endeavor from then on to devote my life to the welfare of others. Exactly how I was to carry out my resolve, I was not certain, but I felt that somehow the way would be found in the writings of Madame Blavatsky. . . . . .

"In December, 1884, Madame Blavatsky and Colonel Olcott again visited Colombo on their way to Madras. I went to my father and told him I wanted to go to Madras and work with them. At first he consented. But, on the day set for my departure, he announced solemnly that he had had a bad dream and could not allow me to go. The high priest, the other priests I had known from childhood, my grandparents, all opposed me. Though I did not know what to do, my heart was determined on the journey, which I felt would lead to a new life for me. Madame Blavatsky faced the priests and my united family. She was a wonderful woman, with energy and will-power that pushed aside all obstacles. She said: ' That boy will die if you do not let him go. I will take him with me anyway.'

" So the family were won over. My mother blessed me and sent me off with the parting words, ' Go and work for humanity'. My father said, ' Go, then, and aspire to be a *Bodhisattva*', and he gave me money to help me in my work.

" In Colombo I had already joined the Theosophical Society. I worked six years for the Society. Madame Blavatsky was a profound student of occult science as well as a strong Buddhist, and in my youth many elderly persons testified to the remarkable things that she had done. At one time she had told me that, since I was physically and mentally pure, I could come in contact with the Himalayan adepts. So in my nineteenth year I had decided to spend a lifetime in the study of occult science. But in Madras Madame Blavatsky opposed my plan. ' It will be much wiser for you to dedicate your life to the service of humanity', she said. 'And, first of all, learn Pali, the sacred language of the Buddha.'

"At that time the Pali writings, which contain the most authoritative account of the Buddha and his doctrines, were little known in comparison with the Sanskrit Buddhist sources. The oldest Pali literature was written on palm leaves in the Sinhalese alphabet. In 1884, when Madame Blavatsky urged me to study this literature, it was not printed but was accessible only in the original palm-leaf writings. Thanks to her advice, I devoted my spare time in Colombo to the study of those beautiful old manuscripts, so difficult to decipher, and thus became familiar with the Buddhist canonical scriptures. Since then the excellent pioneer work of the Pali Text Society of London and of the late Henry Clarke Warren of Harvard University has made Pali literature accessible in translation to English readers. In America it is possible for those interested to examine Pali manuscripts. Brown University has several, in Burmese characters. The complete Buddhist scriptures—the *Tipitaka*, or 'Three Baskets'—are also now available to American scholars. On the twenty-fifth anniversary of his coronation, the father of the late King of Siam presented Harvard University with an edition of the *Tipitaka* in thirty-nine volumes, printed in Siamese characters. Through the self-sacrificing and dignified labors of a few scholars, the West has now been awakened to the importance of Pali as a foundation for a rational and scientific study of Buddhism. . . .

"On May 31, 1891, I started the Maha Bodhi Society, to rescue the holy Buddhist places and to revive Buddhism in India, which for seven hundred years had forgotten its greatest teacher. In 1892 I started the journal of the society, *The Maha Bodhi*, which is still in existence and well known among the Buddhists of Great Britain and the United States.

"A copy of the first issue of this journal was sent to Dr. John Henry Barrows, chairman of the World's

Parliament of Religions at the Chicago World's Colum-
bian Exposition in 1893. In his letter of acknowledgment he invited me to serve on the advisory council of
the congress and asked me if I could send a Buddhist
delegate. . . .

"Finally . . . Dr. Barrows wrote to me ' You come
yourself as a delegate to the congress.' I was only 27
at the time, and I did not consider myself qualified to
take the place of such a venerable bhikkhu as should
have represented our Sinhalese Buddhists. But I
could not disappoint the amiable Dr. Barrows; so I
went, in the white robes of a Buddhist student to the
white city that the people of Chicago had built near
Lake Michigan. . . .

"After the congress I returned to Bodh Gaya.
Actively as I had identified myself with the Buddhist
cause, I still wore only the white robe of a student.
But in October 1895, I put on the yellow robe; I
became an *anâgârika*. . . .

"When I put on the yellow robe after my return to
Bodh Gaya, it was merely that I might serve humanity
more consistently.

"I worked night and day when I was in India. . . .
After ten years of perseverance, I succeeded in obtaining the consent of the Government to the erection of
a comfortable rest-house for Buddhist pilgrims at Bodh
Gaya. . . .

"When I had labored for seventeen years at Bodh
Gaya, the two or three resident monks and I—all of
us Sinhalese Buddhists—were forced by the Government to withdraw. I immediately transferred the
activities of the Maha Bodhi Society to Calcutta. . . .
I was able to erect a beautiful Buddhist vihâra, or
monastery and temple, which was opened by the
Governor of Bengal in November, 1920." *

Thus in great measure the reawakening of Buddhism
in India, in modern times, was due to the efforts of

* Published in *Asia* Magazine, New York City, Vol. XXVII, No. 9,
pages 720-727, issue of September, 1927.

Dharmapâla and the impetus which he received through his contact with H. P. Blavatsky.

How Buddhism came to Tibet and the results of the stimulus gained thereby—achieving as it did such an out-pouring in literary and artistic pursuits, while the religious fervor evoked was greater even than in the land where the religion originated—is narrated in the second chapter, entitled " On Tibet and its Religion."

CHAPTER II

ON TIBET AND ITS RELIGION

The land of Tibet is shrouded in mystery. For centuries it has remained isolated, aloof from the world. Foreigners have not been permitted to enter its domain, least of all to visit Lhasa, which has come to be known as the Forbidden City. So few travellers have entered the land that their names are well known. Recent Americans to make the trip to Tibet, Lowell Thomas and his son, were given special permission to do so and were permitted to bring back colored films of their expedition and their journey to Lhasa. It was hoped that this journey would evoke world interest sufficient to hold back the threatened menace which was overshadowing Tibet—the threat of foreign invasion. Most unfortunately the realization of the danger threatening Tibet was not noticed.

What were the reasons prompting the Tibetans to hold off travellers? Any number of reasons may be given: the desire to be independent, fear of being imposed upon by outsiders, their wish to maintain their own political and religious systems. These and others have been suggested, not to omit the inaccessible nature of the land itself. It is doubtful, however, whether the real reason has been recognised. It was given by H. P. Blavatsky in this significant statement:

" A prophecy of Tsong-Kha-pa is current in Tibet to the effect that the true doctrine will be maintained in its purity only so long as Tibet is kept free from the incursions of western nations, whose crude ideas of fundamental truth would inevitably confuse and obscure the followers of the Good Law. But, when the western world is more ripe in the direction of philosophy, the incarnation of Pban-chhen-rin-po-chhe—the Great Jewel of Wisdom—one of the Teshu Lamas, will take

place, and the splendour of truth will then illuminate
the whole world. We have here the true key to
Tibetan exclusiveness." *

Recent events have brought about an upheaval, and
that which has been feared for centuries has actually
come to pass. Gone is the exclusiveness of Tibet. Reports
in the press have told how Tibet was overrun by the
Chinese army. The world is now aware of the plight of
the Tibetans and what befell their land. The Dalai
Lama was obliged to flee from his home-land, leaving
his sanctuary in Lhasa. What will be the outcome of
this invasion?

The land of Tibet is called Bod, or Bod-yul, by its
inhabitants, and its language, Bod-skad. The word
"Tibet" comes from the frontier lands of China—from
Mongolia and Kashmir—where that country is referred
to as Tö-böt, meaning the high plateau-land, or table-
land. Unquestionably it is the highest table-land in the
world, for it is some 16,000 feet above sea level. Some of
the valleys drop to 12,000 feet, while mountain peaks
rise to 20,000 and even to 24,000 feet in height. To the
north and east of Tibet are the Chinese provinces of
Sinkiang, Chinghai and Sikang; on the west and south
lie the Indian provinces of Kashmir and Ladakh and also
the two free mountain countries of Nepal and Bhutan.

Buddhism was first brought into Tibet in the seventh
century and was well received by the people. It came
about in a rather singular manner. The reigning monarch
of Tibet, Sron-Tsan-Gam-po, had become betrothed to a
Chinese princess, Wencheng, who was an ardent Buddhist.
When she became queen of Tibet, not only did she
convert the king to Buddhism from Bön worship (the
popular religion of the time), but she also went about
the land spreading the "Good Law", as Buddhism is

---

* From an article entitled "Tibetan Teachings", published in
Lucifer, Vol. XV, Sept. and Oct., 1894; republished in *H. P. Blavatsky
Collected Writings*, Vol. VI, p. 105. The term Pban-chhen-rin-po-chhe
is also spelled Panchen Rimpoche.

often called. After her death, Wencheng was deified, being named the white Tārā.

Further, showing his zeal for the Good Law, King Sron-Tsan-Gam-po decided that it was necessary to have the Buddhist scriptures in Tibet. Whereupon he sent Thon-mi, called Sambhota in India, one of his ministers (who was also the monarch's brother) into India to obtain such manuscripts. In due time his ambassador returned, bringing with him the Buddhist canonical scriptures. He it was who devised the Tibetan alphabet, basing it upon the Devanâgarî characters (the name by which Sanskrit writing is known). Yet, even before this era esoteric Buddhism was present within the land, for it is so mentioned by Chinese pre-Buddhistic books. These refer to the fraternity of the great teachers of the snowy mountains, known by the name of *Byang-tsiub* — meaning " the perfect ones ", " the accomplished." *

Thus, while Buddhism became the religion of Tibet, it should be noted that along the fringes of the country, especially in the regions which have been frequently visited by travellers, the customs and religion that have been described are not genuine Buddhistic. Instead these pertain to the primitive religious beliefs and practices, known as Bön worship.

A century later, the Tibetan king, Thi-Sron Detsan, sent an ambassador to India for the purpose of inviting a Buddhist priest to come to his kingdom, in order to establish Buddhism more firmly in Tibet. Padma Sambhava responded to the invitation, and returned to Bodyul with the Tibetan king's messenger. They arrived in 747 A.D. Padma Sambhava forthwith organized Buddhism in Tibet, following the system of the Yogāchārya School, with which he had been identified in India. (The Yogā School is regarded as one of the six Darśanas, or philosophical schools of India). Padma

---

* Cf. *The Complete Works of H. P. Blavatsky*, 1881-2, Vol. III, p. 272, article: " Reincarnations in Tibet ", reprinted from *The Theosophist*. Vol. III, No. 6, March, 1882, pp. 146-8. *Byang-chub* is an alternate spelling which is more frequently used.

Sambhava is thus justly considered to be the founder of
Lamaism, which is the European term for Buddhism in
Tibet. However, the Tibetan word Lama means "the
Superior One". There is no equivalent for Lamaism in
Tibet. Tibetans simply refer to it as "the religion",
signifying "Buddha's religion". Hence, they regard
themselves as *nang-pa* (those belonging to the faith—a word
which may be rendered "Insiders".), whereas those who
are "outside the faith" are termed *p'yi-lin*, usually spelled
peling, *i.e.*, foreigners.

Padma Sambhava built the first monastery at Sam-yäs
in 749 A.D., placing his Hindu assistant, Sânta-rakshita,
as the first abbot. In this manner the founder of Lamaism,
called the Guru Rimpoche (meaning "the precious
teacher") also instituted the order of the Lamas. The first
Tibetan Lama who followed Sânta-rakshita, was named
Pal-bans. After his death Padma Sambhava was deified.

As already stated (but it will bear repetition), the
religious practices described by travellers who have
managed to penetrate Tibet by means of the border-
lands, do not represent the genuine Buddhism (or
Lamaism) for two reasons: (1) It is pervaded by Bön
worship (the religious practices flourishing before the
introduction of Buddhism into Tibet). (2) The Buddhism
colored by Bön worship pertains to the "unreformed
Lamaism"—technically referred to as belonging to the
Red Cap or Red Hat Order (from the color of their
robes and hoods), in contradistinction to the Yellow Cap
or Yellow Hat Order, who inculcates what is termed
"Reformed Buddhism". For it was towards the close of
the fourteenth century that a great religious revival took
place in Tibet—occurring under the administration of
Tsong-Kha-pa. He instituted a purified form of Buddhism, freeing it from the Bön worship that had per-
meated into Lamaism as practised by the Order of the
Red Caps. In order to distinguish the reformed Buddhism from that of the Red Caps, Tsong-Kha-pa instituted
the Order of the Yellow Caps (*i.e.*, Gelukpas).

Although the Reformed Buddhists of Tibet are called
Gelukpas, alone the Dalai-Lama, as chief of that order,

actually wears a yellow hood, and on ceremonial occasions also a yellow robe. The monks usually wear red robes and red hoods, except during ceremonies when they are bare-headed. The Gelukpas are not permitted to marry; the prohibition does not apply to the Red Hats. A legend is still current in Tibet which tells how Tsong-Kha-pa came to use a yellow hood and why the Reformed Buddhists later came to be called Gelukpas.

In his time it was the custom, as it is today, to welcome a young person into the Order by means of an appropriate ceremony, concluding by investing the newcomer or novice with a robe and hood. Since the clothing of the monks consisted of red robes and red hoods, there were also given to the novices. When it came to the youthful Tsong-Kha-pa's turn to receive his marks of investiture, there was no red hood left for him. So, in haste, the hierophant picked up the only hood then available—a yellow one. So ever after, Tsong-Kha-pa wore a yellow hood. Later on, when he made his reforms in Buddhism, his followers were named the Gelukpas, or yellow-hooded ones.

There is no question that the dominant motif in Tibet is religious. This is manifest not only because of the great number of monasteries that flourish throughout the land, but also by the marked religious temperament of the people themselves. Contrary to what may be expected, the monasteries are not only situated in isolated spots, but are present in every large city or town as well. Each one has its cloister. Shigatse, for instance, the second largest city, has its monastery, called Tashi-Lhünpo. It was founded by Gan-den Trup-pa, the successor of Tsong-Kha-pa. In the environs of Lhasa (the capital city) are the three largest and principal monasteries of the land, known as Drebung, Sera and Ganden. The last two named were founded by Trong-Kha-pa. Not only are these three the chief religious centers but they even have a powerful position in the political administration of Tibet. They are regarded as the three Pillars of the State. The chief abbots from these three monasteries, together with eight governing officials, over whom is the

Dalai-Lama, preside over the National Assembly of Tibet. It is understandable, then, that these three abbots see to it that all decisions are made according to the prescribed prevailing pattern. It is for this reason that Tibet has remained as it has for so many centuries, because of the dominating control maintained by the three abbots.

The largest of the three institutions is Drebung. It is situated about five miles from Lhasa. Although called a monastery, it actually consists of many houses, as well as gardens and temples. About 10,000 monks are attached to Drebung. This gives some idea of the prominent position held by this institution. For, naturally, the monasteries are equivalent to schools of religious education, in which the Buddhist teachings are, of course, studied. Those who graduate become candidates for the staffs of the religious institutions which are maintained in the monasteries. Then, too, the monastic or church officials in the government are also selected from the graduates of the monasteries.

The Dalai-Lama is not only the titular head of the Tibetan government, but he is one of the supreme pontiffs of Lamaism. The title " Dalai-Lama " is not Tibetan. It is Mongolian in origin and was first brought into use by the Mongolian ruler, Altan Khan, who several centuries ago became a Buddhist. The word " dalai " (in Mongolian *ta-lai*) signifies ocean or sea—implying the vast extent of knowledge attainable by one who becomes a Buddha. Lama (written *blama* in Tibetan), literally a " superior one " signifies a high priest. The term " Dalai Lama " is not employed in Tibet, instead the title in use is Gyalpo Rinpoche: *rGyal-po* (derived from *rgyal*, victory), is applied to kings and emperors as well as to the Buddha, as the most exalted being; *rin-po-che*,* literally very dear, precious; also jewel. Hence the title signifies

---

* Also spelled, and pronounced, Rimpoche.

The information given in this chapter was, of course, applicable to the period prior to the invasion of Tibet by the Chinese army in 1959.

the most exalted treasured one, or as usually rendered "Treasured King." Within the intimate circle of the family and friends, the sovereign is addressed as Kündün, signifying "the Presence", implying an embodiment of a Living Buddha. In very truth the populace revere and honor their monarch as a "God-King."

CHAPTER III

CONCERNING THE TIBETAN LANGUAGE AND LITERATURE

In a work of this nature where so many Tibetan words appear, a short chapter devoted to the manner of spelling Tibetan terms is certainly necessary. Unfortunately, no specific system or rule can be laid down and implicitly followed, due to the nature of the language. Hence an explanation is required.

There are two systems in use for the spelling of Tibetan words. Most writers on Tibet adopt the system that will be mentioned first, while scholars prefer the second. (1) The first system is that of spelling a word by means of its sound-value as represented by letters of the English alphabet. (2) Spelling a word by means of its transliteration into English from the Tibetan written alphabet. This may not be very clear to one not conversant with the subject, therefore an illustration will clarify the point. The Tibetan word included in the title of this work is customarily spelled according to its sound-value, or the manner in which it is pronounced in Tibet (the first system), hence it is written " Tulku." Following the second system the word would be spelled " sprul-sku." Since there are a great many silent or unpronounced letters (just as in English), this mode of spelling Tibetan words becomes confusing at times. As an instance: the name of the celebrated monastery near Shigatse, in the province of Tsang, founded by Tsong-kha-pa's successor, Ganden Truppa, is written " bkra-śis-lun-po " although pronounced Ta-shi-Lhün-po.

In this work both systems are followed, depending upon the method used by the writer from whom a citation is made. Obviously, when a word has been adopted into the English language it is preferable to follow the spelling which has become familiar in print. A clear example of this may be given in the Tibetan word " Lama ", generally rendered a priest. To spell it " bLama " (literally meaning "superior," hence a title of respect and used as an equivalent of guru, teacher) would be inappropriate.

However, even the method following the pronunciation runs into difficulty, because there are a great many variants in the pronunciation of the language. It is said that there are as many pronunciations as there are provinces in Tibet. Be that as it may, lexicographers are content to list six main systems. The principal system is that which is used in the Central Provinces, in which Lhasa is situated, and is identified with the provinces of Tsang and Ü. These two provinces practically always have the same pronunciation, and more often than not the same mode is followed in the province of Spiti. Differences are to be noted in the Western Provinces—those of Ladak and Lahul—as is also the case in the province of Khams, bordering China in south-eastern Tibet. Writers generally follow the system of pronunciation used in the Central Provinces, which is considered to be the mode followed by educated classes.

The language of Tibet is classified as belonging to the Tibeto-Burman dialectic group—which groupage covers a broad territorial district ranging from Tibet in the north to Burma in the south, including some Himalayan dialects in India as well as some in the Chinese provinces of Sze-chuen and Yünnan in the east. In fact, a larger grouping may be made by the designation Sino-Tibetan, which includes languages spoken in China and Tai. The reason for this larger grouping is clearly discernible when an analysis is made of the Chinese and Tibetan languages. Both have the same characteristic, in that words consist of single syllables. New words are formed by means of joining single-syllabled words into compounds. In the written language each word (consisting of a single syllable) is indicated by means of a dot, called a t'seg. When transliterating into English the t'seg is indicated by means of a hyphen. As an example of the formation of single syllabled words into compounds: in Tibetan

sprin, means a cloud;
char-sprin, a rain-cloud;

        glog-sprin, a thunder-cloud;
        sprin-skyes, lightning;
        sprin-dmar, clouds reddened by the sun.

In addition to this manner of word-formation, prominent also are prefixes, suffixes and even infixes. Suffixes are used to indicate cases (in place of inflection), as well as even to single out a noun or adjective for particular emphasis. Suffixes are also used to denote gender, and likewise plurality.

There also is a similarity between Tibetan and Chinese in the phonetical system as well as in vocabulary and in grammar. One difference is to be noted, namely, in the construction of a sentence: the Chinese language favors the order of the sentence to be that of: subject, verb, object; the Tibeto-Burman group prefers: subject, object, verb.

But when it comes to the written language, there is no similarity whatsoever. The Tibetan writing does not use ideographs as does the Chinese. Instead it uses an alphabet, which was patterned after the Sanskrit Devanâgarî script. This was quite an accomplishment, since the language bears no resemblance to Sanskrit. Furthermore, there are sounds in the Tibetan which are not used in Sanskrit.

The development of Tibetan writing came about in a rather singular manner. In the seventh century A.D., King Srong-tsang-Gam-po was the ruler of Tibet. He had chosen a Chinese princess to be his bride and she was an ardent Buddhist. So devoted was the princess to Buddhism that she importuned the king to spread the faith throughout Tibet. In order to put this in effect the sovereign came to the conclusion that it would be necessary to have the Buddhist Canon. Thereupon he sent his minister, Thonmi Sambhota, to India for the express purpose of learning Sanskrit, so that the texts might be translated into Tibetan. So fascinated was Thonmi Sambhota with the Devanâgarî alphabetical characters, that he determined to adapt the Tibetan written language to them, even using the same alphabetical order. And so it came to pass.

So excellent was his adaptation, that his system has been in use ever since the year 632, when it was introduced into Tibet.

When Thonmi Sambhota returned to his native land, his enthusiasm was passed on to others. This set off a period of literary activity in Tibet. First, their endeavors took the form of translating the Sanskrit texts on Buddhism. Then, later on it spurred others to the writing of original works of historical and legendary character. An example of historical works produced at that time are the *Mani Kah-'*bum scriptures—in fact they are the oldest known manuscripts on the history of Tibet.

This literary activity resulted in the production of the Tibetan Sacred Canon, represented by the scriptures generally known under their Mongolian titles of *Kanjur* and *Tanjur*. In Tibetan Kanjur is written bKa-hgyur, or bKa-'gyur: *bka,* meaning word, order, commandment; while *'gyur* signifies translated; the root meaning of *'gyur* implying " change." The work is generally rendered " the Word of the Buddha." In Tibetan Tanjur is written bsTan-hgyur, or bsTan-'gyur: *bstan* signifying doctrine; hence " the doctrine of the Buddha." Thus the Tanjur represents the commentaries on the Word of the Buddha.

The Chohan-Lama of Rin-cha-tze (Tibet), the Chief of the Archive-registrars of the secret Libraries of the Dalai Lama and the Tashi Lama of Ta-shi-Lhün-po, may be cited authoritatively for the number of volumes comprising the Tibetan Canon:

" the sacred canon of the Tibetans, the *Bka-hgyur* and *Bstan-hgyur,* comprises one thousand seven hundred and seven distinct works—one thousand and eighty-three public and six hundred and twenty-four secret volumes—the former being composed of three hundred and fifty and the latter of seventy-seven folio volumes." *

* Quoted from an article entitled " Tibetan Teachings," republished in *H. P. Blavatsky Collected Writings,* Vol. VI, p. 98. Although written by the Chohan-Lama for *The Theosophist* it was first published in H.P.B.'s magazine *Lucifer,* in London, September, 1894. Vol. XV, No. 85, pp. 9-17.

His views regarding the ability of Westerners to read the secret folios—even if they were procurable—is worthy of note. "Theosophists" are addressed, because of the fact that he was writing for H. P. Blavatsky's journal *The Theosophist*.

"Could they even by chance have seen them, I can assure the Theosophists that the contents of these volumes could never be understood by anyone who had not been given the key to their peculiar character, and to the hidden meaning.

"Every description of localities is figurative in our system; every name and word is purposely veiled; and a student, before he is given any further instruction, has to study the mode of deciphering, and then of comprehending and learning the equivalent secret term or synonym for nearly every word of our religious language. The Egyptian enchorial or hieratic system is child's play to the deciphering of our sacred puzzles. Even in those volumes to which the masses have access, every sentence has a dual meaning, one intended for the unlearned, and the other for those who have received the key to the records." *

A brief comment concerning the Tanjur, made by H. P. Blavatsky, is appropriate:

"The 'Stan-gyour' [bstan-hgyur] is full of rules of magic, the study of occult powers, and their acquisition, charms, incantations, etc.; and is as little understood by its lay-interpreters as the Jewish 'Bible' is by our clergy, or the 'Kabala' by the European Rabbis." †

---

* Quoted from an article entitled "Tibetan Teachings", republished in *H. P. Blavatsky Collected Writings*, Vol. VI, p. 98. Although written by the Chohan-Lama for *The Theosophist* it was first published in H. P. B.'s magazine *Lucifer*, in London, September, 1894, Vol. XV, No. 85, pp. 9-17.

† *Isis Unveiled*, Vol. I, p. 580.

Few in number are the folios that have been translated from the Tibetan Sacred Canon into modern European languages. A pioneer in the field of translating during the last century was the Hungarian philologist Alexander Csoma de Körös (1784-1842), who spent four years in a Buddhist monastery in Tibet. In 1848 the *rGya Tch'er Rol Pa*—signifying the History of Buddha-Sâkyamuni—from the Kanjur, was published in Paris.

In the present century through the efforts of W. Y. Evans-Wentz, four books representing translations of Tibetan manuscripts have been published in London: *The Tibetan Book of the Dead; Tibet's Great Yogî Milarepa; The Tibetan Book of the Great Liberation; and The Tibetan Yoga and Secret Doctrines*—the last work carrying the sub-title "Seven Books of Wisdom of the Great Path." These books have given the Occident an insight into the literary work representative of Tibetan Buddhism—generally referred to as Lamaism.

With regard to the secret folios: a portion of the arcane lore was given to the world through the publication of *The Secret Doctrine*. Some of the secret folios were made available to H. P. Blavatsky, more particularly that portion classed under the title the Book of Dzyan. From it she translated the Stanzas of Dzyan, as well as passages from the Commentaries from the Book of Dzyan. These form the basis for the exposition of *The Secret Doctrine*.

In addition, there is also her devotional book entitled *The Voice of the Silence*, which as she states belongs to the same series as that from which the Stanzas of Dzyan were taken.

Regarding the source of the Stanzas from the Book of Dzyan, H. P. Blavatsky wrote:

"The BOOK OF DZYAN—from the Sanskrit word 'Dhyâna' (mystic meditation)—is the first volume of the Commentaries upon the seven secret folios of *Kiu-te*, and a Glossary of the public works of the same name. Thirty-five volumes of *Kiu-te* for exoteric purposes and the use of the laymen may be found in the possession of the Tibetan Gelugpa Lamas, in the library of any monastery; and also fourteen books of Commentaries and Annotations on the same by the initiated Teachers.

" Strictly speaking, those thirty-five books ought to be termed ' The Popularised Version ' of the SECRET DOCTRINE, full of myths, blinds and errors; the fourteen volumes of *Commentaries*, on the other hand—with their translations, annotations, and an ample glossary of Occult terms, worked out from one small archaic folio, the BOOK OF THE SECRET WISDOM OF THE WORLD— contain a digest of all the Occult Sciences. These, it appears, are kept secret and apart, in the charge of the Teshu Lama of Tji-gad-je [Shigatse]. The Books of *Kiu-te* are comparatively modern, having been edited within the last millennium, whereas, the earliest volumes of the *Commentaries* are of untold antiquity, some fragments of the original cylinders having been preserved. With the exception that they explain and correct some of the too fabulous, and to every appearance, grossly exaggerated accounts in the Books of *Kiu-te*—properly so-called—the *Commentaries* have little to do with these." *

---

* *The Secret Doctrine*, Vol. V, p. 389; Section 47, entitled "The Secret Books of ' Lam-rin ' and Dzyan."

CHAPTER IV

THE DALAI AND TASHI LAMAS AND TULKU

Since Tulku is definitely associated with the Dalai Lamas of Tibet, by inquiring into the commencement of the hierarchy of the Lamas we may also learn of the origin of Tulku in connection with the Dalai Lamas. The date of the establishment of the hierarchical series may be easily ascertained, because the inauguration of the first Dalai Lama was made under the aegis of the Chinese empire. It occurred in 1641, a year after Tibet had been invaded and conquered by a Mongol prince named Gusri Khan. This invasion took place during the era of the fifth Grand Lama (or the fourth Tulku) following the formation of the Gelukpa Order by Tsong Kha-pa in 1417. Therefore it may be asserted that the continuation of the hierarchical series of Grand Lamas by means of Tulku had not occurred before the time of Tsong-Kha-pa.

Before 1641, however, a previous Khan of the Mongols had bestowed the *title* of "Dalai Lama Vajradhara" (which may be rendered "the All-Embracing Lama, the Holder of the Thunderbolt") to the third grand Lama, Sönam Gyatso, because of his efforts in spreading Buddhism not only throughout Tibet but in Mongolia as well. With the formal institution of the fifth Grand Lama by the Chinese emperor as the acknowledged ruler of Tibet, with the title of Dalai Lama, the rule of the priest kings (as they are sometimes called in Western lands) commenced. And the series has continued by means of Tulku to our day.

The birth of Tsong-Kha-pa is given as occurring in 1358 A.D. in the province of Amdo in Northeast Tibet near the lake of Kokonor. It was he who instituted great reforms in the Buddhism of Tibet, coinciding with the establishment of the Gelukpa Order in 1417. The word "Tsong-Kha-pa" signifies "the man from the land of Tsong-Kha," which in turn means "the man from the land of onions"—a rather strange name for the Great Reformer, who was not only a great preceptor but the presiding hierarch of the monastery of Drepung, near Lhasa. During his administration Tsong-Kha-pa also established the monasteries of Sera and Ganden. These two monasteries, along with Drepung, have dominated Tibet not only in religious matters but also in the policy of the land ever since that time. The three monasteries, in fact, are known as the Three Pillars of State—Den-sa Sum.

Following the passing of Tsong-Kha-pa in 1419, his grand nephew, Gan-den Trup-pa (also spelled Gedundub-pa and Geden Tub-pa) was installed as the Gyalwa Rim-poche, to use the Tibetan term—a title signifying the Great Gem of Majesty. Another title in use is Kyam-gön Rimpoche, signifying the Precious Protector. In 1445 Ganden Truppa founded the monastery of Tashi-Lhünpo (the words signifying " mass of glory ") near the city of Shigatse, second in importance to Lhasa. This became the seat of the Tashi Lamas. The latter hierarchical series of Lamas did not commence as early as that of the Dalai Lamas; it originated, in fact, a century later, according to the outer published records.

The official lists of the hierarchical series of both the Dalai and Tashi Lamas have been prepared and printed by the monks of the respective monasteries. First the series of Dalai Lamas, prepared at Lhasa:

OFFICIAL LIST OF DALAI LAMAS *

Name	Birth A.D.	Death A.D.
1. *d*Ge'dun grub-pa	1391	1475
2. *d*Ge-'dun *r*Gya-mts'o	1475	1543
3. *b*Sod-nams ,,	1543	1589
4. Yon-tan ,,	1589	1617

* Published in *Lamaism*, by L. A. Waddell, p. 233, 2nd ed., 1895. Waddell states that the dates were calculated by Lama S'erab Gya-ts'o, of the Gelug-pa monastery in Darjiling, India. The apostrophes (') in the above Tibetan names represent aspirated letters. *r*Gya-*m*ts'o signifies " Ocean."

5.	Nag-dban blo-bsan rGya-mts'o	1617	1682
6.	Ts'ans-dbyans rGya-mts'c	1683	1706
7.	sKal-bzan ,,	1708	1758
8.	'Jam-dpal ,,	1758	1805
9.	Lun-rtogs ,,	1805	1816
10.	Ts'ul K'rims ,,	1819	1837
11.	mK'as grub ,,	1837	1855
12.	' P ' rin-las ,,	1856	1874
13.	T'ub-bstan ,,	1876	1933 *
14.	Ling-Erh Pamo Töntrup Lamu Fankha	1935 June 6	

It will be observed that the official list does not commence with Tsong-Kha-pa, for it is held that the first Tulku took place after the passing of Ganden Truppa, in 1474 or 1475. As tradition has it, his spirit did not leave this earth but instead passed into the body of an infant boy. The series of Grand Lamas has continued in this manner ever since. Thus, the meaning of Tulku in connection with the Dalai Lamas signifies the transference of the spirit from one vehicle to another vehicle. While this idea appears strange in Western lands, it was not considered so in Tibet. Sir Charles Bell in his book, *The Religion of Tibet,* points out that even in early periods of Tibetan history the idea was present. In regard to Ganden Truppa he writes:

" soon after his death the system of incarnation from man to man was developed. The incarnation of God in man was known from the first; we find traces of it in some of the earliest Tibetan records: the inscriptions engraved on the stone monuments at Lhasa.

* To the above Official List has been added the death of the 13th Dalai Lama (as it occurred in 1933). Also added is the name of the 14th Dalai Lama. " Ling Erh " signifies " divine child". The enthronement of the Dalai Lama occurred on February 13, 1940, in the Potala at Lhasa. He was invested with full government powers on November 17, 1950 (when but 15 years old in place of the usual 18 years, due to the crisis in Tibet).

Thus, of a bygone king we can read, ' After having been a god in the heaven he reappeared as a king of human beings in the lofty land with the mountains of snow.'—Inscription on the eastern face of the stone pillar by the Temple in Lhasa." *

The second in the line of the Dalai Lamas, Gedün Gyatso,† carried on the hierarchical series until 1543. His name signifies " Ocean of Yearning for Righteousness." The third, Sönam Gyatso, is known as the propagator of Buddhism, carrying the faith into Mongolia. It was to him that the Mongol chieftain gave the title " Dalai Lama " (or Tala Lama). Passing on to the fifth in the series who is called " the great fifth," Lobsang Gyatso. It was during his rule, under the supervision of his chief minister, that the remarkable edifice called the Potala was erected. This great building is constructed of stone slabs, each one of which was carried from the quarry to the site upon the back of a workman. It is 900 feet in length and taller than St. Paul's cathedral in London. Another noteworthy item about this Dalai Lama is the fact that he travelled all the way to Pekin in order to visit the Emperor of China—quite a journey

---

* *Op. cit.*, p. 107, published by the Clarendon Press, Oxford, 1931. Sir Charles Bell was one of the few Europeans who had been granted the privilege of conversing with a Dalai Lama. He had the opportunity to learn Tibetan when he resided in Lhasa for some years, where he functioned as the representative of the Biritish Empire in Tibet.

† The reason that one finds such a variance in the spelling of Tibetan names is this: many writers prefer to spell the Tibetan words in English (or Roman letters) in the manner that they are pronounced. Again, others, especially scholars, prefer to transliterate Tibetan words in the way that they are written, even though there are many silent letters which are not pronounced, just as in English. For example, in the English word " though," three letters are not pronounced, namely *ugh*. Thus, in the " Official List " of the Grand Lamas (previously given) the first Dalai Lama's name though spelled *d*Ge'dun grub-pa is pronounced Ganden Truppa; the second, *d*Ge-'dun Gya-*m*ts'o is pronounced Gedün Gyatso; the third, Sod-nam, *r*Gya-*m*ts'o is pronounced Sönam Gyatso, and so forth.

in those days. He was received with dignity and was acknowledged as having sovereign rights, because of being supported by the Mongols and Manchus.

By turning to the " Official List," it may be observed that there was a period in which the young lamas of the hierarchical series passed through some strenuous times. In fact, from the era of the ninth up to and including the twelfth of the succession, the Dalai Lamas were all short-lived. Thus, the ninth died when only eleven years old; the tenth attained an age of twenty-three years; the eleventh perished when seventeen; the twelfth not even reaching his majority passed on in his twentieth year. It is held that the reason for the untimely passing of the young Lamas was due to the machinations of the regents. For during the minority of the Rimpoches, the regents were the actual rulers of Tibet.

While these statements may be viewed with suspicion, the following news item reported in the press for the year 1947 is indicative that former regents very likely conspired against the Rimpoches. The dispatch conveyed the news that the ex-regent, Jechong (born 1924), head of the Reting monastery, was ordered to be arrested by the ruling regent of Tibet, Yung Tseng Dala, on the charge of plotting against the Dalai Lama. Further, the report stated that the traitorous Jechong was blinded and died in prison. This news item had reference to the 14th Dalai Lama, who was then but a youth.

The thirteenth in the line of succession, named Lopsang Tupden Gyatso, was born in 1876 in the village of Per-chö-de, situated in the province of Tak-po, about a hundred miles south-east of Lhasa. He was duly insti-tuted as Gyal-po Rimpoche in 1893. The Lama proved to be a very able ruler and became known in the West through the writings of Sir Charles Bell, the British representative who lived in Lhasa. One of Bell's books, in fact, is entitled *Portrait of the Dalai Lama*, and is based upon the ambassador's personal observations and inter-views which he had with the Rimpoche.

The passing of this Grand Lama, in 1933, necessitated once again the appointment of a regent for the land. The story of the selection of the fourteenth Dalai Lama is reserved for Chapter V, which follows the section devoted to the Tashi Lamas.

The Tashi or Panchen Lamas

The Tashi Lamas of Tashi-Lhünpo are not held in the same degree of esteem in the West as are the Dalai Lamas. Doubtless the reason for this is that their real significance has not been understood, since they have not been concerned with civil affairs or with the administration of the kingdom of Tibet. In Bod-yul (as Tibetans call their land), however, they are looked upon with a greater degree of holiness and reverence, for the very reason that they have not been associated with temporal affairs, devoting themselves to spiritual pursuits. Then, too, the Panchen Lamas have always been noted for their lofty aims, their learning and studiousness in Lamaism (as Buddhism in Tibet is called in the West). The very title by which they are known conveys this meaning: Panchen Rimpoche—" the Precious Great Gem of Learning." Panchen has also the connotation of " great teacher," Rimpoche—" gem", or " precious jewel ".

Since both hierarchical series are regarded (popularly) as reincarnations of the Buddha and called " Living Incarnations of Buddha," wherein lies the difference? Tibetans have an explanation, but it deals with subtleties of metaphysics, which are not easily grasped by one schooled in the West. Here is the answer that would most likely be given by a Tibetan, representing the view of the populace: The Dalai Lamas are Incarnations originating from Chenrezi; the Tashi Lamas are Incarnations deriving from Ö-pa-me. Chenrezi is the Tibetan equivalent of the Northern Buddhistic term Avalokiteśvara; Ö-pa-me is the equivalent of Amitâbha. Officialdom might be induced to explain a little further, somewhat in this manner: Since Ö-pa-me is to be regarded

as the enlightener of Chenrezi, therefore the Incarnations
of the Tashi Lamas are to be viewed in a more spiritual
aspect than are the Dalai Lamas. It is unlikely that
an explanation of Chenrezi and Öpame would be forthcoming, and so the matter has hardly been clarified.
Assuredly an inquiry into the popular conceptions of
Chenrezi and Öpame would not yield a satisfactory
interpretation; therefore the subject is usually by-passed.

At this point a Theosophist is sure to ask: Has H. P.
Blavatsky clarified the subject? Here is her answer. It
commences with a reference to the popular idea of
regarding both series of Grand Lamas as Incarnations of
Buddha and continues:

" The expression that the latter ' never dies ' applies
but to the two great incarnations of equal rank—the
Dalai and the Tda-shi Lamas. Both are incarnations
of Buddha, though the former is generally designated
as that of Avalokiteśvara, the highest celestial Dhyân.
For him who understands the puzzling mystery by
having obtained a key to it, the Gordian knot of these
successive reincarnations is easy to untie. He knows
that Avalokiteśvara and Buddha are one as Amita-pho
(pronounced Fo) or Amita-Buddha is identical with
the former. What the mystic doctrine of the initiated
' Phag-pa ' or ' saintly men ' (adepts) teaches upon
this subject, is not to be revealed to the world at
large." *

Regarding Amitâbha, or Amita-Buddha, H.P.B. wrote
that it is:

---

* Quoted from an article entitled " Reincarnations in Tibet ", first
appearing in *The Theosophist*, Vol. III, No. 6, March, 1882, pp. 146-8.
Also published in *The Complete Works of H. P. Blavatsky*, Vol. III,
pp. 267-74.

A footnote was added after the word *Amita-pho*, as follows:

" In Tibetan *pho* and *pha*—pronounced with a soft labial breath-
like sound—means at the same time ' man, father.' So *pha-yul* is
native land; *pho-nyo*, angel, messenger of good news; *pha-me*,
ancestors, etc., etc."

" The Chinese perversion of the Sanskrit *Amrita Buddha*, or the ' Immortal Enlightened,' a name of Gautama Buddha. The name has such variations as Amita, Abida, Amitâya, etc., and is explained as meaning both ' Boundless Age ' and ' Boundless Light'. The original conception of the ideal of an impersonal divine light has been anthropomorphized with time." *

At this point it would be well to add the explanation which was given concerning the term Avalokiteśvara. First as to its literal meaning. The Sanskrit word compounded as follows: *ava*, a prepositional prefix meaning " down "; *lokita*, the past passive participial form of the verb *loch*, to see; *îśvara*, derived from the verbal root *îś*—to rule, to be master, generally rendered lord, hence applicable to the summit of a hierarchy, in connection with a cosmos; in the case of man usually rendered " the Lord within." Thus, Avalokiteśvara is

" ' The on-looking Lord.' In the exoteric interpretation, he is Padmapâni (the lotus-bearer and the lotus-born) in Tibet, the first divine ancestor of the Tibetans, the complete incarnation or Avatar of Avalokiteśvara; but in esoteric philosophy Avaloki, the ' on-looker,' is the Higher Self, while Padmapâni is the Higher Ego or Manas. The mystic formula ' Om mani padme hum ' is specially used to invoke their joint help. While popular fancy claims for Avalokiteśvara many incarnations on earth, and sees in him, not very wrongly, the spiritual guide of every believer, the esoteric interpretation sees in him the Logos, both celestial and human. Therefore, when the Yogâchârya School has declared Avalokiteśvara as Padmapâni ' to be the Dhyâni Bodhisattva of Amitâbha Buddha,' it is indeed, because the former is *the spiritual reflex in the world of forms* of the latter, both being one—one in heaven, the other on earth." †

---

* *The Theosophical Glossary*, p. 19. The Sanskrit word *amrita* signifies " un-dying," *i.e.*, immortal.

† *The Theosophical Glossary*, p. 44.

While the later Yogâchârya School is, strictly speaking, an exponent of Brahmanical teaching, rather than Buddhistic, nevertheless, in the exposition just presented in regard to the Dhyâni Bodhisattva, the two schools of thought are in agreement. It should be pointed out that the *terms* used by H.P.B. in the closing sentence of the extract are Buddhistic rather than Brahmanical. The equivalent Brahmanical term is Manu.

Turning now to the hierarchy of Tashi Lamas. The series commenced, according to popular tradition, when Lob-sang Gyatso, known as "the great fifth" Dalai Lama, made his old, revered teacher the first Grand Lama of Tashi-Lhünpo, and at the same time instituted the title of Panchen Rimpoche. While this may be the version given to the laity, within the temples there is another explanation, which hints that the hierarchy commenced after the passing of Tsong-Kha-pa. To be sure, there is the " Official List " prepared by the lamas and printed in the monastery of Tashi-Lhünpo, near Shigatse, and this indicates that the first recorded Panchen Lama commenced the series in 1569. Here is the official listing:

OFFICIAL LIST OF TASHI LAMAS *

		Born	Died	
1.	*b*Lo-bzan ch'os-kyi rhyal-mts'an	1569	1662	
2.	*b*Lo-bzan ye-she dpal bzan-po	1663	1737	
3.	*b*Lo-bzan dpal-idan ye-s'es	1738	1780	Installed 1743
4.	*r*Je-bstan pahi nima	1781	1854	
5.	*r*Je-dpal-idan ch'os-kyi grags-pa bstan-pahi dban p'yug	1854	1882	Died in August
6.	[name not given]	1883	1937†	Installed in Feb. 1888.

---

* Published in *Lamaism*, by L. A. Waddell, p. 236, 2nd ed. Taken from the list printed at Tashi-Lhünpo monastery.

† The date of the Panchen Lama's passing has of course been added to the Official List. It occurred in China.

8

Regarding the third Tashi Lama on the Official List: it is noteworthy that Lobzan Paldan received George Bogle * —a writer in the employ of the East India Company—as an ambassador for Warren Hastings in 1774, and a cordial relationship was thus established. Ambassador Bogle was thus the first Englishman to visit Tibet, and most likely the first European to meet a Tashi Lama, for while a few missionaries had been in Tibet before that time, none had been accorded a visit with a Grand Lama.

During his embassy to the court of the Tashi Lama at Tashi-Lhünpo, ambassador Bogle also mentions meeting the Panchen Lama's half-sister, Durjiay Panmo, who was regarded as an " Incarnation," that is to say, representing a reincarnation of a series of female embodiments. In other words, tradition has it that the Superior of the nunnery situated close to Lake Yam-dog-cho is maintained by means of a series of Tulkus. H. P. Blavatsky stated that the Chinese Princess who married the Tibetan King who introduced Buddhism into Tibet in the seventh century. was the one who inaugurated the succession of female Lamas or *Rim anis* (" precious nuns "), by means of successive reincarnations—that is, Tulkus.†

Shortly after George Bogle's reception at Tashi-Lhünpo, the Panchen Rimpoche received an embassy from the emperor of China. The purpose of the official call was to extend an invitation to the Panchen Lama to visit the emperor's court in China. The offer was accepted and plans were forthwith made for the long trip. The Rimpoche was attended by 1500 troops and followers and every comfort was prepared for him on the extended journey to Sining, where he met the emperor. However, while still in China the Panchen Lama contracted small-pox (a disease to which Tibetans are very susceptible),

---

* See Chapter V for the account of George Bogle's impression of his visit with the Panchen Lama.

† Cf. *The Theosophist*, III, No. 6, March, 1882, pp. 146-8; or *The Complete Works of H. P. Blavatsky*, III, p. 272.

and he died on November 12, 1780 before being able to return to his homeland.

Since the embassy sent by Warren Hastings to the Tashi Lama had been so successful, a second emissary was delegated to make another trip to Tashi-Lhünpo. Captain Samuel Turner was selected by Hastings to carry out the mission, and he set out for Tibet. On reaching Shigatse in 1783, Captain Turner learned that the Panchen Lama whom he was to meet had died in China. Nevertheless, ambassador Turner carried out his assignment, and met with the new Tashi Lama even though the successor was but an infant of eighteen months.*

It will be noticed that the name of the last Tashi Lama was not given on the Official List, although the date of his birth was supplied as having occurred in 1883, and that he was installed in February 1888. It is related that the Panchen Lama left his official seat at Tashi-Lhünpo in 1924 and resided in China until his death, which occurred in 1937. Because of this, the Chinese were in a position to select the successor for the position of the Grand Lama. Thus, in regard to the present living Panchen Lama, who is two years younger than the present Dalai Lama, it is stated by Harrer † (who spent

---

* For an account of Captain Turner's meeting with the infant Panchen Lama, see Chapter V.

† Heinrich Harrer, an Austrian by birth, has given in his book, *Seven Years in Tibet*, a most fascinating account, not only of his adventurous journey into Tibet on foot, but also of his stay in the Forbidden City (Lhasa). Having escaped with a companion from an internment camp in northern India, the two had a perilous journey lasting for 21 months before reaching Lhasa. There, expulsion was imminent, in fact both were ordered to leave the land. At the last moment, because of his inability to walk—brought on by exposure on icy mountains—Harrer was granted a temporary stay. Because of his knowledge of Tibetan, he and his companion demonstrated their ability to make themselves useful to government officials. After a time recognition of his capableness was rewarded by an interview with the Dalai Lama. This led to his being retained as a tutor of the fourteen-year-old ruler of Tibet—a position he held until 1950 when he was obliged to terminate it because the Dalai Lama decided

seven years in Lhasa) and by William O. Douglas * that the present Panchen Lama was selected in China from a number of young candidates. Instead of being educated in Tibet (as was customary for Grand Lamas), the child was tutored in China. He was declared in Peiping to be the rightful ruler of Tibet, and was introduced at Tashi-Lhünpo by Chinese officials.

Readers who are sympathetic to the traditions of Tibet may take comfort in a portion of a prophecy of Tsong-Kha-pa, stated by H. P. Blavatsky to be current in Tibet, which runs in this manner:

" When the western world is more ripe in the direction of philosophy, the incarnation of Pban-chhen-rin-po-chhe † —the Great Jewel of Wisdom—one of the Teshu Lamas, will take place, and the splendour of truth will then illuminate the whole world." ‡

Thus far an account of the hierarchical series of the Dalai and Tashi Lamas has been presented. However, there is another aspect of the Incarnation Idea which has not yet been brought forward. This theme is very closely connected with Tulku and may, in fact, be stated to furnish a demonstration of the idea. It is true that this aspect is not so well known as is the " living Incarnations" connected with the Grand Lamas, nor has it

---

to leave Tibet when his land was invaded by an army from China. Thus this narrative represents first-hand knowledge of the people of Tibet, more particularly with officialdom, with whom he was in close contact. His book, therefore, gives a personal account of the traditions held in regard to the Grand Lamas and their " Incarnations".

* In his book *Beyond the High Himalayas*, published in 1952. William O. Douglas, Associate Justice of the U.S. Supreme Court since 1939, records his travels in Central Asia made during 1951. He made a trek by foot and pack train from Manali to Leh in the Indian Himalayas. Justice Douglas met and talked with men and women who bring sheep trains from Sinkiang and Tibet, as well as discoursed with lamas and local officials. Quite naturally the topic of the Grand Lamas was foremost in their conversation.

† Usually spelled Panchen Rimpoche.

‡ *H. P. Blavatsky Collected Writings*, Vol. VI, p. 105.

been publicized by writers on Tibet. Yet it is deserving of careful consideration. The subject may best be presented by reference to a scene at which a European scientist affirms he was an eye-witness. He relates that the episode occurred in a Buddhist temple. The account is taken from H. P. Blavatsky's narrative of the incident and she states that the Florentine scientist sent the report of his observation direct to the French Institute in the early part of the 1800's:

" having been permitted to penetrate in disguise to the hallowed precincts of a Buddhist temple, where the most solemn of all ceremonies was taking place, [he] relates the following as having been seen by himself. An altar is ready in the temple to receive the resuscitated Buddha, found by the initiated priesthood, and recognized by certain secret signs to have reincarnated himself in a new-born infant. The baby, but a few days old, is brought into the presence of the people and reverentially placed upon the altar. Suddenly rising into a sitting posture, the child begins to utter in a loud, manly voice, the following sentences: ' I am Buddha, I am his spirit; and I, Buddha, your Dalai-Lama, have left my old, decrepit body, at the temple of . . . and selected the body of this young babe as my next earthly dwelling.' Our scientist, being finally permitted by the priests to take, with due reverence, the baby in his arms, and carry it away to such a distance from them as to satisfy him that no ventriloquial deception is being practised, the infant looks at the grave academician with eyes that ' make his flesh creep,' as he expresses it, and repeats the words he had previously uttered." *

There is yet to be brought forward another aspect connected with the subject of the Incarnation Idea, or Reincarnations of the Lamas, as it is termed by writers on Tibet. This aspect, which may be found current

---

* *Isis Unveiled*, Vol. I, p. 437.

in Tibet, however, expresses but a portion of the doctrine, which is somewhat analagous to the Northern Buddhistic teaching concerning the Dhyâni-Buddhas and their counterparts on earth. Thus, reference is made to the three manifestations of the Buddha, although there are five aspects which form the Lamaic hierarchy. Because of this, therefore, one would be justified in making the statement that there must be teachings regarding Lamaism (or Buddhism in Tibet) which are not expressed publicly. As stated popularly, then, there is a triple manifestation in connection with the Buddha, which is termed the Ku, Tuk and Sung. Sir Charles Bell mentions the subject in his books, stating that Ku represents the " Body", Tuk, the " Mind", and Sung, " Speech". These represent manifestations or " Incarnations" of the Buddha in the following manner: Ku—applicable to the " Incarnation " of the Dalai Lama; Tuk—to the Tashi Lama; Sung—to the Emperor of China. The statement was added that the Jampeyang Incarnation—or the Incarnation of *Sung*—is regarded as no longer occurring.*

Clarification of the theme may best be made by means of a citation:

" And now for the Lamaic hierarchy. Of the living or incarnate Buddhas there are five also, the chief of whom is Dalay, or rather Talay-Lama—from *Tale* ' Ocean ' or Sea; he being called the ' Ocean of Wisdom '. Above him, . . . there is but the ' SUPREME WISDOM '—the abstract principle from which emanated the five Buddhas—Maïtree Buddha (the last Bodhisattva, or Vishnu in the Kalki Avatar) the tenth ' messenger ' expected on earth—included. But this will be *the* One Wisdom and will incarnate itself into the whole humanity collectively, not in a single individual. But of this mystery—no more at present.

---

* Especially so as the Chinese emperors had not supported Buddhism. The idea was expressed, of course, before the Chinese emperor had passed from the world scene.

" These five ' Hobilgans ' * are distributed in the following order:

" (1) Talay-Lama, of Lha-ssa, the incarnation of the ' Spiritual ' ' passive wisdom,'—which proceeds from Gautama or Siddhartha Buddha, or Fo.

" (2) Bande-cha-an Rem-Boo-Tchi, at Djashi-Loombo.† He is ' the *active* earthly wisdom '.

" (3) Sa-Dcha-Fo, or the ' Mouthpiece of Buddha ', otherwise the ' word ' at Ssamboo.

" (4) Khi-sson-Tamba—the ' Precursor ' (of Buddha) at the Grand Kooren.

" (5) Tchang-Zya-Fo-Lang, in the Altai mountains. He is called the ' Successor ' (of Buddha).

" The ' Shaberons ' are one degree lower. They, like the chief *Okhals* of the Druses, are the initiates of the great wisdom or Buddh esoteric religion. . . . It was from the ninth to the fifteenth centuries that modern Lamaism evolved its ritual and popular religion, which serves the Hobilgans and Shaberons as a blind, even against the curiosity of the average Chinaman and Tibetan. " ‡

---

* Hobilgan, also spelled Khubilkhan or Khubilhan by H.P.B.: a Mongolian term equivalent in meaning to the Tibetan term Chutuktu (also spelled Houtouktou), which is explained as follows:

" In the mystical system of the Druses there are five ' messengers ' or interpreters of the ' Word of the Supreme Wisdom ', who occupy the same position as the five chief Bodhisattvas, or Hobilgans of Tibet, each of whom is the bodily temple of the spirit of one of the five Buddhas."—*The Theosophist*, II, No. 9, June, 1881, pp. 193-6; or *The Complete Works of H. P. Blavatsky*, III, p. 22.

† Other spellings of Panchen Rimpoche at Tashi-Lhünpo. Maïtree Buddha is usually spelled Maitreya-Buddha.

‡ *The Theosophist*, Vol. II, No. 9, June, 1881, pp. 193-6; *The Complete Works of H. P. Blavatsky*, Vol. III, pp. 23-4.

CHAPTER V

CONCERNING THE SELECTION OF
THE DALAI LAMA AND TULKU

The present Dalai Lama of Tibet is regarded as the fourteenth in succession, or the fourteenth Incarnation, of the Dalai Lama series. The thirteenth Gyalpo Rimpoche (to use the Tibetan term) was a very progressive individual. He was interested in the activities of the world and would like to have made improvements in the condition of Tibet. His ideas were viewed with disfavour, however, and he was not permitted to put them into practice because of the opposition of the Den-sa Sum in his Cabinet—that is, the three Pillars of the State, representing the three abbots of the three largest monasteries. In spite of objections, however, the Dalai Lama had made trips into China as well as into India. So that in 1910, when a Chinese army marched into Tibet, the Rimpoche did not hesitate to flee from Tibet. He did so, and took sanctuary in India.

While in India, at Darjiling, the Tibetan ruler came into contact with Sir Charles Bell, who held an official position in the British administration of India. Sir Charles was very sympathetic to the situation in Tibet. When peace was restored between China and Tibet, the Dalai-Lama invited the British adminstrator to visit him at Lhasa. The invitation was accepted and Sir Charles spent some time in Tibet. In fact he became the official British representative in Lhasa. This British ambassadorial position continued to be maintained until the present status of India came into being.

Before the thirteenth Dalai-Lama's death, which occurred in 1933, he gave hints regarding his forthcoming birth, inferring that a Tulku would be made manifest. And so it came to pass, as the story is related in Tibet.

After the Rimpoche's passing, his body was placed in state in the manner in which the Buddha is usually represented, looking toward the south. But it was noticed, one morning, that instead of facing south, the head was turned towards the east. Whereupon the Tibetan Oracle was consulted.

One of the positions looked upon with great respect by the Tibetan administrative government is that of the Oracle. It is held by a monk, who is chosen for it because of his aptitude. His sole activity consists in the deliverance of oracles, whenever consulted in connection with government procedures. His services are in constant demand. There is, of course, quite a ritual involved in connection with the consultation, but to state the matter briefly, it may be said that the oracles are delivered during a trance-condition. In this instance the Oracle's message was not at all definite: a white scarf was simply tossed in the direction of the rising sun.

Two years passed by without any further information from the Oracle. The regent of the land, who had been appointed by the Tibetan Cabinet upon the passing of the Dalai Lama, decided that he would make a pilgrimage to a celebrated lake in Tibet, known as Chö Khor Gya. It is said that any person looking into the waters of this lake will see part of a vision of future events. The trip to the lake was made and some days were spent in prayer and meditation before going to the edge of the water. Upon approaching it and looking into the clear surface of the lake, the regent saw the picture of a three-storied monastery having golden roofs. Nearby he noticed a somewhat small house, of the kind in which peasants are accustomed to dwell. His attention, however, was attracted to it because of its uniquely carved gables. He had the feeling that this would be the place where the new Dalai Lama would be found.

On returning to Lhasa, the regent organized several search parties, each party consisting of a group of monks as well as some government officials. They were all given the same instructions: what to look for, what to be governed by, and especially to watch for a child who would be able to identify objects belonging to the late Dalai Lama. All travelled eastward. First, search was

made in Tibet, but without results. One group went on
into China, into the province of Chingnai, and from
there into the district of Amdo. This region once had
belonged to Tibet. It was 'the region from which Tsong-
Kha-pa had come—from the lake of Koko-nor. Even
now many Tibetans still live there. Also monasteries
are there situated. In their search, the party had come
upon many boys, but none seemed to have the qualifying
marks. When about to depart from that locality, they
came upon a three-storied monastery and noticed that
its roofs were golden. Close to it they observed a small
hut and were especially attracted to it because of its
carved gables. This was indeed what they had been
told to look for. But prescribed ritual had to be observed.
Instead of entering the house immediately, the group
withdrew to their resting-place. There, the officials
took on the dress of their servants, and the servants put
on the regalia of their masters. Whereupon the whole
group went to the house by the monastery.

Upon entering the hut the officials were of course shown
into the main room, while the disguised servants were
led to the kitchen. Upon entering the back room a
two-year old boy came running forward calling out:
" Sera Lama, Sera Lama," indicating that in spite of
being born in China, so far distant from Lhasa, the child
had not been taken in by the servant's disguise: he had
recognized a Lama from the great monastery of Sera in
Tibet. But, even more, the little one espied a rosary
around the neck of the disguised Lama and reached for
it. The Lama let him have it for a while. The officials
of the party were quite convinced that they had found
the object of their search. Yet, even so, they still had
to observe the traditional method of procedure. So they
bade farewell to the parents of the child, and requested
that they be allowed to return again in a few days.

On their next call there was no substitution of robes,
the group came in their proper garments. Upon their
arrival they formally requested to see the child, who was
brought into the presence of the four officials of the party.
But there was no shrinking or timidness, no cringing or

mark of fear, so often displayed by children upon seeing unaccustomed persons. When the officials placed four rosaries before the little boy, without hesitation he selected the well-worn rosary of the former Dalai-Lama, in place of the other glittering ones, and danced up and down in joy. Some drums and drum-sticks were displayed, and straightway the child selected the pair which had been used by the Rimpoche to call his servants. Next, walking sticks were brought forth. Instead of choosing a beautiful one with a silver handle, the old one which had been used by the Lama was selected. From four tea-cups, the boy pointed to the one which had been in use as the drinking-cup. Thus, having made the correct indentification of objects belonging to the former Gyalpo Rimpoche, the delegates examined the body of the child for certain characteristic marks. These were found to be present. The officials were quite satisfied that they had found the reincarnated Dalai Lama. They were certain that the Tulku had been effected; everything pointed to it. Forthwith they sent a coded message to Lhasa via India—for there is a telegraph line between India and Lhasa.

The regent's party was given instructions how to proceed. Namely, to continue the search for other likely candidates, instead of asking for official permission to take the child out of China. Had they done so, the Chinese would promptly have placed the child under a military escort, which would have entered Tibet and remained there permanently. After a time permission was requested of the governor of the province, for permission to have the parents accompany the child to Lhasa in order that a boy might be chosen from among the candidates which had been selected. The governor demanded 100,000 Chinese dollars for the privilege. When the sum was paid promptly, the governor suspected that especial attention was being given to the child in his province and thereupon raised the amount to 400,000 dollars.

The Tibetans realized that they had made a mistake. They had been too hasty. Therefore they became cautious. Instead of raising the increased sum, they turned to Mohammedan merchants, borrowing some money—only half the sum asked—and promising to pay the balance when the merchants reached Lhasa. It was stipulated that they would accompany the caravan into Tibet. The Chinese governor agreed to the compromise.

Towards the late summer of 1939 the Tibetan delegation with their servants set out on the return journey to their capital city. The child was not being escorted alone; he was accompanied by his parents, to whom signal honours were also paid. The Mohammedan merchants and their pack animals also formed part of the caravan. Several months were required to make the journey, because it was performed by means of slow stages. Not until the delegation had crossed into the Tibetan frontier did it receive official recognition. This was accorded by a Cabinet Minister himself, who was waiting with a message from the regent of the land, acknowledging the boy as the future Dalai Lama. Later, in 1940, the child was duly installed as the Gyalpo Rimpoche at Lhasa.*

Since Reincarnation is a cardinal tenet in Theosophy, one who is confirmed in the belief does not question the doctrine of rebirth. But in view of the teachings associated with Reincarnation, some explanation is necessary regarding the very rapid return to incarnation in the case of the Dalai Lamas. How is it possible? How can the after-death states and conditions be dispensed with—practically in their entirety? Here is where the doctrine of Tulku comes in. But the explanation of necessity must be given in technical terms,

---

* This story of the selection of the present Dalai Lama has been circulated in the public press. An account of it was given in *The Reader's Digest*. It was narrated in *The Saturday Evening Post* (April 13, 1946) and quoted by William O. Douglas in his book *Beyond the High Himalayas*. Likwise the story was related by Heinrich Harrer in his *Seven Years in Tibet*. Virtually the same tests were required of other young boys in the selection of previous Dalai Lamas, as, for instance, in the account mentioned by Sir Charles Bell in connection with the thirteenth Dalai Lama, whom he came to know so well.

since the terminology of modern languages is insufficient. This will be given in a later chapter. Nevertheless, there is an analagous phase which may now be presented. In fact, it may be regarded as another aspect of Tulku. In the Orient this phase is also referred to in popular language. Similarly, it is called the Incarnation of a Living Buddha. Orientalists are just as skeptical about this phase as they are about the possibility of the reincarnation of the Dalai-Lama—in the manner recounted above. Instead of re-telling the story, a citation will be used, because of the way in which it is worded. It is given in the form of an eye-witness account, couched in the language of a modern skeptic, emphatically denying the possibility of such an occurrence. The skeptical attitude of disbelief is typical of the frame of mind adopted by the person reared in Western civilization. Such a one fortifies himself against the inroads of reports brought by eye-witnesses by wrapping himself in the cloak of disbelief. He regards himself as superior to the credulous believer. Because of this he loses touch with many of the finer things of life. But to the narration.

The episode is related by H. P. Blavatsky, who declares that she witnessed such an Incarnation of a Living Buddha, in the company of an ex-Lutheran minister, whom she calls Mr. K—. The minister is introduced in this manner:

" K—was a positivist, and rather prided himself on this anti-philosophical neologism. But his positivism was doomed to receive a death-blow.

" But one sight seen by him was as good as if he had witnessed the reincarnation of Buddha itself. Having heard of this ' miracle' from some old Russian missionary in whom he thought he could have more faith than in Abbé Huc, it had been for years his desire to expose the ' great heathen ' jugglery, as he expressed it."

" About four days journey from Islamabad, at an insignificant mud village, whose only redeeming feature was its magnificent lake, we stopped for a few days' rest. It was there that we were apprised by our Shaman * that a large party of Lamaic ' Saints', on pilgrimage to various shrines, had taken up their abode in an old cave-temple and established a temporary Vihâra † therein. The holy Bhikshus ‡ were capable of producing the greatest miracles. Mr. K—, fired with the prospect of exposing this humbug of the ages, proceeded at once to pay them a visit, and from that moment the most friendly relations were established between the two camps.

" The Vihâra was in a secluded and most romantic spot, secured against all intrusion. Despite the effusive attentions, presents and protestations of Mr. K—, the Chief (an ascetic of great sanctity), declined to exhibit the phenomenon of the ' incarnation ' until a certain talisman in possession of the writer was exhibited. Upon seeing this, however, preparations were at once made, and an infant of three or four months was procured from its mother, a poor woman of the neighborhood. An oath was first of all exacted of Mr. K—, that he would not divulge what he might see or hear, for the space of seven years. . . .

" On the appointed afternoon, the baby being brought to the Vihâra, was left in the vestibule or reception-room, as K— could go no further into the temporary sanctuary. The child was then placed on a bit of carpet in the middle of the floor, and every one not belonging to the party being sent away, two ' mendicants ' were placed at the entrance to keep out intruders. Then all the lamas seated themselves on the floor, with their backs against the granite walls, so that each was separated from the child by a space, at least, of ten feet. The chief, having had a square piece of leather spread for him by the servant, seated

---

* Shaman—a Tartar or Mongolian priest-magician.

† Vihâra (Sanskrit)—with Buddhists or Jainas, a temple or monastery.

‡ Bhikshus (Sanskrit)—in Buddhism, either monks or mendicants.

himself at the farthest corner.   Alone, Mr. K— placed himself close by the infant, and watched every movement with intense interest.   The only condition exacted of us was that we should preserve a strict silence, and patiently await further developments.   A bright sunlight streamed through the open door.   Gradually the 'Superior' fell into what seemed a state of profound meditation, while the others, after a sotto voce short invocation, became suddenly silent, and looked as if they had been completely petrified.   It was oppressively still, and the crowing of the child was the only sound to be heard.   After we had sat there a few moments, the movements of the infant's limbs suddenly ceased, and his body appeared to become rigid.   K—watched intently every motion, and both of us, by a rapid glance, became satisfied that all present were sitting motionless. The Superior, with his gaze fixed upon the ground, did not even look at the infant; but, pale and motionless, he seemed rather like a bronze statue of a Talapoin * in meditation than a living being. Suddenly, to our great consternation, we saw the child, not raise itself, but, as it were, violently jerked into a sitting posture! A few more jerks, and then, like an automaton set in motion by concealed wires, the four months' baby stood upon his feet! Fancy our consternation, and, in Mr. K—'s case, horror. Not a hand had been outstretched, not a motion made, nor a word spoken; and yet, here was a baby-in-arms standing erect and firm as a man!

"The rest of the story we will quote from a copy of notes written on this subject by Mr. K—, the same evening, and given to us, in case it should not reach its place of destination, or the writer fail to see anything more.

"After a minute or two of hesitation, writes K—, the baby turned his head and looked at me with an expression of intelligence that was simply awful! It

---

* Talapoin (Siamese)—a Buddhist monk and ascetic in Siam.

sent a chill through me. I pinched my hands and
bit my lips till the blood almost came, to make sure
that I did not dream. But this was only the beginning.
The miraculous creature, making, *as I fancied*, two
steps toward me, resumed his sitting posture, and,
without removing his eyes from mine, repeated, sentence
by sentence, in what I supposed to be Tibetan language,
the very words, which I had been told in advance, are
commonly spoken at the incarnations of Buddha,
beginning with ' I am Buddha; I am the old Lama; I
am his spirit in a new body,' etc. I felt a real terror;
my hair rose upon my head, and my blood ran cold.
For my life I could not have spoken a word. There
was no trickery here, no ventriloquism. The infant
lips moved, and the eyes seemed to search my very
soul with an expression that made me think it was the
face of the Superior himself, his eyes, his very look
that I was gazing upon. It was as if his spirit had
entered the little body, and was looking at me through
the transparent mask of the baby's face. I felt my
brain growing dizzy. The infant reached toward me,
and laid his little hand upon mine. I started as if
I had been touched by a hot coal; and, unable to bear
the scene any longer, covered my face with my hands.
It was but for an instant; but when I removed them,
the little actor had become a crowing baby again, and
a moment after, lying upon his back, set up a fretful
cry. The Superior had resumed his normal condition,
and conversation ensued.

" It was only after a series of similar experiments,
extending over ten days, that I realized the
fact that I had seen the incredible, astounding
phenomenon described by certain travellers, but always
by me denounced as an imposture. Among a multitude of questions unanswered, despite my cross-
examination, the Superior let drop one piece of
information, which must be regarded as highly
significant. ' What would have happened,' I inquired,
through the Shaman, ' if, while the infant was speaking,
in a moment of insane fright, at the thought of its

being the "Devil", I had killed it?' He replied that, 'if the blow had not been instantly fatal, the child *alone* would have been killed.' 'But,' I continued, 'suppose that it had been as swift as a lightning-flash?' 'In such case,' was the answer, '*you would have killed me also.*'" *

In this aspect of Tulku, in which a demonstration of its performance was provided by a Shaberon, the Tulku was performed in daylight. No special conditions were required, such as darkness or screened cabinets. It differs from the first phase of Tulku, which was described in connection with the case of the Tibetan Dalai Lama, in that the "individuality-consciousness" as well as the "personality-consciousness" (to coin terms, for lack of English words) were transferred consciously by the Shaberon into the infant. The ability of the Superior to activate the infant's body was demonstrated, the while functioning as the Shaberon—not as an infant! This is the important point to bear in mind. It was referred to in the episode as the Superior's ability to "shine through the transparent mask of the baby's face." Furthermore, the power of the Shaberon was also conclusively manifested in that he was able to depart from the infant *at will*. The concluding questions and answers of the citation give the clue to the performance of Tulku —the ability to project the "individuality-consciousness" as well as to withdraw it *at will*.

In the phase of the Dalai Lamas of Tibet, as related previously, the Tulku is not known until after a few years have elapsed—at least that is the general pattern that has been noted throughout the series of Dalai Lamas as recorded. As only infants have been connected with the Tulku, very little has been ascertained about the status of the infants, for as soon as the "incarnation" is discovered and brought into Tibet, the tot has been placed in strict seclusion and guarded very carefully.

---

* *Isis Unveiled*, II, 599-602.

9

The technical ruler of the land, in such case, is the regent. However, this regent in his turn would be held accountable to, and kept under the surveillance of the all-powerful Cabinet, which again would be under the dominancy of the chief abbots of the three large monasteries—of Ganden, Sera and Drepung.

One testimonial is available, which was given by the second Englishman to visit Tibet, who was accorded an interview with a Tashi Lama, in spite of the fact that at the time the Lama was only eighteen months old. For the sake of clarity it should be repeated here that the Tashi Lamas * of Tibet are also regarded as maintaining the series of lamaistic incarnations through the performance of Tulku, in similar manner to the Dalai Lamas. In response to an invitation, Warren Hastings (then in charge of affairs in India) in 1783 sent an embassy to Tibet under the captaincy of Samuel Turner to visit the Tashi Lama at Shigatse. Before reaching his destination, however, the Tashi Lama who had extended the invitation had passed away. In his publication entitled *An Account of an Embassy to the Court of the Teshoo Lama in Tibet*, published in London in 1800, he refers to this in the following manner:

> " The soul of the late Lama, according to the doctrines of their faith, having passed into, and animated the body of an infant, who, on the discovery of his identity, by such testimonies as their religion prescribes, was acknowledged and proclaimed by the same title and appellation as his predecessor." †

Upon arriving at Shigatse Captain Turner was informed of the passing of the Tashi Lama, nevertheless, he decided to go ahead with the carrying out of his assignment even though it meant that he should present

---

* The Dalai Lama is the titular ruler of Tibet, responsible both for civil and religious affairs, and resides at Lhasa. The Tashi Lama is head of the monastery of Tashi-Lhünpo, near Shigatse, and is regarded as having higher spiritual authority than the Dalai Lama.

† *Op. cit.*, Introduction, p. xvii.

himself to an infant. Turner relates that on the day
arranged for the reception, the parents of the young
Tashi Lama told him that their son had awakened early
and could not be prevailed upon to go back to sleep.
Testifying to the audience, the captain continued:

" Though unable to speak he made most expressive
signs and conducted himself with astonishing dignity
and decorum. . . . His features were good; he had
small black eyes; and an animated expression of
countenance; altogher, I thought him one of the handsomest children I had ever seen." *

In his narrative Captain Turner refers to the first
Englishman to visit Tibet in 1774—also sent by Warren
Hastings on an embassy to the Tashi Lama at Shigatse.
This trip was under the ambassadorship of George Bogle,
a writer of the East India Company. Mr. Bogle wrote
of the Tashi Lama whom he visited nine years previous
to Captain Turner's trip to Shigatse (quoting from the
captain's book):

" I endeavoured to discover in him some of those
defects which are inseparable from humanity, but he
is so universally loved that I had no success, and not
a man could find it in his heart to speak ill of him." †

One more citation from the *Account of an Embassy to
the Court of the Teshoo Lama* is deserving of inclusion here,
in that it testifies to the profound impression that must
have been made upon Captain Turner. He mentions that
the Regent of the Tashi Lama regarded the infant Tashi
Lama with reverence " tending to establish the identity
of the present " Tashi Lama with the previous Lama

" from the unerring signs of wisdom and greatness
stamped upon his brow, and the early traits of his
sublime character which had been already evidently
displayed." ‡

* *Op. cit.*, pp. 335-6

† *Op. cit.*, p. 338.

‡ *Op. cit.*, pp. 252-3.

CHAPTER VI

H. P. BLAVATSKY IN TIBET

There is a fascination about the very word Tibet that intrigues one—that is if a person is at all inclined towards mystical things. Unquestionably it must have so appealed to H.P.B. What was the potent spark that lit the flame within, spurring her onward to make attempt after attempt to enter that forbidden land? Surely it must have been more than the lure to travel in out-of-the-way places, for she had already been in India, in Siam, in Egypt, in Greece, in Canada, in America—even crossing the continent at a time when the only way of making the trip was by covered wagon!—in Turkey, and in little-known places of her Russian homeland. Or again in Texas, in Mexico and Peru—in an era when to travel in those regions was no light task. Had she heard of Swedenborg's declaration that to find the Lost Word one had to search for it in Tartary or Tibet? Or had she come upon a clue that the members of a Secret Brotherhood had their *âsrama* behind the snowy fastnesses of the Himalayas?

Be that as it may, H. P. Blavatsky was determined that she would brook no defeat in pursuing the quest she had set for herself. And if she was not successful in her first attempt, she certainly was not discouraged in making another trial. Neither was she disheartened. That her first entry into Tibet was thwarted by officials, came to light in a rather unusual way. It may never have been made known, but for a chance meeting of Colonel H. S. Olcott with a British official in a train during one of his trips in India. Certain it is that H.P.B. never mentioned the incident to him, and very likely had not told anyone else about that first attempt of hers. It does not seem to have been mentioned in her volume of letters which were written to A. P. Sinnett between the years 1880 and 1887.* Since Col. Olcott was very interested in the travels of H. P. Blavatsky before the founding of The Theosophical Society, he gave careful attention to what his travelling companion had to recount. He recorded the episode in this manner † :

"On the 3rd of March, 1893, S. V. Edge and I met in the train between Nalhati and Calcutta, Major-General C. Murray (retired), late of the 70th Bengal Infantry, now Chairman of the Monghyr Municipality, who met H.P.B. in 1854 or '55, at Punkabaree, at the feet of the Darjeeling Hills. He was then a Captain, commanding the Sebundy Sappers and Miners. She was trying to get into Tibet via Nepal ' to write a book '; and to do it, she wished to cross the Rungit river. Captain Murray had it reported to him by the guard that a European lady had passed that way, so he went after and brought her back. She was very angry, but in vain. She stopped with Captain and Mrs. Murray for about a month when, finding her plan defeated, she left, and Captain Murray heard of her as far as Dinajpore. She was then apparently about thirty years of age.

"The above facts were so interesting that I wrote them out in the railway carriage and got General Murray to append his certificate, as follows: ' The above memo is correct. C. Murray, Major-General.'

"The British Resident probably did have something to do indirectly with her detention, for strict orders had been given by Captain Murray, in military command

---

* These *Letters of H. P. Blavatsky to A. P. Sinnett* were incorporated in book-form under this title, and published after Mr. Sinnett's death under the editorship of A. Trevor Barker in 1925. These letters also formed the basis for the work entitled *Incidents in the Life of Madame Blavatsky*. This book was prepared and published in 1886 by A. P. Sinnett during the lifetime of H. P. Blavatsky.

† In *The Theosophist*, April, 1893. Quoted in *Personal Memoirs of H. P. Blavatsky*, by Mary K. Neff (published in 1937), p. 58, where it is stated that there is a confusion in the dates: it " should be 1853. She was not in India in 1854."

of that Frontier District, to permit no European to cross the Rungit, as they would be almost sure of being murdered by the wild tribes in that country."

Word of another trial to cross the border between India and Tibet is available. In similar fashion it came to Colonel Olcott's attention while at Bareilly. Unfortunately, the Colonel was not so methodical in acquiring the details as in his former journey. He failed to give the name of his informant; nor did he obtain a signed certificate as he did from Major-General Murray. This would have authenticated the fact beyond question. Nevertheless, here is the Colonel's memorandum:

"I got trace of another of her Tibetan attempts from a Hindu gentleman living at Bareilly, while on one of my North Indian official tours. The first time H.P.B. came to that station after our arrival in India, this gentleman recognised her as the European lady who had been his guest many years before, when she was going northward to try and enter Tibet via Kashmir. They had much pleasant chat about old times." *

The first account of Mme. Blavatsky's successful entry into Tibet was made known to the western world by a journalist, shortly after her arrival in New York in July, 1873. The reporter, Anna Ballard, was representing one of the prominent New York newspapers, of the nineteenth century, and had been given the assignment of interviewing someone from Russia. In addition to being a veteran journalist, Miss Ballard was also a life member of the New York Press Club. The reporter's account speaks for itself and is best narrated in her own words, which were put in the form of a letter to Colonel Olcott, in order that he might have this testimonial of the authentic incident. Miss Ballard was visiting Colonel Olcott at Adyar, India, in 1892, which accounts for the date line.

---

* From *The Theosophist*, April, 1893. Quoted in *Personal Memoirs of H. P. Blavatsky*, by Mary K. Neff, pp. 58-9, where it is stated that this second attempt to enter Tibet occurred in 1856.

"Adyar, 17th January, 1892.

" Dear Col. Olcott:

" My acquaintanceship with Mme. Blavatsky dates even further back than you suppose. I met her in July, 1873, at New York, not more than a week after she landed. I was then a reporter on the staff of the New York *Sun*, and had been detailed to write an article upon a Russian subject. In the course of my search after facts the arrival of this Russian lady was reported to me by a friend, and I called upon her; thus beginning an acquaintance that lasted several years. At our first interview she told me that she had had no idea of leaving Paris for America until the very evening before she sailed, but why she came or who hurried her off she did not say. I remember perfectly well her saying with an air of exultation, ' I have been in Tibet.' Why she should think that a great matter, more remarkable than any other of the travels in Egypt, India, and other countries she told me about, I could not make out, but she said it with special emphasis and animation. I now know, of course, what it means.

ANNA BALLARD." *

Nevertheless, before the actual successful accomplishment of entering Tibet and attaining the object of her quest, H. P. Blavatsky had given a narrative of another experience of hers, in which she managed to enter Tibet by means of a disguise. However, this venture landed her in a rather precarious position, to say the least. She contrived to extricate herself from this perilous situation

---

* Quoted in *Old Diary Leaves*, Vol. 1, pp. 21-2 (2nd ed., 1941). The first edition of this work by Henry Steel Olcott was published in 1895, during his lifetime. The book is sub-titled " The True History of the Theosophical Society," a narrative which Col. Olcott was fully qualified to write, since he was one of the Founders and President of the Society, from the time of its founding in New York in 1875 until his death in 1907. Largely autobiographical in character, *Old Diary Leaves* first appeared serially in *The Theosophist*, from March, 1892, until September, 1894, and reached the proportions of a six-volume publication.

by resorting to occult assistance—for ordinary human powers would have been of no avail, as she herself narrates the episode.

" Years ago, a small party of travellers were painfully journeying from Kashmir to Leh, a city of Ladakh (Central Tibet). Among our guides we had a Tartar Shaman, a very mysterious personage, who spoke Russian a little and English not at all, and yet who managed, nevertheless, to converse with us, and proved of great service. Having learned that some of our party were Russians, he had imagined that our protection was all powerful, and might enable him to safely find his way back to his Siberian home, from which, for reasons unknown, some twenty years before, he had fled, as he told us, via Kiachta and the great Gobi Desert, to the land of the Tcha-gars. With such an interested object in view, we believed ourselves safe under his guard. To explain the situation briefly: Our companions had formed the unwise plan of penetrating into Tibet under various disguises, none of them speaking the language, although one, a Mr. K—,* had picked up some Kasan Tartar, and thought he did. As we mention this only incidentally, we may as well say at once that two of them, the brothers N—, were very politely brought back to the frontier before they had walked sixteen miles into the weird

---

* In one of her letters to Mr. Sinnett, mention is made that the minister's name was Külwein and that he was met in Lahore in 1856 (*H. P. Blavatsky's Letters to A. P. Sinnett*, p. 151). It would seem that H.P.B.'s meeting with Külwein was opportune, because the minister was known to her father, Colonel Peter von Hahn—at the time of Helena's birth he was a Captain of Artillery. Colonel von Hahn had requested Külwein, if possible, to contact his daughter, in the event that he should meet her during his travel in the Orient (Cf. William Kingsland's *The Real H. P. Blavatsky*, p. 44). In all likelihood Külwein may have been the means, in one instance, of supplying H.P.B. with funds, since Colonel von Hahn kept providing his daughter with financial assistance, whenever an opportunity presented itself for doing so. Also, cf. Sinnett's *Incidents in the Life of Madame Blavatsky*, pp. 44-5 (2nd ed.).

land of Eastern Bod; * and Mr. K—, an ex-Lutheran
minister, could not even attempt to leave his miserable
village near Leh, as from the first days he found himself
prostrated with fever, and had to return to Lahore
via Kashmere. . . .

"We . . . [had] a kind of carnelian stone † in
our possession, which had such an unexpected and
favourable effect upon the Shaman's decision. Every
Shaman has such a talisman, which he wears attached
to a string, and carries under his left arm.

" ' Of what use is it to you, and what are its virtues? '
was the question we often offered to our guide. To
this he never answered directly, but evaded all explanation, promising that as soon as an opportunity was
offered, and we were alone, he would ask the stone to
answer for himself. With this very indefinite hope, we
were left to the resources of our own imagination.

" But the day on which the stone ' spoke ' came
very soon. It was during the most critical hours of
our life; at a time when the vagabond nature of a

---

* The Tibetans call their land *Bod*, or again *Bod-pa.*

† " The talisman is a simple agate or carnelian known among the
Tibetans and others as *A-yu*, and naturally possessed, or had been
endowed with very mysterious properties. It has a triangle engraved
upon it, within which are contained a few mystical words.

" These stones are highly venerated among Lamaists and Buddhists;
the throne and sceptre of Buddha are ornamented with them, and
the Dalai Lama wears one on the fourth finger of the right hand.
They are found in the Altai Mountains, and near the river Yarkuh.
Our talisman was a gift from the venerable high-priest, a *Heiloung*,
of a Kalmuck tribe. Though treated as apostates from their primitive Lamaism, these nomads maintain friendly intercourse with their
brother Kalmucks, the Chokhots of Eastern Tibet and Kokonor,
and even with the Lamaists of Lhasa. The ecclesiastical authorities,
however, will have no relations with them. We have had abundant
opportunities to become acquainted with this interesting people of
the Astrakhan Steppes, having lived in their *Kibitkas* in our early
years, and partaken of the lavish hospitality of the Prince Tumene,
their late chief, and his Princess. In their religious ceremonies, the
Kalmucks employ trumpets made from the thigh and arm bones of
deceased rulers and high priests."—*Isis Unveiled*, II, p. 600

traveller had carried the writer to far-off lands, where neither civilization is known, nor security can be guaranteed for one hour. One afternoon, as every man and woman had left the *yourta* (Tartar tent), that had been our home for over two months, to witness the ceremony of the Lamaic exorcism of a Tshoutgour,* accused of breaking and spiriting away every bit of the poor furniture and earthen-ware of a family living about two miles distant, the Shaman, who had become our only protector in those dreary deserts, was reminded of his promise. He sighed and hesitated; but, after a short silence, left his place on the sheepskin, and, going outside, placed a dried-up goat's head with its prominent horns over a wooden peg, and then dropping down the felt curtain of the tent, remarked that now no living person would venture in, for the goat's head was a sign that he was ' at work'.

" After that, placing his hand in his bosom, he drew out the little stone, about the size of a walnut, and, carefully unwrapping it, proceeded, as it appeared, to swallow it. In a few moments his limbs stiffened, his body became rigid, and he fell, cold and motionless as a corpse. But for a slight twitching of his lips at every question asked, the scene would have been embarrassing, nay—dreadful. The sun was setting, and were it not that dying embers flickered at the centre of the tent, complete darkness would have been added to the oppressive silence which reigned. We have lived in the prairies of the West, and in the boundless steppes of Southern Russia; but nothing can be compared with the silence at sunset on the sandy deserts of Mongolia; not even the barren solitudes of the deserts of Africa, though the former are partially inhabited, and the latter utterly void of life. Yet, there was the writer alone with what looked no better than a corpse lying on the ground. . . .

---

* "An elemental demon, which every native of Asia believes." —*Isis Unveiled*, II, 626.

"For over two hours, the most substantial, unequivocal proofs that the Shaman's astral soul was travelling at the bidding of our unspoken wish, were given to us. . . . .

"We had directed the Shaman's inner *ego* to the . . . Kutchi of Lhasa, who travels constantly to British India and back. *We knew* that he was apprised of our critical situation in the desert; for a few hours later came help, and we were rescued by a party of twenty-five horsemen who had been directed by their chief to find us at the place where we were, which no living man endowed with common powers could have known. The chief of this escort was a Shaberon, an 'adept' whom we had never seen before, nor did we after that, for he never left his *soumay* (lamasery), and we could have no access to it. But *he was a personal friend of the Kutchi*.

"The above will of course provoke naught but incredulity in the general reader. But we write for those who will believe; who, like the writer, understand and know the illimitable powers and possibilities of the human astral soul. In this case we willingly believe, nay, we know, that the 'spiritual double' of the Shaman did not act alone, for he was no adept, but simply a medium. According to a favorite expression of his, as soon as he placed the stone in his mouth, his 'father appeared, dragged him out of his skin, and took him wherever he wanted,' and at his bidding." *

As may be gleaned from the narrative, H.P.B. had been led by the Shaman into a district of eastern Tibet, which even in the twentieth century is regarded as dangerous. For that region is called the land of the Khampas—the very name of which is uttered fearfully by the nomads of Tibet, as it conveys the meaning that it is a land inhabited by robbers and cut-throats.

---

* From *Isis Unveiled*, Vol. II, pp. 598-9, and II, 626-8.

It is but natural to deduce that this third attempted entry into Tibet was unsuccessful. Since H.P.B. has given no sequential accounts of her travels and has left only a narrative of her adventurous exploits, it is difficult to give any precise information as to when she was actually at the place in Tibet which she had endeavored to reach. In fact, instead of passing the matter off lightly, she expressed herself vehemently in this manner:

" I say . . . to the world: ' Ladies and gentlemen, I am in your hands and subject and subordinate to the world's jury, *only since I founded the T.S.* Between H. P. Blavatsky from 1875 and H.P.B. from 1830 to that date, is a veil drawn and you are in no way concerned with what took place behind it, before I appeared as a public character. . . .' "

". . . The whole of my life except the weeks and months I passed with the Masters in Egypt or in Tibet, is so inextricably full of events with whose secrets and real actuality the dead and the living are concerned, and I made only responsible for their outward appearance, . . ." *

In the above extract the hint is given that she had attained her quest, not only in Tibet, but in Egypt as well. Thus we are led to conclude that Mme. Blavatsky definitely had accomplished the feat of entering Tibet and of contacting the custodians of the Ancient Wisdom. And from them she learned the process of evoking powers and potencies which are at present not only unknown to the Western world, but are dormant as well.

The suggestion is offered by the writer—and it is a novel one, in that he has not seen it expressed previously in any of the biographical data or books on H.P.B.— that her entrance into Tibet was made through China. We have evidence that she was in Japan and had contact with a little known religious order, known as the Yamabûshi. She refers to this in *The Secret Doctrine*:

---

* *Letters of H. P. Blavatsky to A. P. Sinnett,* p. 145.

" The seven ' mysteries ' are called by the Japanese *Yamabûshi*, the mystics of the Lao-Tze sect and the ascetic monks of Kioto, the Dzenodoo—the ' seven jewels.' Only the Japanese and Chinese Buddhist ascetics and Initiates are, if possible, even more reticent in giving out their ' Knowledge ' than are the Hindus." *

The journey from Japan to China could very easily have been accomplished. At all events, corroboration of the fact that Mme. Blavatsky *was in China*, is to be obtained from the following letter, which was written by an individual in China to a Hindu prince, who in turn forwarded the missive to Colonel Olcott. Because of its content the letter is given in full. The Colonel introduced the letter, which speaks for itself, in this manner:

" Through the kindness of an Indian Prince, we have received a letter written by a gentleman from Simla who was travelling in China, to an Indian friend. The reference to H.P.B. makes it specially interesting. We omit the names from the original letter, which is in our possession:

---

* *The Secret Doctrine*, Vol. I, pp. 173-4 (or. ed.); I, 226, 6 vol. ed.; I, 197-8, 3rd ed.

In the opening story of the book known as *Nightmare Tales*, collected and published after H.P.B.'s passing, the proficiency in the occult arts of the Yamabûshis is told with dramatic consequences. The story is entitled " A Bewitched Life " and gives detailed descriptions of tenets held by the Yamabûshis, which must have been gained by first-hand contact with them.

Then, referring to machines " which represented the night-sky with the planets and all their revolutions, with the angels presiding over them," the comment is added:

" Whether produced by *clockwork* or *magic* power, such machines —whole celestial spheres with planets rotating—were found in the Sanctuaries, and some exist to this day in Japan, in a secret subterranean temple of the old Mikados, as well as in two other places." (S.D., Vol. V, p. 322)

" RUNG JUNG, MAHAN, China,
JANUARY 1, 1900.

" Dear————

" Your letter addressed through His Highness, Rajah
Sahab Hira Singh, reached me while traversing the
Spiti Mts. Now I have crossed these Mts. and am in
the territory of Mahan, China. This place is known
by the name of Rung Jung, and lies within the territory
of the Chinese Empire. The place has a great cave
and is surrounded by high mts. It is the chief haunt
of lamas and the favourite resort of Mahatmas. Great
Rishis have chosen it on account of its antiquity and
beautiful scenery.

" The place is suited for divine contemplation. A
man can nowhere find a place better suited for focussing
one's mind. The great Lama Kut Te Hum is the guru
of all lamas, and has absorbed his attention in the form
of *samâdhi* for the last two and a half months. He is
expected to be out of *samâdhi* after some three and a
half months, so it is my chief desire to wait here for
that period, and personally converse with him. His
chelas also are ever meditating and trying to absorb
themselves in the great Divide.

" From conversation with them, I came to know
that Mme. Blavatsky had visited this place and medi-
tated here for some time. Formerly I had doubts as
to her arrival here, but all my misgivings have now
been removed, and I feel confident of her divine
contemplation at this holy and sacred place.

" The lesson and *Updesha* I received from these lamas
show that the views of the Theosophical Society are
not merely visionary and theoretical, but are practical
schemes. But after long experience I felt that it is
difficult to practise Yoga in the plains of Hindustan;
that it is possible to do so only in these high mountains.
Formerly I used to contemplate for two or three hours
per day, and that even with difficulty; now I can sit
easily for eight or nine hours and even more. I am,
nowadays, quite healthy and feel myself better than
before.

"A Bengali Babu named——is here with me, and has come here for the sake of contemplation, and we two will together proceed to Lhasa. These Lamas have got with them a valuable library, which I cannot describe to you within this short space." *

It is quite apparent that the writer of the letter did not wish to be too precise in his statements. Nevertheless, the document is a valuable testimonial regarding H.P.B. and her work in the Theosophical Society.

The next account of an incident concerning Mme. Blavatsky's stay in Tibet is in connection with one of the processes she witnessed performed by Tibetan shepherds, namely the liberation of the soul and of the astral body in animals. Although writing the account to a French journal H.P.B. does not give any clue as to the time-period when the event took place, nor does she mention the locality in which the experiences occurred. She writes:

" Please look in *La Revue Spirite* for July, 1878, and for October, 1878, where you have translated my interview with a reporter from the *New York World*, and compare it with what I told the reporter in regard to the liberation of the soul from the body and of the liberation of the soul and of the astral body in animals by the Tibetan shepherds, who have possessed the secret for ages. And I added, ' I predict that, within a year, *science will have discovered that method with the lower animals.*' Exactly a year afterwards Rotura discovered it.† Am I a medium? No. It was not a

---

* From *The Theosophist*, August, 1900.   Quoted in *Personal Memoirs of H. P. Blavatsky*, pp. 106-7.

Updesha (in the preceding paragraph): more correctly Upadeśa signifying instruction, teaching; also initiation.

† " Have you read in the French papers the account of the last great discovery in Australia, made by Professor Rotura? He plunges animals into a trance—deathly to all appearance—which lasts for about twenty days, two months, ten months, or more, as he wishes, and then he makes them revive at his will, perfectly well and happy; the whole thing is done by the manipulation of one of the arteries in the neck, in which he makes a tiny puncture with a needle dipped

prophecy, for in a letter from India from one of our Brothers and Chiefs there, they directed me to announce it to the world and I did so. I contradicted the reporter in my article in October, because I never said I had *myself helped in the operation done by the Tibetan shepherds*, who live in the Himalayas at 28,000 feet above sea-level, nor have I done it myself. But, as, until this day, it was one of the secrets of our Adepts I did not think I had the right to speak about it more than was necessary.

" I have seen that operation done by our ' Brothers ' fifty times, on human beings. They have operated on me, and I once slept for eleven weeks, believing myself to be awake the whole time and walking around like a ghost of Pontoise, without being able to understand why no one appeared to see me and to answer me. I was entirely unaware that I was liberated from my old carcase which, at that time, however, was a little younger. That was at the beginning of my studies.

" As far as the animals are concerned science will learn the secret—for human beings it will have to wait, materialistic as it is. It is the great secret known to fakirs, who bury themselves for months and revive after a certain time. During our latest journey, three months ago, we saw this phenomenon at Jeypoor (Radjpootana), the land of the *Children of the Solar Race*: a fakir, or rather a Hindu yogi (for the fakirs are usually Mussulmans), put himself in a trance, and in the presence of a great crowd, including well educated, but as usual skeptical, persons, allowed himself to be immured in a chamber, and remained therein for twenty days; the officials of the Maharaja's Government opened the chamber and brought out the cadaver. At the end of a quarter of an hour the man came to himself and

in the juice of a plant; it *anaesthetises* them. . . . . This paper, I say, published this matter on January the first." (This citation was made from another portion of the same article, published in *La Revue Spirite*, Paris, December, 1879. Published in *The Complete Works of H. P. Blavatsky*, Vol. II, p. 45).

greeting the public, went away. He accomplished this act of phenomenalism as a penitence." *

Even during Mme. Blavatsky's lifetime word had got around that she had been in Tibet for seven years. The exact manner in which her stay in Tibet should be regarded is given in reponse to a critic. The statement is made in an article sent to the editor of a magazine, entitled *Light*,† under the title " Mr. A. Lillie's Delusions", and published therein:

" I will tell him [Arthur Lillie] also that I have lived at different periods in Little Tibet as in Great Tibet, and that these combined periods form more than seven years. Yet, I have never stated either verbally or over my signature that I had passed seven consecutive years in a convent. What I have said, and repeat now, is, that I have stopped in Lamaistic convents; that I have visited Tzi-gadze, the Tashi-Lhünpo territory and its neighbourhood, and that I have been further in, and in such places of Tibet as have never been visited by any other European, and that he can ever hope to visit."

Arthur Lillie's article in *Light* contains several mis-statements. Only one more need be considered here, since it concerns Tibet and initiations. It is corrected in this manner:

" Mr. Lillie asks for ' information about the seven years' initiation of Madame Blavatsky.' The humble

---

* From an article entitled: " Letter of Mme. Blavatsky—Dr. Rotura's Discovery " published in *La Revue Spirite* (Paris), December, 1879. Reproduced in *The Complete Works of H. P. Blavatsky*, Volume II, page 46.

† *Light*, a journal of Spiritual Progress and Psychic Research published in London, issue of August 9, 1884, Vol. IV, No. 188, pp. 323-4; republished in *H. P. Blavatsky Collected Writings*, Vol. VI, pp. 269-80. H.P.B.'s article was written in response to an article published in the August 2nd, 1884 issue of *Light* (IV, No. 187, pp. 214-5), entitled " Koot Hoomi Unveiled."

individual of this name has never heard of an initiation lasting seven years. Perhaps the word ' initiation '—with that *accuracy* in the explanation of esoteric terms that so preeminently characterises the author of *Buddha and Early Buddhism*—may be intended for ' instruction '? If so, then I should be quite justified in first asking Mr. Lillie what right he has to cross-examine me? But since he chooses to take such liberties with my name, I will tell him plainly that he himself knows nothing, not only of initiations and Tibet, but even of *exoteric*—let alone *esoteric*—Buddhism. What he pretends to know about Lamaism he has picked up from the hazy information of travellers, who, having forced themselves into the *borderland* of Tibet, pretend on that account to know all that is *within* the country closed for centuries to the average traveller. Even Csoma de Körös * knew very little of the *real gelukpas* † and Esoteric Lamaism, except what he was permitted to know; for he never went beyond Zanskar, and the

---

* Alexander Csoma de Körös (in Hungarian: Körösi Csoma Sandor—1784-1842) was a Hungarian philologist and traveller. He left his native city, Körös, and his homeland, Transylvania, about 1820 for the Orient, with the avowed purpose of discovering the origin of the Magyars. After visiting Egypt without accomplishing his quest, he travelled to Tibet, where he settled for a time. Cloistered in a Buddhist monastery, he studied the language, customs and literature. After four years the realization dawned upon him that he could not solve his mission there, so he left Tibet for India, taking up his residence in Bengal. There he contributed to the *Journal of the Asiatic Society of Bengal*, and his knowledge of Tibetan enabled him to translate Buddhist scriptures and write an analysis of the *Kanjur*—the principal Tibetan work. De Körös continued his study of other Oriental languages in addition to Sanskrit, and in Calcutta published a Tibetan-English dictionary and grammar in 1834. Shortly thereafter the philologist decided to reinstitute his search for the origin of the Magyars and travelled to Darjiling, where he died in 1842.

† Gelukpas—the Reformed Buddhists (lit. *dge-lugs-pas*, the virtuous ones), popularly called Yellow Caps, instituted by Tsong-Kha-pa; in contradistinction to the Ñingmapas, (lit. *rnying-ma-pas*, the most ancient ones), the original Buddhist School, deriving from Padma Sambhava—also known as the Red Hats or Red Caps.

lamasery of Phag-dal—erroneously spelt by those who pretend to know all about Tibet, *Pugdal*, which is incorrect. . . ." *

One more citation from the letter to the editor of *Light* may be added now, since it bears directly on the theme of entry into Tibet. Nevertheless, it should be borne in mind that the time period under consideration is that of the 1860's, whereas the date of the forthcoming citation has reference to the year 1882. It may be observed, however, that when the required conditions had been complied with, arrangements would be taken care of so that there would be no difficulties encountered by H.P.B. for passing into Tibet and making contact with her Teachers.

" Only two years back, as I can prove by numerous witnesses, when journeying from Chandernagor to Darjeeling, instead of proceeding to it direct, I left the train half way, was met by friends with a conveyance, and passed with them into the territory of Sikkim, where I found my Master and Mahatma Koot Hoomi. Thence five miles across the old borderland of Tibet." †

Having provided H.P.B.'s own statement of the fact that she was in Tibet, the best source for adducing evidence of this is to turn to the closing chapter of *Isis Unveiled*. Here the author draws upon intimate experiences for the purpose of enriching her narrative. Instead of condensing this account of a portion of her travels, the citations (although somewhat lengthy) are given in full, in order that the significance of the stay in Tibet may be appreciated.

" Both in Western and Eastern Tibet, as in every other place where Buddhism predominates, there are two distinct religions, the same as it is in Brahmanism

---

* *Light*, August 9, 1884, pp. 323-4.

† *Light*, August 9, 1884, pp. 323-4.

—the secret philosophy and the popular religion. The former is that of the followers of the doctrine of the sect of the Sûtrântika.* They closely adhere to the spirit of Buddha's original teachings which show the necessity of *intuitional* perception, and all deductions therefrom. These do not proclaim their views, nor allow them to be made public.

" ' All *compounds* are perishable,' were the last words uttered by the lips of the dying Gautama, when preparing under the Sâl-tree to enter into Nirvâna. ' Spirit is the sole, elementary, and primordial unity, and each of its rays is immortal, infinite, and indestructible. Beware of the illusions of matter.' Buddhism was spread far and wide over Asia, and even farther, by Dharma-Aśoka.†. . . The Buddhism of Nepal being the one which may be said to have diverged less than any other from the primeval ancient faith, the Lamaism of Tartary, Mongolia, and Tibet, which is a direct offshoot of this country, may be thus shown to be the purest Buddhism; for we say it again, Lamaism properly is but an external form of rites.

" The Upâsakas ‡ and Upâsikâs, or male and female semi-monastics and semi-laymen, have equally with the lama-monks themselves, to strictly abstain from

---

* Sûtrântika: a Sanskrit compound; *sûtra*, literally a thread, but in Buddhism the term has the significance of a precept or maxim; *antika*, vicinity, proximity, near. Hence the compound is applied to those adherents of Buddhism who cling closely to Buddha's teachings.

† Aśoka is the celebrated Buddhist emperor of India: 264 to 228 or 227 B.C.; grandson of Chandragupta, the founder of the Maurya dynasty. " From a reckless profligate and atheist, he had become Priyadarśin, the ' beloved of the gods', and never was the purity of his philanthropic views surpassed by any earthly ruler. His memory has lived for ages in the hearts of the Buddhists."—*Isis Unveiled*, II, 607-8.

‡ Upâsaka: a Sanskrit word, derived from the verb-root *upa-âs*— to sit by the side of, to worship; hence, a worshipper. In Buddhism the term is applied to a lay worshipper, as distinguished from a Bhikshu (derived from the verb-root *bhiksh*, meaning to wish to share,

violating any of Buddha's rules, and must study *Meipo* and every psychological phenomenon as such. Those who become guilty of any of the ' five sins ' lose all right to congregate with the pious community. The most important of these is *not to curse upon any consi-deration, for the curse returns upon the one that utters it, and often upon his innocent relatives who breathe the same atmosphere with him.* To love each other, and even our bitterest enemies; to offer our lives even for animals, to the extent of abstaining from defensive arms; to gain the greatest of victories by conquering one's self; to avoid all vices; to practice all virtues, especially humility and mildness; to be obedient to superiors, to cherish and respect parents, old age, learning, virtuous and holy men; to provide food, shelter, and comfort for men and animals; to plant trees on the roads and dig wells for the comfort of travellers; such are the moral duties of Buddhists. Every Ani or Bhikshunî (nun) is sub-jected to these laws.

"Numerous are the Buddhist and Lamaic saints who have been renowned for the unsurpassed sanctity of their lives and their ' miracles.'. . . Then the Lamaists had their great reformer, the Shaberon Tsong-Kha-pa, who is claimed to have been immaculately conceived by his mother, a virgin from Kokonor (fourteenth century), who is another wonder-worker. The sacred tree of Kounboum, the tree of the 10,000 images, which, in consequence of the degeneration of the true faith had ceased budding for several centuries, now shot forth new sprouts and bloomed more vigorously than ever from the hair of this avatar of Buddha, says the

---

hence to beg). In Buddhism the term signifies a mendicant; also applied to a monk.

The feminine form of the word is Upâsikâ, hence in Buddhism a female lay votary in contradistinction to a Bhikshunî, a female mendicant, also a nun.

H.P.B.'s Teachers in writing to Mr. Sinnett often referred to her as Upasika (more correctly Upâsikâ), thus stressing the fact that she was acting in the capacity of their chela.

legend. The same tradition makes him (Tsong-Kha-pa) ascend to heaven in 1419. Contrary to the prevailing idea, few of these saints are *Khubilhans*),* or Shaberons—reincarnations.

"Many of the lamaseries contain schools of magic, but the most celebrated is the collegiate monastery of the Shu-tukt, where there are over 30,000 monks attached to it, the lamasery forming quite a little city. Some of the female nuns possess marvellous psychological powers. We have met some of these women on their way from Lhasa to Candi, the Rome of Buddhism, with its miraculous shrines and Gautama's relics. To avoid encounters with Mussulmans and other sects they travel by night alone, unarmed, and without the least fear of wild animals, *for these will not touch them.* At the first glimpses of dawn, they take refuge in caves and vihâras † prepared for them by their co-religionists at calculated distances; for notwithstanding the fact that Buddhism has taken refuge in Ceylon, and nominally there are but few of the denomination in British India, yet the secret Byauds (Brotherhoods) and Buddhist vihâras are numerous, and every Jain feels himself obliged to help, indiscriminately, Buddhist or Lamaist.

"Ever on the lookout for occult phenomena, hungering after sights, one of the most interesting that we

---

* Khubilhans: also Khubilkhans, or Chubilgans—a Mongolian term equivalent to the Tibetan Shaberons or Chutuktus. According to the Lamaists these individuals are regarded as Living Incarnations of the Buddha. H.P.B. explains the Tibetan term Chutuktu in this manner:

"An incarnation of Buddha or of some Bodhisattva, as believed in Tibet, where there are generally five manifesting and two *secret* Chutuktus among the high Lamas."—*Theosophical Glossary*, p. 85.

† Vihâra: the literal meaning of this Sanskrit word is walking, or roaming for pleasure (being derived from the verb-root *vi-hri*, to walk, to roam); by extension of meaning: a pleasure-ground. With Buddhists the word, however, signifies a temple or a monastery; originally: a hall where monks walked about; hence a hall used as a temple.

have seen was produced by one of these poor travelling Bhikshunîs. It was years ago, and at a time when all such manifestations were new to the writer. We were taken to visit the pilgrims by a Buddhist friend, a mystical gentleman born at Kashmir, of Katchi parents, but a Buddha-Lamaist by conversion, and who generally resides at Lhasa.

" ' Why carry about this bunch of dead plants? ' inquired one of the Bhikshunîs, an emaciated, tall and elderly woman, pointing to a large nosegay of beautiful, fresh, and fragrant flowers in the writer's hands.

" ' Dead? ' we asked, inquiringly. ' Why they just have been gathered in the garden? '

" ' And yet, they are dead,' she gravely answered. ' To be born in this world, is this not death? See, how these herbs look when alive in the world of eternal light, in the gardens of our blessed Foh? '

" Without moving from the place where she was sitting on the ground, the Ani took a flower from the bunch, laid it in her lap, and began to draw together, by large handfuls as it were, invisible material from the surrounding atmosphere. Presently a very, very faint nodule of vapor was seen, and this slowly took shape and color, until, poised in mid-air, appeared a copy of the bloom we had given her. Faithful to the last tint and the last petal it was, and lying on its side like the original, but a thousand-fold more gorgeous in hue and exquisite in beauty, as the glorified human spirit is more beauteous than its physical capsule. Flower after flower to the minutest herb was thus reproduced and made to vanish, reappearing at our desire, nay, at our simple thought. Having selected a full-blown rose we held it at arm's length, and in a few minutes our arm, hand, and the flower, perfect in every detail, appeared reflected in the vacant space, about two yards from where we sat. But while the flower seemed immeasurably beautified and as ethereal as the other spirit flowers, the arm and hand appeared like a mere reflection in a looking-glass, even to a large spot on the forearm, left on it by a piece of damp earth which had stuck to one of the roots." *

Passing from this type of exhibition of Meipo to another —to that which is closely associated with, if not directly connected with, Tulku. The subject is introduced by reference to lamas who have worked for and attained the ability of demonstrating the feat to be mentioned.

" A number of lamas in Sikkim produce *meipo*— ' miracle '—by magical powers. The late Patriarch of Mongolia, Gegen Chutuktu, who resided at Urga, a veritable paradise, was the sixteenth incarnation of Gautama, therefore a Bodhisattva. He had the reputation of possessing powers that were phenomenal, even among the thaumaturgists of the land of miracles *par excellence*. Let no one suppose that these powers are developed without cost. . . .

" Within the cloisters of Tashi-Lhünpo and Si-Dzang, these powers, inherent in every man, called out by so few, are cultivated to their utmost perfection. Who, in India, has not heard of the Banda-Chan Ramboutchi,† the *Houtouktou* of the capital of Higher Thibet? His brotherhood of Khe-lan was famous throughout the land. . . .

" The greatest of the *meipo*—said to be the object of the ambition of every Buddhist devotee—was, and yet is, the faculty of walking in the air. The famous King of Siam, Pia Metak, the Chinese, was noted for his devotion and learning. But he attained this ' supernatural gift ' only after having placed himself under the direct tuition of a priest of Gautama Buddha." ‡

---

* *Isis Unveiled*, Vol. II, pp. 607-10.

† Also spelled Panchen Rimboche. For meaning of Houtouktou —an alternate form of Chutuktu—see under Khubilhan (footnote on page 126).

‡ *Isis Unveiled*, Vol. II, pp. 617-8.

Those who are familiar with the injunctions given in the " Book of the Golden Precepts " (better known under the title of *The Voice of the Silence*) will recall the ślokas where the faculty of walking in the air—or in the sky—is connected with Kundalinî:

" Let not thy ' Heaven-born', merged in the sea of Mâyâ, break from the Universal Parent (SOUL), but let the fiery power retire into the inmost chamber, the chamber of the Heart and the abode of the World's Mother." *

Notes are added in explanation of the Fiery Power and the Chamber of the Heart, but first reference should be made to the significance of the " Heaven-born "—âtman, man's divine principle—linked as it is, even during earth-life, with its Universal Parent, Paramâtman. Âtman is regarded as merged in the sea of Mâyâ (Illusion) during the interval of a life-time. The śloka enjoins the disciple not to " break the connection " with Paramâtman, which certainly would be the case were he to permit himself to be " weaned from the rest " of the disciples by " the great dire heresy of separateness " (which forms the context of the previous śloka). The Fiery Power is Kundalinî:

" *Kundalinî* is called the ' Serpentine ' or the *annular* power on account of its spiral-like working or progress in the body of the ascetic developing the power in himself. It is an electric fiery occult or *Fohatic* power, the great pristine force, which underlies all organic and inorganic matter." †

" The *inner* chamber of the Heart, called in Sanskrit *Brahmapura*." ‡

---

* *The Voice of the Silence*, p. 9, or. ed.

† *Op. cit.*, pp. 77-8.

‡ *Op. cit.*, p. 76. Brahma-pura: a compound signifying Brahma's abode (*pura*—abode). In the Upanishads the term signifies " the heart".

Resuming the ślokas, which now describe the evocation of the Fiery Power: and the resultant achievement:

"Then from the heart that Power shall rise into the sixth, the middle region, the place between thine eyes, when it becomes the breath of the ONE-SOUL, the voice which filleth all, thy Master's voice.

"'Tis only then thou canst become a 'Walker of the Sky' who treads the winds above the waves, whose step touches not the waters." *

Continuing the explanation:

"The 'Power' and the 'World-mother' are names given to *Kundalini*—one of the mystic 'Yogi powers'. It is *Buddhi* considered as an active instead of a passive principle (which it is generally, when regarded only as the vehicle, or casket of the Supreme Spirit ÂTMAN). It is an electro-spiritual force, a creative power which when aroused into action can as easily kill as it can create."

"*Khechara*, 'sky-walker' or 'goer'. As explained in the 6th Adhyâya of that king of mystic works, the *Jñâneśvarî*—the body of the Yogi becomes as one *formed of the wind*; as 'a cloud from which limbs have sprouted out,' after which—'he (the Yogi) beholds the things beyond the seas and stars; he hears the language of the Devas and comprehends it, and perceives what is passing in the mind of the ant.'" †

---

* *Op. cit.*, p. 9.

† *Op. cit.*, pp. 76-7. The mystic Yoga powers here signify the Siddhis. The literal meaning of the Sanskrit word Kundalinî is "circular", "annular".

Khechara, a Sanskrit word, gives the clue to its meaning in its literal translation: *khe*, the locative form of the noun *kha*, signifying "in the sky"; *chara*, from the verb-root *char*, to go, to walk. When Khechara is used in connection with Siddhi or Gati, it signifies the magical power of flying.

Adhyâya is a Sanskrit noun, meaning a chapter, or a lesson. It is compounded of the preposition *adhi*, meaning "in", "towards", and the verb-root *i*, to go; hence to go inwards; to turn the mind inwards; hence study, lesson, chapter.

Returning to H.P.B.'s narrative in *Isis Unveiled*, the projection of the Self, resulting in Khechara, by means of the evocation of Kundalinî—which is a necessary requirement for Tulku—is considered in this manner:

" One phase of magical skill is the voluntary and conscious withdrawal of the inner man (astral form) from the outer man (physical body). In the cases of some mediums withdrawal occurs, but it is unconscious and involuntary. With the latter the body is more or less cataleptic at such times; but with the adept the absence of the astral form would not be noticed, for the physical senses are alert, and the individual appears only as though in a fit of abstraction—' a brown study', as some call it.

" To the movements of the wandering astral form neither time nor space offer obstacles. . . .

" But, while the astral form can go anywhere, penetrate any obstacle, and be seen at any distance from the physical body, the latter is dependent upon ordinary methods of transportation." *

One of the first Europeans to visit Tibet (in 1846), a Roman Catholic missionary, Evariste Huc, recorded an instance of such an aerial journey which came to his attention when he was a guest at the lamasery of Kounboum. Here is the account of his experience, as told in *Isis Unveiled*:

" At the time when Abbé Huc was living in Paris, after his return from Tibet, he related, among other unpublished wonders, to a Mr. Arsenieff, a Russian gentleman, the following curious fact that he had

---

Jñâneśvarî—a Sanskrit compound: *jñâna*, knowledge; *îśvara*, the Lord; applied to the Lord within, the Self; hence Self-Knowledge. The name of a treatise in which Krishna speaks in allegorical manner on the attainment of wisdom and the Siddhis.

In Tibet this faculty of the projection of the Self—so as to become a Khechara, " a walker in the sky "—is termed Hpho-wa (or 'Pho-*ba*.)

* *Isis Unveiled*, II, 588-9.

witnessed during his long sojourn at the lamasery of
Kounboum. One day while conversing with one of
the lamas, the latter suddenly stopped speaking, and
assumed the attentive attitude of one who is listening
to a message being delivered to him, although he
(Huc) heard never a word. 'Then, I must go',
suddenly broke forth the lama, as if in response to the
message.

" ' Go where? ' inquired the astonished ' lama of
Jehovah ' (Huc). ' And with whom are you talking? '

" ' To the lamasery of——,' was the quiet answer.
' The Shaberon wants me; it was he who summoned
me.'

" Now this lamasery was many days' journey from
that of Kounboum, in which the conversation was
taking place. But what seemed to astonish Huc the
most was, that, instead of setting off on his journey,
the lama simply walked to a sort of cupola-room on
the roof of the house in which they lived, and another
lama, after exchanging a few words, followed them to
the terrace by means of the ladder, and passing between
them, locked and barred his companion in. Then
turning to Huc after a few seconds of meditation,
he smiled and informed the guest that ' he had
gone.'

" ' But how could he? Why you have locked him in,
and the room has no issue? ' insisted the missionary.

" ' And what good would a door be to him? ' answered the custodian. ' It is he himself who went away;
his body is not needed, and so he left it in my charge.'

" Notwithstanding the wonders which Huc had witnessed during his perilous journey, his opinion was that
both of the lamas had mystified him. But three days
later, not having seen his habitual friend and enter-
tainer, he inquired after him, and was informed that
he would be back in the evening. At sunset, and just
as the ' other lamas ' were preparing to retire, Huc
heard his absent friend's voice calling as if from the
clouds, to his companion to open the door for him.
Looking upward, he perceived the ' travellers's '

outline behind the lattice of the room where he had been locked in." *

While this last incident from the narrative of Evariste Huc may have no direct bearing on the theme of the chapter— H. P. Blavatsky's stay in Tibet—it does give an idea as to one of the reasons for her sojourn in that far-off land under the tutelage of her Preceptors, namely, becoming proficient in the Siddhis. The next anecdote gives the desired information. It is one of the few direct references given by H.P.B. herself to the time when she was actually with her Teachers in Tibet. It is to be found in a letter addressed to A. P. Sinnett, written in Würzburg, and bearing the date January 6, 1886. By means of a stated number of years in one of the sentences the episode may be stated to have occurred in 1870. The letter opens with the injunction: " I am impressed to give you the following." Then follows one of the most delightful reminiscences yet, withal, conveying a touch of pathos:

" I went to bed and I had the most extraordinary vision . . . in my sleep I saw them (the Masters) both, I was again (a scene of years back) in Mah. K.H.'s house. I was sitting in a corner on a mat and he walking about the room in his riding dress, and Master was talking to someone behind the door. ' *I remind can't* ' —I pronounced in answer to a question of His about a dead aunt.— He smiled and said ' Funny English you use.' Then I felt ashamed, hurt *in my vanity,* and began thinking (mind you, in my *dream* or *vision* which was the *exact* reproduction of what had taken place word for word 16 years ago) ' now I am here and speaking *nothing but English* in verbal phonetic language I can perhaps learn to speak better with Him.' (To make it clear with Master I also used English, which whether bad or good was the same for Him as he does not speak it but understands every word I say out of

---

* *Isis Unveiled,* II, 604-5.

my head; and I am made to understand Him—*how* I could never tell or explain if I were killed *but I do*. With D.K. I also spoke English, he speaking it better even than Mah. K.H.) Then, in my dream still, *three months after* as I was made to feel in that vision—I was standing before Mah. K.H. near the old building taken down he was looking at, and as Master was not at home, I took to him a few sentences I was studying in Senzar * in his sister's room and asked him to tell me if I translated them correctly—and gave him a slip of paper with these sentences written in English. He took and read them and correcting the interpretation read them over and said ' Now your English is become better—*try to pick out of my head even the little I know of it*.' And he put his hand on my forehead in the region of memory and squeezed his fingers on it (and I felt even the same trifling pain in it, as then, and the cold shiver

---

* Senzar is defined as: " The mystic name for the secret sacerdotal language or the ' Mystery-speech ' of the initiated Adepts, all over the world."—*Theosophical Glossary,* p. 295.

Regarding the origin of Senzar, we read:

" there was a time when its language (the *Sen-zar*) was known to the Initiates of every nation, when the forefathers of the Toltec understood it as easily as the inhabitants of the lost Atlantis, who inherited it, in their turn, from the sages of the 3rd Race, the *Manushis,* who learnt it direct from the *Devas* of the 2nd and 1st Races."—*The Secret Doctrine,* I, p. xliii or ed.; I, 64; 6 vol. ed.; I, 26, 3rd ed.

In addition to being a language, the very alphabet of Senzar had an unusual significance:

" The Senzar and Sanskrit alphabets, and other Occult tongues, besides other potencies, have a number, colour, and distinct syllable for every letter."—*The Secret Doctrine,* V, 505.

Moreover, there was more than one cipher or code connected with the writing, the clue to which had to be provided in order that the document could be read:

" The system of the so-called Senzar characters is still more wonderful and difficult, since each letter is made to yield several meanings, a sign placed at the commencement showing the true meaning."—*The Secret Doctrine,* V, 117.

I had experienced) and since that day He did so with my head daily, for about two months. Again, the scene changes and I am going away with Master who is sending me off, back to Europe. I am bidding good-bye to his sister and her child and all the chelas. I listen to what the Masters tell me. And then come the parting words of Mah. K.H. . . . . " *

A corroboration of the fact that H.P.B. had been in Shigatse, the second city in importance in Tibet and the seat of the Tashi Lama, is available, although this testimonial was obtained by means of psychometry. † The object used for the psychometric reading was a letter from a Mahatma which Dr. Franz Hartmann had received during his stay at Adyar, India. When returning to Europe the doctor requested a German peasant woman residing near Kempton, who was proficient in psychometry, to tell him what impressions she received upon being handed the letter. Later, Dr. Hartmann sent this account to Mme. Blavatsky, while she was at Ostende in 1886, who in turn commented upon the psychometer's description. First the psychometric reading:

---

* *The Mahatma Letters to A. P. Sinnett*, pp. 478-9. The date when H. P. B. first met the Mahatma K.H. is available. It occurs in a sentence written in her article entitled " Mr. Arthur Lillie " (published in *Light*, October 11, 1884, Vol. IV, pp. 418-9). The Mahatma is referred to as " Mr. Sinnett's correspondent ":

" I had never seen Mr. Sinnett's correspondent before 1868."— *H. P. Blavatsky Collected Writings*, Vol. VI, p. 292.

† Psychometry signifies the ability to receive from any object, whether held in the hand or placed against the forehead, the impressions with which that object had previously been in contact. Images of events are imbedded in the all-permeating, universal and ever-retaining medium called Âkâśa. This all-pervasive principle is also known as the Anima Mundi, or the Soul of the World, which in its lower reaches is termed the Astral Light.

" When the psychometer examines his specimen, he is brought in contact with the current of the astral light, connected with that specimen, and which retains pictures of the events associated with its history. These pass before his vision with the swiftness of light."—*Isis Unveiled*, I, 184.

" ' Ah,' she exclaimed, ' what is this? I never saw anything so beautiful in my life! I see before me a high but artificially made elevation or hill, and upon that hill a building which looks like a temple, with a high Chinese roof. The temple is of a splendid white, as if it were made of pure white marble, and the roof is resting upon these pillars. On the top there is a shining sun—but now!—it only looks like a sun; it seems to be some kind of animal. . . . There is a beautiful walk of smooth stones and some steps leading to the temple, and I am going up to it. Now I am there, and lo! the floor is a lake, in which the light of that sun on the top of the roof is reflected! But no—I am mistaken; it is no water at all; it is a kind of yellowish marble, which shines like a mirror. Now I see it plainly! it is a square marble floor, and in the centre there is a dark round spot. . . . .

" Now I am in the temple, and I see two gentlemen looking at something on the wall. One is a very fine-looking gentleman, but he is dressed quite differently from the people in this country. He is dressed in a loose flowing robe of pure white, and the fore-part of his shoes is pointed upward. The other one is smaller and bald-headed; he wears a black coat and silver buckles. . . . . It (a vase) stands in the corner, and there are ornamental paintings on it. . . .

" There are some paintings and drawings on the wall. Below the ceiling, where the roof begins, there is a field, or panel, on which there are some curious figures. Some look like a 15 and one like a V, and others like squares and ciphers. . . . . They look as if they were numbers, but I do not think they are. They may be some strange letters or characters. Above that field or panel there is another one, on which there are some square pictures or plates, with some very queer things painted on them. They are movable; at least, I think they are. . . .

" Now these gentlemen are going out, and I am following them. There are a great many trees looking like pine-trees. I think they are pines. There are others with big fleshy leaves and spikes, something like prickly-pears. There are mountains and hills and a lake. They are taking me away from that temple. . . . There is a big ravine, and there are some trees which I take to be olive-trees. Now I have arrived at a place where I can see a wide expanse of country. The two gentlemen have gone away.

"Here is some antiquity looking like an old ruined wall, and something like what I saw on that paper you showed me. I believe you call it a Sphinx. There is a sort of pillar, and on the top of it a statue whose upper part looks like a woman, while the lower part of her body seems to be a fish. She seems to be holding some moss in her hands, or resting them upon it. . . What a funny sight! There are lots of queer people! They are little women and children. They have *soles* tied to their feet! They are collecting something from the shore and putting it into baskets. Now the whole scene dissolves into a cloud." *

Here is Mme. Blavatsky's comment written to Dr. Hartmann:

"This looks like the temple of the Tashi Lama, near Shigatse—made of the ' Madras cement- ' like material; it does shine like marble and is called the snowy ' Shakang ' † (Temple)—as far as I remember. It has no ' sun or cross ' on the top, but a kind of algiorno dagoba, triangular, on three pillars, with a dragon of gold and a globe. But the dragon has a swastika on it. . . . I don't remember any ' gravel walk '—nor is there one, but it stands on an elevation (artificial) and a stone path leading to it, and it has steps—how many I do not remember (I was never allowed inside); saw from the outside, and the interior was described to me.

---

* From *The Theosophist*, March 1887, quoted in *Personal Memoirs of H. P. Blavatsky*, pp. 142-3.

† Shakang—in Tibetan, *mChod-khang*.

11

" The floors of nearly all Buddha's (Sangyas) temples
are made of yellow polished stone, found in those
mountains of Oural and in Northern Tibet towards
Russian territory. I do not know the name but it
looks like yellow marble. The ' gentleman ' in white
may be Master, and the ' bald-headed gentleman ' I
take to be some old ' shaven-headed ' priest. . . . .

" In those temples there are always movable ' pictures ' on which various geometrical and mathematical
problems are placed for the disciples who study astrology and symbolism. The ' vase ' must be one of
many Chinese queer vases about in temples, for various
objects. In the corners of the temples there are numerous statues of various deities (Dhyânis). The roofs are
always (almost always) supported by rows of wooden
pillars dividing the roof into three parallelograms, and
the mirror ' Melong' of burnished steel (round like
the sun) is often placed on the top of the kiosque on
the roof. I myself took it once for the sun.

" Also on the cupolas of the dagobas, there is sometimes a graduated pinnacle, and over it a disk of gold
placed vertically, and a pear-shaped point, and often
a crescent supporting a globe and the swastika upon it.
Ask her whether it is this she saw: *Om tram ah hri hum,*
which figures are roughly drawn sometimes on the
Melon ' mirrors '—(a disc of brass) against evil spirits
—for the mob.

" Or perhaps what she saw was a row of slips of
wood (little cubes) on which such things were seen.
(She illustrates.) If so, then I will know what she
saw. ' Pinewoods ' are all round such temples, the
latter built expressly where there are such woods, and
prickly pear, and trees with Chinese fruits that the
priests use for making inks. A lake is there, surely,
and mountains plenty—if where Master is; if near
Shigatse—only little hillocks. The statues of Meilha
Gualpo, the androgyne Lord of Salamanders or the
Genii of the Air, looks like the ' sphinx '; but her lower
body is lost in clouds, not fish; and she is not beautiful,
only symbolical. Fisherwomen do use soles alone, like

the sandals, and they wear all fur caps. That's all;
will this do?" *

Evidence of another type that H.P.B. had been in
Tibet was brought to light when a traveller, Major
Cross by name, was in Toronto, Canada, and gave this
endorsement:

"Major Cross, who with his wife, Dr. Cross, and
their daughter, have been visiting Toronto . . . . gave
a long, graphic and intensely interesting account of his
travels in northwestern Tibet, during which he traced
the progress of a white woman in 1867, through the
most difficult country to a lamasery far north, through
the recollections of various old people who were impressed by the personality of this unusual visitor. He
identified her with Mme. Blavatsky, and the date was
settled by those he talked with as having been ten
years after the Mutiny. Major Cross said he was not
a Theosophist, but could not help being interested in
the story of Mme. Blavatsky's journey, as it had been
related to him. . . . . He is manager or factor of tea
and other estates of the Dalai Lama of Tibet, to which
he is returning." †

Two testimonials have been recorded, showing that
H.P.B. was undergoing tuition in Tibet. These bear
even greater weight than if they had been penned by
Mme. Blavatsky herself. The documents were provided
by those who sent H. P. Blavatsky to the western world
as their agent for announcing the teachings of the Ancient
Wisdom, under the name of Theosophy, during the last
quarter of last century. Although regarded as custodians
of the teachings of the Esoteric Philosophy, they were
more often referred to by Mme. Blavatsky as her Teachers,
or Masters.

---

* From *The Path*, January, 1896; quoted in *Personal Memoirs of
H. P. Blavastky*, p. 143.

† Published in *The Canadian Theosophist* of June, 1927; quoted in
Personal Memoirs of H. P. Blavatsky, p. 162.

The first document is in the form of a letter which was enclosed within an envelope which was addressed as follows:

" À l'Honorable,
   Très Honorable Dame—
   Nadyéjda Andréewna
      Fadeew.
         Odessa.

The letter itself was written in French, upon what is known as " rice paper " (in use in Tibet and Northern India), and bore this message—in translation:

" The noble relatives of Mad. H. Blavatsky have no cause whatsoever for grief. Their daughter and niece has not left this world at all. She is living and desires to make known to those whom she loves that she is well and feels very happy in the distant and unknown retreat she has selected for herself. She has been very ill, but is so no longer; for owing to the protection of the Lord Sang-gyas she has found devoted friends who take care of her physically and spiritually. Let the ladies of her house, therefore, remain calm. Before 18 new moons shall have risen—she will have returned to her family." *

At the time of its receipt a notation was made upon the envelope, written in Russian and signed by the writer. It reads, in translation:

" Received at Odessa November 7, about Lelinka probably from Tibet—November 11, 1870. Nadyezhda F." †

---

* Published in *H. P. Blavatsky Collected Writings*, Vol. VI, p. 275. The translation of the address on the envelope reads: "To the Honourable, Most Honourable Lady—Nadyejda AndreewnaFadeew." Fadeew (anglicized as Fadeyev) was the maiden name of H.P.B.'s mother; Nadyejda was Helena's aunt's given name.

† *Op. cit.*, p. 277.

À l'Honorable,
Très Honorable Dame—

Nadyéjda Andréevna

Fadeew.

Odessa.

получена въ Одессе
ноября 7, отъ Лёлиньки французски
въ русто изъ Тибета —
" апр. 1, 1870 Надежда да †

Les nobles parents de Mad. H. P. Blavatsky n'ont aucune cause de se désoler. Leur fille et nièce n'a point quitté ce monde. Elle vit et désire faire savoir à ceux qu'elle aime, qu'elle se porte bien et se sent fort heureuse dans la retraite lointaine et inconnue qu'elle s'est choi-sie. Elle a été bien malade, mais, ne l'est plus: car grâce à la protection du Seigneur Sang-gyas elle a trouvé des amis dévoués qui en prennent soin physiquement et spirituellement. Que les dames de Sa maison se tranquillisent donc. Avant que 18 lunes nouvelles se lèvent — Elle sera revenue dans sa famille.

FACSIMILE No. 1 (Exact size)
The Address on the Envelope and the First Mahatma Letter:
Received November 7, 1870.

Adyar, Madras, 5 August '88

My dear Leadbeater.

I give over into your exclusive charge the _Theosophist_ until my return. You will be the sole judge as to the admission of matter and its sequential order. The only limitation I impose is that you shall not admit anything of a personally aggravating nature (anything calculated to provoke unpleasant controversy); or any announcements of resignations of membership, with or without reasons given unless they are first submitted to me.

FACSIMILE No. 2

A reproduction of the handwriting of H. S. Olcott. A portion of a letter addressed to Charles W. Leadbeater, dated 5 August, 1888.

Lelinka is the Russian " pet name " of Yelena (the Russian form of Helena). The date of 1870 is important in two ways: (1) It definitely states that Miss de Fadeyev's niece was in a distant and unknown retreat. Since she was stated to be under the protection of Lord Sang-gyas —the Tibetan title for the Lord Buddha, it further establishes the fact that the retreat was in Tibet. (2) The date definitely places the letter as being the very first " Mahatma Letter " to be received. It is written in the script which had come to be associated with the letters sent by the Mahatma known as K.H. (Koot Hoomi), although his customary signature is not present. A symbol was used in place of a signature. A third factor may be instanced. The letter was written in French, not in English; nevertheless it bears a singular peculiarity present in all of these Mahatma's letters: over every *m* appears a line similar to a macron accent. This is a distinctive feature which is very necessary in Russian handwriting, but it is not required when writing in English or French. For that matter it is not used in any European language. This would indicate that this particular trait had been adopted from someone who was very familiar with Russian handwriting—namely, H.P.B.

Since the letter was undated, it was very fortunate that Miss de Fadeyev placed the pencilled notation on the envelope four days after its receipt. Also of great value is the memorandum regarding the manner in which the letter was received, since it was not sent by means of the customary manner of sending letters—through the post office. This notation was recorded in a letter addressed to Col. Olcott, dated June 26, 1884, from Paris, at which time Miss de Fadeyev was visiting her niece Helena.

"Two or three years ago I wrote to Mr. Sinnett in reply to one of his letters, and I remember telling him what happened to me about a letter which I received phenomenally, when my niece was on the other side of the world, and because of that nobody knew where she was— which made us deeply anxious. All our researches had ended in nothing. We were ready to believe her dead, when—I received a letter from Him Whom I believe you call ' Kouth Humi ', which was brought to me in the most incomprehensible and mysterious manner, in my house by a messenger of Asiatic appearance, *who then disappeared before my very eyes.* This letter, which begged me not to fear anything, and which announced that she was in safety—I have still, but at Odessa. Immediately upon my return I shall send it to you, and I shall be very pleased if it can be of any use to you." *

One more item may be added in regard to the delivery of the letter to Miss de Fadeyev. In a letter addressed to A. P. Sinnett by the Mahatma M., upon which the notation was made that it was " received at Allahabad, India, about February 1882," mention is made concerning the visit to H.P.B.'s aunt. The Mahatma makes the suggestion that Mr. Sinnett should write to her and send her his autograph, since she was desirous of having the autograph of a celebrated writer:

" Tell her I—the ' *Khosyayin* ' (her niece's *Khosyayin* she called me as I went to see her—thrice) gossiped the thing to you advising you to write to her furnishing her thus with your autograph. . . ." †

The next testimonial is in the script associated with the Mahatma K.H. It was sent to both of the Mahatma's correspondents: Allan O. Hume and Alfred P. Sinnett. The notation was added that it was " received at Simla, India, in the autumn of 1881." It is a most significant letter in that it deals with the triple aspect which forms the title of this work, namely: H. P. Blavatsky, her stay in Tibet, and Tulku—more particularly that aspect of it

---

* *Op. cit.*, p. 274. Col. Olcott received both letters and placed them in the archives of The Theosophical Society, Adyar, India.

† *The Mahatma Letters to A. P. Sinnett*, p. 254. Khosyayin is a Russian word meaning the master of the house, landlord, host, also applicable to an employer. This was a title used by Miss de Fadeyev when writing to her niece about her teacher.

which was especially connected with her. It is a forth-right letter, immediately entering into the reason for its writing without preliminaries:

" I am painfully aware of the fact that the habitual incoherence of her statements—especially when excited —and her strange ways make her in your opinion a very undesirable transmitter of our messages. Nevertheless, kind Brothers, once that you have learned the truth; once told, that this unbalanced mind, the seeming incongruity of her speeches and ideas, her nervous excitement, all that in short, which is so calculated to upset the feelings of sober minded people, whose notions of reserve and manners are shocked by such strange outbursts of what they regard as her temper, and which so revolt you,—once that *you know* that nothing of it is due to any fault of hers, you may, perchance, be led to regard her in quite a different light. Not-withstanding that the time is not quite ripe to let you entirely into the secret; and that you are hardly yet prepared to understand the great Mystery, even if told of it, owing to the great injustice and wrong done, I am empowered to allow you a glimpse behind the veil. This state of hers is intimately connected with her occult training in Tibet, and due to her being sent out alone into the world to gradually prepare the way for others. After nearly a century of fruitless search, our chiefs had to avail themselves of the only oppor-tunity to send out a European *body* upon European soil to serve as a connecting link between that country and our own. You do not understand? Of course not. Please then, remember, what she tried to explain, and what you gathered tolerably well from her, namely the fact of the *seven* principles in the *complete* human being. Now, no man or woman, unless he be an initiate of the ' fifth circle,' can leave the precincts of *Bod-Las* * and return back into the world in his integral whole— if I may use the expression. *One*, at least of his seven

---

* *Bod-Las* is one of the names by which Tibet is known.

satellites has to remain behind for two reasons: the
first to form the necessary connecting link, the wire of
transmission—the second as the safest warranter that
certain things will never be divulged.   She is no exception to the rule, and you have seen another exemplar
—a highly intellectual man—who had to leave one of
his skins behind; hence, is considered highly eccentric.
The bearing and status of the remaining *six* depend
upon the inherent qualities, the psycho-physiological
peculiarities of the person, especially upon the idio-
syncracies transmitted by what modern science calls
' atavism.'   Acting in accordance with my wishes, my
brother M. made to you through her a certain offer,
if you remember.   You had but to accept it, and at
any time you liked, you would have had for an hour
or more, the real *baitchooly* to converse with, instead of
the psychological cripple you generally have to deal
with now." *

---

* *The Mahatma Letters to A. P. Sinnett*, Third Edition pp. 201-2

CHAPTER VII

H. P. BLAVATSKY AND HER WRITINGS

It is maintained that the writings of H. P. Blavatsky are the principal means of demonstrating that she possessed the ability of utilizing powers not normally employed in literary productions. For that reason the major portion of this work will be devoted to that theme.

H. P. Blavatsky's entry into the literary field occurred in a rather singular manner. The causes which brought this about have a definite bearing upon her career as a writer; therefore they should be reviewed briefly.

Into the smug complacency of nineteenth century thought, a most disturbing element had been injected: the possibility that there was some sort of survival after death. Nothing definite had as yet been formulated. The idea was altogether too shocking to be harbored by staunch believers in orthodoxy. Nevertheless, the Press, eager to make a hue and cry about something that would entice the public into giving more attention to their domain, was making much out of this news item which had burst in upon their humdrum recounting of daily affairs.

From a remote farm-house situated in the township of Chittenden, in the northwestern part of Vermont, reports had gone forth that forms of the dear departed had been seen in the farm-house. " Spirits " they had been dubbed, since they were not of flesh and blood. Not only had they been seen, but they had even conversed with those present. In itself this was nothing new. Believers in what had been called " Spiritualism " had grouped themselves together into an association and had even started a journal to which they had given the name *The Banner of Light*. But the manifestations of forms at the Eddy farm-house in Vermont were far more interesting than were the " intelligent raps," regarded as messages from the " other world," and usually associated with Spiritualism. These "intelligent raps," as they were called, had been brought to the attention of the Press in association with a family living at Hydesville near Rochester, New York, apparently the first recorded notice of that phenomenon in America, occurring in 1848. Therefore the Boston journal, *The Banner of Light*, published an account of the Vermont manifestations.

People had become interested in the apparitions. A New York newspaper had sent a reporter to give an account of what was to be seen at the Vermont farm-house. And Mme. Blavatsky had read the account in the newspaper.

Such happenings were nothing new for Mme. Blavatsky. She had been brought up on Russian folk-lore and the tales that servants and peasants had to tell of similar weird happenings, because she had lost her mother during her childhood. Nevertheless, she had received her "orders" (as she called the intimations she had received) to be present at the investigations of this after-death survival that was being publicized by the press. So off she went to Vermont.

After visiting the Eddy farm-house in Chittenden and witnessing the manifestations that had appeared before the assembled group there, she believed she was justified in writing in defense of the Eddys, when they were attacked in the public press by a skeptical doctor by the name of George M. Beard. Therefore she penned an article and sent it off to the newspaper. It was accepted for publication by the New York *Daily Graphic* * under the heading: " The Eddy Manifestations."

The reporter who had been sent by the New York *Daily Graphic* to cover the Vermont " manifestations "

---

* Issue of October 30, 1874, Volume V, p. 873. The Editor supplied the following introductory note:

" The following letter was addressed to a contemporary journal by Mme. Blavatsky, and was handed to us for publication in *The Daily Graphic*, as we have been taking the lead in the discussion of the curious subject of Spiritualism."—Quoted in *The Complete Works of H. P. Blavatsky*, Vol. I, p. 13, along with the letter to the Editor entitled " The Eddy Manifestations."

was eager enough to capitalize upon his assignment.   It
meant more to him than just another story.   He was
interested in Spiritualism, yes.   He was also intrigued by
the number of strange individuals he contacted there.
Why not take advantage of the situation offered and
describe some of the characters seen?—for people had
been coming from far and near to see the apparitions.
The reporter prided himself upon his ability as well as
his talent for analysing every phase of the subject he was
delegated to cover.   He certainly would not be deceived
by any bogus apparitions or other fraudulent practices.
In fact he introduced tests so that there should be no
frauds perpetrated during his presence.   And yet, a bit
of sensationalism was certainly permissible, nay, necessary
to capture public attention.   After all, was he not a
reporter, writing for the public?   So we read:

" The dinner hour at Eddy's was noon, and it was
from the entrance door of the bare and comfortless
dining-room that Kappes* and I first saw H.P.B.
She had arrived shortly before noon with a French
Canadian lady, and they were at table as we entered.
My eye was first attracted by a scarlet Garibaldian
shirt the former wore, as in vivid contrast with the
dull colours around.   Her hair was then a thick blond
mop, worn shorter than the shoulders, and it stood out
from her head, silken-soft and crinkled to the roots,
like the fleece of a Cotswold ewe.   This and the red
shirt were what struck my attention before I took in
the picture of her features.   It was a massive Calmuck
face, contrasting in its suggestion of power, culture,
and imperiousness, as strangely with the commonplace
visages about the room as her red garment did with
the grey and white tones of the walls and woodwork

---

* Kappes was an artist delegated by *The Daily Graphic* to make
sketches of the apparitions which appeared at the Eddy farm-house.
This, be it remembered, was taking place in the era before the advent
of the press photographer, when newspapers utilized " on the spot "
coverage performed by professional sketch-makers.

and the dull costumes of the rest of the guests. All sorts of cranky people were continually coming and going at Eddy's to see the mediumistic phenomena, and it only struck me on seeing this eccentric lady that this was but one more of the sort. Pausing on the door-sill, I whispered to Kappes, ' Good gracious! look at *that* specimen, will you.' I went straight across and took a seat opposite her to indulge my favorite habit of character-study. The two ladies conversed in French, making remarks of no consequence, but I saw at once from her accent and fluency of speech that, if not a Parisian, she must at least be a finished French scholar. Dinner over, the two went outside the house and Madame Blavatsky rolled herself a cigarette." *

This was the very opportunity that the colonel had hoped he would have. Quickly stepping forward, in his most gallant reportorial manner he extended a lighted match: " Permettez-moi, s'il vous plaît, madame."

The reporter was none other than Colonel H. S. Olcott, who certainly had no idea as to what the future had in store for him when he set out so blithely to cover his Vermont farm-house assignment.

Since Colonel Olcott is a prominent figure in this narrative, a brief biographical account will aid in evaluating his testimony, which of necessity is called upon from time to time, because of his constant association with H. P. Blavatsky for over a decade.

Henry Steel Olcott was born on August 2, 1832, in Orange, New Jersey. As an investigator (to use the modern term for his Civil War assignment) he had made a name for himself for his scrupulous attention to detail, enabling him to uncover fraudulent practices that were prevalent among the petty officials he had been obliged to contact in the service of his country.

---

* *Old Diary Leaves*, by Henry Steel Olcott; Vol. I, pp. 4-5, 2nd ed. (1941, published by Theosophical Publishing House, Adyar, India). Mary K. Neff in *Personal Memoirs of H. P. Blavatsky*, p. 196, suggests that the French Canadian lady was Mrs. Magnon.

HENRY STEEL OLCOTT

President and Co-Founder of The Theosophical Society.
A reproduction from a portrait first published in
The Word, October, 1915.

DR. ANNIE BESANT, COL. HENRY S. OLCOTT AND WILLIAM Q. JUD

A photo taken in the garden outside of 19 Avenue Road, St. John's Wood, Lond
(N.W.), England. Reproduced from a print published in
Old Diary Leaves, Vol. IV, p. 412.

This service commenced in the spring of 1861, when Henry S. Olcott enlisted in the Grand Army of the Republic (the official title of the Northern forces) shortly after the outbreak of the Civil War. In 1862 Edwin Stanton, Secretary of War, appointed Olcott to the position of a Special Commissioner of the War Department of the Mustering and Disbursing Office, with the delicate and arduous task of detecting and exposing the " gross frauds and crimes which during the war had been attempted or perpetrated by unprincipled speculators regardless of the welfare of soldiers and sailors."

His work in this branch of the service proved to be so excellent that by request of the Navy Department in Philadelphia, he was loaned to that branch of the service. The Colonel was complimented by those in authority for his honorable service and unfaltering courage, his integrity, patriotism, and uncompromising faithfulness to duty.* During the administration of his duties he was awarded the rank of Colonel, although did not have occasion to serve on the battlefield. After the conclusion of the Civil War, when it became necessary to disband the army, Col. Olcott resigned from active service.

It was on the 14th of October, 1874, that Col. Olcott met H. P. Blavatsky at the farm-house in Chittenden, Vermont (as narrated) and from that time until his death he devoted himself to the cause of Theosophy. He was one of the Founders of The Theosophical Society and was also its first President, holding that office until his passing at Adyar, India, on February 17, 1907.

After concluding his assignment at the Eddy farm-house, Col. Olcott's newspaper reports were gathered together and published under the title *People from the Other World*. The book created a good deal of interest at the time that it was published.

Resuming the account of how H. P. Blavatsky entered the literary field. About a fortnight after the publication

---

* Cf. *A Short History of The Theosophical Society*, pp. 38-9, compiled by Josephine Ransom.

of her first letter to the newspaper,* Mme. Blavatsky visited the offices of *The Daily Graphic* and was there interviewed by a reporter. His account of the visit was published in the November 13, 1874, issue of the *Graphic*, and it was followed by an article " About Spiritualism " written by H. P. Blavatsky.

The following month *The Spiritual Scientist* of Boston, Massachusetts, had an article in its columns entitled " Madame Blavatsky". This consisted of extracts made from a letter which H. P. Blavatsky had addressed to that journal. Following this published item, articles from Mme. Blavatsky appeared regularly in the *Scientist* for the next two years. Unfortunately, the journal was obliged to discontinue publication in 1878 because of bankruptcy—H.P.B. remarking that she was several hundred dollars out of pocket because of it.

Before the last issue of *The Spiritual Scientist* had been published, however, H. P. Blavatsky was well on her way towards establishing herself in the literary field through the writing and publication of *Isis Unveiled*, her two-volume work which she subtitled: " A Master-Key to the Mysteries of Ancient and Modern Science and Theology." Also she had written some of her occult stories for *The New York Sun*. An account of the writing of *Isis Unveiled* will be given later in an appropriate chapter, for the reason that the next seven chapters will be devoted to H.P.B.'s writings. These will be considered by means of phases, or processes, instead of reviewing specific works.

That H.P.B. looked forward eagerly to the publication of her first book may be seen by this extract from a letter addressed to N. A. Aksakoff, dated October 4, 1877:

" Well, my book has appeared at last, my darling was born last Saturday, September 29th, but a week

---

* Her first letter was addressed from 124 East 16th St., New York, Oct. 27, 1874; her second letter was from 23 Irving Place, New York, Nov. 10, 1874. It was at 46 Irving Place that a proposal was made for the formation of The Theosophical Society (Sept. 7, 1875). On the next evening the formation of The Theosophical Society took place.

earlier my publisher had sent pre-publication copies to the editors of all the papers." *

This enthusiasm was also conveyed to others, for she eagerly accepted every opportunity for corresponding with anyone who concerned himself with the cause of Spiritualism. Thus in a letter to Professor H. Corson of Cornell University, who had written to H. P. Blavatsky showing interest in the Spiritualistic movement of the day, because of having lost a daughter, there is a passage referring to *Isis Unveiled*:

" The first edition (1,000 copies) was sold in nine days, and the two others have been long sold out. My publisher, Bouton, has had printed a fourth edition for October. The English journals have praised it even more than the American critics." †

Isis Unveiled was expressly written for The Theosophical Society, which was founded on September 8, 1875, the dedicatory page conveying the message in these words:

" The author dedicates these volumes to The Theosophical Society which was founded at New York, A.D. 1875, to study the subjects on which they treat."

A sudden interruption curtailed literary activities, but it was not for long. This was occasioned by the departure on December 18, 1878, of Madame Blavatsky and Colonel Olcott from America to India. It was as though this temporary inactivity called for a greater degree of production. So, work was soon resumed after they had

---

* Quoted in *A Modern Priestess of Isis* by V. S. Solovyoff, London, 1895 (pp. 276-7).

N. Alexander Aksakoff was an eminent St. Petersburg publisher, the former tutor to the Tsarevitch. Col. Olcott states that Aksakoff had commissioned H. P. Blavatsky to translate into Russian his newspaper reports of the Chittenden séances, for publication in Russia. The reports were also published as a book, entitled *People from the Other World*. (Cf. p. 452 *op. cit.*).

† *Some Unpublished Letters of Helena Petrovna Blavatsky*, p. 201.

become settled in Bombay, India, by means of articles written to journals interested in Spiritualism and Theosophy. When all these articles are gathered together they form a good-sized book, as may be seen by viewing the first volume of the series entitled *The Complete Works of H. P. Blavatsky.* *

But the realization must have come to H.P.B. that this spasmodic method of sending an article here or there, as occasion required, was not a satisfactory method of broadcasting the message which had been entrusted to her to deliver to the world at large. Therefore, she decided to have a means whereby she could proclaim her message in her own way: she would have a magazine, which she could devote solely to the cause of Theosophy. Such a periodical was therefore established, and it was named *The Theosophist.* The first issue of her monthly appeared in October, 1879. Then literary activities were carried on in earnest, every issue carrying articles from her pen.

Regarding the establishment of her magazine she wrote:

" The foundation of this journal is due to causes which, having been enumerated in the Prospectus, need only be glanced at in this connection. They are —the rapid expansion of the Theosophical Society from America to various European and Asiatic countries; the increasing difficulty and expense in maintaining correspondence by letter with members so widely scattered; the necessity for an organ through which the native scholars of the East could communicate their learning to the Western world, and, especially, through which the sublimity of the Aryan, Buddhistic, Parsi, and other religions might be expounded by their own priests or pandits, the only competent interpreters; and

---

* Published by Rider & Company, London, England, 1933. A somewhat similar compilation had already been published earlier under the title *A Modern Panarion* (London, 1895)—long out of print.

finally, to the need of a repository for the facts—
especially such as relate to Occultism—gathered by the
Society's Fellows among different nations. . . . ." *

H. P. BLAVATSKY'S WRITINGS IN RUSSIAN

In addition to writing for her own magazine, articles
were sent to other journals, as occasion demanded. In
November, 1879, a lengthy series was commenced for a
Russian journal, the *Moskovskiya Vyedomosti* (i.e., the
" Moscow Chronicle"). This was published regularly
under the title " *Iz peshcher i debrey Indostana* " (meaning,
in translation, " From the Caves and Jungles of Hindostan "), and carrying a sub-title: " *Pisma no rodinu* "
(" Letters to the Fatherland "), until the end of the
year 1882. An English translation, carrying a portion of
Part I of the story, was made by Mrs. Vera Vladimirovna
Johnston (the daughter of H.P.B.'s sister, Vera Petrovna
de Zhelihovsky). This was published in book-form a
year after the author's passing.†

There was no doubt about the popularity of Radda-
Bai's (H.P.B.'s) writing. This was borne out by the fact
that the *Russkiy Vestnik* (i.e., the " Russian Messenger ")
commenced republishing *From the Caves and Jungles of
Hindostan* in January, 1883, and continued publishing
instalments in the form of Supplements until August,

---

* From an article entitled " Namastae " (which may be rendered
" Salutation," from the Sanskrit *namas*, signifying reverential salutation), in the first issue of *The Theosophist*, October, 1879, Vol. I,
No. 1. This journal is still being published monthly by the Theosophical Publishing House, Adyar, Madras, India.

† Under the title *From the Caves and Jungles of Hindostan*, by the
Theosophical Publishing Society, London, 1892. This series, written
specifically to entertain the public, represents H.P.B. at her peak
of descriptive writing. An edition in Russian had already appeared
in Moscow in 1883, produced by the University Printing House
(508 pages), but covering Part I only. In 1912 another Russian
edition was published by A. C. Suvorin in St. Petersburg (438 pages),
and profusely illustrated. Both publications carried the author's
pen-name, Raddai-Bai.

1883. With the August Supplement, which commenced Part II of the story, publication was temporarily discontinued because the author had not had time to prepare further instalments. However, publication was resumed in the November, 1885, issue of the *Russkiy Vestnik* by the reprinting of the 32 pages of the Part II instalment (published in August, 1883). Three more instalments appeared, in February, March and August of 1886; and although the story was supposed to have been continued after the above-mentioned issue, there were no further instalments.

Another series appearing in the *Russkiy Vestnik* under the title "The Durbar in Lahore," was completed in three instalments: May, June and July, 1881. This story had not been published in English until 1960, when it was printed serially.*

A third series, prepared for the Russian journal *Russkiy Vestnik* was printed serially in five instalments, commencing in December, 1884, and concluding in April, 1885 (Vol. 176). It had a very intriguing title: "*Zagadochniya plemena na Golubih Gorah*" (signifying in translation: "The Enigmatical Tribes on the Azure-Blue Hills.") This series was also translated into English by Mrs. Charles Johnston. †

---

* In *The Theosophist*, Adyar, Madras, India, commencing August, 1960 (Vol. 81, No. 11) and running through March, 1961 (Vol. 82, No. 6). The translation from the Russian was made by Boris de Zirkoff, editor of *H. P. Blavatsky Collected Writings*.

† A copy is extant in printed form, although unbound and dated 1897; apparently it was never placed on the market as a published work. This translation bore the title of "The Magicians of the Blue Hills."

This series, together with the "Durbar in Lahore," carried the over-all title "From the Caves and Jungles of India" and was published in Russian in Book-form by V. I. Gubinsky at St. Petersburg (passed by the Censor February 18, 1893—but with no publication date). This was reprinted in Berlin by Olga Dyakova & Co., 1925, with the addition of a biographical sketch by the author's sister, Vera P. de Zhelihovsky. Following the author's name, "Radda-Bai," H. P. Blavatsky was added in parentheses.

Another translation of this story was made and was published serially in *The Theosophist* (Adyar, India), from the issue of April, 1909, to November, 1910.*

"FIVE YEARS OF THEOSOPHY"

The literary effort of publishing a journal for five years blossomed forth in a unique volume, reflected in its title *Five Years of Theosophy.* While this work is not entirely from the pen of H. P. Blavatsky, nevertheless she was the editor of *The Theosophist*, and certainly took care of the literary activity of the journal. In fact the major portion of the volume is hers. Unfortunately, the title of the book does not convey any idea as to its value and significance, other than five years of endeavor. True, the sub-title gives some assistance to the reader, in stating that the book consists of " Mystical, Philosophical, Theosophical, Historical, and Scientific Essays, Selected from *The Theosophist*," but it is a mystery how the publishers, Reeves & Turner, London, 1885, failed to have a Preface prepared for such an important work.

Strangely enough, *Five Years of Theosophy* has never received the acclaim to which it is entitled. Some of its essays contain an exposition of the teachings of the Esoteric Philosophy not to be found elsewhere. Understandably, it was eclipsed by *The Secret Doctrine.* However, of especial significance is the series of inquiries suggested by a reading of Mr. Sinnett's book *Esoteric Buddhism.* Originally published in *The Theosophist* under the title " Replies to an English F.T.S." these answers present an amazing

---

* Several years later this translation was published in book-form by the Theosophical Press, Wheaton, Illinois, in 1930. If the translator's art is an indication of the nature of his work, instead of an enticing title, the name chosen for the story was simply: " The People of the Blue Mountains." This title omits the first adjective "zagadochniya," which besides " enigmatical " could also be rendered "strange," or ' puzzling "; whereas the second adjective, *golubih,* should endeavor to render the kind of blue: either azure blue or light blue. In any event the translation is incomplete.

amount of information; they were in fact dictated to H.P.B. by a Mahatma.*

STILL MORE LITERARY UNDERTAKINGS

Next in the series of published work is H.P.B.'s greatest literary achievement, *The Secret Doctrine.* † Planned first as an expansion and elucidation of *Isis Unveiled*, it soon took on its own unique character. The four volumes planned for the work were never completed in published form, but the two volumes which were published in London in 1888 carried the sub-title: "The Synthesis of Science, Religion, and Philosophy"—Volume I, Cosmogenesis; Volume II, Anthropogenesis.

Although leaving India for Europe on March 31, 1885 (never to return there), H.P.B. continued writing for *The Theosophist* as well as sending occasional articles for publication in William Q. Judge's magazine, *The Path* (New York), as well as to other Theosophical journals. When definitely settled in London, in May, 1887, the writing of *The Secret Doctrine* was the chief concern of the author. However, even before its publication, literary work had been further expanded by the establishment of another "Theosophical" monthly journal, entitled *Lucifer*. The first issue appeared on September 15, 1887, the title-page bearing the following description: "A Theosophical Magazine, designed to 'bring to light the hidden things of darkness.'" The names of H. P. Blavatsky and Mabel Collins were listed as the editors; the publisher, George Redway, York Street, Covent Garden, London. In September, also, The Theosophical Publishing Company was organized in London.

---

* This remarkable series of "Replies to an English F.T.S." has been republished in *H. P. Blavatsky Collected Writings*, Volume V, pp. 143-262. Other essays by H.P.B. which were included in *Five Years of Theosophy* have been republished in the "Collected Writings" series.

† Published by The Theosophical Publishing Co., Ltd., London. The writing of *The Secret Doctrine* is covered in a later chapter.

Even more remarkable essays flowed from the busy pen of the author: to mention but one outstanding example, " The Esoteric Character of the Gospels."

Another volume to appear from this period is entitled *The Key to Theosophy,* " being a Clear Exposition, in the form of Question and Answer, of the Ethics, Science and Philosophy, for the Study of which The Theosophical Society has been founded." First published in 1889, a second edition soon followed, to which a copious glossary was added.

About this time H. P. Blavatsky demonstrated her versatility by preparing a little work, the title of which adequately indicates its contents: *Gems from the East.* Those who love aphorisms, and who treasure the wisdom of the Orient, will be delighted by this compilation of H.P.B.'s. Sub-titled " A Theosophical Birthday Book of Precepts and Axioms " it carries a message for every day in the year. Its publication date is 1890.

Before concluding her literary career, another gem of inestimable value was added to enhance her endeavour: an incomparable devotional work bearing the paradoxical title of *The Voice of the Silence.* Albeit, its title-page carries this explanatory passage: " Being Chosen Fragments from the ' Book of the Golden Precepts ' for the Daily Use of Lanoos (Disciples). Translated and Annotated by H.P.B." Published in 1889.

Another work, entitled *Transactions of the Blavatsky Lodge,* was first published in London and New York in two parts; the first in 1890, the second in 1891. It is of particular value to students of *The Secret Doctrine.* In view of the importance of this work its title is singularly misleading, because no clue is given as to its content; furthermore, no preface nor introduction was provided. The title, of course, announces that it presents what transpired at meetings of the Blavatsky Lodge of London, but it does not state that the lodge had the inestimable privilege of having H.P.B. herself present at its assemblies. Moreover, she answered questions which were asked upon the Stanzas of Dzyan. But the striking feature of these questions and answers—which were taken down in shorthand by a stenographer—was the fact that the queries were upon the most difficult portion of the Stanzas, namely, upon the opening slokas dealing with cosmogenesis in its pre-manifestation stages, covering Stanzas I, II, III and IV of Volume I of *The Secret Doctrine*. Unfortunately, the published "Transactions" did not complete the seven Stanzas of Dzyan dealt with in Volume I of *The Secret Doctrine*: nor were included any portion of the Stanzas contained in Volume II. Thus *Transactions of the Blavatsky Lodge*, as published, represents an unfinished work. In spite of this drawback, this book is a most valuable contribution to H.P.B.'s presentation of the Esoteric Philosophy.

Posthumous Works

While the preceding account represents the volumes published during the lifetime of H.P.B., additional works appeared after her passing. Some of these have already been mentioned: *A Modern Panarion*, and the books enumerated under the heading of her Russian writings. These need not be repeated.

First to appear was *Nightmare Tales*: a collection of occult stories, published by The Theosophical Publishing Society (London, New York, Madras, 1892). The stories had the following intriguing titles:

1. An Unsolved Mystery.
2. A Story of the Mystical.
3. The Luminous Circle.
4. The Cave of the Echoes.
5. The Ensouled Violin.
6. A Bewitched Life.
7. From the Polar Lands.

All but the seventh in this compilation had already been published either in newspapers or magazines. They are available either under this title, or else in the "Collected Writings" series.*

---

* For a detailed explanation of the contents of this work, see *H. P. Blavatsky Collected Writings*, Vol. VI, pp. 354-5.

Next: *The Theosophical Glossary*, published by The Theosophical Publishing Society (London, New York, Madras, 1892). An extract from the Preface is appropriate:

" *The Theosophical Glossary* labours under the disadvantage of being an almost entirely posthumous work, of which the author only saw the first thirty-two pages in proof. This is all the more regrettable, for H.P.B., as was her wont, was adding considerably to her original copy, and would no doubt have increased the volume far beyond its present limits. . . ."

Along with a revision of *The Secret Doctrine* (which became known as the Third and Revised Edition), was added an additional volume which was entitled *Volume III of The Secret Doctrine*. This was published posthumously in London in 1897 with a preface written by Annie Besant. It should be understood, however, that this volume is not *the* third volume contemplated by H.P.B. As a matter of fact Mme. Blavatsky intended the manuscript which she had prepared as *her first volume* to be on data concerning the Mystery-Schools of antiquity, as well as information regarding " the history of occultism as contained in the lives of the great Adepts." But when she turned over her manuscript to the Keightleys to arrange for the printer, they suggested altering the sequence. As well as arranging the manuscript into three parts (1) the Stanzas and Commentaries, (2) Symbolism; (3) Science, and typewriting it, they suggested placing Cosmogenesis as Volume I of the series; Anthropogenesis as Volume II; historical data of Occultists as Volume III.* H.P.B. acquiesced and the first two volumes alone were published in 1888.

In the present six volumes edition, as published at Adyar, India, the posthumous third volume (so-called) is

---

* Cf. Bertram Keightley's Account of the Writing of *The Secret Doctrine*, published in *Reminiscences of H. P. Blavatsky and The Secret Doctrine*, by Countess Wachtmeister, page 91.

represented by Volume V of the six volume set; Volume VI is solely an Index. The opening sentences of Annie Besant's Preface clearly indicate the status of the contents of the volume:

" The task of preparing this volume for the press has been a difficult and anxious one, and it is necessary to state clearly what has been done. The papers given to me by H.P.B. were quite unarranged, and had no obvious order: I have therefore, taken each paper as a separate Section, and have arranged them as sequentially as possible. With the exception of the correction of grammatical errors and the elimination of obviously un-English idioms, the papers are as H.P.B. left them, save as otherwise marked." (page 7)

The above citation should be read in conjunction with what H.P.B. wrote in her Preface to *The Secret Doctrine* (published in 1888):

" Even the two volumes now issued do not complete the scheme, and these do not treat exhaustively of the subjects dealt with in them. A large quantity of material has already been prepared, dealing with the history of occultism as contained in the lives of the great Adepts of the Aryan Race, and showing the bearing of occult philosophy upon the conduct of life, as it is and as it ought to be. Should the present volumes meet with a favourable reception, no effort will be spared to carry out the scheme of the work in its entirety." (p. vii, orig. ed.)

The Letters of H. P. Blavatsky to A. P. Sinnett, " and other Miscellaneous Letters: Transcribed, Compiled, and with an Introduction " by A. T. Barker: Published by T. Fisher Unwin Ltd., London, 1925. Intended to form a companion volume to *The Mahatma Letters to A. P. Sinnett* (published 1923). A valuable source of information regarding H.P.B. herself, given in her own inimitable manner. These letters were the basis for A. P. Sinnett's published book *Incidents in the Life of Madame Blavatsky* (first published in 1886).

H. P. BLAVATSKY

Reproduced from a print first published in *The Review of Reviews*, New York, Vol. VIII, p. 659, December, 1893. One of the little known portraits of Mme. Blavatsky, probably taken during her forties.

H. P. B. AT THE TIME OF THE FOUNDING OF
THE THEOSOPHICAL SOCIETY

Taken by a professional photographer, Beardsley of Ithaca, New York,
during a visit to that city in September, 1875.

Some Unpublished Letters of Helena Petrovna Blavatsky, by Eugene Rollin Corson, B.S., M.D., published by Rider & Co., Paternoster House, London (no publication date given, but produced some time between 1925 and 1935). This book is of interest in that it gives H. P. Blavatsky's own account of her closing endeavors in the cause of Spiritualism in America and the transition to the founding to The Theosophical Society—which occurred on September 8, 1875. Five lengthy chapters serve to introduce the fourteen letters included in the book. Twelve of the letters were written by H. P. Blavatsky to H. Corson, the father of Eugene Corson. Professor Corson held the chair of Anglo-Saxon and English literature at Cornell University. As well as being a teacher he was considered to be an authority on English poetry. The first letter is dated February 9, 1875; the twelfth, March 22, 1876. The other two letters were written to Mrs. Corson, and dated March 12, 1876 and August 28, 1878. Dr. Corson states that his mother was French.

Some of the letters indicate that Mr. and Mrs. Corson had extended to H. P. Blavatsky an invitation to visit them at Ithaca. This actually eventuated, and the professor's son fixes the date of H. P. Blavatsky's visit at Ithaca as taking place on September 17, 1875. Of interest is the fact that one of the best photographs taken of H. P. Blavatsky was made by a professional photographer, by the name of Beardsley of Ithaca, New York, during this Ithaca visit. H. P. Blavatsky herself ordered several dozen copies of the photograph.

Dr. Corson mentions that H. P. Blavatsky stayed four weeks at the Corson residence, which was situated very near to Cornell University. Most likely she left during the early part of the fourth week, because she was present in New York on Saturday, October 16, 1875. On October 30th occurred the election of the officers of The Theosophical Society, and H. P. Blavatsky was elected to the post of Corresponding Secretary.

Dr. Corson, however, never met H. P. Blavatsky himself, as he was then studying medicine at Philadelphia, yet he treasured the memory of her visit with his parents. He relates that:

"My mother described to me how H.P.B. would sit down at the piano and improvise with great skill, showing a remarkable efficiency for one who played but at odd times as the spirit might move her. Her biographers have not dwelt at any length on her musical talent. . . . .

"My mother on several occasions spoke of the charm of her playing.

"To H.P.B. many incidents in her eventful and stormy life during her younger days were a sealed book to her friends and acquaintances. In a casual way she mentioned to my mother that she had fought in Garibaldi's army and had slept in the Pontine marshes." *

"H.P.B.'s phenomena with a few exceptions were not a feature of her visit. She showed the raps as produced by her will-power sometimes through a stack of hands, and again on different parts of the room. My father was familiar with the phenomenon in the séance room through the ordinary medium, but was much more impressed when produced by conscious will-power. On another occasion he had asked if she could place me and tell what I was doing, then a student of medicine in Philadelphia, and she gave him an accurate account of where I was and what was taking place. It happened to be that I was visiting my preceptor on Green Street. She said I was much under his influence, which was true, and a very good

---

* *Some Unpublished Letters of Helena Petrovna Blavatsky*, pp. 33-34. Dr. Corson adds this footnote concerning Mentana—which was the battle at which H.P.B. was present, and in which she was also wounded:

"13 miles N.E. of Rome, noted from the battle which took place there November 3rd, 1867. On this occasion Garibaldi himself was taken prisoner. See Johnson's Universal Encyclopaedia, article, 'Mentana.'"

influence it was too. On another occasion she caused a heavy table to rise up in the air without touching it, and she repeatedly said that this was all due to her will-power, and was not to be classed with the ordinary mediumistic phenomena.

"One evening a frost was predicted, and my mother was anxious to get in her potted plants from the porch, when H.P.B. told her not to worry, and she would get 'John' to bring them in. So they went to bed without any concern, and in the morning all the plants were found inside.

"I mention these incidents, not that I think them of much importance at this late day, but because these phenomena became a part of her activities, both in New York and India and later in Europe." *

Following the letters, Dr. Corson has added a chapter entitled "Commentary on the Letters," some fifty pages in the book, which adds to the value of the work.

THE H. P. BLAVATSKY COLLECTED WRITINGS SERIES

By far the most important of the posthumous publications is the series which is still in process of publication. It is known under two titles, as will be explained in the narrative.

Early in the 1930's by an arrangement with a publishing firm in London, an endeavor by a group of Theosophists was made to start the publication of a series of volumes under the editorship of A. Trevor Barker, entitled *The Complete Works of H. P. Blavatsky*. The intention was to produce a uniform collection of all writings findable which had come from the pen of H.P.B. The first volume contained the articles included in the work known as *A Modern Panarion*, as well as additional material. Four volumes were issued serially, as follows:

---

* *Op. cit.*, pp. 35-6.

Volume I—1874-1879 (publisher: Rider & Co.,
London, 1933);
Volume II, December 1879—May 1881 (published
1933);
Volume III, 1881-1882 (published 1935);
Volume IV, 1882-1883 (published 1936).

Then came World War II and the project had to be
discontinued. Not to be discouraged by the vicissitudes
which had befallen "The Complete Works" series—
such as the destruction of all the plates and the stock of
books in the London war-time bombings—Boris de Zirkoff himself undertook the task of continuing the publication of the series. Commencing as a private undertaking, in 1950 he accomplished the feat of bringing forth
another volume of the series under the more logical title
of *H. P. Blavatsky Collected Writings*. Thus, Volume V,
covering the year 1883, was published by the Philosophical Research Society, Inc., Los Angeles, California,
in 1950. This provided the stimulus for bringing forth
Volume VI, which continued the writings of 1883 and
on through the years of 1884 and 1885. The book was
published in 1954 by the Blavatsky Writings Publication
Fund, Los Angeles, California.

With Volume VII, the compiler was able to assure
Theosophists that the series which he had inaugurated
and carried on so devotedly would be continued—as was
expressed in his Foreward to Volume VII:

"With the present Volume, the publication of the
Collected Writings is being undertaken by The Theosophical Publishing House, Adyar, Madras, India, at
the suggestion of our esteemed Brother and Friend,
N. Sri Ram, President of The Theosophical Society,
Adyar. His offer to undertake the publication of the
remaining volumes in this Series comes as a fitting
culmination to many years of valuable collaboration
between the Officials of The Theosophical Society,
Adyar, and the Compiler. It augurs well for the
ultimate success of the entire venture, and contributes

greatly towards an earlier completion of the task at hand." (Page xxiii) *

Volume VII consists of articles prepared for *The Theosophist* during the years 1886-87. It was published in 1958.

Volume VIII (published in 1960) introduced a new feature: it consists of the essays and articles written by H. P. Blavatsky for her new magazine, *Lucifer*. H.P.B. had left India in March, 1885, and commenced work on *The Secret Doctrine* in the spring of that year in Würzburg, Germany. In May, 1886, she left Würzburg for Ostend, Belgium, continuing writing on *The Secret Doctrine* as well as contributing articles to *The Theosophist*. In May, 1887, she left Ostend for London, England, and after moving to 17 Landsdowne Road in September, she founded the Theosophical magazine entitled *Lucifer*. Its title-page described it as a periodical designed to "bring to light the hidden things of darkness." The essays prepared for this monthly organ represent H.P.B. at the peak of her literary career—both in regard to their content as well as the manner in which they were written. Volume VIII comprises the articles written in 1887, commencing with the first issue of *Lucifer*, bearing the date September 15, 1887, and continuing in the October, November and December issues. Also included chronologically are some articles which were written during this period but published posthumously. Especial mention should be made of the outstanding series of three essays entitled "The Esoteric Character of the Gospels." Another important contribution from H.P.B.'s pen is included in this volume:

---

* Theosophists the world over are indeed grateful to Boris de Zirkoff, whose zeal and unflagging efforts have brought about the publication of H. P. Blavatsky's literary works—first under the title of *The Complete Works* and continuing as *H. P. Blavatsky Collected Writings*. It is his purpose to have the first four volumes of the series re-published at Adyar, India, as these works have been unprocurable since World War II. Further information regarding the series is adequately covered in the Preface to each volume.

the first one of a series known as the literary controversy with the Abbé Rocca. It was first published in *Le Lotus*, December, 1887, and written in French.

Volume IX continues the articles prepared for *Lucifer*, covering the period January to June, 1888. A good portion of the volume is devoted to the series of articles referred to as the literary controversy with the Abbé Rocca.

Volume X is devoted to the essays and articles written for *Lucifer*. It covers the years 1888-1889. It was published at Adyar in 1964.

The enumeration that has been made of the years associated with each volume does not give any idea whatsoever of the wealth of information contained in each one of the books. The scope of this lavish literary production could only be given by means of naming each article. The list, however, is so multitudinous that it would require a volume to catalogue and explain it.

The compiler's Preface to the " Collected Writings " series states that the search for H. P. Blavatsky's literary work was extended to cover publications in English, French, Russian and Italian. This in itself is a noteworthy feat. It is estimated that close to one thousand articles will be included in the series. It should be borne in mind that this remarkable literary output was accomplished without secretarial assistance of any kind, and that every page was written by hand. What an astonishing achievement; it is positively outstanding!

When all of H. P. Blavatsky's writings are gathered together their scope is indeed phenomenal; they truly represent a prodigious undertaking, considering the time-period involved—not quite seventeen years.

Processes involved in Writing

In order to call attention to the different facets utilized by H. P. Blavatsky in her writing, it is considered advantageous to divide her writings into seven categories. Perhaps it might be clearer to phrase it in this manner: " the processes involved in her writing." These seven categories will be considered in seven chapters—one for each chapter.   In enumeration:

1. Descriptive Writing—in which H.P.B. displayed her talents as a writer.
2. Writing by means of Instruction.
3. Writing by Dictation.
4. Writing by *Directive* Clairvoyance.
5. Writing by Psychometry.
6. Writing by means of Precipitation.
7. Writing by means of a process analogous to Tulku.

These seven categories should be clear enough, except the wording of the seventh.   It is admitted that this is somewhat vague, for the simple reason that the writer knows of no proper word in English to describe the idea that is intended to be conveyed.   But by the time that the exposition of this seventh category will have been completed, it is hoped that the idea will be conveyed to the reader.   In any event, there is more to the subject than a mere listing of categories, as will be shown as the theme unfolds.

CHAPTER VIII

ON H. P. BLAVATSKY'S DESCRIPTIVE WRITING

As more and more of H. P. Blavatsky's writings are made available through the publication of the *H. P. Blavatsky Collected Writings* series, there is no question but that she was pre-eminent in the field of descriptive writing. She was indeed superb! Innumerable passages from her major works might be chosen to display this talent, for it shines forth in her way of writing. Who has not read her collected stories—published under the awesome title of *Nightmare Tales* *—but can agree that these are some of the wierdest tales ever penned! Her versatility was well displayed in her stories. Occasionally her love of fun and wit would crop out to enliven her account. Witness this example, from one of her early newspaper articles entitled "The Knout," in which she wields this instrument of punishment not only on those deserving of the lash, but also upon herself!

"The 'Protest' of Mr. W. Emmette Coleman, entitled 'Sclavonic Theosophy *v.* American Spiritualism' is the musky rose in an odoriferous bouquet. Its pungent fragrance would give the nose-bleed to a sensitive whose olfactories would withstand the perfume of a garden full of the Malayan flower-queen —the tuberose; and yet, my tough, pug-Mongolian nose, which has smelled carrion in all parts of the world, proved itself equal even to this emergency.

"'From the sublime to the ridiculous,' says the French proverb, 'there is but a single step.' From sparkling wit to dull absurdity, there is no more. An attack, to be effective, must have an antagonist to strike, for to kick against something that exists only

---

* Published in 1892 (London, New York and Madras).

in one's imagination, wrenches man or beast. Don Quixote fighting the ' air-drawn ' foes in his windmill, stands for ever the laughing-stock of all generations, and the type of a certain class of disputants, that, for the moment, Mr. Coleman represents. . . .

"I never claimed that magic was anything but psychology practically applied. That one of your mesmerizers can make a cabbage appear a rose, is only a lower form of the power you all endow me with. You give an old woman—whether forty, fifty, sixty or ninety years old (some swear I am the latter, some the former), it matters not; an old woman whose Kalmuco-Buddhisto-Tartaric features, even in youth, never made her appear pretty; a woman whose ungainly garb, uncouth manners and masculine habits are enough to frighten any bustled and corseted fine lady of fashionable society out of her wits—you give her such powers of fascination as to draw fine ladies and gentlemen, scholars and artists, doctors and clergymen, to her house by the scores, to not only talk philosophy with her, not merely to stare at her as though she were a monkey in red flannel breeches, as some of them do, but to honor her in many cases with their fast and sincere friendship and grateful kindness!" *

---

* From the *Religio-Philosophical Journal*, Chicago, Vol. XXIV, March 16, 1878, p. 8; republished in *The Complete Works of H. P. Blavatsky*, Vol. I, pp. 185-8.

It might be well to add here Elizabeth G. K. Holt's impressions of H.P.B., as she lived for a time in the same apartment house, at 222 Madison Street, New York, in 1873:

"Mme. Blavatsky . . . was certainly an unusual figure. I think she must have been taller than she looked, she was so broad; she had a broad face and broad shoulders; her hair was a lightish brown and crinkled like that of some negroes. Her whole appearance conveyed the idea of power. I read somewhere lately an account of an interview with Stalin; the writer said that when you entered the room you felt as if there was a powerful dynamo working. You felt something like that when you were near H.P.B.

13

Turning from her ability to use the pen in the capacity of a knout, to a different type of writing, albeit in the descriptive vein, we find it captivatingly and delightfully exhibited in the publication entitled *From the Caves and Jungles of Hindostan*.* In this work there is nothing to hamper her facile pen, which seems to revel in entertaining her readers. In order to demonstrate a sample of this type of writing, first choice should go to the account of one of her journeys which she named " An Isle of Mystery." It is an outstanding example.

" The island was a tiny one, and so overgrown with tall reeds that from a distance it looked like a pyramidal basket of verdure. With the exception of a colony of

---

" Madame referred often to her life in Paris; for one thing she told us that she had decorated the Empress Eugenie's private apartments. I thought of her as dressed in blouse and trousers, mounted on a ladder and doing the actual work, and I think this is what she told us; but I cannot be sure whether she said that she did the actual painting, frescoing, etc., or whether she merely designed it. Later she gave practical demonstration that she had ability in the arts. I had a piano, and Madame sometimes played, usually because somebody pressed her to do so.

" She described their past life to the people who asked her to do so, and these accounts must have been accurate, they made such a profound impression. I never heard that she told them their future, but she may have done so without my knowing it. . . . .

"' I never looked upon Madame as an ethical teacher. For one thing, she was too excitable; when things went wrong with her, she could express her opinion about them with a vigour which was very disturbing. I would say here that I never saw her angry with any person or thing at close range. Her objections had an impersonality about them. . . . In mental or physical dilemma, you would instinctively appeal to her, for you felt her fearlessness, her unconventionality, her great wisdom and wide experience and hearty good will—her sympathy with the under dog."— Quoted in *Personal Memoirs of H. P. Blavatsky by Mary K. Neff*, pp. 190-1; from *The Theosophist* of December 1931.

* This English translation was made by H.P.B.'s niece Mrs. Charles Johnston (née Zhelihovsky), published in 1892 by The Theosophical Publishing Society (London, New York and Madras).

monkeys, who bustled away to a few mango trees at our approach, the place seemed uninhabited. In this virgin forest of thick grass there was no trace of human life. . . . . The *grass* under which we stood, like insects under a rhubarb leaf, waved its feathery many-coloured plumes much above the head of Gulab-Sing (who stood six feet and a half in his stockings) and of Narayan, who measured hardly an inch less. From a distance it looked like a waving sea of black, yellow, blue, and especially of rose and green. On landing, we discovered that it consisted of separate thickets of bamboos, mixed with the gigantic sirka reeds, which rose as high as the tops of the mangoes.

" It is impossible to imagine anything prettier and more graceful than the bamboos and sirka. The isolated tufts of bamboos show, in spite of their size, that they are nothing but grasses, because the least gush of wind shakes them, and their green crests begin to nod like heads adorned with long ostrich plumes. There were some bamboos there fifty or sixty feet high. From time to time we heard a light metallic rustle in the reeds, but none of us paid much attention to it. . . . .

" The sun had set, and we were told that the supper was ready. . . . As the last golden ray disappeared on the horizon, a gauze-like veil of pale lilac fell over the world. . . . The phosphoric candles of the fire-flies began to twinkle here and there, shining brightly against the black trunks of the trees, and lost again on the silvery background of the opalescent evening sky. But in a few minutes more, thousands of these living sparks, precursors of Queen Night played round us, pouring like a golden cascade over the trees, and dancing in the air above the grass and the dark lake.

" And behold! here is the queen in person. Noise-lessly descending upon earth, she reassumes her rights. With her approach, rest and peace spread over us; her cool breath calms the activities of the day. Like a fond mother, she sings a lullaby to nature, lovingly wrapping her in her soft black mantle. . . . . Nature

sleeps, but man is awake, to be a witness to the beauties
of this solemn evening hour. Sitting round the fire,
we talked, lowering our voices as if afraid of awaking
night. We were only six; the colonel, the four Hindus
and myself. . . .

" We were waiting for the 'concert' which the
Takur had promised us. ' Be patient,' he said, ' the
musicians will not appear before the moon rises.'
The fickle goddess was late: she kept us waiting
till after ten o'clock. Just before her arrival . . . a
sudden wind rose. . . . In the general silence, we
heard again the same musical notes, which we had
passed unheeded when we first reached the island, as
if a whole orchestra were trying their musical instruments before playing some great composition. All
round us, and over our heads, vibrated strings of
violins, and thrilled the separate notes of a flute.

" In a few moments came another gust of wind
tearing through the reeds, and the whole island
resounded with the strains of hundreds of Aeolian
harps. And suddenly there began a wild unceasing
symphony. It swelled in the surrounding woods,
filling the air with an indescribable melody. Sad
and solemn were its prolonged strains, like the *arpeggios*
of some funeral march; then changing into a trembling
thrill, they shook the air like the song of a nightingale,
and died away in a long sigh. They did not quite
cease, but grew louder again, ringing like hundreds of
silver bells; then changing from the heart-rending
howl of a wolf deprived of her young, to the precipitate
rhythm of a gay tarantella, forgetful of every earthly
sorrow; from the articulate song of a human voice to
the vague majestic accords of a violoncello; from merry
child's laughter to angry sobbing. And all this was
repeated on every side by mocking echo. . . . .

" There was a short interval, after which the invisible
orchestra started again with renewed energy. The
sounds poured and rolled in unrestrainable, overwhelming waves. . . . Listen! A storm in the open
sea, the wind tearing through the rigging, the swish of

the maddened waves rushing over each other, or the whirling snow wreaths on the silent steppes. Suddenly the vision is changed; now it is a stately cathedral and the thundering strains of an organ rising under its vaults. The powerful notes now rush together, now spread out through space, break off, intermingle, and become entangled like the fantastic melody of a delirious fever, some musical fantasy born of the howling and whistling of the wind.

"Alas! the charm of these sounds is soon exhausted, and you begin to feel that they cut like knives through your brain. A horrid fancy haunts our bewildered heads; we imagine that the invisible artists strain our own veins, and not the strings of imaginary violins; their cold breath freezes us, blowing their imaginary trumpets, shaking our nerves and impeding our breathing.

" ' For God's sake stop this, Takur! This is really too much,' shouted the colonel, at the end of his patience, and covering his ears with his hands. ' Gulab-Singh, I tell you you must stop this.'

" The three Hindus burst out laughing; and even the grave face of the Takur lit up with a merry smile.

" ' Upon my word,' said he, ' do you really take me for the great Parabrahm? Do you think it is in my power to stop the wind, as if I were Marut, the lord of storms, in person? Ask for something easier than the instantaneous uprooting of all these bamboos.'

" ' I beg your pardon; I thought these strange sounds were some kind of psychological influence.'

" ' So sorry to disappoint you, my dear colonel. . . . Don't you see that this wild music is a natural acoustic phenomenon? Each of the reeds round us—and there are thousands on this island—contains a natural musical instrument; and the musician, Wind, comes here daily to try his art after nightfall, especially during the last quarter of the moon.'

" ' The wind! ' murmured the colonel. ' Oh, yes! But this music begins to change into a dreadful roar. Is there no way out of it? '

" ' I at least cannot help it. But keep up your patience, you will soon get accustomed to it. Besides, there will be intervals when the wind falls.'

" We were told that there are many such natural orchestras in India. The Brahmans know well their wonderful properties, and calling this kind of reed *vina-devi*, the lute of the gods, keep up the popular superstition and say the sounds are divine oracles. The sirka grass and the bamboos always shelter a number of tiny beetles, which make considerable holes in the tiny reeds. The fakirs of the idol-worshipping sects add art to this natural beginning, and work the plants into musical instruments. The islet we visited bore one of the most celebrated *vina-devis*, and so, of course, was proclaimed sacred.

" ' Tomorrow morning,' said the Takur, ' you will see what deep knowledge of all the laws of acoustics was in the possession of the fakirs. They enlarged the holes made by the beetles according to the size of the reed, sometimes shaping it into a circle, sometimes into an oval.. These reeds in their present state can be justly considered as the finest illustration of mechanism applied to acoustics. However, this is not to be wondered at, because some of the most ancient Sanskrit books about music minutely describe these laws, and mention many musical instruments which are not only forgotten, but totally incomprehensible in our days.'

" All this was very interesting, but still, disturbed by the din, we could not listen attentively.

" ' Don't worry yourselves,' said the Takur. ' After midnight the wind will fall, and you will sleep undisturbed. However, if the too close neighbourhood of this musical grass is too much for you, we may as well go nearer the shore. There is a spot from which you can see the sacred bonfires on the opposite shore. . . .'

" We arrived at a small glade some distance from the bamboo forest. The sounds of the magic orchestra reached us still, but considerably weakened, and only from time to time. . . . We sat down, and only then I realized how tired and sleepy I was—and no wonder, after being on foot since four in the morning." *

It is a pity that one must turn away *From Caves and Jungles.* It would be so easy to select passage after passage from that entertaining narrative. Nevertheless, the purpose of calling attention to Radda-Bai's talent as a descriptive writer has been accomplished. This was H.P.B.'s pen-name when writing in Russian periodicals. It may also be noted here that her mother had also made a name for herself in the literary field. But, unfortunately, the mother's experience could not be passed on to her daughter, because she died while Helena was still a child. And little Sedmichka † was usually referred to as an orphaned child, because her father was so often away from home captaining his regiment.

In order to show that beauty of description may serve to heighten a philosophical exposition, one selection from *The Secret Doctrine* will suffice as an illustrative example:

"Just as milliards of bright sparks dance on the waters of an ocean above which one and the same moon is shining, so our evanescent personalities—the illusive envelopes of the immortal MONAD-EGO—twinkle and dance on the waves of Mâyâ. They last and appear, as the thousands of sparks produced by the moon-beams, only so long as the Queen of the Night radiates

---

* *From the Caves and Jungles of Hindostan*, quoted in *Personal Memoirs of H. P. Blavatsky*, by Mary K. Neff, pp. 89-91.

† A person born in the seventh month of the year and during the night between July 30-31 (Russian style—equivalent to August 11-12, in the year of 1831) would customarily receive the nickname Sedmichek—or Sedmichka if a girl—signifying in Russian, literally " the little seven-numbered one." It may be observed that H.P.B. certainly upheld the traditions of folk-lore which associated unusual powers with a " Sedmichka "—among which was the ability of being able to control the *domovoy* (a term which may be equated with the *poltergeist*, or " racket-sprite "). Significantly enough, in her major works the number 7 was assuredly predominant.

her luster on the running waters of life: the period of a Manvantara; and then they disappear, the beams—symbols of our eternal Spiritual Egos—alone surviving, re-merged in, and being, as they were before, one with the Mother-Source." *

The full significance of the passage may not be grasped, without explanation, since profound philosophy has been introduced in allegorical manner. It would be well to pause and consider the meaning while reflecting upon the beauty of the paragraph, which was called forth in order to explain one of the Stanzas of Dzyan (Stanza VII, śloka 4):

"It is the root that never dies, the three-tongued flame of the four wicks. . . . The wicks are the sparks, that draw from the three-tongued flame (*their upper triad*) shot out by the seven, their flame; the beams and sparks of one moon reflected in the running waves of all the rivers of the earth (Bhûmi, or Prithivî)." †

The root that never dies signifies Âtman—the divine counterpart, or Spirit, in the sevenfold constitution of a human being (commonly referred to as the seven principles of man). It is represented as a three-tongued flame, since Âtman is unable to manifest in physical realms without a vehicle (to be further explained later under the term "Monad-Ego.") The three-tongued flame, then, stands for man's immortal triad: Âtman; Buddhi, the discriminating principle; Manas, the mind principle (the seventh, sixth and fifth principles in the sevenfold enumeration of the "seven principles" comprising the septenary human constitution). The four wicks signify the perishable components, the lower quaternary, consisting of the four lower principles of the sevenfold constitution: (1) Sthûla-śarîra, the physical body, or vehicle; (2) Linga-śarîra, the model body; (3) Prâna, the life

---

* *The Secret Doctrine,* Vol. I, p. 237; I, 283, 6 vol. ed.; I, 258, 3rd ed.
† *Ibid.*

principle, or vitality; (4) Kâma, the desire principle, providing the energic stimulus in man. The wicks are likened to sparks because during an earth-life a spark (or the evanescent personality) is enabled to exist so long as the wick is sustained by means of its contact with the three-tongued flame. In its turn the wick transmits the good, the true and the beautiful (to use the familiar Platonic triad) to Higher Manas (Manas-Taijasî) when the four wicks are extinguished at death. It is Lower Manas (that is to say, the mind principle in conjunction with the desire principle, Kâma) along with the four wicks that fashions the evanescent personality during a life-time on earth. This is described as an illusive envelope of the immortal Monad-Ego. Notice the compound word here, employed in order to designate the three-tongued flame, the root that never dies: that is, the Monad (which technically signifies Âtman and Buddhi) plus the Ego (standing for Higher Manas)—again enumerating the immortal triad (Âtman-Buddhi-Manas). It is the evanescent personalities which twinkle and dance on the waves of Mâyâ—appearing and disappearing. Mâyâ, of course, here signifies earth-life; one evanescent personality following after another in incarnation after incarnation on earth.

Assuredly, during the period of a Manvantara—that is to say a period of activity of the planetary system of Earth (Bhûmi)—the personalities that compose the illusive envelopes of the Monad-Ego may indeed appear as thousands of sparks, yet the *spiritual aroma* of each personality—referred to as a beam of the Monad-Ego—is garnered during the after-death state, and becomes linked with the immortal triad as Manas-Taijasî and constitutes that which is experienced in the Devachanic interlude. It is for that reason that this is referred to as the spiritual beams of the spiritual Ego. The closing words of the descriptive passage have reference to the teaching that during the pralaya, following a Manvantara (a Solar Manvantara), the monad re-merges for a period with its Mother-Source (this signifying Paramâtman—the Source of Âtman).

Thus, in this one descriptive passage there is contained an epitome of the teaching concerning the seven principles of man, reference to the significance of the after-death state, as well as directing attention to the origin and goal of man.

CHAPTER IX

WRITING BY MEANS OF INSTRUCTION

The second category in the writing processes of H.P.B. is listed as writing by means of instruction. The words should provide the idea that is desired to be conveyed, although more is implied than might be suspected. This is particularly applicable to the preparation of H.P.B.'s principal work, *The Secret Doctrine*. During its writing the author for the most part was alone, situated in a small house on Ludwigstrasse at Würzburg, Germany, until a single companion came to stay with her. Later, by request of her sister and niece she moved to Ostend, Belgium, carrying on her labor. At neither place did she have access to any library and her visitors were few in number. The work was concluded London, when English Theosophists rallied to her support, providing a residence and financial support for the publication of her writings. In every case she carried on her writing in pen and ink. Yet it is stated that she wrote under instruction. How was this guidance provided? In a most singular manner. Orally, from her Teachers—which she jocularly referred to at times as coming by spiritual telegraphy; but more frequently by means of written slips.

The focus for this "spiritual telegraph" was located in a rather strange place, to put it mildly, but it is indicative of anything connected with H.P.B.: that one should be alert to look for the unsuspected. The companion referred to above had this to say about the spiritual telegraph and the labors of the author:

"It seems to me that by showing some of the details of H.P.B.'s life at that time, one gains a better comprehension of the woman who wrote that stupendous work. Day after day she would sit there writing through all the long hours, and nothing could be more monotonous and wearisome than her life regarded from an outside point of view. But, I suppose, at that time she lived much in the inner world, and there saw sights and visions which compensated for the dreariness of her daily life. She had, however, a distraction of rather a peculiar nature. In front of her writing table, attached to the wall, was a cuckoo clock, and this used to behave in a very extraordinary manner. Sometimes it would strike like a loud gong, then sigh and groan as if possessed, cuckooing in the most unexpected way. Our maid, Louise, who was the most dense and apathetic of mortals, was very much afraid of it, and told us solemnly one day that she thought the devil was in it. ' Not that I believe in the devil,' she said, ' but this cuckoo almost speaks to me at times.' And so it did. One evening I went into the room and saw that appeared to me like streams of electric light coming out of the clock in all directions. On telling H.P.B. she replied, ' Oh, it is only the spiritual telegraph, they are laying it on stronger tonight on account of tomorrow's work.' Living in this atmosphere and coming into contact so continually with these, usually unseen, forces, this all seemed the true reality, to me, and the outer world was that which appeared vague and unsatisfactory." *

With regard to the written slips of paper: witnesses have testified to the fact that slips of paper bearing writing either in red ink or in blue ink would appear on Mme. Blavatsky's writing table. Generally these slips would be present the first thing in the morning, although it was known that the writing table had been cleared and tidied when work had been completed for the day. How did the papers get there, and from whom did they come? " These are my writing assignments, placed there by my Teachers," H.P.B. would explain.

" Was it *fraud? Certainly not.* Was it written and produced by elementals? *Never.* It was delivered, and

---

* *Reminiscences of H. P. Blavatsky and " The Secret Doctrine,"* by Countess Constance Wachtmeister, pp. 55-6.

the *physical* phenomena are produced by elementals used for the purpose, but what have they, those senseless beings, to do with the intelligent portions of the smallest and most foolish message ? " *

Countless Wachtmeister, † who lived with H.P.B. during the autumn and winter of 1885 and spring of 1886, and was therefore present at the time that *The Secret Doctrine* was being written, supplied this testimonial:

" Another incident of frequent occurrence came under my notice from time to time, and marks another mode in which guidance and aid were given to H.P.B.

---

* From a letter written by H. P. Blavatsky and published in *The Path*; quoted in *Reminiscences*, etc., p. 38.

† Countess Constance Wachtmeister (1838-1910) is frequently referred to as a Swedish Countess, because her husband Count Karl Wachtmeister (who was also her cousin) was the Minister of Foreign Affairs for Sweden and resided in Stockholm.   Prior to that appointment he had been a Minister to the Danish Court at Copenhagen, and still earlier the Swedish and Norwegian Minister at the Court of St. James in England.   It was during the period of this assignment that he married Constance de Bourbel de Monpinçon.   As her maiden name indicates, she was born into a French family, her father bearing the title of Marquis, while residing in Florence, Italy. As her parents died during her childhood, Constance was sent to her mother's sister, Mrs. Bulkley of Lindel Hall, Berkshire, England, who reared the orphan.   Being interested in Spiritualism, after coming in contact with some Theosophical books, the Countess joined the Theosophical Society in 1881.   She first met Mme. Blavatsky in 1884 while on a visit to London, at the home of Mr. and Mrs. A. P. Sinnett.

In her book entitled *Reminiscences of H. P. Blavatsky and " The Secret Doctrine "* (published by the Theosophical Publishing Society, London, 1893), Countess Wachtmeister narrates how she came to live with H.P.B. at Würzburg and then in Ostend (1885-6).   Her *Reminiscences* are valuable in that they are an eye-witness account of the writing of *The Secret Doctrine*, as well as an intimate picture of the author at the pivotal point of her career.

Portions of the manuscript of *The Secret Doctrine*, copied in the handwriting of the Countess Wachtmeister and sent by direction of H.P.B. to Col. Olcott at Adyar, are preserved in the archives of The Theosophical Society at the Headquarters in Adyar, India.

in her work. Often, in the early morning, I would
see on her writing-table a piece of paper with unfamiliar
character traced upon it in red ink. On asking her
what was the meaning of these mysterious notes, she
replied that they indicated her work for the day.

"These were examples of the 'precipitated' messages which have been the subject of so much heated
controversy, even within the ranks of the Theosophical
Society." *

An instance is provided of " instruction " in a different
manner, indicating, moreover, that as already mentioned,
superintendence of the actual writing of *The Secret Doctrine*
was being carried on, and that it was under careful
supervision. In view of the character of the work this is
an important point to bear in mind. The recorded
incident is noteworthy:

"When I walked into H.P.B.'s writing room, I found
the floor strewn with sheets of discarded manuscript.
I asked the meaning of this scene of confusion, and she
replied: 'Yes, I have tried twelve times to write this
one page correctly, and each time Master says it is
wrong. I think I shall go mad, writing it so often;
but leave me alone; I will not pause until I have
conquered it, even if I have to go on all night.'

"I brought a cup of coffee to refresh and sustain
her, and then left her to prosecute her weary task.
An hour later I heard her voice calling me, and on
entering found that, at last, the passage was completed
to satisfaction, but the labour had been terrible, and
the results were often at this time small and uncertain." †

Continuing the theme with regard to the care that was
being shown on the manuscript. This supervision, at
times, called for a somewhat drastic procedure, and was
rather bewildering to the Countess. But she assures us

---

* *Op. cit.*, p. 35.

† Countess Wachtmeister's *Reminiscences*, etc., pp. 32-3.

that H.P.B. always heeded the instruction or messages,
when they were received. She says that:

"To her they came direct, and the injunctions they
contained were always met by her with submission and
obedience, even when she would have preferred to act
otherwise.

"How often, then, did I grieve over reams of manuscript, carefully prepared and copied, and, at a word,
an intimation from the Masters, consigned to the
flames—stores of information and commentary that it
seems to me would be of priceless value to us now that
we have lost our Teacher. *

"At that time, it is true, I understood very little of
what I copied, and did not realise the value of the
teachings as I do now. I have often since thought
that I was the more fitted for my task on that very
account, since, as only fragments and hints are given
out in *The Secret Doctrine*, H.P.B. may in the early days
have set down much that it was not advisable to make
known to anyone, even to one who, like myself, was
an earnest though untried pupil. Indeed, I know for
a fact that much really esoteric teaching had to be
weeded out of her original writings, and, as I have
said, much both of her MSS. and my copies was
destroyed. At that time, too, I never got any satisfactory answers to my enquiries, so that at last I learned
to be silent and rarely or never asked a question." †

An example of "writing under instruction" from the
pen of H.P.B. herself emphasizes the theme that has
been depicted. Although short, it is succinct and clearly
illustrates the chief point under consideration, namely,
the supervision that was exercised in regard to the manuscript of *The Secret Doctrine*. In addition, the citation also
indicates the manner in which some of her instructions

---

* The Countess' *Reminiscences* were published in 1893—two years
after the passing of Mme Blavatsky.

† *Reminiscences, etc.*, pp. 38.

were received, that is to say, by means of notes on paper, as already mentioned and described in this section. The "authorities"—characteristically doubly underlined by the pen of the writer—are, of course, the Mahatmas. The extract is the opening paragraph of a letter, the address and date (one of the rare times that these were included) indicates that it was penned during the writer's stay in Belgium, at the time that she was engaged in writing *The Secret Doctrine*. Its opening words demand attention, bursting in upon the recipient in this fashion:

> "17, Rue d'Ouest, Ostend.
> January 10th, 1887.

"My dear Mr. S.,

"You want to know what I am doing? Atoning for my sins of having sent to you my *Archaic Doct.** before it was ready. Rewriting it, adding to it, posting and reposting, scratching out and replacing with notes from my AUTHORITIES. I was told to send you the MS.—but not told when. . . .

"The year 1887 and you 47? Well this is good. There are two roads for you, I see, and your luck and unluck depend on the one you will select. We all have quite a cargo of bad Karma around us, so we need not complain. But you have your health, something I will never have—and that's a blessing for you.

"You are wrong in attributing to *my neglect* the review of your 'United.'† It is there two-thirds done ever

---

* It was H.P.B.'s plan to have what she here calls her *Archaic Doctrine* as Volume II of her arrangement of *The Secret Doctrine*. Following the suggestion of the Keightley's this became Volume I of the published work

† *United* is the title of a novel written by A. P. Sinnett and published by George Redway, 1886, in two volumes. The title hardly gives an inkling of the story, which H.P.B. characterizes as a "remarkable work—remarkable as a psychic production besides its undeniable literary worth." The story revolves around the theme of a man who seeks to save the life of a girl. He does so in a unique way: by transferring his vitality to the girl. By means of this self-sacrifice her savior raises the girl's life to a higher scale of being.

H. P. B. AT WORK; 17 LANSDOWNE ROAD,
HOLLAND PARK, LONDON

During the fall of 1887 a photographer took this picture before
H. P. B. commenced her morning work on *The Secret Doctrine*—the
papers before her being part of her manuscript. The pen in her
hand was presented to her by a Theosophist in New York; it was
manufactured by John Foley. The photo was first published in
The Path, magazine, New York, Vol. VII, p. 39, May, 1892.

HELENA PETROVNA BLAVATSKY

Reproduced from a photograph taken by Enrico Resta in London,
January 8, 1889. First printed in *The Path*, Vol. IV, Feb. 1890.

since you went away * but I wanted to do it well, or leave it alone. Two pages *were dictated to me*—the rest left to my own brilliant pen. Hence it clashes like a star with a rush-light. I am on it again however and this time *will finish it*. Ah, my poor Boss, you are young, VERY VERY young in *matters occult*; and very apt to judge everything and everyone on the wrong rub, according to your own worldly notions. That's the trouble. Judge *me* as much as you like; only do not judge others, those one thousand times greater than I ever will be in ten Manvantaras, from the same standpoint; for the year 1887 would then be worse than the dead departed one, 1886. . . ." †

This is indeed a trenchant document. It is deserving of careful thought and calls for fitting comments. For as well as giving desired emphasis upon the theme, it draws attention to the fact that ever before us lie two roads: which one will we choose? And then comes the thought: *Why* have we chosen the wrong road so often, so that " a cargo of bad Karma hangs around us "? Goodness knows when this " bad Karma " was generated, and yet, there it is, hanging around us, thwarting us when we least expect it! Then the pathos attaching to the statement of her poor health! Do we realize the agony,

---

H.P.B.'s review was published in *The Theosophist*, Vol. VIII, No 92, May, 1887, pp 514-20; republished in *H. P. Blavatsky Collected Writings*, Vol. VII, pp 306-17.

* Sinnett had come to visit H.P.B. in Ostend. In a letter to Countess Wachtmeister H. P. Blavatsky comments: " I am trying to write *The Secret Doctrine*. But Sinnett, who is here for a few days, wants all my attention directed to the blessed Memoirs." Then later: " My poor legs have parted company with my body. It is a limitless if not an eternal ' furlong,' as they say in India. Whatever the cause may be, I am now as legless as any elemental can be. No, except Louise and my landlady with her cat and robin I do not know a soul in Ostend."—Wachtmeister's *Reminiscences*, etc., p. 63. Louise was H.P.B.'s maid, and was also with her at Würzburg. The Memoirs, just mentioned, were published by Sinnett under the title *Incidents in the Life of Madame Blavatsky*, in 1886.

† *The Letters of H. P. Blavatsky to A. P. Sinnett*, p. 227.

14

misery and heart-ache that was H.P.B.'s when she literally struggled to keep on day after day with her task of penning *The Secret Doctrine*? And that she should have been misjudged by Sinnett at this critical juncture—so critical that she would have died had she not been actually snatched from the jaws of death by her Teacher not long after penning this letter. How poignant is the closing sentence, at the same time showing such reverence to her Teachers! How easily the mind falls into the habit of misjudging others, thereby obscuring the vision and raising a fog that clouds one's understanding!

Returning to the theme of illustrating " writing under instruction " by means of documents: one sentence from a letter simply dated " Sunday," pointedly draws attention to this, and also refers to Mr. Sinnett's visit at Ostend:

> " It is true that ever since you left, Master has made me add something daily to the old MSS so that much of it *is* new and much more that I do not understand myself." *

The opportunity should not be missed of including H.P.B.'s own words upon the writing of *The Secret Doctrine*, since it will be seen that the citation definitely fits into the category of writing under instruction:

> " I have finished an enormous Introductory Chapter, or *Preamble*, Prologue, call it what you will; just to show the reader that the text as it goes, every Section beginning with a page of translation from the Book of *Dzyan* and the Secret Book of ' Maitreya Buddha ' *Champai chhos Nga* † (in prose, not the five books in verse known, which are a blind) are no fiction. I was ordered to do so, to make a rapid sketch of what *was* known historically and in literature, in classics and in

---

* *Op. cit.*, p. 226.

† *Champai chhor Nga* may be rendered from the Tibetan: " The Whole Doctrine in its Essentiality " (*champai*, from *cham* signifies whole, unimpaired, *chhos*—doctrine; *ngang*—essentiality).

profane and sacred histories—during the 500 years that preceded the Christian period and the 500 y. that followed it: of *magic*, the existence of a Universal Secret Doctrine known to the philosophers and Initiates of every country and even to several of the Church fathers such as Clement of Alexandria, Origen, and others, who had been initiated themselves. Also to describe the Mysteries and some rites: and I can assure you that most extraordinary things are given out now, the whole story of the Crucifixion, etc., being shown to be based on a rite as old as the world—the Crucifixion on the *Lathe* of the Candidate—trials, going down to Hell etc., all Aryan. The whole story hitherto unnoticed by Orientalists is found even exoterically, in the Puranas and *Brahmanas* and then explained and supplemented with what the *Esoteric* explanations give. How the Orientalists have failed to notice it passes comprehension. Mr. Sinnett, dear, I have *facts* for 20 Vols. like *Isis*; it is the language, the cleverness for compiling them, that I lack. Well you will soon [see] this Prologue, the *short* survey of the forthcoming Mysteries in the text—which covers 300 pages of foolscap." *

It is imperative that certain facts should be noted, which are clearly indicated in the citation: (1) The Prologue described here by H.P.B. is not the "Introductory" section that was published in Volume I of *The Secret Doctrine* for these reasons: (*a*) Volume I's "Introductory" does not correspond with the description given in the citation; (*b*) The Introductory consists of but 31 printed pages; (*c*) The Proem occupies but 24 pages; (*d*) Neither the Introductory nor the Proem are divided into sections; (*e*) There are no citations made from the *Champai chhos Nga*.

(2) It was H.P.B.'s intention to have this material, as well as other sections pertaining to the Mystery-Schools, in what she planned for Volume I. Following the

---

* *The Letters of H. P. Blavatsky to A. P. Sinnett*, p. 195. This letter is dated simply " Mar. 3 "—most likely 1886.

suggestions made by the Keightleys, however, who also rearranged the manuscripts, Cosmogenesis was placed as Volume I, Anthropogenesis as Volume II (both as now published); while Volume III was reserved for the Mystery-Schools.

(3) The description penned by H.P.B. does not tally with the material comprising the so-called " Volume III " (or Volume V of the Adyar 6-volume edition) published posthumously.

(4) The unsolved question persists: What became of the 300 pages of foolscap? and the rest of the material prepared by H.P.B. for *her* first volume, which was never re-arranged nor typewritten by the Keightleys?

Therefore, any information in connection with H.P.B.'s manuscript of her third volume of *The Secret Doctrine*, as well as any personal reminiscences regarding it, would have an importance not to be gainsaid—especially in a work of this nature. It is unlikely, however, that there are any persons now living who knew H.P.B., or who may have contacted her. The next best thing, then, would be testimony that would have been passed on to the present generation by those who did know H.P.B. Testimony of such a nature may be presented. The present writer is able to testify to the fact of knowing three of H.P.B.'s students (who belonged to her Inner Group): Henry T. Edge, Dr. Herbert Coryn, and Reginald W. Machell; and that he had daily contact with two of them for some years.

In discussing the publication of *The Secret Doctrine* with Dr. Herbert Coryn at Point Loma, California, the information was volunteered that he himself had seen the manuscript of H.P.B.'s third volume on her desk. He was definitely not referring to what was published after H.P.B.'s passing, for Dr. Coryn was well aware of what the posthumous printed volume contained. The doctor was not able to say what had become of the manuscript which he saw.

Regarding H. T. Edge, the writer often heard him relate how he had first met H.P.B., and that the result of that meeting had changed his whole life.

CHAPTER X

WRITING BY DICTATION

Three simple words; but they need a great deal of explanation to convey the meaning intended. In the first place it should be stated that these words are not intended to convey the usual meaning attaching to them —such as an author dictating a section to his stenographer. Nor do they apply to the case of an author who phrases a passage for his secretary and then requests the steno-grapher to "type it up" for him. Nor yet do they signify the case of an author who jots down an idea, or an outline of a paragraph and requests his assistant to fill it in and complete the paragraph. Perhaps the desired meaning may be grasped by stating that "writing by dictation" is intended to apply to three categories:

(a) Writing by Clairaudient Dictation
(b) Writing by Receptive Dictation
(c) Writing by Perceptive Dictation

These three categories are distinct, even though they may appear to be similar. Obviously these three requirements are beyond the ability of normal writers and may correctly be designated as requiring the use of powers beyond the ken of normal individuals. Hence an explanation is necessary.

Since "powers" are mentioned, it might be well to digress for a moment and respond to the query which arises: What is meant by "powers"? Replying directly: The ability to use Siddhis—which again calls for an explanation. Nevertheless, by pursuing this theme an answer will be forthcoming to the problem before us, namely, *How* H.P.B. was able to "write by dictation". Siddhis is a Sanskrit word which has the connotation of phenomenal powers. The literal meaning of the word is that of "attainment," since the verbal root *sidh* means to attain. Obviously, when something is attained which is superior to that which may be demonstrated by use of the five senses it may be regarded as phenomenal—a phenomenal power.

Since there are various classes or kinds of Siddhis, attention need be given solely to the Siddhis which would be required in connection with the subject under discussion. These may be enumerated as: (1) the ability to see clairvoyantly; (2) the ability to hear clairaudiently; (3) the ability to place oneself *en rapport* with persons having similar capabilities; (4) the power of Receptivity; (5) the power of Perceptivity. A person who can demonstrate the use of these powers and corresponding faculties, has the ability of using Siddhis.

Fortunately, an explanation is available concerning the above-mentioned Siddhis. As it is provided by one who had knowledge of these " powers " and was able to demonstrate their use, it will carry more weight to have the explanation given by direct quotation: In introducing the citation it should be stated that the passage comes from a letter written by a Mahatma in response to a question which was asked, quite obviously inquiring whether it would be possible for the querent * to be taught by means of occult methods—hence the opening words:

---

* The querent was Alan O. Hume, C. B., (1829-1912), Secretary to the Government of India from 1870 to June, 1879. He was interested in ornithology, which he pursued as a hobby, although he did acquire a scientific standing in this field of study. In December of 1879 Mr. Hume along with Mr. A. P. Sinnett met H. P. Blavatsky at Allahabad and later at Simla, the summer capital of India. Both gentlemen became interested, if not actually fascinated by the new ideas which flooded in upon them when they had witnessed some phenomena produced by H.P.B. and had heard her discourse on the subject. Not satisfied with her statements they determined to go to the source from which she obtained her knowledge. Because of having given the required prerequisite, namely a willingness to assist in spreading the teachings of Theosophy, they were enabled to contact the Mahatmas through correspondence. The rise, growth and decline of these two " lay-chelas " as they were characterized by the Mahatmas may be followed in the volume named *The Mahatma Letters to A P. Sinnett*. The title might well have included the name of A. O. Hume. He later became famous in India because of his efforts in establishing the Indian National Congress.

ALLAN OCTAVIAN HUME

Commissioner of Customs (1867-1870);
Secretary to the Government of India (1870-1879);
General Secretary of the Indian National Congress (1884-1891).
(Reproduced from the *Life of Allan Octavian Hume*, by Sir William
Weddenburn, London, F. Fisher Unwin, 1913).

ALFRED PERCY SINNETT
The recipient of the Mahatma Letters
in the volume bearing his name.

" ' Converse with you and teach you through astral light?' Such a development of your psychical powers of hearing, as you name,—the Siddhi of hearing occult sounds would not be at all the easy matter you imagine. It was never done to any one of us, for the iron rule is that what powers one gets *he must himself acquire*. And when acquired and ready for use the powers lie dumb and dormant in their potentiality like the wheels and clockwork inside a musical box; and only then does it become easy to wind up the key and set them in motion. . . . Yet every earnestly disposed man *may* acquire such powers practically. That is the finality of it; there are no more distinctions of persons in this than there are as to whom the sun shall shine upon or the air give vitality to. There are the powers of all nature before you; *take what you can*." *

In addition to the above citation it is recorded that the Mahatma's other correspondent, A. P. Sinnett,† was

---

* *The Mahatmas Letters to A. P. Sinnett*, p. 65.

† Anything written about H. P. Blavatsky must of necessity bring in the name of Alfred Percy Sinnett (1840-1921). In the first place he was her biographer, in fact, his biography (although not so named) was actually published during her lifetime, in 1886. It was called *Incidents in the Life of Madame Blavatsky* because the title of Memoirs was objectionable to H.P.B., even though she so referred to the book in correspondence (published by George Redway, London; 2nd ed. 1913, by Theosophical Publishing House). In the second place Sir Percy (as H.P.B. sometimes addressed him) was the recipient of voluminous letters, as may readily be seen in the work named *The Letters of H. P. Blavatsky to A. P. Sinnett* (transcribed and compiled by A. T. Barker, published by Frederick A. Stokes Co., New York, 1925, 404 pages). In the third place he was the recipient of letters from H.P.B.'s teachers containing an exposition of the Esoteric Philosophy. This correspondence was published in the book known as *The Mahatma Letters to A. P. Sinnett* (transcribed and compiled by A. T. Barker, 3rd rev. ed., T. P. H., Adyar, 1962). Fourthly, from this correspondence Mr. Sinnett was able to publish the books which made him famous, the first one being *The Occult World*, (Trübner & Co., London, 1881), followed by *Esoteric Buddhism*, 1883, by the same publisher. Two novels were also published:

also inquiring along the same line as was Mr. Hume, for another letter is available which goes more deeply into the required conditions as well as requirements necessary for communicating by occult means. Three categories are enumerated (evidently applicable to three questions which were asked):

"I must tell you now that for opening 'direct communication' the only possible means would be: (1) For each of us to meet in our own *physical* bodies. I being where I am, and you in your own quarters, there is a material impediment *for me*. (2) For both to meet in our astral form—which would necessitate your 'getting out' of yours, as well as my leaving my body. The spiritual impediment to this is on *your part*. (3) To make you hear my voice either within you or near you as 'the old lady' does. This would be feasible in either of two ways: (*a*) My chiefs have but to give me permission to set up the conditions—and this for the present they refuse; or (*b*) for you to hear my voice, i.e., my *natural voice* without any psycho-physiological *tamasha* being employed by me (again as we often do among ourselves).* But then, to do this, not only have one's *spiritual* senses to be abnormally opened, but one must himself have mastered the great

---

Karma (Chapman & Hall, London, 1885); *United* (George Redway, London, 1886).

At the time that H.P.B. left America, in December of 1878, in order to conduct Theosophical activities in India, Mr Sinnett was the editor of *The Pioneer*, a Government periodical published for Anglo-Indians. A year later he met Mme. Blavatsky at Allahabad, and then, later, at Simla. Mr. Sinnett's career, in connection with H.P.B. and The Theosophical Society, may be followed in the two volumes of Letters mentioned above, so that there is no need to delineate it here.

* Compare this śloka from *Yoga Aphorisms* of Patañjali: "By concentrating his mind upon the relations between the ear and Ākāśa, the ascetic acquires the power of hearing all sounds, whether upon the earth or in the aether, and whether far or near." (Book III, śloka 42; W. Q. Judge's recension.)

secret—yet undiscovered by science—of, so to say, abolishing all the impediments of space; of neutralising for the time being the natural obstacle of intermediary particles of air and forcing the waves to strike your ear in reflected sounds or echo. Of the latter you know as yet only enough to regard this as an unscientific absurdity. Your physicists, not having until recently mastered acoustics in this direction, any further than to acquire a perfect (?) knowledge of the vibration of sonorous bodies and of reverberations through tubes, may sneeringly ask: ' Where are your indefinitely continued sonorous bodies, to conduct through space the vibrations of the voice?' We answer that our tubes, though invisible, are indestructible and far more perfect than those of modern physicists, by whom the velocity of the transmission of mechanical force through the air is represented as at the rate of 1,100 feet a second and no more—if I mistake not. But then, may there not be people who have found more perfect and rapid means of transmission, from being somewhat better acquainted with the occult powers of air (*Âkâśa*) and having *plus* a more cultivated judgment of sounds?'' *

It is to be noted that in the three conditions mentioned by the Mahatma, the second requirement was listed as the ability of meeting by means of the astral form. It was explained that this would necessitate " getting out " of the physical body—stating the matter in easily understood words without technical terms. Nevertheless, this forms one of the aspects, if not an actual requirement in connection with Tulku. It is maintained that H.P.B. had this ability. This is an important point to bear in mind, as it goes directly to the crux of the problem, and it is also necessary in arriving at an understanding of Tulku. The subject will be elaborated further under the seventh category to be considered in Chapter XIV. It was

* *The Mahatma Letters to A. P. Sinnett*, pp. 28-29.

brought up now as it formed one of the constituents in the matter of " occult instruction "—the matter now under review.

The third condition mentioned the ability of hearing the Mahatma's voice " within you or near you." It was specifically stated that H.P.B. (i.e., " the old lady ") had this power. By means of listening to this voice it would be a simple matter to take down what was heard—thus exemplifying " writing by dictation," and fulfilling the condition listed in this category.

The Mahatma continued his exposition by pointing out to Mr. Sinnett, painstakingly and at great length, the difficulty he was having in making himself understood to his correspondent. Finally, to illustrate his point, an example was given of what the result would be of suddenly confronting an Alexandrian Neo-Platonist with modern scientific concepts. Then, this was followed by indicating the requirements necessary for " seeing at a distance," that is to say, clairvoyant perception—a subject also under consideration.

" How shall I teach you to read and write or even comprehend a language of which no alphabet *palpable*, or words *audible* to you have yet been invented! How could the phenomena of our modern electrical science be explained to—say, a Greek philosopher of the days of Ptolemy were he suddenly recalled to life—with such an unbridged *hiatus* in discovery as would exist between his and our age? Would not the very technical terms be to him an unintelligible jargon, an abracadabra of meaningless sounds, and the very instruments and apparatuses used, but ' miraculous ' monstrosities? And suppose, for one instant, I were to describe to you the hues of those colour rays that lie *beyond* the so-called ' visible spectrum '—rays invisible to all but a very few even among us; to explain, how we can fix in space any one of the so-called subjective or *accidental* colours—the *complement*, (to speak mathematically) *moreover, of any other given colour of a dichromatic body* (which alone sounds like an absurdity), could you comprehend, do you think, their optical effect or even my meaning? And, since you see them not, such rays, nor can know them, nor have you any names for them as yet in Science, if I were to tell you:—' My good friend Sinnett, if you please, without moving from your writing desk, try, search for, and produce before your eyes the whole solar spectrum decomposed into fourteen prismatic colours (seven being complementary), as it is but with the help of that occult light that you can see me from a distance as I see you ' . . . what think you, would be your answer?. What would you have to reply? Would you not be likely enough to retort by telling me in your own quiet, polite way, that as there never were but seven (now three) primary colours, which, moreover, have never yet by any known physical process— been seen decomposed further than the seven prismatic hues—my invitation was as ' unscientific ' as it was ' absurd '? Adding that my offer to search for an imaginary solar ' complement ' being no compliment to your knowledge of physical science—I had better, perhaps, go and search for my mythical ' dischromatic ' and solar ' pairs ' in Tibet, for modern science has hitherto been unable to bring under any theory even so simple a phenomenon as the colours of all such dichromatic bodies. And yet—truth knows—*these* colours are objective enough!

" So you see, the insurmountable difficulties in the way of attaining not only *Absolute* but even primary knowledge in Occult Science, for one situated as you are. How could you make yourself understood— *command* in fact, those semi-intelligent Forces, whose means of communicating with us are not through spoken words but through sounds and colours, in correlations between the vibrations of the two? For sound, light and colours are the main factors in forming these grades of Intelligences, these beings, of whose very existence you have no conception. . . . . " *

* *Op. cit.*, pp. 30-31.

So much for the exposition of the processes involved in occult communication. It is clear that not only is the knowledge of the process a requirement, but also the vehicle must be made adaptable, if not already receptive.

Resuming the consideration of the subsidiary categories enumerated in regard to writing by dictation.

(a) Clairaudient Dictation: for this to be effective, it would be necessary for a person on the " receiving end " to be able to hear the person who was dictating, as well as to be en rapport with the transmitter. Thus the necessary preparation of the instrument would be required, or, expressed technically, the required components of the sevenfold constitution would need to be developed. At this point an illustration of a familiar apparatus may be used to assist in clarifying the idea: that of a radio instrument. A broadcasting station sends forth its signal, which is broadcast by means of an electric dsicharge. It depends upon the force given to the signal on a given frequency whether the message may be picked up solely in a restricted area or at a great distance. Granted, then, that the barrier of distance is eliminated, any radio apparatus may catch the broadcast signal by tuning in to the proper wave-length that is being used by the broadcasting station. So long as the receiving instrument is tuned in to the appropriate signal, it will continue to receive signals on this frequency. Should a radio announcer be broadcasting a message, it would be a simple matter for a stenographer to take down the announcer's message by tuning in to the frequency which the broadcaster was using in his station. The radio instrument, of course, has supplied the means for assisting the stenographer to write by dictation—even though the broadcaster may be in Central India.

Applying the idea to the case in hand: H.P.B. had the ability of making her vehicle responsive, so that she could hear the message clairaudiently and write what was dictated to her. Or to put it in other words, she was able to tune in to the frequency which a Mahatma would employ in sending her a message; then she would put it down in writing.

(b) Receptive Dictation. This process, although akin to Clairaudient Dictation, is different. It may be described as follows. Primary importance is focused upon the receptivity of the instrument. It is necessary that it be attuned to and be in consonance with the one dictating. The transmitter, then, would be able to impress his thought directly upon the receiver's attuned instrument, so that the recipient would then put down the message received. The impress of the transmitter's thought, then, conveys the message, rather than spoken words uttered by voice and heard clairaudiently, as in the first category. Of course, this would be analagous to " Writing by Dictation."

(c) Perceptive Dictation. This describes a different process from that of Receptive Dictation. Also required is the synchronization between sender and receiver. In this process, however, instead of the need for a transmissal of the message, the receiver would have the ability to *perceive* the message, and take down the result of the perception.

Examples may be supplied indicating that H. P. Blavatsky herself stated that she wrote by dictation. The first instance refers to her first major work, *Isis Unveiled*, commenced during the period of the founding of The Theosophical Society, in the autumn of 1875. The extract is from a letter written to A. P. Sinnett and dated, January 6, 1886, Würzburg (at the time that *The Secret Doctrine* was in process of being written):

" I am [at] 47th Street, New York, writing *Isis* and His voice dictating to me. In that dream or *retrospective* vision I once more *rewrote* all *Isis* and could now point out all the pages and sentences Mah. K. H. dictated—as those that Master [M.] did—in my bad English, when Olcott tore his hair out by handfuls in despair to ever make out the meaning of what was intended. I again saw myself night after night in bed—writing *Isis* in my dreams, at New York, positively *writing it in my sleep* and felt sentences by Mah. K. H. impressing themselves on my memory." *

---

* *The Mahatma Letters to A. P. Sinnett*, p. 479.

It may be observed that two of the categories above considered are distinctly referred to: (a) Clairaudient Dictation—hearing " His voice dictating." (b) Receptive Dictation: " and felt sentences by Mahatma K. H. impressing themselves on my memory."

Here is a passage referring to the writing of *The Secret Doctrine*: from a letter to A. P. Sinnett:

" M. . . . .r dictates all the time about one ' Grove, F.R.S.' (1855-6) who wrote *Correlations of Physical Forces*. Never heard of the man before! . . . . his occult insight was remarkable—*he* says." *

" M. . . . .r " stands for the Master M. Grove's work is referred to in Book I—Part III in the section entitled " Science and The Secret Doctrine Contrasted." Another reference in the writing of *The Secret Doctrine*:

" You must have written your *Transaction*—in *sulks*. However it may be I am sorry to have to contradict you in the *Secret D*. I have written that long ago— and it is diametrically opposite to what you say and as it was *dictated* to me." †

The outstanding example of writing by dictation, with the exception of the two major works, is without doubt the lengthy series published in *The Theosophist*, ‡ entitled

---

* *The Letters of H. P. Blavatsky to A. P. Sinnett*, p. 236.

† *Op. cit.*, p. 238.

‡ First published in *The Theosophist*, September, October and November, 1883; republished in *Five Years of Theosophy*, pp. 235-364, and again in *H. P. Blavatsky Collected Writings*, Vol. V, pp. 143-259. The Replies to an English F.T.S. were written in response to an article written by Frederic W. H. Myers entitled " Some Inquiries Suggested by Mr. Sinnett's *Esoteric Buddhism*," published in *The Theosophist*, Vol. IV, September 1883. Mr. Myers (1843-1901) was one of the Co-Founders of the Society for Psychical Research in 1882. He joined the Theosophical Society on June 3, 1883. Largely due to his agency and interest, the S.P.R. instituted an inquiry into the phenomena connected with Mme. Blavatsky in 1884, the out-come of which was the issuance of their infamous " Report".

" Replies to an English F.T.S." In reference to these Replies H.P.B. herself wrote:

" What do you mean by saying that ' their Lordships ' write too much for your London Society. It is my Boss and two others you do not know. It is *against* science, not for your members that they write." *

As an example of " writing by dictation," a passage is chosen from the " Replies to an English F.T.S." The citation is selected because it has a specific bearing upon the main theme under consideration, namely, the use of senses and powers beyond the use of " ordinary " men:

" the gradual development of man's seven principles and physical senses *has* to be coincident and on parallel lines with Rounds and Root-races. Our *fifth* race has so far developed but its *five* senses. Now, if the *Kâma* or *Will*-principle of the ' Fourth-rounders ' has already reached that stage of its evolution when the automatic acts, the unmotivated instincts and impulses of its childhood and youth, instead of following external stimuli, will have become acts of will framed constantly in conjunction with the mind (*Manas*), thus making of every man on earth of that race *a free agent*, a *fully* responsible being—the *Kâma* of our hardly adult *fifth* race is only slowly approaching it. As to the 6th sense of this, our race, it has hardly sprouted above

---

Evidently swayed by Richard Hodgson's prejudicial and unsubstantiated assertions, Myers had a change of heart and added his vilifications to those of Hodgson.

* *Letters of H. P. Blavatsky to A. P. Sinnett*, p. 68. The reference to " my Boss " signifies the Mahatma M. And the closing sentence of a letter from the Mahatma K.H. to Sinnett states: " I have naught to do with the *Replies* to Mr. Myers, but, you may recognise in them, perhaps, the brusque influence of M." (*Mahatma Letters*, p. 396). The second of the three Mahatmas responsible for the " Replies " is referred to by H.P.B. in this sentence: " Maitland would not have attributed to ' Mad. Blavatsky ': a sentence written by the Tiravellum Mahatma in *Reply* No. 2 of October, page 3, I have his MSS." (*Letters of H. P. Blavatsky to A. P. Sinnett*, p. 63)

the soil of its materiality. It is highly unreasonable, therefore, to expect for the men of the 5th to sense the nature and essence of that which will be fully *sensed* and perceived but by the 6th—let alone the 7th race —*i.e.*, to enjoy the legitimate outgrowth of the evolution and endowments of the future races with only the help of our present limited senses. The exceptions to this quasi universal rule have been hitherto found only in some rare cases of constitutional, abnormally precocious individual evolutions; or, in such, where by early training and special methods, reaching the stage of the 5th rounders, some men in addition to the natural gift of the latter have fully developed (by certain occult methods) their sixth, and in still rarer cases their seventh sense. As an instance of the former class may be cited the Seeress of Prevorst; a creature *born out of time*, a rare precocious growth, ill adapted to the uncongenial atmosphere that surrounded her, hence a martyr ever ailing and sickly. As an example of the other, the Count St. Germain may be mentioned. Apace with the anthropological and physiological development of man runs his spiritual evolution. To the latter, purely intellectual growth is often more an impediment than a help. . . ." *

One more citation refers specifically to the process involved in writing by dictation. It forms a fitting conclusion to the subject. It is taken from an article entitled " My Books," and is one of the last, if not the very last one, penned by H.P.B., since it is dated April 27, 1891—just 11 days before her passing. The words " this work " in the opening sentence refer to *Isis Unveiled*.

" every word of information found in this work or in my later writings, comes from the teachings of our Eastern Masters; and that many a passage in these works has been written by me *under their dictation*. In saying this no *supernatural* claim is urged, for no *miracle*

---

* *H. P. Blavatsky Collected Writings*, Vol. V, pp. 144-5.

is performed by such a dictation. . . . . Space and
distance do not exist for thought; and if two persons
are in perfect mutual psycho-magnetic *rapport*, and of
these two, one is a great Adept in Occult Sciences,
then thought-transference and dictation of whole pages
become as easy and as comprehensible at the distance
of ten thousand miles as the transference of two words
across a room." *

---

* *Lucifer*, London, Vol. VIII, No. 45, May 15, 1891, pp. 241-47.
15

CHAPTER XI

WRITING BY DIRECTIVE CLAIRVOYANCE

A distinction is here made between Process No. 3 and Process No. 4. Process No. 3 was listed as Writing by Dictation, the third of the seven categories in connection with the processes involved in H. P. Blavatsky's writings, and was considered in Chapter X. Process No. 4 is termed Writing by Directive Clairvoyance, inasmuch as there is a difference between clairaudience and clairvoyance, especially so in regard to these two processes as utilized by H.P.B. in her writings. Of course, it may be maintained that the subsidiary categories already defined under Process No. 3 pertain more to clairvoyance than to clairaudience. This is quite understandable. Nevertheless, it may be pointed out, that faculties and processes are being considered for which no English words have been coined, consequently the reader should not be too particular about the " words " which are being employed, but rather should attempt to grasp the ideas which are being presented. Had someone asked H.P.B. to explain the difference between the processes involved in what has been set down in the third category and the present fourth category, unquestionably she could have given a precise answer. Be that as it may, that which is termed writing by directive clairvoyance is in a class by itself: the results speak for themselves. This testimony is not to be gainsaid.

First, attention should be given to the word " directive " preceding clairvoyance. This signifies that more is involved in the process than that which generally comes under the appellation of clairvoyance. *Directive* clairvoyance (as the term is used here) signifies the ability of employing a specific faculty, which may be described in the following manner. The ability to select a book on a specific theme. Then, although never having seen the volume before, from any page in the work choose a selective, appropriate passage on a predetermined subject. Having selected a citation, the ability to copy it verbatim, and then give its correct page. Continuing the process: in the event that it would be needful to give support to the citation by means of another author, an extract from another book would be required—and it would be forthcoming in the same manner. In either case there would be no need to see the book itself, nor handle it, nor search through its pages: it would be a matter solely of visualizing the page from which the desired extract was to be copied. In any event this would all be done without so much as stirring from a chair and without actually turning a single page of a book, or even glancing at an index. Such in very truth was the phenomenal achievement, accomplished by the author of *Isis Unveiled* and *The Secret Doctrine*.

Moreover, it should be borne in mind that some of the works required for citation are not to be found in libraries in the Western world. How was H.P.B. able to accomplish this remarkable feat? By being trained in this type of clairvoyance by her Teachers. She relates the process whereby she was able to accomplish this seemingly impossible achievement.

" Well, you see, what I do is this. I make what I can only describe as a sort of vacuum in the air before me, and fix my sight and my will upon it, and soon scene after scene passes before me like the successive pictures of a diorama, or, if I need a reference or information from some book, I fix my mind intently, and the astral counterpart of the book appears, and from it I take what I need. The more perfectly my mind is freed from distractions and mortifications, the more energy and intentness it possesses, the more easily I can do this." *

In addition to this accomplishment Mme. Blavatsky relates that she was able to employ another method,

---

* *Reminiscences of H. P. Blavatsky and The Secret Doctrine* by Countess Wachtmeister, p. 33.

different from that of copying citations, yet coming under the classification of Directive Clairvoyance. She described this phase of her work, used in the writing of both *Isis Unveiled* and *The Secret Doctrine*, in a letter which she wrote to her sister, Vera; * from New York:

"Well, Vera, whether you believe me or not, something miraculous is happening to me. You cannot imagine in what a charmed world of pictures and visions I live. I am writing *Isis*; not writing, rather copying out and drawing that which She personally shows to me. Upon my word, sometimes it seems to me that the ancient Goddess of Beauty in person leads me through all the countries of past centuries which I have to describe. I sit with my eyes open and to all appearances see and hear everything real and actual around me, and yet at the same time I see and hear that which I write. I feel short of breath; I am afraid to make the slightest movement for fear the spell might be broken. Slowly century after century, image after image, float out of the distance and pass before me as if in a magic panorama; and

---

* Vera Petrovna von Hahn (1834-1896), H.P.B.'s sister, was three years younger than Helena. She was married to Nikolay Nikolay-evich de Yahontoff (who died in 1858) and is therefore referred to as Mme. Yahontoff until her second marriage to Vladimir Ivano-vich de Zhelihovsky (who was her first cousin). By her second marriage she had a son and three daughters, one of whom was named Vera, who was married to Charles Johnston. It was Vera Vladimirovna Johnston who translated into English her aunt's Russian series of stories known under the title *From the Caves and Jungles of Hindostan* (published in 1892). Another translation of her aunt's stories entitled *The Magicians of the Blue Hills* (1897) was never placed on the market.

According to Mr. Sinnett, Mme. Jelihovsky (as he transliterates the Russian name) wrote a work entitled *Juvenile Recollections Compiled for My Children*, which he describes as " a thick volume of charming stories selected by the author from the diary kept by herself during her girlhood " (*Incidents, etc.*, p. 24). He quotes copiously from this work for his chapters on the early life of H.P.B. in his book, *Incidents in the Life of Madame Blavatsky.*

meanwhile I put them together in my mind, fitting
in epochs and dates, and know *for sure* that there can
be *no mistake*. Races and nations, countries and cities,
which have for long disappeared in the darkness of
the pre-historic past, emerge and then vanish, giving
place to others; and then I am told the consecutive
dates. Hoary antiquity makes way for historical
periods; myths are explained to me with events and
people who have really existed, and every event which
is at all remarkable, every newly-turned page of this
many-colored book of life, impresses itself on my brain
with photographic exactitude. My own reckonings
and calculations appear to me later on as separate
colored pieces of different shapes in the game which
is called *casse-tête* (puzzles). I gather them together
and try to match them one after the other, and at the
end there always comes out a geometrical whole. . . .
Most assuredly it is not I who do it all, but my Ego,
the highest principle which lives in me. And even
this with the help of my Guru and teacher who helps
me in everything. If I happen to forget something
I have just to address him, or another of the same
kind, in my thought, and what I have forgotten rises
once more before my eyes—sometimes whole tables
of numbers passing before me, long inventories of
events. They remember everything. They know
everything. Without them, from whence could I
gather my knowledge?" *

During the period that *Isis Unveiled* was being written,† Colonel Olcott was Mme. Blavatsky's constant

---

* From a series entitled "Letters From H. P. Blavatsky," published serially in *The Path*, New York, 1895 (Vol. IX, No. 10, Jan.,
pp. 300-1). The letters were supplied to *The Path* by H.P.B.'s niece,
Vera Johnston.

† In all the accounts telling of the writing of *Isis Unveiled*, not one
has given credit to a young man who assisted H.P.B. in a very capable
way. Therefore, the writer considers it a privilege to honor the
memory of William Q. Judge's younger brother, John, for the service

companion, and observed her at work. His testimonial
is recorded in his *Old Diary Leaves*:

"To watch her at work was a rare and never-to-
be-forgotten experience. We sat at opposite side of
one big table usually, and I could see her every
movement. Her pen would be flying over the page,
when she would suddenly stop, look out into space
with the vacant eye of the clairvoyant seer, shorten
her vision as though to look at something held invisible
in the air before her, and begin copying on her paper
what she saw. The quotation finished, her eyes would
resume their natural expression, and she would go on
writing until again stopped by a similar interruption." *

An incident is related by the Colonel which is illustra-
tive of both Directive Clairvoyance and Precipitation.
Since the episode is especially applicable at this point,
Colonel Olcott's narrative is once more cited:

"I remember well two instances when I, also, was
able to see and even handle books from whose astral
duplicates she had copied quotations into her

---

he rendered in the matter of preparing Mme. Blavatsky's manuscript
for the printer, by copying a good portion of the work. This was
not a light task, for typewriters were unknown in those days, and
it was necessary to prepare manuscripts for publication by means of
handwritten copy.

Young John Judge met H.P.B. when he was only seventeen years
of age, so he related to the students who had gathered to greet him
on the occasion of his visit to the Râja-Yoga College and School at
the Point Loma Theosophical Headquarters in California. He went
on to say that he had a great admiration for H.P.B. and considered
it a great privilege to assist her in preparing *Isis Unveiled* for the
publisher. Mr. John H. Judge visited Point Loma on August 25,
1914, and the writer was present when he told of the assistance
which he rendered H. P. Blavatsky. The account of the reception
accorded to the brother of one of the founders of the Theosophical
Society was recorded in the *Râja-Yoga Messenger* for October, 1914,
Vol. X, No. 10, pp. 16-17—the magazine published by students of
the College.

* *Old Diary Leaves*, Vol. I, pp. 208-9.

manuscript, and which she was obliged to ' materialise '
for me, to refer to when reading the proofs, as I refused
to pass the pages for the ' strike-off ' unless my doubts
as to the accuracy of her copy were satisfactory. One
of these was a French work on physiology and psychology; the other, also by a French author, upon
some branch of neurology. The first was in two
volumes, bound in half calf, the other in pamphlet
wrapper. It was when we were living at 302 West 47th
Street—the once-famous ' Lamasery,' and the execu-
tive headquarters of the Theosophical Society. I said
' I cannot pass this quotation, for I am sure it cannot
read as you have it.' She said: ' Oh don't bother;
it's right; let it pass.' I refused, until finally she said:
' Well, keep still a minute and I'll try to get it.' The
far-away look came into her eyes, and presently she
pointed to a far corner of the room, to an *étagère* on
which were kept some curios, and in a hollow voice
said: ' There! ' and then came to herself again.
' There, there; go look for it over there! ' I went,
and found the two volumes wanted, which, to my
knowledge, had not been in the house until that very
moment. I compared the text with H.P.B.'s quotation,
showed her that I was right in my suspicions as to the
error, made the proof correction and then, at her
request, returned the two volumes to the place on the
étagère from which I had taken them. I resumed my
seat and work, and when, after awhile, I looked again
in that direction, the books had disappeared! " *

Another eye-witness, Dr. Hübb-Schleiden,† who
stayed some time with Mme. Blavatsky during the period

---

* *Old Diary Leaves*, Vol. I, pp. 209-10.

† Dr. William Hübbe-Schleiden (1846-1916) was born in Ham-
burg, Germany. His title of doctor was gained in the field of law
—in jurisprudence and political economy. During the Franco-
Prussian War of 1870-1 he was an attaché to the German Consulate
General in London. Dr. Hübbe-Schleiden demonstrated his interest
in Theosophy by becoming the first president of the Germania

that she was writing *The Secret Doctrine*, relates what he observed:

" Four or five times I have spent periods of different lengths with her. The first time from September to December, 1884 (about three months) when she stayed with the Gebhards in Elberfeld, where I had before met her for a few days in August of the same year. After that I remained with her in Würzburg about a week or ten days in October, 1885, and I saw her last, one afternoon and night, early in January, 1886. Thus I had many opportunities to learn a good deal from her and about her, all the more so as she was always exceedingly kind to me and very seldom grew tired of my many questions. . . ." *

Dr. Hübbe-Schleiden's narrative is interrupted for a moment to direct attention to the next paragraph, which alludes to the extreme paucity of books for a writer covering the field of religion, philosophy and science—not even a Bible being present in the house. In the second paragraph confirmation is also given to what has been considered in Chapter IX—Writing by means of Instruction. The word " it " in the first sentence, immediately following, refers to *The Secret Doctrine*.

" When I visited her in October, 1885, she had just begun to write it, and in January, 1886, she had

---

Theosophical Society. This was the name of the first branch of the Society in Germany, and was organized by Col. H. S. Olcott at Elberfeld in 1884. Shortly thereafter the president of Germania founded a Theosophical magazine bestowing the name of " The Sphinx " upon it. It continued to be published from 1886 to 1896.

It was to Dr. Hübbe-Schleiden that the Mahatmas sent documents regarding the writing of *The Secret Doctrine*. These documents have come to be known as " certificates " and are reproduced herein in the chapter on Precipitation. Furthermore, even before the doctor had made H.P.B.'s acquaintance, he testified to the fact that he was the recipient of a communication from a Mahatma, via Colonel Olcott. This letter was sent to him in response to one which he had addressed to the Master. At a later date the doctor received a fourth letter from the same source.

* *Reminiscences of H. P. Blavatsky and The Secret Doctrine*, pp. 110-1.

finished about a dozen chapters. . . she was writing
at her manuscript almost all day, from the early
morning until the afternoon and even until night,
unless she had guests. At that time she wrote articles
for *The Theosophist* as well. But she had scarcely any
books, not half a dozen, and I had to procure for her
an English Bible, either to quote some text correctly
or to control the correctness of some quotation.

". . . I also saw her write down sentences as if she
were copying them from something before her, where,
however, I saw nothing. I did not pay much attention to the manner of her work from the standpoint
of a hunter of phenomena, and did not control it for
that purpose; but I know that I saw a good deal of
the well-known blue K. H. handwriting as corrections
and annotations on her manuscripts as well as in books
that lay occasionally on her desk. And I notice this
principally in the morning before she had commenced
to work." *

An example of H.P.B's writing by Directive Clairvoyance may be instanced by turning to the opening
sentences of *Isis Unveiled*:

"There exists somewhere in this wide world an old
Book—so very old that our modern antiquarians might
ponder over its pages an indefinite time, and still not
quite agree as to the nature of the fabric upon which
it is written. It is the only original copy now in
existence. The most ancient Hebrew document on
occult learning—the *Sipphra Dzeniouta* †—was compiled

---

* *Op. cit.*, pp. 112-3.

† *Siphra Dzeniouta* (also transliterated *Dtzeniuthah*): originally a
Chaldean work; later incorporated in the Zohar by the Hebrew
compiler of the Kabbala. The Zohar (or Sohar, literally the Book
of Splendor) is composed of a number of Kabbalistic works. In
English translations of some portions of the Zohar, the *Siphra Dzeniouta*
is translated "The Book of Concealed Mystery" or simply "The
Book of Mysteries." The latter translates the medieval Kabbalist
Knorr von Rosenroth's Latin work entitled *Liber Mysterii*—adortion

from it, and that at a time when the former was already considered in the light of a literary relic. One of its illustrations represents the Divine Essence . . . like a luminous arc proceeding to form a circle; and then, having attained the highest point of its circumference, the ineffable Glory bends back again, and returns to earth, bringing a higher type of humanity in its vortex. As it approaches nearer and nearer to our planet, the Emanation becomes more and more shadowy, until upon touching the ground it is as black as night." *

No finer illustration may be given of the facility with which the operation of Directive Clairvoyance was utilized than by calling attention to the tremendous scope and magnitude of the task demonstrated in the writing of *Isis Unveiled*. It was a stupendous performance. Listed below are the number of the works, alphabetically arranged, which are cited in the two volumes. In explanation: the numbers following each letter of the alphabet indicate the number of books

---

of his *Kabbala Denudata*. Referring to this portion of the Kabbala, H.P.B. remarks that "The Book of Mystery" is "the oldest book of the Kabalists." (*Isis Unveiled*, II, 42)

* *Isis Unveiled*, I, 1. Commenting on this citation in a letter to Mr. Sinnett, the Mahatma K.H. writes:

"'the Divine Essence (Purusha) like a luminous arc' proceeds to form a circle—the Mahâmanvantaric chain; and having attained the highest (or its first starting point) bends back again and returns to earth (the first globe) [i.e., Globe A of the Earth planetary chain] bringing a higher type of humanity in its vortex—thus seven times. 'Approaching our earth it grows more and more shadowy until upon touching ground it becomes as black as night'—i.e., it is matter *outwardly*, the Spirit or Purusha being concealed under a quintuple armour of the first five principles.

". . . 'Isis' was *not* unveiled but rents sufficiently large were made to afford flitting glances to be completed by the student's own intuition. In this curry of quotations from various philosophic and esoteric truths purposely veiled, behold our doctrine, which is now being partially taught to Europeans for the first time." (*The Mahatma Letters to A. P. Sinnett*, pp. 120-1)

quoted commencing with that letter.* Of course, the listing does not show how *many times* a particular book was cited; the ensuing enumeration mentions each book only once.

A—	115	N—	50
B—	65	O—	28
C—	117	P—	144
D—	46	Q—	7
E—	76	R—	54
F—	25	S—	121
G—	51	T—	54
H—	52	U—	8
I—	34	V—	21
J—	38	W—	16
K—	20	X—	1
L—	54	Y—	3
M—	133	Z—	6

The list totals 1339 different works. What an array these volumes would have made in a person's room! Imagine if one had to search through a thousand books to find a reference upon a specific topic! Only a person engaged in a literary undertaking knows how tedious such a search becomes, and how frustrating when one simply cannot find a desired citation!

Hence the assertion is made: the only way that these citations were obtained was by means of utilizing the

---

* This enumeration is based upon the splendid compilation made by Fred J. Dick, M. Inst. C. E., entitled "Bibliographical Index, with Author and Title Key," appended to the Point Loma edition of *Isis Unveiled*. The present writer made the computation at the time that he was engaged in setting up the work while preparing the above-mentioned edition for publication by means of the monotype process at the Aryan Theosophical Press. (For those not familiar with printing processes it may be explained that the process designated signifies the equivalent of "typewriting" every single letter of the volumes upon a paper ribbon. From the perforated ribbon single metal types are cast in lines. Then, when arranged into page-form, the pages are printed in sections.)

process of Directive Clairvoyance. It signified that H. P. Blavatsky was able to read the "Ākâśic Records"— to make use of the term she employed in this connection—

"The (to us) invisible tablets of the Astral Light, 'the great picture-gallery of eternity'— a faithful record of every act, and even thought, of man, of all that was, is, or ever will be, in the phenomenal Universe. As said in ' Isis ', this divine and unseen canvas is the BOOK OF LIFE." *

---

* The Secret Doctrine, Vol. I, 104; I, 165, 6 vol. ed.; I, 130, 3rd ed.

CHAPTER XII

WRITING BY PSYCHOMETRY

In order to make a distinction between Writing by Directive Clairvoyance (listed as category No. 4, or Process No. 4) and that of the present process, the title of the fifth in the classification of seven categories has been given the name of Writing by Psychometry. There is, of course, a similarity between the two aspects, in view of the fact that clairvoyant faculties are demonstrated in both processes; nevertheless, a distinction is considered to be appropriate. Moreover, a difference in the manner in which clairvoyant faculties are used may be noted. Thus, for example, one individual may "see" a person's aura and may observe a focal point of disturbance therein (which would thereupon manifest in the physical body of the individual as a disease). Another clairvoyant may see things at a distance—such as Swedenborg, who had the vision of a great fire taking place in Stockholm when he himself was at Göteborg. Then, too, Apollonius was stated to have seen the murder of the Emperor Domitian in Rome, at the time it was occurring, when he himself was addressing a multitude at Ephesus.* Another has the "second sight" of seeing accidents which occur at the spot predicted; and so on.

Bearing directly upon the particular point under consideration: in the documented passages concerning individuals who possess the ability to make psychometric readings, not one of the persons who demonstrated this singular faculty could have duplicated what H.P.B. performed in what has been termed her writing by Directive Clairvoyance. Her exceptional power was unique, albeit she could as easily exhibit psychometric abilities. An example of the latter faculty may be cited

---

* Cf. *The Secret Doctrine*, V, 147.

to prove the point. It is given by Mr. Judge,* who related the incident which he himself "prepared "— somewhat in the nature of a test.

"My first acquaintance with H. P. Blavatsky began in the winter of the year 1874. She was then living in apartments in Irving Place, New York City, United States. . . . .

---

* William Quan Judge (who thus perpetuated his mother's maiden name as well as his father's), was born at Dublin, Ireland on April 13, 1851. During his thirteenth year his parents emigrated with their family to the United States of America. The Judges arrived in New York on July 14, 1864, settling in Brooklyn, and young Judge continued residence in that city until 1893. (The writer can testify to the fact of having seen a member of the family—John Judge, William's brother—during his visit to Point Loma, California.) On becoming of age, Mr. Judge became naturalized as an American citizen. In May of the same year (1872) he was admitted to the Bar of New York and specialized in Commercial Law. It is of interest to note that the same cause which led Colonel Olcott to come in contact with Mme. Blavatsky was also instrumental in bringing Mr. Judge to meet the two Theosophists. It came about in this way.

Reading about the incidents that were occurring at the Eddy farmhouse in Chittenden, Vermont, which Col. Olcott was publicizing in the newspapers, Mr. Judge wrote to the Colonel inquiring whether he could supply him with the address of a good medium. This was in 1874. Instead of giving the desired information, Col. Olcott responded by sending Mr. Judge an invitation to meet Mme. Blavatsky. The invitation was accepted and a friendship immediately resulted. Thenceforward Mr. Judge was a regular visitor at Irving Place, New York. He was present at the gatherings which were being held at H.P.B.'s suite of rooms for the purpose of attracting people who were interested in Occultism. And it was at one of such gatherings, on the evening of September 7, 1875, that Mr. Judge acted as chairman in announcing the intention of forming a society for the purpose of studying and investigating the unexplained laws of nature. He then made a motion requesting Col. Olcott to preside during the organization of such a society. This developed into the founding of the Theosophical Society. The activities of William Q. Judge in connection with the Theosophical Society need not be entered into since they are available in published form in the magazine which he founded in April, 1886, entitled *The Path*, and which he continued to publish monthly until his death, which occurred on March 21, 1896.

WILLIAM QUAN JUDGE—ONE OF THE FOUNDERS OF
THE THEOSOPHICAL SOCIETY

(Reproduced from a print first published in *The Word*,
New York, Vol. XV, April, 1912.)

H. P. BLAVATSKY ABOUT 1887

A portrait first published in *Unter den Adepten und Rosenkreuzern*
("Among the Adepts and Rosicrucians")
by Dr. Franz Hartmann.

" Very much was said on the first evening that arrested my attention and enchained my imagination. I found my secret thoughts read, my private affairs known to her. Unasked, and certainly without any possibility of her having inquired about me, she referred to several private and peculiar circumstances in a way that showed at once that she had a perfect knowledge of my family, my history, my surroundings, and my idiosyncrasies. . . .

" The next day I thought I would try an experiment with Mme. Blavatsky. I took an ancient scarabaeus that she had never seen, had it wrapped up and sent to her through the mails by a clerk in the employment of a friend. My hand did not touch the package, nor did I know where it was posted. But when I called on her at the end of the week the second time, she greeted me with thanks for the scarabaeus. I pretended ignorance. But she said it was useless to pretend, and then informed me how I had sent it, and where the clerk had posted it. During the time that elapsed between my seeing her and the sending of the package no one had heard from me a word about the matter." *

At this point it would be appropriate to explain why a psychometer is able to describe events that occurred in the proximity of an object. First in the words of a geologist who made a detailed study of psychometry:

" Not a leaf waves, not an insect crawls, not a ripple moves, but each motion is recorded by a thousand faithful scribes in infallible and indelible scripture. This is just as true of all past time. From the dawn of light upon this infant globe, when round its cradle the steamy curtains hung, to this moment, nature has been busy photographing everything. What a picture-gallery is hers! " †

---

* Quoted by A. P. Sinnett in his *Incidents in the Life of Madame Blavatsky*, pp. 145-7.

† Quoted in *Isis Unveiled*, I, 183 from *The Soul of Things; or Psychometric Researches and Discoveries*, by W. and E. M. F. Denton, Boston, 1873.

"It appears to us the height of impossibility to imagine that scenes in ancient Thebes, or in some temple of prehistoric times should be photographed only upon the substance of certain atoms. The images of the events are imbedded in that all-permeating, universal, and ever-retaining medium, which the philosophers call the 'Soul of the World,' and Mr. Denton 'The Soul of Things.' The psychometer, by applying the fragment of a substance to his forehead, brings his *inner-self* into relations with the inner soul of the object he handles. It is now admitted that the universal aether pervades all things in nature, even the most solid. It is beginning to be admitted, also, that this preserves the images of all things which transpire. When the psychometer examines his specimen, he is brought in contact with the current of the astral light, connected with that specimen, and which retains pictures of the events associated with its history." *

"Thus a manuscript, painting, article of clothing, or jewelry—no matter how ancient—conveys to the sensitive, a vivid picture of the writer, painter, or wearer; even though he lived in the days of Ptolemy or Enoch. Nay, more; a fragment of an ancient building will recall its history and even the scenes which transpired within or about it. A bit of ore will carry the soul-vision back to the time when it was in process of formation." †

Unquestionably H.P.B. had psychometric ability. In her girlhood this faculty exuded spontaneously, so to speak, bubbling forth effervescently at times. After having received tuition, however, this capability no longer issued forth unpromoted; it was held in check and directed in appropriate channels. Thus it found service in her writing. What a pity that Mme. von Hahn (Helena's mother) was not present to have preserved her daughter's

---

* *Isis Unveiled*, I, 183-4.

† *Op cit.*, I, 182.

rapturous accounts of the wonders she "saw" in the objects around her. Fortunately, Vera did record some of Helena's romantic "stories" (as the younger sister termed the psychometric narrations). The first example of Writing by Psychometry, then, comes from the pen of the sister.

"At about ten versts from the Governor's * villa there was a field, an extensive sandy tract of land, evidently once upon a time the bottom of a sea or a great lake, as its soil yielded petrified relics of fishes, shells, and teeth of some (to us) unknown monsters. Most of these relics were broken and mangled by time, but one could often find whole stones of various sizes on which were imprinted figures of fishes and plants and animals of kinds now wholly extinct, but which proved their undeniable antediluvian origin. The marvellous and sensational stories that we, children and schoolgirls, heard from Helena during that epoch

---

* H. P. Blavatsky's maternal grandfather, Privy Councillor Andrey Mihailovich de Fadeyev, was the civil Governor of Saratov. Before this assignment he had been Governor of Astrakhan. When Helena was eleven, her grandmother, née Princess Helena Pavlovna Dologrukov, took over the care of her granddaughter, and five years were spent at Saratov. Here is Vera's description of their dwelling place:

"'The great country mansion (datche) occupied by us at Saratov was an old and vast building, full of subterranean galleries, long abandoned passages, turrets, and most weird nooks and corners. It had been built by a family called Pantchoolidzef, several generations of whom had been governors at Saratov and Penja—the richest proprietors and noblemen of the latter province. It looked more like a medieval ruined castle than a building of the past century. . . . We had been permitted to explore, under the protection of half-a-dozen male servants and a quantity of torches and lanterns, those awe-inspiring 'Catacombs'. True, we had found in them more broken wine bottles than human bones, and had gathered more cobwebs than iron chains, but our imagination suggested ghosts in every flickering shadow on the old damp walls." (Quoted by A. P. Sinnett in his Incidents in the Life of Madame Blavatsky, pp. 21-2) Verst: a Russian linear measure, equal to 2/3 of a mile or about 3,500 feet.

were countless. I well remember when stretched at
full length on the ground, her chin reclining on her
two palms, and her two elbows buried deep in the soft
sand, she used to dream aloud and tell us of her visions,
evidently clear, vivid, and as palpable as life to her!
. . . How lovely the description she gave us of the
submarine life of all those beings, the mingled remains
of which were now crumbling to dust around us. How
vividly she described their past fights and battles on
the spot where she lay, assuring us she saw it all; and
how minutely she drew on the sand with her finger
the fantastic forms of the long-dead sea-monsters, and
made us almost see the very colours of the fauna and
flora of those dead regions. While listening eagerly to
her descriptions of the lovely azure waves reflecting
the sunbeams playing in rainbow light on the golden
sands of the sea bottom, of the coral reefs and stalactite
caves, of the sea-green grass mixed with the delicate
shining anemones, we fancied we felt ourselves the cool,
velvety waters caressing our bodies, and the latter
transformed into pretty and frisky sea-monsters; our
imagination galloped off with her fancy to a full
oblivion of the present reality. She never spoke in
later years as she used to speak in her childhood and
early girlhood. The stream of her eloquence has
dried up, and the very source of her inspiration is now
seemingly lost! She had a strong power of carrying
away her audiences with her, of making them see
actually, if even vaguely, that which she herself saw.
. . . Once she frightened all of us youngsters very nearly
into fits. We had just been transported into a fairy
world, when suddenly she changed her narrative from
the past to the present tense, and began to ask us to
imagine that all that which she had told us of the cool,
blue waves with their dense populations was around
us, only invisible and intangible, so far. . . . ' Just fancy!
A miracle!' she said; ' the earth suddenly opening,
the air condensing around us and rebecoming sea
waves . . . Look, look . . . there, they begin already
appearing and moving. We are surrounded with

water, we are right amid the mysteries and the wonders of a submarine world! . . .'

" She had started from the sand, and was speaking with such conviction, her voice had such a ring of real amazement, horror, and her childish face wore such a look of a wild joy and terror at the same time, that when, suddenly covering her eyes with both hands, as she used to do in her excited moments, she fell down on the sand screaming at the top of her voice, ' There's the wave . . . it has come! . . . The sea, the sea, we are drowning! . . .' Every one of us fell down on our faces, as desperately screaming and as fully convinced that the sea had engulfed us, and that we were no more! " *

The second example selected for Writing by Psychometry more closely approximates Writing by Directive Clairvoyance than the first selection. Yet a distinction is to be noted, as previously remarked. In Directive Clairvoyance the process necessitated bringing into view a specific text from a book. Psychometry also requires looking into the Astral Light, but focalized by means of an object. The " appearance " is more like a viewing of pictures (as in cinematography) and does not require the reading of texts. The extract is taken from one of Mme. Blavatsky's letters to A. P. Sinnett:

" Master finds that it is too difficult for me to be looking consciously into the astral light for my *S.D.*, and so, it is now about a fortnight, I am made to see all I have to as though in my dream. I see large and long rolls of paper on which things are written and I recollect them. Thus all the Patriarchs from Adam to Noah were given me to see—parallel with the Rishis; and in the middle between them, the meaning of their symbols—or personifications. Seth standing

---

* Quoted by A. P. Sinnett from Mme. Vera de Zhelihovsky's " Juvenile Recollections Compiled for my Children," in *Incidents in the Life of Madame Blavatsky*, pp. 26-28.

with Brighu for first *sub*-race of the Root race, for inst.: meaning, *anthropologically*—first *speaking* human sub-race of the 3rd Race; and *astronomically*—(his years 912 y.) meaning at one and same time the length of the solar year in that period, the duration of his race and many other things— (too complicated to tell you now). Enoch, finally, meaning the solar year when our present duration was settled, 365 days— ('God took him when he was 365 years old') and so on." *

The third example definitely illustrates the process under consideration. At the same time it explains why the psychometer can determine the character of the individual by means of an object associated with that individual, especially so if there has been an intense feeling manifested at the time that there was contact between the object and the person.

" Is or is not that which is called magnetic effluvia a something, a stuff, or a substance, invisible, and imponderable though it be? If the learned authors of *The Unseen Universe* † object to light, heat and electricity, being regarded merely as imponderables, and show that each of these phenomena has as much claim to be recognized as an objective reality as matter itself —our right [so] to regard the mesmeric or magnetic fluid which emanates from man to man or even from

---

* *The Letters of H. P. Blavatsky to A. P. Sinnett,* p. 194.

† "The learned authors of *The Unseen Universe*" were two physicists: Balfour Stewart (1828-1887) and Peter Guthrie Tait (1831-1901). Professor Tait, the better known of the collaborators, was a Scottish physicist, professor of natural philosophy at Edinburgh from 1860 to 1901. Prior to that he collaborated with Thomas Andrews in research work on the density of ozone and the action of electrical discharges on oxygen and other gases. Professor Tait published a series of papers (1886-1892) on the kinetic theory of gases. In 1875, in collaboration with Balfour Stewart, he published *The Unseen Universe, or, Physical Speculations on a Future State.*" In this work the statement is made that " energy has as much claim to be regarded as matter itself." (Quoted in " Transmigrations of the Life-Atoms." See the next footnote.)

man to what is termed an *inanimate* object, is far greater. It is not enough to say that this fluid is a species of molecular energy like heat for instance, for it is vastly more. Heat is produced whenever visible energy is transformed into molecular energy, we are told, and it may be thrown out by any material composed of sleeping atoms or inorganic matter as it is called: whereas the magnetic fluid protected by a living human body *is life itself.* ' Indeed it is life atoms ' that a man in a blind passion throws off, unconsciously, and though he does it quite as effectively as a mesmeriser who transfers them from himself to any object consciously and under the guidance of his will. Let any man give way to any intense feeling, such as anger, grief, etc., under or near a tree, or in direct contact with a stone; and many thousands of years after that any tolerable Psychometer will see the man and sense his feelings from one single fragment of that tree or stone that he had touched. Hold any object in your hand, and it will become impregnated with your life atoms, indrawn and outdrawn, changed and transferred in us at every instant of our lives. Animal heat is but so many life atoms in molecular motion. It requires no adept knowledge, but simply the natural gift of a good clairvoyant subject to see them passing to and fro, from man to objects and *vice versa* like a bluish lambent flame. . . . The processes of nature are acts of incessant borrowing and giving back." *

* From the article entitled " Transmigration of the Life-Atoms " first published in *The Theosophist*, Vol. IV, No. 11, August 1883, 286-8. Republished in *Five Years of Theosophy*, pp. 533-9; also in *H. P. Blavatsky Collected Writings*, Vol. V, pp. 115-6.

CHAPTER XIII

WRITING BY PRECIPITATION

The subject of Precipitation is bound to take in a wider field than intended; yet it is such an important theme that it should be dealt with comprehensively. First of all, as to the word itself. Precipitation is usually defined, from the scientific standpoint, as signifying a condensation, particularly in chemistry. In a sense, this meaning bears a close relationship to the derived meaning of the word as used in Spiritualism, rather than its literal significance, which is "headlong" (from the Latin compound: *prae*, forward; *ceps* from *caput*, a head) the meaning which is present in the cognate word "precipice." In connection with meteorology the falling down process is implied as well as a condensation, when used in connection with rain, snow, hail, fog, or dew. In Spiritualism, however, the word conveys the meaning of a materialization, which is the signification intended here. Therefore, when employed in connection with writing it generally signifies the materialization of a message on paper (or other substance).

Because of the nature of the subject presented under the sixth of the seven categories, entitled Writing by means of Precipitation, it becomes necessary to consider all the aspects connected with the process of Precipitation, therefore the subject of " Mahatma letters " is included. Moreover, since it is maintained that H.P.B. was able to demonstrate precipitation, that which is applicable in her case is applicable to the " Mahatma letters " and vice versa. In other words, explain the one and the other is also explained.

Actually, two processes are involved in connection with the precipitation of a letter: (1) the materialization of the message; (2) the delivery of the message. These will be considered separately, enumerated under the heading of Classification (1) and (2) respectively for ease in identification, and further by means of subsequent subdivisions. To these will be added a third classification: the three to be defined as follows:

Classification (1) The ability to make writing appear on paper (or other substance) without the application of pen, pencil, crayon or brush (or for that matter any of the normal methods used in writing).

Classification (2) The ability to deliver the message —whether written or precipitated—at any desired location.

Classification (3) The ability to have an intermediary, or agent, fulfil the requirements.

In further explanation of the three Classifications, by means of subdivisions—each of which will be considered separately and in detail:

Classification (1) The materialization of the message:

(a) In regard to the precipitation that appears to be made on the surface of the paper.

(b) In regard to the precipitation that is imbedded, or seems to be incorporated in the substance on which it has been made to appear.

(c) The quality of the precipitation, i.e., whether of pen, pencil, crayon or brush, or other substance.

(d) The color of the precipitation: blue (of various hues), black, red (of various shades), or other colors.

(e) The caligraphy of the message, i.e., the distinctive penmanship employed by each sender of the message.

(f) The permanence or impermanence of the precipitation.

(g) The ability to " erase " a message and re-precipitate it.

Classification (2) The delivery of the message. Since senders of messages may be a thousand or so miles from the recipient, delivery of precipitations deals with these factors:

(a) The ability to disassemble the material composing a piece of paper (or other substance), and send the material to the desired location; there to re-assemble it into the normal substance of the paper—with the message thereon.

(b) Delivery by means of normal procedures—such as by telegram over the telegraph system; or by the normal mail delivery system of the country.

(c) Delivery at any specified spot.

(d) Delivery in person—whether by a Mahatma himself, or by his chela.

Classification (3): Fulfilment of the requirements by an intermediary. This calls for a greater degree of understanding than the words would seem to imply. For the statement is tantamount to a declaration that the intermediary possesses the ability to act in the capacity of a precipitator as well as a transmitter—otherwise the processes could not be accomplished. When designated to be an agent, the intermediary must decide which of the methods are to be employed, as listed under Classification (1), subdivisions (a) to (e); and under Classification (2), (a), (b) or (c).

Taking up the consideration of Classification (1) in detail: subdivision (a): In regard to the precipitation that appears to be made on the surface of the paper. First, it should be remarked that the listing has not included reference to the quality of the paper on which precipitations have been made. This is because little mention has been made on this point. Certain it is that H.P.B. did not require any special paper for precipitation. The majority of the " Mahatma letters " have been described as being written on what is known as " rice paper " (a kind of paper available in North India and Tibet). However, in the early days of the Theosophical Society in New York, Col. Olcott received letters on distinctive paper. One such was a green colored paper which would have been difficult for him either to acquire or duplicate in New York. Testifying to this coloured paper he relates this anecdote:

" After finishing my washing I turned toward the shaving-stand, behind me and just in front of the window, to brush my hair, when I saw something of a green colour reflected in the glass. A second glance showed it to be a sheet of green paper with writing upon it, and to be attached to the wall just over the washing-stand where I had the moment before been occupied without seeing anything save the blank wall before my eyes. I found the paper attached to the plastering by pins at the four corners, and the writing to be a number of Oriental texts from *Dhammapada* and Sûtras, written in a peculiar style and signed at the lower corner by one of the Masters." *

Since little information has been supplied concerning precipitation on the surface of paper, two instances will have to suffice. The first one is an example of writing described as being made by a lead-pencil (although the narrator of the incident is unable to explain the matter or account for the manner in which the pencilling appeared on the surface of the paper). At all events, here is the manner in which the anecdote is related by Col. Olcott:

" One day, on my way home, I bought a reporter's note-book, and, on getting to the house, showed it to her [H.P.B.] and explained its intended use. She was seated at the time and I standing. Without touching the book or making any mystical pass or sign, she told me to put it in my bosom. I did so, and after a moment's pause she bade me take it out and look within. This is what I found: inside the first cover, written and drawn on the white lining paper in lead pencil:

' JOHN KING, HENRY DE MORGAN,
his book.
4th of the Fourth month in A.D. 1875.'

" Underneath this, the drawing of a Rosicrucian jewel; over the arch of the jewelled crown, the word FATE; beneath which is her name, ' Helen,' followed by a symbolical drawing . . . . . no one but myself had touched the book after it was purchased; I had had it in my pocket until it was shown to H.P.B.,

---

* *Old Diary Leaves*, Vol. I, pp. 414-5.

from the distance of two or three feet, had myself held
it in my bosom, removed it a moment later when
bidden, and the precipitation, of the lead-pencil writing
and drawing had been done while the book was inside
my waistcoat.   Now the writing inside the cover of my
notebook is very peculiar; the e's being all like the
Greek *epsilon*, and the n's being all like the Greek *pi*:
it is a quaint and quite individual handwriting, not
like H.P.B.'s, but identical with that in all the written
messages I had from first to last from ' John King.'
H.P.B. having, then, the power of precipitation, must
have transferred from her mind to the paper the
images of words traced in this special style of script;
or, if not she, by some other expert in this art. . . . ." *

The second example of a message which is regarded
as being on the surface of the paper is that of a letter
which is in the writing associated with the Mahatma
K.H.   It is described as " written in black ink, the
original being now somewhat faded.   It is on one sheet,
and written on both sides." †

Subdivision (*b*):   In regard to the precipitation that is
imbedded, or seems to be incorporated in the substance
on which it has been made to appear.   More often than
otherwise, precipitations apparently display this characteristic.   It should be mentioned that " imbedded
precipitation " (as it may be termed) is applicable not
solely to writing but to other examples as well, such as
portraits.   Thus, two examples of portraits precipitated
by H.P.B., which are preserved in the Theosophical
archives, exhibit this feature.   The first example is the
likeness of an individual purported to be Chevalier Louis.‡

---

* *Old Diary Leaves*, Vol. I, pp. 40-2.

† *H. P. Blavatsky Collected Writings*, Vol. VI, p. 24.   This letter
is preserved in the archives of The Theosophical Society at Adyar.
A facsimile reproduction of the entire letter appears on pages 25-8
of the work cited.   The delivery and receipt of this letter are considered under Classification 2 (d).

‡ For H.P.B.'s caustic comments and castigation of this " bogus
adept " see *The Key to Theosophy*, pp. 302-3 (or. ed.).

This portrait was precipitated in the presence of Colonel
Olcott and Mlle. Liebert. * In addition to demonstrating H.P.B.'s ability to precipitate a portrait by request
(which the self-styled medium thought was impossible,
because she knew that there was no portrait of Chevalier
Louis in the suite of rooms), it also illustrates the process
in subdivision (f) designated as the ability to make a
precipitation impermanent or permanent—as desired.
This is also a singular feature in regard to precipitation:
it is within the power of the precipitator to determine
whether a materialization will be permanent or impermanent. The suggestion is offered that less " power "
would be required in the fixation process, when the
message is not required to be made permanent. Be that
as it may, this is how Col. Olcott relates the story:

" One cold evening (Dec. 1, 1875), after a fresh day
of failures at Mr. Mason's laboratory, Mlle. Liebert
was, as usual, shuffling over her grimy photographs,

* Mlle. Pauline Liebert, a French Spiritualist from Leavenworth,
Kansas. Originally from Paris, in which city she had become
acquainted with H.P.B. Upon reading Mme. Blavatsky's articles
in the Leavenworth newspapers on Dr. Beard in connection with
the spiritualistic manifestations that had occurred in the Eddy farm-
house at Chittenden, Vermont, Mlle. Liebert sought to revive her
acquaintanceship by writing to H.P.B., relating that she had had
success in St. Louis and Kansas in having spirits photographed.
Col. Olcott was taken in by the pretended claims of the self-styled
medium. At his expense he arranged to have Mlle. Liebert come
to New York and stay at the suite of rooms which he maintained.
He also arranged to have the pretensions of the dissembler tested by
Mr. H. J. Newton, the first Treasurer of the Theosophical Society,
who was an amateur photographer as well as the president of the
spiritualist society in New York. After 50 trials, in which he
endeavoured to take the picture of the spirit guide (alleged by the
supposed medium to be the spirit of Napoleon Bonaparte), Mr.
Newton gave up in disgust. Nevertheless, he arranged with Col.
Olcott to have Mr. Mason, a member of the Photographic Section
of the American Institute, continue the photographic experiments.
After 75 more attempts to capture the elusive apparition on a photographic plate, Mr. Mason was likewise of the opinion that the effort
was a hoax.

sighing and arching her eyebrows into a despairing expression, when H.P.B. burst out: 'Why will you persist in this folly? Can't you see that all those photographs in your hand were swindles on you by photographers who did them to rob you of your money? You have had every possible chance now to prove your pretended power,—more than one hundred chances have been given you, and you have not been able to do the least thing. Where is your pretended guide, Napoleon, and the other sweet angels of Summerland; why don't they come and help you? Pshaw! it makes me sick to see such credulity. Now see here: I can make a " spirit picture " whenever I like and—of anybody I like. You don't believe it, eh? Well, I shall prove it on the spot!' She hunted up a piece of cardboard, cut it to the size of a cabinet photograph, and then asked Mlle. Liebert whose portrait she wished. ' Do you want me to make your Napolean?' she asked. ' No,' said Mlle. L., ' please make for me the picture of that beautiful M. Louis.' H.P.B. burst into a scornful laugh, because, by Mrs. Britten's request, I had returned to her through the post the Louis portrait three days previously, and it being by that time in Boston, 250 miles away, the trap set by the French lady was but too evident. ' Ah!' said H.P.B., ' you thought you could catch me, but now see!' She laid the prepared card on the table before Mlle. Liebert and myself, rubbed the palm of her hand over it three or four times, turned it over, and lo! on the underside we saw (as we then thought) a facsimile of the Louis portrait. In a cloudy background at both sides of the face were grinning elemental sprites, and above the head a shadowy hand with the index-finger pointing downward. I never saw amazement more strongly depicted on a human face than it was upon Mlle. Liebert's at that moment. She gazed in positive terror at the mysterious card, and presently burst into tears and hurried out of the room with it in her hand, while H.P.B. and I went into fits of laughter. After a half hour she returned, gave me the picture, and on retiring for the night I placed it as a bookmark in a volume I was reading in my own apartment. On the back I noted the date and the names of the three witnesses. The next morning I found that the picture had quite faded out, all save the name ' Louis,' written at the bottom in imitation of the original: the writing, a precipitation made simultaneously with the portrait and the elves in the background. That was a curious fact—that one part of a precipitated picture should remain visible, while all the rest had disappeared, and I cannot explain it." *

William Q. Judge's account of the episode takes up the story at this point:

"A week or two later, seeing this blank card lying in Colonel Olcott's room, I took it to Mme. Blavatsky, and requested her to cause the portrait to reappear. Complying, she again laid the card under another sheet of paper, placed her hand upon it, and presently the face of the man had come back as before; this time indelibly imprinted." †

The second precipitated portrait is superior to the first. In addition to its artistic effects, it displays a unique method of application, which no pencil or crayon work would be able to duplicate. The story in connection with its precipitation is also told by Colonel Olcott:

"At the close of dinner we [W. Q. Judge, L. M. Marquette, M.D., and H. S. Olcott] had drifted into talk about precipitations, and Judge asked H.P.B. if she would not make somebody's portrait for us. As we were moving towards the writing-room, she asked him

---

* *Old Diary Leaves*, Vol. I, p. 199. The portrait is reproduced therein, next to page 199. The precipitation is at present in the archives at Adyar.

† *Incidents in the Life of Madame Blavatsky*, p. 148. Mr. Judge relates, also, that he himself returned the " original portrait " of Chevalier Louis to Mrs. E. H. Britten by " posting it in the nearest post-box ".

whose portrait he wished made, and he chose that of this particular yogi, whom we knew by name as one held in great respect by the Masters. She crossed to my table, took a sheet of my crested club-paper, tore it in halves, kept the half which had no imprint, and laid it down on her own blotting paper. She then scraped perhaps a grain of the plumbago of a Faber lead pencil on it, and then rubbed the surface for a minute or so with a circular motion of the palm of her right hand; after which she handed us the result. On the paper had come the desired portrait and, setting wholly aside the question of its phenomenal character, it is an artistic production of power and genius. . . . The yogi is depicted in Samâdhi, the head drawn partly aside, the eyes profoundly introspective and dead to external things, the body seemingly that of an absent tenant. There is a beard and hair of moderate length, the latter drawn with such skill that one sees through the upstanding locks, as it were—an effect obtained in good photographs, but hard to imitate with pencil or crayon. The portrait is in a medium not easy to distinguish: it might be black crayon, without stumping, or black lead; but there is neither dust nor gloss on the surface to indicate which, nor any marks of the stump or the point used: hold the paper horizontally towards the light and you might fancy the pigment was below the surface, combined with the fibres." *

Subdivision (c) dealing with the quality of the precipitation has already been partially considered. As already

---

* *Old Diary Leaves*, Vol. I, pp. 367-8. A reproduction of the precipitation appears in Olcott's book, facing p. 368. Since the substance for the production was supplied by providing a lead-pencil, the color of the portrait is, of course, black: A well-known American artist of that epoch provided this testimonial: it is " unique, distinctly an ' individual ' in the technical sense; one that no living artist within his knowledge could have produced." (Le Clear, quoted in O.D.L., p. 368). The yogi's name is Tiruvalluvar. At the time that Col. Olcott wrote his book the portrait was hanging in the Picture Annex to the Adyar Library.

shown by means of her portrait precipitations, H.P.B. did not confine her materialization solely to specimens similar to handwriting by pencil, pen, or crayon, because she was able to materialize objects of varied description. These need not be included here, as they would digress too far from the principal theme, although a fascinating account could be presented. The next example shows her ability to simulate handwriting like that produced by pen and ink. The narration is by W. Q. Judge:

" This precipitation of messages or sentences occurred very frequently, and I will relate one which took place under my own hand and eyes, in such a way as to be unimpeachable for me.

" I was one day, about four o'clock, reading a book by P. B. Randolph, that had just been brought in by a friend of Colonel Olcott. I was sitting some six feet distant from H. P. Blavatsky, who was busy writing. I had carefully read the title-page of the book, but had forgotten the exact title. But I knew that there was not one word of writing upon it. As I began to read the first paragraph I heard a bell sound in the air, and looking saw that Mme. Blavatsky was intently regarding me.

" ' What book do you read? ' said she.

" Turning back to the title-page, I was about to read aloud the name, when my eye was arrested by a message written in ink across the top of the page which, a few minutes before, I had looked at and found clear. It was a message in about seven lines, and the fluid had not yet quite dried on the page—its contents were a warning about the book. I am positive that when I took the volume in my hand, not one word was written in it." *

The next example is unusual in that it demonstrates the ability to produce by precipitation the duplication of a letter which was in handwriting. H.P.B. had

---

* *Incidents in the Life of Madame Blavatsky*, p. 149.

received a letter from W. Stainton Moses * dated
December 22, 1877, in which he addressed her as " My
dear Sphinx." Evidently she was very pleased by the
words of the letter, for she told Col. Olcott that she
would make a duplicate of the epistle. So he did not
hesitate about making preparations for the manifestation.
As he narrates the incident:

" I took from the desk five half-sheets of foreign
letter-paper of the same size as Oxon's and gave her
them. She laid them against the five pages of his
letter, and then placed the whole in a drawer of the
desk just in front of me as I sat. We went on with
our conversation for some time, until she said she
thought the copy was made and I had better look and
see if that were so. I opened the drawer, took out

---

* Rev. Stainton Moses, who wrote under the nom-de-plume of
M. A. Oxon, by which pen-name he was probably better known
than under his own name, was editor of the spiritualist magazine
Light, and a member of the Staff of University College, London.
In an autobiographical account sent to H. S. Olcott in April, 1876,
he narrates that he was an eager student at college—a likely First
and Fellowship to follow. But ten days before the examinations
he broke down from overwork and could not read or write for two
years, during which he wandered all over Europe. Then he worked
for his degree and passed. Next, six years were spent in theological
work and the reverend became a preacher. After a period of illness,
from which he almost died, Stainton Moses accepted a post in a
London University as a lecturer in philology. During this period
of his life he contacted Spiritualism and followed it with enthusiasm.
In fact, Rev. Moses became a medium, maintaining that he was
taught by beings of the spirit world, which he named as Imperator,
Kabbila, Mentor, Magus, Sadi and others.

Shortly after the founding of the Theosophical Society in 1875
Rev. Moses joined the parent society, but resigned therefrom. Later
he affiliated with the London Lodge, but evidently was more
impressed with his mediumistic teachings than with the message
coming from H P. Blavatsky's Teachers. Wrote H.P.B.: " In
Mâyâ he lives, in Mâyâ he will die, and in Mâyâ he will pass a long
period before his next rebirth." (The Letters of H. P. Blavatsky to
A. P. Sinnett, p. 24. See also The Mahatma Letters to A. P. Sinnett,
pp. 39-40 et seq.)

the papers, and found that one page of each of my five pieces had received from the page with which it was in contact the impression of that page. . . . The writings are almost duplicates, yet not quite so. They are rather like two original writings by the same hand. If H.P.B. had had time to prepare this surprise for me, the explanation of forgery would suffice to cover the case; but she had not. The whole thing occurred as described, and I submit that it has an unquestionable evidential value as to the problem of her possessing psychical powers. I have tried the test of placing one page over the other to see how the letters and marks correspond. I find they do not, and that is proof, at any rate, that the transfer was not made by the absorption of the ink by the blank sheet from the other; moreover, the inks are different, and Oxon's is not copying-ink. The time occupied by the whole phenomenon might have been five or ten minutes, and the papers lay the whole time in the drawer in front of my breast, so there was no trick of taking it out and substituting other sheets for the blank ones I had just then handed her." *

Here is an illustration of another type, which may be termed the ability to " re-create " an advertised message of a firm. The episode is related by William Q. Judge:

" On one occasion the address of a business firm in Philadelphia was needed for the purpose of sending a letter through the mail, and no one present could remember the street or number, nor could any directory of Philadelphia be found in the neighbour-hood. The business being very urgent, it was proposed that one of us should go down nearly four miles to the General Post Office, so as to see a Philadelphia directory. But H.P.B. said: 'Wait a moment, and perhaps we can get the address some other way.' She

---

* *Old Diary Leaves*, Vol. I, pp. 353-4. Both the original letter and the precipitated duplicate are on file in the archives at Adyar.

17

then waved her hand, and instantly we heard a signal bell in the air over our heads. We expected no less than that a heavy directory would rush at our heads from the empty space, but no such thing took place. She sat down, took up a flat tin paper-cutter japanned black on both sides and without having any painting on it. Holding this in her left hand, she gently stroked it with her right, all the while looking at us with an intense expression. After she had rubbed thus for a few moments, faint outlines of letters began to show themselves upon the black, shining surface, and presently the complete advertisement of the firm whose address we desired was plainly imprinted upon the paper-cutter in gilt letters, just as they had had it done on slips of blotting paper such as are widely distributed as advertising media in America—a fact I afterwards found out. On a close examination, we saw that the street and number, which were the doubtful points in our memories, were precipitated with great brilliancy, the other words and figures being rather dimmer. Mme. Blavatsky said that this was because the mind of the operator was directed almost entirely to the street and number, so that their re-production was brought about with much greater dis-tinctness than the rest of the advertisement, which was, so to speak, dragged in in a rather accidental way." *

A description of another type of precipitation is that in which letters are made to appear on wood. Again Mr. Judge narrates the occurrence:

"Well, over the top of the doors of the bookcase was a blank space, about three inches wide, and running the breadth of the case. One evening we were sitting talking of magic as usual, and of ' the Brothers,' when Madame said, ' Look at the bookcase!'

"We looked up at once, and as we did so, we could see appear, upon the blank space I have described, several letters apparently in gold, that came out upon

---

* *Incidents in the Life of Madame Blavatsky*, pp. 149-50.

the surface of the wood. They covered nearly all of the space. Examination showed that they were in gold, and in a character that I had often seen upon some of her papers." *

The next instance comes from the pen of a reporter, who prepared his write-up for the *Hartford Daily Times*, of Connecticut. It was published in the issue of December 2, 1878, under the heading of New York correspondence. The reporter had spent an evening at H.P.B.'s suite of rooms in company with a group of people, from one of whom—an English artist—he obtained his "story".

" ' I know it will seem incredible to you, my dear fellow,' said my friend, ' for it does to me as I look back upon it; yet, at the same time, I know my senses could not have deceived me. Besides, another gentleman was with me at the time. I have seen Madame create things.' ' Create things? ' I cried. ' Yes, create things,—produce them from nothing. I can tell you of two instances.

" Madame, my friend, and myself were out one day looking about the stores, when she said she desired some of these illuminated alphabets which come in sheets, like the painted sheets of little birds, flowers, animals, and other figures, so popular for decorating pottery and vases. She was making a scrap-book, and wished to arrange her title page in these pretty colored letters. Well, we hunted everywhere but could not find any, until at last we found just one sheet, containing the twenty-six letters, somewhere on Sixth Avenue. Madame bought that one and we went home. She wanted several, of course, but not finding them proceeded to use what she could of this. My friend and I sat down beside her little table, while she got her scrap-book and busily began to paste her

---

* *Op. cit.*, p. 149.

letters in. By and by she exclaimed, petulantly,
' I want two S's, two P's, and two A's.' I said,
' Madame, I will go and search for them downtown.
I presume I can find them somewhere.'

" ' No, you need not,' she answered. Then,
suddenly looking up, said: ' Do you wish to see me
make some ? '

" ' Make some ? How ? Paint some ? '

" ' No, make some exactly like these.'

" ' But how is that possible ? These are printed by
machinery.'

" ' It is possible—see ! '

" She put her finger upon the S and looked upon it.
She looked at it with infinite intensity. Her brow
ridged out. She seemed the very spirit of will. In
about half a minute she smiled, lifted her finger, took
up two S's exactly alike, exclaiming, ' It is done ! '
She did the same with the P's.

" Then my friend thought: ' If this is trickery, it
can be detected. In one alphabet can be but one
letter of a kind. I will try her.' So he said:
' Madame, supposing this time, instead of making
two letters separately, you join them together thus
A—A—? '

" ' It makes no difference to me how I do it,' she
replied indifferently, and placing her finger on the
A, in a few seconds she took it up, and handed him
two A's, joined together as he desired. *They were as
if stamped from the same piece of paper.* There were no
seams or (artificial) joinings of any kind. She had
to cut them apart to use them. This was in broad
daylight, in the presence of no one but myself and
friend, and done simply for her own convenience.

" We were both astounded and lost in admiration.
We examined them with the utmost care. They
seemed as much alike as two peas. But if you wish,
I can show you the letters this moment. ' Madame,
may we take your scrap-book to look at ? '

" ' Certainly, with pleasure,' returned Madame,
courteously. We waited impatiently until Mr. P.

could open the volume. The page was beautifully arranged, and read thus, in brilliant letters:

THIRD VOLUME. SCRAP-BOOK OF THE THEOSOPHICAL SOCIETY
New York, 1878
THEIR TRIBULATIONS AND TRIUMPHS

" ' There,' said he, pointing to the S in Scrap and the S in Society, ' those are the letters she used, and this is the one she made.' There was no difference in them." *

From the accounts recorded about precipitations it would seem that it is not an easy matter to determine just what is the quality of the materialized product, since it simulates so closely the writing made by means of pen and ink, or crayon, or pencil, as well as duplicating coloured printed products. Unquestionably, the most striking feature—that which has caught the attention of all observers—is that which is considered under category (*d*): the color of the precipitation. Before presenting the best known examples—the Mahatma letters, so well known to be in the colors of red and blue—another type of precipitation will illustrate the use of color. The remarkable fact about this precipitation is that the colors which were manifested in the materialization were all produced at the moment of precipitation—not by means of repeated applications (as is the case in the painting of a picture). Again one must resort to Col. Olcott for his testimonial, the precipitated portrait being reproduced in his book in black and white:

" One evening, in the autumn of 1876 . . . she did the very best thing by offering to show me in a picture how Oxon's evolution was proceeding, and at once made good her promise. Rising from the table, she

---

* Quoted in *Old Diary Leaves*, Vol. I, pp. 417-20. The Scrapbook is preserved in the archives at Adyar.

went and opened a drawer from which she took a
small roll of white satin—the remnant, I believe, of a
piece she had had given her at Philadelphia—and
laying it on the table before me, proceeded to cut off
a piece of the size she wanted; after which she returned
the roll to its place and sat down. She laid the piece
of satin, face down, before her, almost covered it with
a sheet of clean blotting-paper, and rested her elbows
on it while she rolled for herself and lighted a fresh
cigarette. Presently she asked me to fetch her a glass
of water. I said I would, but first put her some
question which involved an answer and some delay.
Meanwhile I kept my eye upon an exposed edge of
the satin, determined not to lose sight of it. Soon
noticing that I made no sign of moving, she asked me
if I did not mean to fetch her the water. I said:
' Oh, certainly.' ' Then what do you wait for? ' she
asked. ' I only wait to see what you are about to do
with that satin,' I replied. She gave me one angry
glance, as though seeing that I did not mean to trust
her alone with the satin, and then brought down her
clenched fist upon the blotting-paper, saying: ' I
shall have it now—this minute! ' Then, raising the
paper and *turning over the satin,* she tossed it over to me.
Imagine, if you can, my surprise! On the sheeny side
I found a picture, in colours, of a most extraordinary
character. There was an excellent portrait, of the
head only, of Stainton Moses as he looked at that age,
the almost duplicate of one of his photographs that
hung ' above the line ' on the wall of the room, over
the mantel-shelf. From the crown of the head shot
out spikes of golden flame; at the places of the heart
and the solar plexus were red and golden fires, as it
might be bursting forth from little craters; the head
and the place of the thorax were involved in rolling
clouds of pure blue aura, bespeckled throughout with
flecks of gold; and the lower half of the space where
the body should be was enwrapped in similarly rolling
clouds of pinkish and greyish vapour, that is, of auras
of a meaner quality than the superior cumuli.

". . . The blue clouds would represent the pure but not most luminous quality of the human aura—described as shining, or radiant; a silver nimbus. The flecks of gold, however, that are seen floating in the blue, typify sparks of the spirit, the 'silvery spark in the brain,' that Bulwer so beautifully describes in his *Strange Story*; while the greyish and pinkish vapours of the inferior portions show the auras of our animalistic, corporeal qualities." *

It has been established that the principal characteristic of the letters received from the Mahatmas was the fact that the messages were in distinctive scripts and in different colors. The epistles from H.P.B.'s direct Guru were usually precipitated in red, while Mahatma K.H.'s correspondence was in blue. It would seem, however, that insufficient attention was directed to this fact: that there are differing shades of red as well as varying hues of blue. In addition, other colors were also used. To emphasize the point a listing is supplied based upon a careful examination made of the original Mahatma letters, which are now the property of the British Museum.†

1. Fiery red ink (or precipitated substance equivalent in appearance to ink)—in Mahatma M.'s script
2. Faded red ink ,,
3. Red pencil ,,
4. Dark blue ink ,,
5. Faded sepia ink ,,
6. Light blue ink in Mahatma K.H.'s script
7. Blue pencil ,,
8. Light blue pencil ,,
9. Greenish ink ,,
10. Green pencil ,,

---

* *Old Diary Leaves*, Vol. I, pp. 363-6.

† This listing is provided by the compiler of *The Collected Writings of H. P. Blavatsky*, whose meticulous attention to detail is so well attested to in those splendid volumes, containing as they do a mine of information not obtainable elsewhere.

11. Red ink   in Mahatma K.H.'s script
12. Light black-brownish ink   „
13. Black ink   „
14. Greenish-blue—in J. K.'s (or Djual Khul's) script
15. Light brown-yellow ink   „

It would be a fascinating theme to follow the procedure involved in each of the instances in which a variance of color is noted, but this digression would extend the subject more than is necessary. Nevertheless, at this point it is of interest to observe that in an early letter to Mr. Sinnett an inquiry was made in regard to the composition of blue ink, for the request came: " Could you oblige me with some receipt for blue ink? " *

From among the number of witnesses that might be cited with regard to the color of the Letters, only one will be selected. It will furnish both clarity and expressiveness. The citation is from a rather lengthy interview, written in the form of a dialogue between Charles Johnston † and H. P. Blavatsky. The first question in the citation is asked by Mme. Blavatsky, and the response is given by Mr. Johnston:

" ' But you have seen some of the occult letters? What do you say? '

" ' Yes,' I replied; ' Mr. Sinnett showed me about a ream of them; the whole series that the *Occult World* and *Esoteric Buddhism* are based on. Some of them are in red, either ink or pencil, but far more are in blue. I thought it was pencil at first, and I tried to smudge it with my thumb; but it would not smudge.'

" ' Of course not! ' she smiled; ' the colour is driven into the surface of the paper. But what about the writings? '

---

* *The Mahatma Letters to A. P. Sinnett*, p. 34.

† Charles Johnston first met H.P.B. in the spring of 1887, as he states in his interview, which, however, remained unpublished until 1900. In this dialogue he also states that he was present in London at the meeting of the Psychical Research Society when their " Report " was first made public in 1885. Earlier he was in the

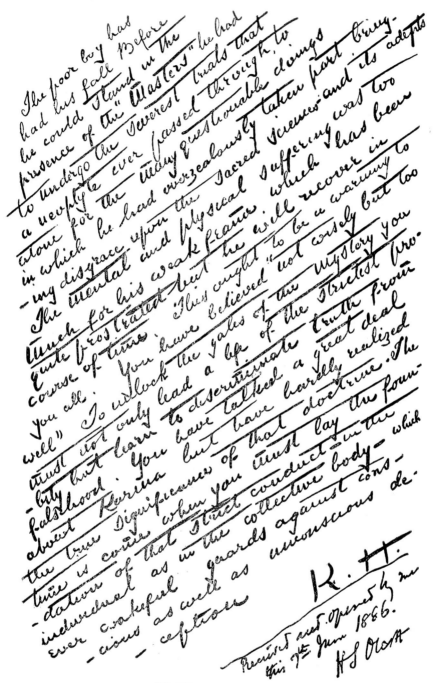

The poor boy had had his fall before he could stand in the presence of the "Masters" he had to undergo the severest trials that a neophyte ever passed through, to atone for the many questionable doings in which he had overzealously taken part being too much for his weak frame which had been mental and physical suffering was too in disgrace upon the sacred sciences and its adepts.

The course of time he will recover in — ing you all. This ought to be a warning to unto prostrated but he believed not wisely but too well. To unlock the gates of the mystery you must not only lead a life of the strictest pro- bity but learn to discriminate truth from falsehood. You have talked a great deal about Karma but have hardly realized the true significance of that doctrine. The time is come when you must lay the foun- dation of that strict conduct in the individual as in the collective body — which Ever careful as guards against uncons- — cious as well as unconscious de- — ception

K. H.

Received and opened by me this 7th June 1886.

H S Olcott

FACSIMILE No. 3

A reproduction of a letter received by H. S. Olcott. A fine example of the K. H. script—usually precipitated in blue ink. Col. Olcott added his signature as well as the date when he received the message.

Do not feel so dejected, my poor boy, we need you for that. As Mr. Sinnett rightly says in his Esoteric Buddhism, the higher spiritual progress cannot be accompanied by intellectual development on a parallel line. You have now the best opportunities for doing that where you are working. For your devotion & unselfish labour, you are receiving help, silent tho' it be. Your time is not yet come. When it does, I shall be recommended to you. I'll then make the best of the present favourable opportunity to improve yourself intellectually while developing your intuitions. Remember that we lost and that for an ocean that there effort is

FACSIMILE No. 4

A reproduction—exact size—of a letter from the Mahatma K. H. received by Damodar. The notation in the upper left-hand corner was added by Damodar indicating the time of its receipt: 5 A.M., February 27, 1884.

" ' I am coming to that. There were two; the blue writing, and the red; they were totally different from each other, and both were quite unlike yours. I have spent a good deal of time studying the relation of hand-writing to character, and the two characters were quite clearly marked. The blue was evidently a man of very gentle and even character, but of tremendously strong will; logical, easy-going, and taking endless pains to make his meaning clear. It was altogether the hand-writing of a cultivated and very sympathetic man.'

" ' Which I am not,' said H.P.B., with a smile; ' that is Mahatma Koothoomi; he is a Kashmiri Brahmin by birth, you know, and has travelled a good deal in Europe. He is the author of the *Occult World* letters, and gave Mr. Sinnett most of the material of *Esoteric Buddhism*. . . . But what about the other writing?'

" ' The red? Oh! that is wholly different. It is fierce, impetuous, dominant, strong; it comes in volcanic outbursts, while the other is like Niagara Falls.

Civil Service employ of the British Government in India. After H.P.B.'s passing, Johnston was of great assistance to William Q. Judge in New York, with editorial work on *The Path* and especially in an educational series published by Mr. Judge in pamphlet form, entitled *Oriental Department Papers*, during the years 1894-96. It was for this series that Johnston translated from the Sanskrit Śankarāchārya's celebrated treatise " The Crest-Jewel of Wisdom ".

In introducing Charles Johnston as the translator of Sanskrit works and as a member of the Theosophical Society, W. Q. Judge wrote:

"Of his qualifications there is no doubt, as he has had experience in this field, has also for some time been teaching Sanskrit, and brings to the work a sincere sympathy with Indian thought as well as devotion to the Society which will without question make the matter furnished of value as well as of interest."
—Quoted in the Preface to the publication in book form of Charles Johnston's translation of *The Crest-Jewel of Wisdom* (by Theosophical University Press, Covina, 1946).

Charles Johnston further had the distinction of being related to Mme. Blavatsky—through his marriage to Vera Zhelihovsky, the daughter of H. P. B.'s sister, Vera.

One is fire, and the other is the ocean. They are wholly different, and both quite unlike yours. But the second has more resemblance to yours than the first.'

" 'This is my Master,' she said, 'whom we call Mahatma Morya.' "

". . . He was a Rajput by birth, she said, one of the old warrior race of the Indian desert, the finest and handsomest nation in the world. Her Master was a giant, six feet eight, and splendidly built; a superb type of manly beauty." *

The citation, of course, had reference to category (d), as well as to (e): the caligraphy of the precipitated Mahatma Letters. This theme is continued in the following extract, which also includes a specific reference to the main sectional title, "Writing by Precipitation". The testimonial is provided by Dr. Hübbe-Schleiden concerning the writing of *The Secret Doctrine*:

" I saw a good deal of the well-known blue K.H. handwriting as corrections and annotations on her manuscripts as well as in books that lay occasionally on her desk. And I noticed this principally in the morning before she had commenced to work. I slept on the couch in her study after she had withdrawn for the night, and the couch stood only a few feet from her desk. I remember well my astonishment one morning when I got up to find a great many pages of foolscap covered with that blue pencil handwriting lying on her own manuscript, at her place on her desk. How these pages got there I do not know, but I did not see them before I went to sleep and no person had been bodily in the room during the night, for I am a light sleeper." †

---

* This interview was first published in *The Theosophical Forum*, New York, Vol. V, No. 12, April, 1900 and continued in the May, June and July issues. It is republished in *H. P. Blavatsky Collected Writings*, Vol. VIII, pp. 398-99.

† *Reminiscences of H. P. Blavatsky and The Secret Doctrine*, pp. 112-113.

FACSIMILE No. 5

A reproduction of a portion of a letter which was received by Dr. Franz Hartmann in January, 1885. An example of Mahatma M.'s script—usually precipitated in red ink.

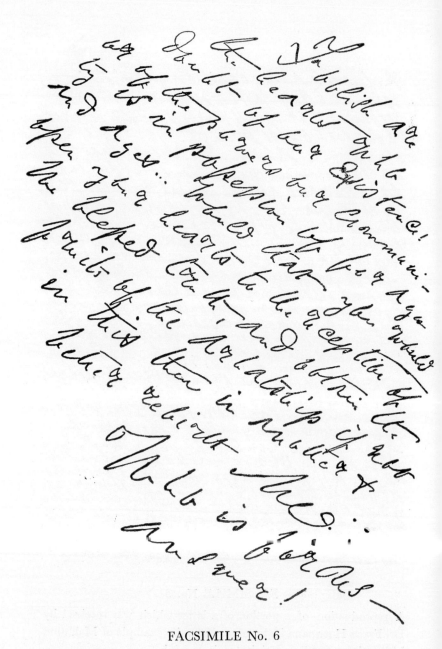

FACSIMILE No. 6

A reproduction of a letter which was dropped in the midst of a group of doubters, during a discussion held at Bhavnagar, India. Another example of Mahatma M.'s script (exact size).

In regard to the writing of *Isis Unveiled*, Col. Olcott stated that he had witnessed a similar display:

" Most perfect of all were the manuscripts which were written for her while she was sleeping. The beginning of the chapter on the civilization of Ancient Egypt (Vol. I, chap. xiv) is an illustration. We had stopped work the evening before at about 2.00 a.m. as usual, both too tired to stop for our usual smoke and chat before parting; she almost fell asleep in her chair while I was bidding her good-night, so I hurried off to my bedroom. The next morning, when I came down after my breakfast, she showed me a pile of at least thirty or forty pages of beautifully written H.P.B. manuscript, which, she said, she had had written for her by. . . . . ." *

One of the most interesting of the examples of caligraphy, and certainly the most unusual of any that were recorded, took place in connection with a diploma. Upon affiliation with The Theosophical Society, each member is issued a diploma acknowledging membership in the Society. During Colonel Olcott's administration, he had instituted a formal initiation ceremony accompanying the granting of the diploma together with appropriate notifications. But the circumstances connected with one particular diploma are distinctly noteworthy and may be retold in this manner.

During the late summer of 1880, when Colonel Olcott and Madame Blavatsky were visiting the Sinnetts at Simla, a great number of occult phenomena were produced. Among the group of Anglo-Indians whom the Sinnetts had invited to their home was a major, who was duly impressed with what he had observed. In fact he had even intimated that he was in sympathy with the objects of the Society. One day while on a picnic party, after witnessing an occult phenomenon the conversation of the group centered upon membership in the Society

---

* *Old Diary Leaves*, Vol. I, p. 211. The name of the Mahatma was not supplied by Col. Olcott.

and Major Henderson was asked by one of the circle if he would be willing to affiliate with the organization. Major Henderson entered into the spirit of the gathering by declaring that he would do so right then and there if the official diploma would be presented to him on the spot—the major knowing full well that as they were on a picnic party in the woods no diploma could possibly be produced immediately. All eyes focussed on H.P.B.

" How about it, H.P.B.? Can you produce a diploma for the Major? " queried one.

" Well, now, may be that can be arranged," was the rejoinder. " Go and look for one out there," extending her arm and pointing towards the woods. " It will be rolled up and there will be a lot of string around the roll, and also it will be bound up in the leaves of a creeping plant." Then, after a pause she added. " but only the one for whom the diploma is intended will find it."

And so it came to pass. Major Henderson did in fact find the diploma, rolled and wrapped as had been indicated. And to cap it all, it was correctly filled in with the major's name, and that day's date (October 3, 1880), together with an official letter from Colonel Olcott welcoming him to membership in The Theosophical Society.

In regard to this incident, Colonel Olcott entered the following notation in his diary:

" the official letter found by Major H. in the deodar shrub along with his diploma, in answer to his demand, was signed ' Faithfully yours . . . (the name in Tibetan characters), for H. S. Olcott, President of the Theosophical Society.' The body of the letter was, how ever, in a facsimile of my handwriting, and, if I had not known the contrary, I should have been ready to swear that I had myself written it." *

Thus, not only had the diploma as well as the letter been precipitated and transmitted to the woods near

---

* *Old Diary Leaves*, Second Series, 1878-83, 2nd ed., p. 237. A facsimile of H. S. Olcott's handwriting is reproduced on the page which faces page 141, in Chapter VI.

Simla, but the caligraphy of the letter was in the Colonel's handwriting—even though he had not handled the diploma nor the letter himself.

Because of the publication of the work entitled *The Mahatma Letters to A. P. Sinnett*, attention has been focused on these letters, and deservedly so. Nevertheless, it should be borne in mind that facsimile reproductions of other precipitated letters have been published, illustrating varied types of caligraphy. *

Col. Olcott was aware of the fact that H.P.B.'s manuscripts, which were written by hand, revealed striking changes in the style of handwriting. He came to the conclusion that the handwriting showed these marked differences in keeping with the personality that was manifested during that interval. (This theme will be further considered in Chapter XIV. †) His views were outlined in this fashion:

" The ' copy ' turned off by H.P.B. presented the most marked dissemblances at different times. While the handwriting bore one peculiar character throughout, so that one familiar with her writing would always be able to detect any given page as H.P.B.'s yet, when examined carefully, one discovered at least three or four variations of the one style, and each of these persistent for pages together, when it would give place to some other of the caligraphic variants. That is to say, there would not often—never, as I now remember—be more than two of the styles on the same page, and even two only when the style which had been running through

---

* Reference is made to the series entitled *Letters from the Masters of the Wisdom*, 1881-1888. Transcribed and Compiled by C. Jinarâjadâsa. First Series: 1st ed. published 1919 by the Theosophical Publishing House, 124 pp. 4th ed. 1948 (with additional Letters). Second Series: published 1925. Also to the work entitled *Did Madame Blavatsky Forge the Mahatma Letters?* by C. Jinarâjadâsa, published by the Theosophical Publishing House, 1934, containing 30 illustrations of caligraphy.

† Chapter XIV is entitled: Writing by means of a Process Analogous to Tulku.

the work of, perhaps, a whole evening or half an evening, would suddenly give place to one of the other styles which would, in its turn, run through the rest of an evening, or the next whole evening, or the morning's ' copy.' One of these H.P.B. handwritings was very small, but plain; one bold and free; another plain, of medium size, and very legible; and one scratchy and hard to read, with its queer, foreign-shaped a's and x's and e's." *

Since the subject of caligraphy in connection with H.P.B. has been a much debated issue, an appropriate place has arrived for the presentation of important documents bearing directly on the subject of handwriting. These documents also deal with the statement previously made, and now repeated: that the handwriting in which a message appears is the least important aspect of precipitation. The first two documents to be cited (following the extract from a letter referring to them) were stated to have been received by Dr. Hübbe-Schleiden, in the manner indicated, at the time he visited Mme. Blavatsky:

" on the night of my last parting from H.P.B., the two *certificates*, which were printed for the first time in the last April number of *The Path*, page 2, were given to me.† At least I found them in my copy of Hodgson's S.P.R. Report ‡ after I had left her. I am the person who showed them to Mr. Judge in London last August. From the advice given me in the one signed K.H. I was not to publish them, but Mr. Judge was authorized to do so by the instructions which he received." §

---

* *Old Diary Leaves*, Vol. I, pp. 210-1.

† April, 1893, Vol. III, published by W. Q. Judge in New York, two years after H.P.B.'s passing.

‡ The S.P.R. Report referred to is the Report of Richard Hodgson's investigations of phenomena at Adyar, India—during H.P.B's absence —published in the Proceedings of the Psychical Research Society, London, Vol. III, Part IX, December, 1885.

§ Extract from a letter received by the Countess Wachtmeister from Dr. Hübbe-Schleiden, published in *Reminiscences of H. P. Blavatsky and The Secret Doctrine*, p. 113.

Brother Henry — Greeting!

..... : _"Be courageous and hopeful"_ ... Blessed words! The divine, ever working Law of compensation whose humble ministry we are has not overlooked the tiny seed, cast by the charitable hand of our brother . on the soil of the future harvests — of Good and Evil — The above words will come back to this brother. Thou hast created — happiness — and happiness must be created unto thee The seed will grow and thrive — and under the beneficent shade of the heavenly shrub planted by thine own hands will thou one day seat thyself with thy beloved boys — and may be find rest for thy weary head . :

Brother — wise beginnings ought to grow in size as in beauty. Advise thy youngest brother of the city of Boston "to try" and increase his paper to XVI pages . :

June 11/75

FACSIMILE No. 7

A reproduction of a letter received in America, June 11, 1875, by Henry S. Olcott, before the founding of The Theosophical Society. It is in the script associated with the Master Serapis, who often used the symbol depicted in place of his signature.

FACSIMILE No. 8

A reproduction of a letter received by Henry S. Olcott in America in the autumn of 1875. Another example of the script of the Master Serapis (exact size).

Attention is called to the statement made by Dr. Hübbe-Schleiden that Mr. Judge was authorized to publish the certificates. The authorization was given, be it noted, two years after H.P.B.'s passing. William Q. Judge was able to publish the documents because in his turn he had received the same certificates, which, he affirmed, had been sent to him by H. P. Blavatsky. The point is this, that although he declared these documents to be *copies*, they were actually precipitations. Were the precipitations produced by H.P.B.? Be that as it may, certain it is that she transmitted them. At all events, the documents appeared in *The Path*, as indicated, when sanctioned. † The first certificate is written in what appears to be blue crayon:

" I wonder if this note of mine is worthy of occupying a select spot with the documents reproduced, and which of the peculiarities of the ' Blavatskian ' style of writing it will be found to most resemble? The present is simply to satisfy the Dr. that—' the more proof given the less believed.' Let him take my advice and not make these two documents public. It is for his own satisfaction that the undersigned is happy to assure him that *The Secret Doctrine* when ready, will be the triple production of M.·., Upasika and the Doctor's most humble servant. S.B.C. K.H." †

The significant fact about this certificate is that the *handwriting* is NOT in the familiar " K.H. script," although his special characteristic of placing a diagonal line over the " lower case m's " is employed *in some cases*—not in all! The reference to " the Dr." in the second sentence is, of course, to Dr. Hübbe-Schleiden, the editor of *The Sphinx*, to whom the document was given, admonishing

* Facsimile reproductions of the two certificates which had been precipitated for Mr. Judge, were published in *The Theosophical Forum*, Vol. XXVI, April, 1948 (by the Theosophical Society at Covina, California).

† Republished in *Reminiscences*, etc., pp. 114-15 (from *The Path*).

him not to publish it in his magazine. His attention
was directed to the different handwriting employed in the
message itself in the words: " which of the peculiarities
of the ' Blavatskian ' style of writing it will be found to
most resemble?" because it does NOT resemble any of
the previously known styles—which were published in the
S.P.R. Report! It would seem that the precipitator was
specifically calling the Doctor's attention to the fact that
the handwriting of a message was not the criterion for
judging the validity of a document, especially so as the
certificate had been placed in the Doctor's copy of the
S.P.R. Report alongside the " documents reproduced "
therein—as mentioned in the message. However, some
of the facsimilies of purported letters which were reproduced in the Report were forgeries: they had been prepared for, and given to, Richard Hodson by Mme.
Coulomb! *

The following deduction is certainly permissible. One
who is able to precipitate a message would be able to
" create " a message in any style of handwriting desired.

Upāsikā (which may be rendered " female disciple "),
mentioned in the last sentence of the certificate has
reference, of course, to H.P.B.—a term applied to her
by her Teachers. The word is also present in the second
document, precipitated in red and in the script associated
with Mahatma M. (who refers to himself as a Fakir):

" If this can be of any use or help to Dr. Hübbe
Schleiden—though I doubt it—I, the humble undersigned Fakir certify that the ' Secret Doctrine ' is dictated to Upāsikā partly by myself and partly by my
Brother K.H.   M∴" †

---

* For verification of this statement, interested readers should
turn to *H. P. Blavatsky Collected Writings*, Vol. VI, pp. 295-308, article
entitled " H.P.B. on the Coulomb Forged Letters." The matter
is too lengthy to go into here and would serve to detract from the
theme under consideration.

† Republished in *Reminiscences*, etc., p. 115, from *The Path*.

When these two certificates were published in *The Path* in 1893, they were accompanied by this significant statement, and by a third document:

"A year after this, certain doubts having arisen in the minds of individuals, another letter from one of the signers of the foregoing was sent, and read as follows. As the prophecy in it has come true, it is now the time to publish it for the benefit of those who know something of how to take and understand such letters. For the outside it will all be so much nonsense:
"The certificate given last year saying that the Secret Doctrine would be when finished the triple production of Upasika, M.·. and myself was and is correct, although some have doubted not only the facts given in it but also the authenticity of the message in which it was contained. Copy this and also keep the copy of the aforesaid certificate. You will find them both of use on the day when you shall, as will happen without your asking, receive from the hands of the very person to whom the certificate was given, the original for the purpose of allowing you to copy it; and then you can verify the correctness of this presently forwarded copy. And it may then be well to indicate to those wishing to know what portions in the Secret Doctrine have been copied by the pen of Upasika into its pages, though without quotation marks, from my own manuscript and perhaps from M.·. though the last is more difficult from the rarity of his known writing and greater ignorance of his style. All this and more will be found necessary as time goes on but for which you are well qualified to wait.   K.H." *

Attention is directed to this sentence: "You will find them both of use on the day when you shall, as will happen without your asking, receive from the hands of the very person to whom the certificate was given." It

---

* Republished in *Reminiscences*, etc., pp. 115-16, from *The Path*. A facsimile reproduction was published in *The Theosophical Forum*, Vol. XXVI, April, 1948 (Covina, California).

18

should be borne in mind that the first two certificates were received by W. Q. Judge in 1885 or 1886. The prophecy in the above indicated sentence was fulfilled exactly as foretold. For when Mr. Judge was in London, a year after the passing of H.P.B., Dr. Hübbe-Schleiden came to him and handed him the certificates. Mr. Judge noted the incident in his Diary, under the date of July 21, 1892: " H. S. arrives and had conference. He lends me Masters' letters to him. Same as copies sent me by H.P.B." It should be noted that Dr. Hübbe-Schleiden himself mentioned the incident of showing his certificates to Mr. Judge—as indicated in his letter to Countess Wachtmeister (previously quoted).

The next point to be dwelt on is the statement in the third document reading: " and then you can verify the correctness of this presently forwarded copy." This would seem to indicate that a *second copy* was sent to Mr. Judge: (1) because he had already received one copy from H.P.B., (2) because the present certificate was stated to have been written a year later than the first two certificates. The query arises: What mode of precipitation was used in this second copy? Is there a different type of precipitation? That is the most significant factor: this very procedure did occur! A published facsimile reproduction * shows that this second copy was also a precipitation, but this time in the *script associated with the* Mahatma M., in what seems to be black pencil or crayon. This is indeed a unique situation. Here is a message which has been precipitated *three times*! This can be demonstrated. (1) because there are slight varia tions between the first and second precipitations; (2) there is a striking change in the third precipitation. It definitely points to this factor: the handwriting of a precipitated message is not the criterion of validity!

---

* A facsimile reproduction was published in *The Theosophical Forum*, for April, 1948, Vol. XXVI (Covina, California). The three precipitated documents are preserved in the archives of the Theosophical Society (now at Pasadena, California).

Another question arises: Why should this third precipitation have been sent? The suggestion is offered in response: that the third precipitation indicates the script referred to in the document that accompanied it, as being the handwriting which "last is more difficult from the rarity of his known writing and greater ignorance of his style."

The third document also calls attention to the fact that had we the original handwritten manuscript of *The Secret Doctrine*, a person would be able to tell by the handwriting "what portions in *The Secret Doctrine* have been copied by the pen of Upasika"—H.P.B.

It hardly seems necessary to pursue the subject further. This section on calligraphy may therefore be concluded with this observation. Although some calligraphists have declared that H.P.B. could have written the Mahatma letters (e.g., the calligraphist Netherclift), on the other hand there is the statement of Ernst Schütze, Calligraphist to the Court of H.M. The Emperor of Germany. In regard to two letters given to him for examination— "A," in the handwriting of Mahatma M., "B," in the script of Mahatma K.H.—he testified:

"The differences between the two are so glaring that I absolutely cannot come to the conclusion that they have been written by the same hand. While the one A, covering eight pages and written in ink comes from a more than hasty (careless?) handwriting, the other B, in blue pencil has been written by a more firm though fluent handwriting, which makes the reading of it not near as difficult as that of the first......

". . . . This my expert testimony I take on the oath given by me once for all as expert of writing.

" Sign. Berlin, February 7th 1886, Ernst Schütze,
" Sworn expert of writing for the Courts." *

One of the most interesting as well as instructive examples of the precipitation of a message, especially so with

---

* Quoted in *The Letters of H. P. Blavatsky to A. P. Sinnett*, pp. 349-50.

regard to the calligraphy of the message, was demonstrated
by H.P.B., when persuaded to do so by a Hindu official,
who was a member of the Theosophical Society. In
order to convey the full significance of the demonstration,
it will be necessary to make a somewhat lengthy introductory statement. It happened in this way.

In June, 1882, H.P.B. and Col. Olcott were invited by
Judge Gadgil, F.T.S., and other high Durbaris * to visit
Baroda. They accepted the invitation. At the time the
Gaikwar † of Baroda was holding a Durbar. ‡ The
travellers were met at the railway station by the Durbaris
with the news that Col. Olcott had been invited to attend
the Durbar. He accepted the honor. It turned out that
the Gaikwar was interested in the objects of the Theosophical Society. Contrariwise, his English tutor was
very unfriendly. The Gaikwar's Dewan, § or Prime
Minister, was a very able and distinguished looking
official—especially when clad in his court costume—and
asked intelligent, philosophical questions. Showing interest in the philosophical exposition concerning the dual
nature of man and her contention that certain superior
men had the ability to use powers that could be called
super-physical, the Dewan requested Mme. Blavatsky to
demonstrate this for him. H.P.B. responded by producing a few raps on tables and some bell-sounds.

---

* *Durbaris*: the title by which native officials were known in India
in those days.

† Gaikwar or Gaekwar: the title of the ruling native prince of
Baroda. Baroda was formerly one of the independent states of
India, situated north of Bombay. Its capital was also named
Baroda.

‡ Durbar signifies an official reception, or audience held by a
native prince. (Durbar in Hindustani and Persian, *darbâr*, signifies
a ruler's court: *dar* portal; *bâr*, court.)

§ Dewan (from the Turkish *dîwân*, or Persian *dîvân*;) originally a
bundle of written sheets; accounts; hence also the "holder of the
accounts," an official; also the room for the accounts, hence a
council-room. The alternate form of the word *divan* is better known
in its secondary meaning, namely, a sofa, or a low couch without
back and arm-rests.

Whereas the Dewan was only politely inquisitive, his Naib,* Mr. Kirtane, was very much interested. Judge Gadgil was of the opinion that Mr. Kirtane might even join The Theosophical Society. In fact the two had been having a pleasant visit with Mme. Blavatsky. Not only had they been able to draw from her an explanation concerning the precipitation of messages, but they had even obtained from her the promise of having one exhibited for them. Fortunately, Col. Olcott arrived just in time to witness the experiment and to record the proceedings:

"I had been out to see the Gaikwar, and on my return found Kirtane and Gadgil standing at the threshold of H.P.B.'s open door, while she was in the middle of the room with her back towards us. Our two friends told me not to step inside, as Madame B. was doing a phenomenon and had just turned them out on the verandah where I found them. The next minute she came towards us, and taking a sheet of paper from the table, told the gentlemen to mark it for identification. Receiving it back, she said: 'Now turn me in the direction of his residence.' They did so. She then laid the paper between her palms (held horizontally), remained quiet a moment, then held it towards us and went and sat down. Cries of amazement broke from the two Durbaris on seeing, on the just before clean sheet of paper, a letter addressed to me in the handwriting and bearing the signature of the then British Resident at that Court. It was a most peculiar, small calligraphy, and the signature more like a tiny tangle of twine than a man's name. They then told me their story. It seems that they were asking H. P. B. to explain the scientific rationale of the process of precipitating upon paper, cloth, or any

---

* Naib: the plural form of *nabob* is perhaps better known. The word is derived from the Hindustani *navvāb*, Arabic, *nuwwāb*, plural of *nābi*, meaning a native provincial deputy; also an assistant. Here the word signifies the Assistant Dewan.

other surface, a picture or writing, then invisible to the onlooker, and without the help of ink, paints, pencils, or other mechanical agents. . . . She explained that inasmuch as the images of all objects and incidents are stored in the Astral Light, it did not require that she should have seen the person or known the writing, the image of which she wished to precipitate; she had only to be put on the trace and could find and see them for herself and then objectivate them. They urgently begged her to do the things for them. ' Well, then,' she finally said, ' tell me the name of some man or woman most unfriendly to the Theosophical Society, one whom neither Olcott nor I could have ever known.' At once, they mentioned Mr. . . . . the British Resident, who held us and our Society in especial hatred, who never missed the chance of saying unkind things of us, and who had prevented the Gaikwar from inviting H.P.B. and myself to his enthronement, as he had otherwise intended, on the suggestion of Judge Gadgil. They thought this a poser. That it was not, the sequel proved. I thought they would explode with laughter when they read the contents of the note. It was addressed to ' My dear Colonel Olcott,' begged my pardon for the malicious things he had said against us, asked me to enter him as a subscriber to our ' world renowned magazine, *The Theosophist*,' and said he wished to become a member of the Theosophical Society: it was signed ' Yours sincerely,' and with his name. She had never seen a line of the gentleman's writing nor his signature, never met him in the flesh, and the note was precipitated on that sheet of paper, held between her hands, as she stood in the middle of the room, in broad daylight, with us three witnesses looking on." *

Without doubt, the precipitation just recorded may be listed as pertaining also to the next category, entitled

---

* *Old Diary Leaves*, Vol. II, 2nd ed., pp. 365-7.

Category (f)—the permanence or impermanence of the precipitation; for in due time the message would have vanished from the paper—not having been "fixed" thereon. This aspect of precipitated messages will now be considered.

Category (f) deals with the permanence or impermanence of the precipitation. It will be recalled that in the first instance recorded previously concerning the precipitation of a portrait, after a day or two the image vanished. By request of Mr. Judge, however, this portrait was re-precipitated and made permanent. One more item may now be added, since it is closely allied to what has been termed the permanence or impermanence of a precipitation. The present example is chosen from a letter addressed by H.P.B. to T.B. (i.e., Tuitit Bey—an Adept member of the Brotherhood of Luxor) concerning a letter sent to Col. Olcott during the spring of 1875. She wrote:

"My suggestion was to let you have one of our parchments on which the contents appear [materialized] *whenever you cast your eyes on it to read it,* and disappear every time as soon as you have done. . . ." *

A suggestion may be offered in explanation. This closely parallels the familiar example of radio waves which, as is well known, are broadcast on specific frequencies. In order to hear a message that is being broadcast, a radio receiving set is required. When the set is turned on, the instrument becomes receptive to the frequencies for which it was designed. The set, however, will not "speak" until the desired frequency is correctly dialed (or, to use more familiar speech, unless it is tuned to the right station).

So also with the "prepared parchment." By concentrating in the correct manner, the appropriate "beam" will reveal the message to the student. Obviously a message must be already precipitated upon the

---

* Quoted in *Personal Memoirs of H. P. Blavatsky,* p. 220.

magnetized surface; yet an ordinary observer will see nothing but a blank piece of paper.

Closely allied to this category is (g): the ability to " erase " a message and re-precipitate it. What a boon an eraser is to a writer who uses a lead-pencil! If one is inclined to wonder whether a precipitator has the same privilege of " rubbing out " a message once that it has been made to appear upon paper, a hint is given that he has such an ability. For example:

> " Besides, bear in mind, that these my letters, are not written but *impressed* or precipitated and then all mistakes corrected." *

A second instance narrates that this procedure was followed in a specific place in one of the letters which was in process of transmittal to Mr. Sinnett. This evidently intrigued him to such an extent that he inquired of his correspondent for more details on the subject—as the reply clearly indicates:

> " If you are so anxious to find out the particular spot where I erased and precipitated instead another sentence last night at post-office I can satisfy your curiosity, Mr. Sinnett, ...†

While it would seem that the major consideration of the subject of Precipitation has been devoted to the Mahatma letters, it may be observed that the messages which H.P.B. did precipitate (when necessary, or when required to do so), come under the same class. Therefore, that which has been presented is just as applicable

---

* *The Mahatma Letters to A. P. Sinnett*, p. 19. The extract is from one of the early letters received from the Mahatma K.H. Another sentence is appropriate here: " we have to first arrange our sentences and impress every letter to appear on paper in our minds before it becomes fit to be read." (*Op. Cit.*, p. 22)

† *The Mahatma Letters to A. P. Sinnett*, p. 375. The rest of the short letter which was precipitated by Mahatma M. calls attention to the portion of an epistle which was " erased " and indicates the substitution that was made by means of another precipitation.

to her precipitated letters, because the methods employed and conditions governing would be the same.

THE DELIVERY OF THE MESSAGE

Proceeding now to the second phase of the subject, which deals with the second process connected with Precipitation, defined as:

Classification (2) The delivery of the message. Consideration will continue under the following categories:

(*a*) The ability to disassemble the material composing a piece of paper (or other substance) used for the deposition of the message, and to transmit the material to the desired location, there to reassemble it into the natural substance of the paper, with the message thereon.

(*b*) Delivery by means of normal procedures—such as by telegram over the telegraph system; or by means of the mail delivery system of the country.

(*c*) Delivery at any specified spot, or location.

(*d*) Delivery in person—whether by a Mahatma himself, or by his chela.

Further explanation of the process for the delivery of a precipitation, as stated under category (a) above, may be given. It is available in an article entitled " Some Scientific Questions Answered "—the queries being raised by an " eminent Australasian Fellow." *

---

* The eminent Australian F.T.S. was the celebrated educator John Smith (1822-1885). Born in Scotland, he early showed his ability in scholarly pursuits by acquiring the degree of M.A at Aberdeen University, and later an M.D. He never followed the medical profession, however. Instead he became an educator in a new land. Responding to a request for qualified educators, Dr. Smith accepted an assignment as Professor of Chemistry and the chair of Philosophy of Physics at the newly incorporated University of Sydney, New South Wales, Australia, being present at the inaugural ceremony in 1852. The following year Dr. Smith was appointed a member of the Board of National Education, and in 1866 accepted the nomination of a position on the Council of Education, of which body he was president for nine consecutive terms.

Dr. Smith joined the Theosophical Society in January 1882, while on a visit to the Headquarters of the Society, then in Bombay, India. During his visit he narrated an incident which occurred during his presence at Headquarters. This was written in a letter to the editor

" The phenomenon of ' osmosing ' [extracting—*Ed. Theos.*] your note from the sealed envelope in which it was sewn with thread, and substituting for it his own reply, without breaking either seal or thread, is to be considered first. It is one of those complete proofs of the superior familiarity with and control over atomic relations among our Eastern Adepts as compared with modern Western men of science, to which custom has made me familiar. It was the same power as that employed in the formation of the letter in the air of your room at——; * in the case of many other air-born letters; of showers of roses. . . ." †

---

of " The Harbinger of Light," who published it in June, 1882. The letter testified to the receipt of a precipitation from the Mahatma M. The professor related that H.P.B.

" asked Col. Olcott and myself to sit down on two chairs which happened to be near the middle of the room, while she stood before me and held both my hands; immediately a letter fell at my feet from some level above my head. The Colonel, who had a better point of view, said it came from a height of six or seven feet from the ground.

" Picking it up I found a plain envelope (gummed), and inside there was a sheet of note-paper, bearing a Government stamp of the Northwest Provinces and Oudh, and containing writing in pencil." (p. 15)

Here is the message:

" No chance of writing to you inside your letters, but I can write direct. Work for us in Australia, and we will not prove ungrateful, but will prove to you our actual existence, and thank you." (Published in *How Theosophy Came to Australia*, p. 17)

* At Bombay, on February 1, 1882—as related by Professor John Smith in the preceding footnote.

| Published in *The Theosophist*, Vol. V. No. 1, October, 1883, p ??
The editor of the magazine, H.P.B., added this illuminating note:

" A letter was recently received by the Editor from one of our most eminent Australasian Fellows, asking some questions in science of such importance that the replies are, with permission, copied for the edification of our readers. The writer is a Chela who has a certain familiarity with the terminology of Western science. If we mistake not, this is the first time that the rationale of the control exercised by an Adept Occultist over the relations of atoms, and of the phenomena of the ' passage of matter through matter,' has been so succinctly and yet clearly explained." (Republished in *H. P. Blavatsky Collected Writings*, VI, pp. 123-4)

An explanation regarding this passage is provided in a prefatory note to the article. In March of 1882 while on a visit at Naples, Professor John Smith wrote a letter to H.P.B., enclosing a note which he had addressed to a Mahatma, requesting that an answer be placed within his securely *sewn* envelope. As he related the incident in " The Harbinger of Light ": *

" I wished that this might be answered without being opened, and so I got my wife to stitch up the note, which she did most effectually with a double thread of coloured silks, a specimen of which I preserved. The note could not be opened or read without either cutting the paper or undoing the stitching; and if the stiching had been undone, it was impossible by any known means to restore it to its original condition."

---

* In the August issue, 1883. *The Harbinger of Light* was a Spiritualistic magazine, published in Melbourne, Australia, founded by William H. Terry (1836-1913), who became an F.T.S. in March, 1880. The first issue was published on September 1, 1870. During the editorship of Wm. H. Terry, *The Harbinger of Light* not only covered the field of Spiritualism but also carried a history of the activities of The Theosophical Society and its founders. It was in answer to queries by Mr. Terry that the series entitled " Fragments of Occult Truth " was published in *The Theosophist*, commencing October, 1881. This series was based on the teachings given in the correspondence published under the title of *The Mahatma Letters to A. P. Sinnett*. The first three " Fragments " were written by Alan O. Hume and then continued by A. P. Sinnett by request of the Mahatma. The " Fragments " also formed the basis for Mr. Sinnett's book *Esoteric Buddhism*.

In a letter from H. P. Blavatsky to W. H. Terry (which he received in Melbourne on December 12, 1881), she requested him to forward an epistle, which she had enclosed, addressed to Professor John Smith of the University of Sydney. On this same letter was added a precipitation by Mahatma M., which has come to be known as a " psychic extra." The message read:

" For very good reasons I beg leave to ask you the favour to ascertain the whereabouts of the Professor. I have some business with him and a promise to redeem. Yours M.∴ (mis)named the 'Illustrious' by Mr. Sinnett, tho' I be but a poor Tibetan *Fakir*. Private and confidential." (Quoted in *How Theosophy Came to Australia and New Zealand*, p. 6, by Mary K. Neff.)

Mme. Blavatsky replied to the letter which Prof. Smith had written to her from Naples. And what a memorable letter it was—destined to travel for half a year! It was dated Bombay, July 23, 1882, and was addressed to his home at Melbourne. Because of his absence from Australia, the missive was forwarded to London, where it failed to reach him. So from London it went on to Cannes, France, and was delivered to him on January 18, 1883. Nevertheless, the letter was well worth waiting for, because tucked within Mme. Blavatsky's letter what was Prof. Smith's surprise but to find, so he narrates:

" a smaller one addressed to me in red ink. The envelope was so curiously folded and gummed that I could find no proper opening, and I had to cut it with a knife. Inside this envelope was the note I had sent to the Brother, absolutely intact. I examined it with great care, using magnifying glasses, and I got some ladies (including my wife, who had sewn it up) to examine it, and we all came to the conclusion that the sewing had not been disturbed, nor the paper tampered with in any way. I then slit open the paper along one side and extracted a piece of blue Chinese paper, about six inches by five, folded three times. The paper had a faint picture on it of the nature of a watermark, and some writing in red ink round the margin, beginning thus:

" ' Your ladies, I see, are unbelievers, and they are better needle-women than our Hindu and Tibetan lasses,' with a few words more, having reference apparently to the letter I got from the same writer in India. I say the ' same writer ' because the handwriting and signature were identical." *

Continuing now the answering of the problem termed " the phenomenon of osmosing your note from the sealed envelope ":

---

* The Harbinger of Light, August, 1883, quoted in How Theosophy Came to Australia and New Zealand, pp. 22-23. Also published in H. P. Blavatsky Collected Writings, Vol. VI, pp. 122-23.

" The solution is found in the fact that the ' attraction of cohesion ' is a manifestation of the Universal Divine Force, and can be interrupted and again set up as regards any given group of atoms in the relation of substance by the same Divine power as that localised in the human monad. Ātman, the eternal spiritual principle in man, has the same quality of power over brute force as has the Universal Principle of which it is a part. Adeptship is but the crown of spiritual self-evolution, and the powers of spirit develop themselves successively in the ratio of the aspirant's progress upward, morally and spiritually. . . .

" Note that no Adept even can disintegrate and reform any organism above the stage of vegetable: the Universal *Manas* has in the animal begun and in man completed its differentiation into individual entities: in the vegetable it is still an undifferentiated universal spirit, informing the whole mass of atoms which have progressed beyond the inert mineral stage, and preparing to differentiate. There is movement even in the mineral, but it is rather the imperceptible quiver of that Life of life, than its active manifestation in the production of form. . . . . .

" Before closing, a word more about the ' passage of matter through matter.' Matter may be defined as condensed Âkâśa (Ether); and in atomizing, differentiates, as the watery particles differentiate from super-heated steam when condensed. Restore the differentiated matter to the state *ante* of undifferentiated matter, and there is no difficulty in seeing how it can pass through the interstices of a substance in the differentiated state, as we easily conceive of the travel of electricity and other forces through their conductors. The profound art is to be able to interrupt at will and again restore the atomic relations in a given substance; to pull the atoms so far apart as to make them invisible, and yet hold them in polaric suspense, or within the attractive radius, so as to make them rush back into their former cohesive affinities, and re-compose the substance. And since we have had a thousand proofs that this knowledge and power is possessed by our Adept-Occultists, who can blame us for regarding as we do those Adepts as the proper masters in science of the cleverest of our modern authorities?"*

The second subdivision, or category (b) of Classification (2), deals with the delivery of a precipitated message by means of normal procedures. There is on record the fact that Mr. Sinnett actually received a telegram from one of the Mahatmas. In itself the receipt of a telegram may seemingly not be a matter of importance, although it does show that normal methods of delivery of messages may be resorted to when they are available—namely, proximity to a telegraph office. Nevertheless, a very significant fact may be brought to light by relating the events connected with the sending and receipt of the telegram. The first point to consider, then, is not with regard to the content of the message sent over the public wires, but rather that the telegram was sent in response to a letter which had been written by Mr. Sinnett at Simla, India. In this missive, which he mailed to H.P.B. at Amritsar, he requested her to forward an epistle which he had enclosed and addressed to a Mahatma. Mr. Sinnett's letter was received at Amritsar on October 27, 1880, as he discovered by means of the post-mark on the envelope, which was forwarded to him by Mme. Blavatsky (under instruction), advising him to preserve this envelope—much to his mystification. Fortunately he complied with the request.

Here is the important factor connected with the correspondence: the forwarding and receipt of Mr. Sinnett's letter by the Mahatma was acknowledged by means of an epistle bearing the date and place: October 29, Amritsar. A notation made by the recipient, A. P. Sinnett, states that it came to hand on November 5, 1880. With regard to the specific point, a citation from Mahatma K.H.'s letter gives the necessary clue:

---

* The Theosophist, V, 22.   Also H. P. Blavatsky Collected Writings, Vol. VI, pp. 124-26.

" I turn my face homeward tomorrow.

" The delivery of this letter may very possibly be delayed for a few days, owing to causes which it will not interest you for me to specify. Meanwhile, however, I have telegraphed you my thanks for your obliging compliance with my wishes in the matters you allude to in your letter of the 24th inst. . . . But I must say, that your promise was well and loyally fulfilled. Received at Amritsar on the 27th inst., at 2 p.m., I got your letter about thirty miles beyond Rawalpindi, five minutes later, and had an acknowledgment wired to you from Jhelum at 4 p.m., on the same afternoon. Our modes of accelerated delivery and quick communications are not then, as you will see, to be despised by the Western world, or even the Aryan, English-speaking and skeptical Vakils." *

Allahabad, the metropolis where A. P. Sinnett, the editor of *The Pioneer*, made his home, is one of the major cities in what was termed the United Provinces somewhat in the centre of India (although more easterly than westerly and bordering Nepal). Amritsar, in north-west India, is one of the principal cities in the province of Punjab, bordering Tibet, in the region termed Trans-Himalaya. Jhelum is considerably north of Amritsar, but not far from Rawalpindi. Both of these towns are close to the border of Kashmir, which is the most northerly of India's provinces, adjacent to China and Tibet. So much for the topography of the cities, indicating that they are far apart.

In his reply to the receipt of the Mahatma's third long letter, as Mr. Sinnett described it, the latter evidently did not catch the significance attaching to the telegram which he had received. An extract from the fourth long letter gives conclusive evidence that this statement is correct. It commences with a significant statement,

---

* *The Mahatma Letters to A. P. Sinnett*, pp. 12-13. Vakil (or Vakeel) is an Anglo-Indian term applied to a native attorney, or law-pleader. In the East Indies the word signifies an ambassador.

exhibiting the same process required for the delivery of a precipitated message, but now demonstrated as a reverse procedure and termed " osmosis."

" I have your letter of November 19th, abstracted by our special *osmosis* from the envelope at Meerut . . .

" So the *test* of the 27th was *no* test phenomenon? Of course, of course. But did you try to get, as you said you would, the original MSS. of the Jhelum dispatch? Though our hollow but plethoric friend, Mrs. B., were even proved to be my *multum in parvo*, my letter-writer, and to manufacture my epistles, yet, unless she were ubiquitous or had the gift of flying from Amritsar to Jhelum—a distance over 200 miles —in two minutes, how could she have written for me the dispatch in my own hand-writing at Jhelum hardly two hours after *your* letter was received by her at Amritsar? This is why I was not sorry that you said you would send for it, for, with this dispatch in your possession, no ' detractors ' would be very strong, nor even the sceptical logic of Mr. Hume prevail." *

Mr. Sinnett relates in his *Occult World* † that he did obtain the original telegram in Mahatma K. H.'s own handwriting.

Passing on to the next portion of category (*b*). It would seem that the delivery of precipitated messages

---

* *The Mahatma Letters to A.P. Sinnett*, pp. 17-19. The Latin phrase " multum in parvo " means literally " much in little," applicable, of course, to H.P.B. in that she could accomplish much in her position. The previous phrase " hollow but plethoric " is significant and is worth thinking over. While it is true that the adjectival use of the last word has come to have a derogatory meaning, the word was very likely used in its original sense: from the Greek *plethora*, fullness, excessive (doubtless implying that H.P.B. was excessive in her praise of her Teachers).

† On page 118 of the American edition: " a message of about twenty words . . . in Koot Hoomi's own handwriting and it was an answer from Jhelum to a letter which the delivery post-mark on the envelope showed to have been delivered at Amritsar on the same day the message was sent."

by means of the postal route would be such an obvious method that it would scarcely need to be mentioned. Yet, there is the case of the precipitated certificates (previously mentioned) which were forwarded to Mr. Judge—most probably by means of ordinary channels. While it was certainly no problem at all for H.P.B. to make use of the postal routes, nevertheless, to have a Mahatma letter delivered by this means, when the sender would not have access to such a route, would require phenomenal powers in very truth!

It is to be noted that consideration was given to ordinary means for the exchange of correspondence, although reference was also made to another mode— which pertains to process (c). The first suggestion was not followed up, at least there is no further reference to it. The citation is from the third of the letters received by A. P. Sinnett.

"The difficulty you spoke of last night with respect to the interchange of our letters I will try to remove. One of our pupils will shortly visit Lahore and the N.W.P. and an address will be sent to you which you can always use; unless, indeed, you really would prefer corresponding through—pillows. Please to remark that the present is not dated from a ' Lodge ' but from a Kashmir valley." *

The reference to " correspondence through pillows " is explained by Mr. Sinnett in his book entitled *The Occult World*. Having been apprised by Mahatma K.H. that an object would be delivered to any desired specified location, Mr. Sinnett requested that the object be delivered inside his wife's pillow—since it had been under observation all morning. Shortly after the specified

---

* *The Mahatma Letters to A. P. Sinnett*, pp. 10-11. Lahore is a large city situated close to Amritsar in the Punjab province—quite a distance from Allahabad. N.W.P. signifies the North-West Frontier Province, beyond the Punjab province, between Kashmir and Baluchistan provinces.

19

location had been passed on to the Mahatma by H.P.B., she intimated that the pillow could be examined. Mr. Sinnett relates that he set to work to cut it open himself.

" I did this with a penknife, and it was a work of some time, as the cushion was very securely sewn all round, and very strongly, so that it had to be cut open almost stitch by stitch, and no tearing was possible. When one side of the cover was completely ripped up, we found that the feathers of the cushion were enclosed in a sepaiate inner case, also sewn round all the edges. There was nothing to be found between the inner cushion and the outer case; so we proceeded to rip up the inner cushion; and this done, my wife searched among the feathers.

" The first thing she found was a little three-cornered note, addressed to me in the now familiar handwriting of my occult correspondent. It ran as follows:

' My " dear Brother,"—This brooch, No. 2, is placed in this very strange place, simply to show you how very easily a real phenomenon is produced, and how still easier it is to suspect its genuineness. Make of it what you like, even to classing me with confederates.' . . .

" While I was reading this note, my wife discovered, by further search among the feathers, the brooch referred to, one of her own, a very old and very familiar brooch. . . . ." *

At this point a testimonial may be provided of a letter which was precipitated by H.P.B.—then situated in her suite of rooms in New York City—and delivered to William Q. Judge, at a time when he was sitting in his office. In narrating the episode he asserted:

" My office was at least three miles away from her rooms. One day, at about 2 p.m., I was sitting in my

* _The Occult World_, pp. 110-1, American edition, publ. Houghton Mifflin Co., Boston and New York, 1885.

office engaged in reading a legal document, my mind
intent on the subject of the paper.   No one else was
in the office, and in fact the nearest room was separated
from me by a wide opening, or well, in the building,
made to let light into the inner chambers.   Suddenly
I felt on my hand a peculiar tingling sensation that
always preceded any strange thing to happen in the
presence of H.P.B., and at that moment there fell
from the ceiling upon the edge of my desk, and from
there to the floor, a triangularly-folded note from
Madame to myself.   It was written upon the clean
back of a printed Jain *sûtra* or text.   The message
was in her handwriting, and was addressed to me in
her writing across the printed face." *

By the testimony that has thus far been presented it
should be clear that when a specified location has been
determined, it makes little difference *where* the place of
delivery is situated, whether it be in a New York office
(as just mentioned in the previous citation), or in a
pillow on Prospect Hill near Simla, India.   Therefore,
in the matter of the delivery of a precipitation there is
no need to offer further testimonials as to the location of
the spot for the transmission of a precipitated message.
As to the process of the transportation of the missive,
that has already been explained.

An extract from a letter may now be adduced, written
by Alan O. Hume to A. P. Sinnett, indicating the manner
in which letters were delivered:

" That the Brothers exist I now know, but the proofs
that I have had have been purely subjective and
therefore useless to any but myself—unless indeed you
consider it a proof of their existence that I here, at
Simla, receive letters from one of them, my immediate
teacher, dropped upon my table, I living alone in

---

* *Incidents in the Life of Madame Blavatsky*, pp. 154-55.

my house and Madame Blavatsky, Col. Olcott and all their chelas, etc., being thousands of miles distant." *

However, in spite of this communication to Mr. Sinnett which was written by Mr. Hume, he must have had another idea regarding the delivery of his letters by other means than simply by having them "dropped" upon his table. In fact, Mr. Hume must have written about this to his Mahatma correspondent, because we may read a reply which he received on this very point:

"Your suggestion as to the box I will think over. There would have to be some contrivance to prevent the discharge of power when once the box was charged, whether during transit or subsequently: I will consider and take advice or rather permission. But I must say the idea is utterly repugnant to us as everything else smacking of spirits and mediumship. We would prefer by far using natural means as in the last transmission of my letter to you." †

This gives the clue to the process that was involved in connection with the transmission and receipt of letters which occurred at Adyar, after the Headquarters had been established there. By means of the magnetization provided in a specific repository, a "magnetic field" was prepared for the transmission of communications. In a certain sense this is somewhat similar to that which occurs in radio broadcasting. By means of a transmitter electric waves are broadcast at a specified frequency. In order to receive the message that has been sent, one must have a receiving set, which must be tuned to the correct frequency. When properly tuned the message that is broadcast is received. Thus, because of the prepared

---

* *The Letters of H. P. Blavatsky to A. P. Sinnett,* p. 353. In their early correspondence both Alan O. Hume and Alfred P. Sinnett referred to the Mahatmas as "the Brothers." So did Col. Olcott and W. Q. Judge in the early years of the T.S. in America.

† *The Mahatma Letters to A. P. Sinnett,* p. 65.

" magnetic field " the message is carried along the âkâśic currents to the one who prepared the " field " and who possesses the required receptivity, enabling him to perceive the message that was placed for transmission.

Soon after the Headquarters of The Theosophical Society had been moved from Bombay to Adyar, Madras —the transference occurring in December, 1882—a means of communication was established between H.P.B. and the Mahatmas. Mr. Sinnett testified to this in March, 1883. While en route to England, he and Mrs. Sinnett stopped off at Adyar where they spent some days. Mr. Sinnett had commenced writing his second book, to which he gave the title *Esoteric Buddhism*. He had it published in London—June 11, 1883. Uncertain about some points in the book, he had prepared some questions which he desired to place before the Mahatma. So, one morning, he asked Mrs. Sinnett to take the questions to Mme. Blavatsky and request her to transmit them. Mrs. Sinnett complied. Pointing to an ornamental cupboard, some three feet square, which hung on the wall between two rooms, Mme. Blavatsky told Mrs. Sinnett to place the questions within the cupboard. After Mrs. Sinnett had done this, the two remained seated and entered into conversation. In about ten minutes, during which interval Mrs. Sinnett had had the cupboard under constant observation, Mme. Blavatsky informed Mrs. Sinnett that she could withdraw her husband's papers from the cupboard. Doing so, she found that a letter had been placed upon the note which she had placed within the cupboard.* This cupboard came to be called " the Shrine " by those in the household.

The cupboard had been made by M. Coulomb, a clever carpenter, by request of Mme. Blavatsky. It was constructed of several pieces of wood in such a manner that when taken down from the wall it could be easily

---

* Cf. *The Early Days of Theosophy in Europe*, pp. 39-40; and *A Short History of The Theosophical Society* by Josephine Ransom, p. 179, The Theosophical Publishing House, Adyar, 1938.

disassembled, as well as reassembled. The reason for this construction was so that the cupboard could be carried with her when Mme. Blavatsky went on her travels.*

William Kingsland describes " the Shrine " in this manner:

" The so-called Shrine was a wooden cupboard between three feet and four feet in width and height, and one foot or fifteen inches in depth, with a drawer below the cupboard portion, and with corner brackets. . . . It was hung, not fixed, against a double partition wall between the Occult Room and Mme. Blavatsky's private rooms, and there appears to have been a space about twelve inches in depth between the two portions of this double partition wall. There appears also to have been a space of some inches between the Shrine itself and the wall against which it was hung. The Shrine contained portraits of two of the Masters, and some other ' sacred ' articles, and was an object of great veneration by the native *chelas*." †

Besides Mr. Sinnett, other members of the staff at Headquarters had opportunities of observing the receipt of communications in connection with the cupboard, notably Damodar and Dr. Franz Hartmann. In Dr. Hartmann's case, it may be noted that he arrived at Madras on December 4, 1883, went immediately to Adyar, and resided there until March 31, 1885; departing at the same time that Mme. Blavatsky left India. Just three weeks after his arrival he had an opportunity to test the efficacy of the Shrine and gave this testimonial. He states that on December 25, 1883, he placed a very brief letter in the Shrine:

" Revered Master! The undersigned offers you his services. He desires that you would kindly examine

---

* Cf. *A Short History, etc.*, p. 213.

† *The Real H. P. Blavatsky*, p. 286, John M. Watkins, London, 1928.

his mental capacity and if desirable give him further instruction.

"Respectfully yours, Franz Hartmann." *

Here is a portion of the response which Dr. Hartmann received from the Shrine:

"Blessings! Were we to employ in our service a man of no intelligence, we would have to point out to him, as you say in the West, chapter and verse, *i.e.*, give him special assignments and definite orders; but a mind like yours, with a background of much experience, can find the way by itself, when given a hint in regard to the direction which leads to the goal. Make for yourself a clear picture of what a man is, in what relation this particular life stands to the sum-total of his former existences, and that his future is entirely within his own power, and you will not be in doubt any longer as to what you should do. . . . I placed in H. S. Olcott's head the idea to suggest to you to come here. Remain in Asia. Take part in the work of the Theosophical Society. Make known without reservations the principles of the philosophy which speaks the loudest in your own heart. Help others, so that you may be helped yourself. . . . Live according to the highest Ideal of Manhood. Think and work. In this lie the conditions of satisfaction for both yourself and others. . . . . M." †

---

* *Report of Observations made during a Nine Months' Stay at the Headquarters of The Theosophical Society at Adyar (Madras), India, by* F. Hartmann, M.D., F.T.S. (*An American Buddhist*). Madras: Printed at The Scottish Press, by Graves, Cookson & Co., 1884, 60 pages. Quoted in *H. P. Blavatsky Collected Writings*, Vol. VIII, p. 445. Dr. Hartmann became an American citizen in 1867. He became a Buddhist on Dec. 26, 1883.

† An English rendition of the German text published in *Lotusblüthen*, Vol. LXV, pp. 142-43; quoted in *H.P. Blavatsky Collected Writings*, Vol. VIII, pp. 444-45. Dr. Hartmann stated that the passages which were omitted had reference to his private affairs and were not known by anyone in India.

In his turn, Colonel Olcott had occasion to test the Shrine for himself. He recorded this testimonial in his diary, under date of June 6, 1883:

" Had nice test this a.m. Couldn't decide whether to accept invitations to Colombo or to Allahabad first. Put Avinas Ch. Bannerji's letter in shrine, locked door, instantly reopened it and got the written orders of Maha Sahib through Hilarion in French. Done while I stood there and not half a minute had elapsed." *

When placing this testimonial in his book entitled *Old Diary Leaves*, the Colonel added this sentence:

" So far as it goes, that pretty effectually disposes of the pretence that these communications were fabricated in advance and passed through a sliding panel at the back of the shrine." †

Here is a translation from the French of the response which the Colonel received in answer to the epistle which he submitted:

" Maha Sahib, with whom I am at the moment, orders me to say that the most reasonable plan would be to make a tour of about a month in the neighbouring districts. From Tinnevelly or even from Malabar the Colonel could go to Colombo for a few days—but *only for a few days*—to encourage them and to recharge them with his *personal Âkâśa*—which could not fail to be beneficial to them. The Societies of the South are in need of his vivifying presence. Going round about within the Presidency, he could thus be recalled at any time to *Headquarters*, should there be need. July 17 would be the proper time to go to the Northern

---

* *Did Madame Blavatsky Forge The Mahatma Letters?* p. 44, by C. Jinarājadāsa (publ. The Theosophical Publishing House, 1934). " Maha Sahib " is an appellation given to the Master Serapis. (*Letters from the Masters of the Wisdom*, Second Series, p. 68.)

† Op. cit., Vol. II, p. 441.

Saïb avec qui je suis
pour le moment, m'ordonne de
dire que le plan le plus raisonnable
serait de faire un tour des pays
adjacents — pour un mois. De Tinnevelly ou bien le Malabar, le
Col. pourrait se rendre pour quelques jours à Colombo — mais
seulement pour quelques jours —
pour les encourager et les remplir
de son AKASA personnel — Ce qui
ne pourrait que leur faire du
bien. Les Sociétés du Midi ont
besoin de la présence vivifiante.
Cerclant tout autour dans la
Présidence - il pourrait être
ainsi rappelé à tout moment
au headquarter si besoin il
y avait. Le 17 Juillet serait
le vrai temps d'aller aux plu

FACSIMILE No. 9

A reproduction of a letter received by Henry S. Olcott in the Shrine at
the T.S. Headquarters, Adyar, Madras, India. An example of the script
of Master Hilarion: the first page of a letter written in French and transmitted in response to the Colonel's request as to the best method of procedure.

vinces du Nord, visitant toutes
les Sociétés sur-son chemin, —
depuis Bareilly jusqu'au Roone
etc.
    Mahu Sahib prie le Col.
de ne pas risquer trop sa santé.
Son bois serait de donner d'une
tricé que que tu que sur la tête de
trois quatre personnes ici et tâches
d'entrer en relation avec Venkatesi
ri et le Vizionagrom, Il y a
assez de temps pour cela jusqu'au
Juin 17. Qu'il fait un plan
et le dise.

Rec'd 11/6/83 formed
instantaneously
in Shrine
madras

FACSIMILE No. 10

A reproduction of the conclusion of Master Hilarion's letter. The notation at the foot of the letter was placed there by Col. Olcott: "Rec'd
11/6/83—instantaneously formed in Shrine, Madras," thus demonstrating
the immediate precipitation of the answer to his question.

Provinces, visiting all the Societies on the road, from Bellary to Poona, etc.

" Maha Sahib begs the Colonel not to risk his health too much. His advice would be to use a magnetic tile on the heads of three or four people here and to try to enter into relation with [the Rajas of] Venkatagiri and Vizianagram. For that there is enough time till June 17. Let him make a plan and present it ."

Taking up category (d) of Classification (2), namely, the delivery of correspondence in person. The writing and transmission of the *first known* Mahatma letter has already been recorded—occurring in 1870, five years before the formation of the Theosophical Society. Its method of conveyance is now again emphasized. It was delivered in person to Mme. Fadeyev (H.P.B.'s aunt) at her home in Russia, as she testified. From a notation given to Mr. Sinnett, in all likelihood the letter was delivered by the Mahatma M.:

" Tell her I—the ' *Khosyayin* ' (her nieces' *Khosyayin* she called me as I went to see her thrice). . . ." *

The second instance of the delivery of a letter in person is testified to by Col. Olcott, who narrates that the missive was conveyed to him in person by a Mahatma himself, not by means of his Mâyâvi-rûpa,† but in his physical body.‡ Here is his notation, made in his Diary under date of November 20, 1883:

---

* *The Mahatma Letters to A. P. Sinnett*, p. 254. It was well known by members of H.P.B.'s family that she had what she called a guardian during her childhood—clearly visible to her, although not by her family. Her aunt here referred to this guardian as *Khosyayin*.

† Mâyâvi-rûpa: this Sanskrit compound literally signifies the illusory form (*mâyâvi*—the adjectival derivative from the noun *mâyâ*; *rûpa*, form). The compound may well be rendered " the vehicle of projection ".

‡ H.P.B. refers to the fact that at the time Col. Olcott recorded this incident the Mahatma K.H. was passing through Southern India (*Letters of H.P.B.* etc., pp. 72-73).

" 1.55 a.m. Koot Hoomi came in body to my tent. Woke me suddenly out of sleep, pressed a note (wrapped in silk) into my left hand, and laid his hand upon my head. He then passed into Brown's compartment and integrated another note in his hand (Brown's). He spoke to me. Was sent by Maha Chohan." *

The letter is described as written in black ink, the original being now somewhat faded, written on both sides of a sheet of paper. Extracts from the letter on the specific point under consideration now follow:

" Of course, by your own canons of evidence you have not until now been a thoroughly qualified witness, since we have never previously—to your knowledge —met in the flesh. But at last you are, and one object in view in my making the journey from the Ashrum to Lahore was to give you this last substantial proof. You have not only seen and conversed with, but touched me, my hand has pressed yours, and the K.H. of fancy becomes the K $\triangle$ of fact. . . . .

" I come to you not alone of my own accord and wish, but also by order of the Maha Chohan, to whose insight the future lies like an open page. At New York you demanded of M. an objective proof that his visit to you was not a maya—& he gave it; unasked, I give you the present one; tho' I pass out of your sight this note will be to you the reminder of our conferences. I now go to young Mr. Brown to try his intuitiveness." †

W. T. Brown, who was accompanying Col. Olcott on one of his tours in India in 1883, and sharing a tent with the Colonel outside Lahore, describes his impression of the visit and the unique manner in which he received

---

* Quoted in *H. P. Blavatsky Collected Writings*, Vol. VI, p. 23.

† Facsimile reproduction of this letter appears on pp. 25-28, *op. cit.* The letter is preserved in the archives of the T.S.

the letter which was delivered to him in person by the Mahatma K. H. His account of the manner in which he received his message is more detailed than Col. Olcott's.

" On the 19th of Nov. 1883, for instance, *at Lahore* I see a man who impresses me as being Koot Hoomi and on the morning of the 20th I am awakened by the presence of someone in my tent. A voice speaks to me and I find a letter and silk handkerchief within my hand. I am conscious that the letter and silk handkerchief are not placed in my hand in the customary manner. They grow ' out of nothing'. I feel a stream of ' magnetism ' and lo! it is ' materialized '. I rise to read my letter and examine the handkerchief. My visitor is gone. The handkerchief is a white one of the finest silk, with the initials K. H. marked in blue. The letter is also in blue in a bold hand." *

Regarding the matter of the delivery of messages personally by an agent, or a chela, instances may also be cited. First, in a letter sent to Mr. Hume by the Mahatma K. H.:

" We would prefer by far using natural means as in the last transmission of my letter to you. It was one

---

* Quoted from *H. P. Blavatsky Collected Writings*, p. 29. The text of the letter is also published, pp. 29-30, quoted from an autobiographical pamphlet, *My Life* (1885).

William Tournay Brown (1857-?) was born in Glasgow, Scotland. After graduating from the Glasgow University in April, 1882, he went to London, where he heard of the Theosophical Society and applied for membership via A. P. Sinnett. Following a strong urge to go to India he left London in 1883. On his arrival he received a warm welcome by Col. Olcott and H.P.B. Immediately he decided to accompany Col. Olcott on his tour, thereby obtaining the unprecedented opportunity of meeting a Mahatma in his physical body, although communications had already been received by Mr. Brown. On the evening of January 7, 1884, Mr. Brown narrates that he decided to present himself for probation as a chela. Unfortunately the young man was unprepared for the trials that befell him. His calamitous career is described in *Collected Writings*, Vol. VI, pp. 428-29 and 31-32.

of M.'s chelas who left it for you in the flower-shed, where he entered invisible to all yet in his natural body, just as he had entered many a time your museum and other rooms, unknown to you all, during and after the ' Old Lady's ' stay." *

Towards the end of the same letter:

" Yes, I am quite ready to look over your 50 or 60 pages and make notes on the margins: have them set up by all means and send them to me either through little ' Deb ' or Damodar, and Djual Kul will transmit them ".†

In another letter, this time to Mr. Sinnett, the Mahatma K. H. refers to the fact that he sent two of his chelas to deliver letters in person:

" The present will be delivered at your house by Darbhagiri Nath, a young Chela of mine, and his brother Chela, Chandra Cusho. . . . They have their mission and beyond that they must not go to deliver into your hands my ' answers to the famous contradictions '. . . ." ‡

The citations are sufficient to show that the delivery of the letters offered no problems: whichever method that was convenient at the time was utilized.

An Agent Fulfilling the Requirements

Passing on to the next Classification (3): the ability to have an intermediary, or agent, fulfil the requirements. To one who has followed the sequence that has been presented by means of Classification (1) and (2), it should be apparent that H. P. Blavatsky was duly empowered and acted as the agent or intermediary for the Mahatmas. She was eminently capable of fulfilling the requirements

---

* *The Mahatma Letters to A. P. Sinnett*, p. 65. The " Old Lady " here signifies H.P.B.

† *Op. cit.*, p. 66.

‡ *Op. cit.*, pp. 446-47.

that have been thus far considered, namely: (1) to produce a precipitation (whether a message or a portrait); (2) to render it permanently, or impermanently, as desired; (3) to transmit the precipitation; (4) to have the precipitation delivered.

At this point a commendation is appropriate. Could a better one be given than that so well expressed by one of her Teachers?

" She can and did produce phenomena, owing to her natural powers combined with several long years of regular training and her phenomena are sometimes better, more wonderful and far more perfect than those of some high, initiated chelas, whom she surpasses in artistic taste and purely Western appreciation of art —as for instance in the instantaneous production of pictures: witness—her portrait of the ' fakir ' Tiravalla mentioned in *Hints* . . . she has most undeniably been *helping* us in many instances; saving us sometimes as much as two-thirds of the power used, and when remonstrated—for often we are unable to prevent her doing it on her end of the line—answering that she had no need of it, and that her only joy was to be of some use to us. And thus she kept on killing herself inch by inch, ready to give—for our benefit and glory, as she thought—her life-blood drop by drop, and yet invariably denying before witnesses that she had anything to do with it." *

In order to strengthen the testimony already given, reference will be made to two further incidents. They

---

* *The Mahatma Letters to A. P. Sinnett*, pp. 312-13. The reference to *Hints*, is to a pamphlet or an article published in *The Theosophist*. The portrait of the " fakir Tiravalla " is the second portrait precipitated by H.P.B. at the request of W. Q. Judge in New York— described in Classification (1) in this chapter. The concluding portion of the citation gives the clue to the reason why H.P.B. suffers so much physically in her later years. Evidently her physical body became impaired because of not being able to withstand the psychic forces which must be exerted for the production of occult phenomena, and in turn react upon the physical body deleteriously.

are related by Mr. Sinnett in his book first on occult subjects, entitled *The Occult World*, with especial regard to the specific subject of this Classification. They illustrate H.P.B.'s ability to transmit messages to persons at a distance.

In the first incident it should be pointed out that the case cited was not as simple as might appear on first reading. In fact it is somewhat complicated, in that a third party was involved, who was not even present. That is to say, in explanation, the incident showed that it was not a matter of communication between disciple and teacher, but involved transmission of *someone else's* correspondence. Because of this factor H.P.B. elicited assistance in her turn from an agent—as will be shown in the extract. The person requesting aid from Mr. Sinnett in the forwarding of the letter via H.P.B. was his friend, Alan O. Hume. The member of the great Fraternity to whom he wished the letter sent was the Mahatma K.H.:

"A lady, a guest at another house in Simla, had been dining with us, when about eleven o'clock I received a note from her host, enclosing a letter which he asked me to get Madame Blavatsky to send on by occult means to a certain member of the great fraternity to whom both he and I had been writing. . . . We were all anxious to know at once—before the lady with us that evening returned up the hill, so that she could take back word to her host—whether the letter could be sent. . . . The question was whether a certain person, a half-developed brother then in the neighbourhood of Simla, would give the necessary help. Madame Blavatsky said she would see if she could 'find him,' and taking the letter in her hands, she went out into the verandah, where we all followed her. Leaning on the balustrade, and looking over the wide sweep of the Simla valley, she remained for a few minutes perfectly motionless and silent, as we all were; and the night was far enough advanced for all commonplace sounds to have settled down, so that the stillness was perfect. Suddenly, in the air before us, there sounded the clear note of an occult-bell. ' All right,' cried Madame, ' he will take it.' And duly taken the letter was shortly afterwards." *

The second incident relates not only to the delivery of a message by H.P.B., but also deals with its transmission, precipitation, re-transmission and receipt in a very singular manner. The episode has come to be known as the pink-note incident.

"About the end of September [1880] my wife went one afternoon with Madame Blavatsky to the top of a neighbouring hill. They were only accompanied by one other friend. I was not present myself on this occasion. While there Madame Blavatsky asked my

---

* *The Occult World*, pp. 59-60 (American edition). Mr. Sinnett did not mention the name of his lady guest. With regard to the " occult bell, " or bell sounds, Mr. Sinnett had this to say:

" By some modification of the force employed to produce the sound of raps on any object, Madame Blavatsky can produce in the air, without the intermediation of any solid object whatever, the sound of a silvery bell—sometimes a chime or little run of three or four bells on different notes. . . . I heard them on scores of occasions and in all sorts of different places—in the open air and at different houses where Madame Blavatsky went from time to time. . . . If you lightly strike the edge of a thin claret glass with a kinfe you may get a sound which it would be difficult to persuade anyone had come from another room; but the occult bell-sound is like that, only purer and clearer, with no sub-sound of jarring in it whatever. . . .

" The bell-sounds are not mere sportive illustrations of the properties of the currents which are set in action to produce them. They serve the direct, practical purpose among occultists of a telegraphic call-bell. It appears that when trained occultists are concerned, so that the mysterious magnetic connection, whatever it may be, which enables them to communicate ideas is once established, they can produce the bell-sounds at any distance in the neighbourhood of the fellow-initiate whose attention they wish to attract. I have repeatedly heard Madame Blavatsky called in this way. . . ." (*Op. cit.*, pp. 56-59)

wife, in a joking way, what was her heart's desire. She said at random and on the spur of the moment, ' to get a note from one of the Brothers.' Madame Blavatsky took from her pocket a piece of blank pink paper that had been torn off a note received that day. Folding this up into a small compass she took it to the edge of the hill, held it up for a moment or two between her hands and returned saying that it was gone. She presently, after communicating mentally by her own occult methods with the distant Brother, said he asked where my wife would have the letter. At first she said she should like it to come fluttering down into her lap, but some conversation ensued as to whether this would be the best way to get it, and ultimately it was decided that she should find it in a certain tree. . . .

" At first Madame Blavatsky seems to have made a mistake as to the description of the tree which the distant Brother was indicating as that in which he was going to put the note, and with some trouble my wife scrambled on to the lower branch of a bare and leafless trunk on which nothing could be found. Madame then again got into communication with the Brother and ascertained her mistake. Into another tree at a little distance, which neither Madame nor the one other person present had approached, my wife now climbed a few feet and looked all round among the branches. At first she saw nothing, but then, turning back her head without moving from the position she had taken up, she saw on a twig immediately before her face—where a moment previously there had been nothing but leaves—a little pink note. This was stuck on to the stalk of a leaf that had been quite freshly torn off, for the stalk was still green and moist—not withered as it would have been if the leaf had been torn off for any length of time. The note was found to contain these few words: ' I have been asked to leave a note here for you. What can I do for you?' It was signed by some Thibetan characters. The pink paper on which it was written appeared to be the

FACSIMILE No. 11

A reproduction of a message transmitted to Mrs. Patience Sinnett in response to her request to have it placed on the twig of a tree on Prospect Hill outside of Simla, India. The first Mahatma letter received in India, on September 29, 1880.

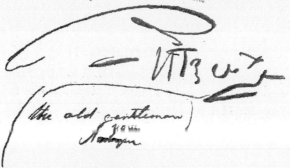

You may — & ought to be kind
to & lenient with an insane person, But
not even for the sake of such a kindness
have you the right to keep back your
religion & allow him even for one twinkling
of the eye to believe you are a Christian
or that you may be one. You have to
make therefore now your choice —
Either your duty to the Lodge or
your own personal ideas

(the old gentleman)
Narayan

FACSIMILE No. 12

A reproduction of a message received by Henry S. Olcott in New York
in 1875. The only known example of the script of the Tiravellum
Mahatma, called Narayan.

same which Madame Blavatsky had taken blank from her pocket shortly before." *

Careful consideration of the preceding missive, the first epistle received *in India* from the Brothers (as the Mahatmas were first designated in the early days of the Theosophical Society by its Founders) reveals some interesting features. These will be pointed out presently. It was received in the early autumn of 1880. Attention is directed to the statement "first epistle received in India," because letters had already been received by Colonel Olcott in America before the Founders had left that land for India. Also it should be noted that the first letter received by Mr. Sinnett, published by him first in his book which he named *The Occult World* and then later in the work entitled *The Mahatma Letters to A. P. Sinnett,* was not the first message received in India. *His* epistle was received a fortnight later, in response to a letter he had written and addressed, as he states, " to the Unknown Brother, " during the period when Colonel Olcott and Madame Blavatsky were his guests at his mountain residence in Simla. The first missive came in response to a verbal request, and not in answer to a written letter. A description of its receipt was also recorded by Colonel Olcott. He penned the memorandum in his *Old Diary Leaves* † as taking place " on the 29th of September, when Mrs. Sinnett, H.P.B. and I went to the top of Prospect Hill "—one of the hills outside the city of Simla. During that era Simla was the summer residence of the viceroy of British India, as well as all the officials of the Anglo-Indian government. The city is situated on the lower Himalaya mountains at a height of about 7,000 feet. The Simla mountains form part of the great central chain of the East Himalayas. The hills are forest-clad and abound with deodars. Also masses of rhododendrons cover the mountain-slopes right

---

* *The Occult World*, pp. 61-3.

† *Op. cit.*, II. 231-2.

20

up to the regions of perpetual snow, enhancing the beauty of the scene. Five rivers run through the district of Simla, adding to the panoramic grandeur.

The Sinnetts were gracious hosts and were accustomed to entertaining in truly Anglo-Indian fashion. Among other means of entertainment they had arranged outings for their guests, and it was during one of such outings that the incident occurred.

Appended is a photographic reproduction made from the original document * which now is filed in the British Museum. The official seal of the Museum is easily discernible. The numbers 266 and 42, in the right-hand corner of the document, were of course also added either by the former custodians or at the Museum. The photographic reproduction is able to show the manner in which the paper was originally folded, as well as the several holes where the paper was punctured when it was placed upon the twig of the tree—thus testifying to the authenticity of the account as narrated by Mr. Sinnett. Evidently the Anglo-Indian editor's flair for journalistic description was uppermost in his mind, so much so that he failed to record the following significant points in connection with the missive:

1. No mention was made concerning the substance used in the written message; that is to say, whether pen, pencil, or other substance was used.

2. No recognition was given with regard to the color of the written missive.

3. No notation was made as to whether the message was on the surface of the paper or imbedded in it.

---

* The photographic reproduction was made by Clarence Q. Wesner during a visit to the British Museum in 1963 direct from the original document by permission of the custodians. The kodachrome picture made from the color film was able to reproduce the original pink color of the paper—which gave rise to its being called "the pink note." Unfortunately, the printed reproduction herewith does not give the original color of the paper. The facsimile reproduction is printed on the insertion which faces page 280.

25.

....Do not indulge in unbrotherly comparisons between the task accomplished by yourself & the work left undone by your neighbour or brother, in the field of Theosophy, as none is held to weed out a larger plot of ground than his strength & capacity will permit him.... "Do not be too severe on the merits or demerits of one who seeks admission among your ranks, as the truth about the actual state of the inner man can only be known to, and dealt justly by Karma alone. Even the simple presence amidst you of a well-inten-tioned & sympathising individual may help you magne-tically.... You are the Free-workers on the Domain of Truth & as such, must leave no obstructions on the paths leading to it."....... [The letter closes with the following lines which have now become quite plain as they give the key to the whole situation.].... " The degree of success or failure are the landmarks we shall have to follow, as they will constitute the barriers placed with your own hands bet-ween yourselves and those whom you have asked to be your teachers. The nearer your approach to the goal contemplated — the shorter the distance between the student & the Master......."

A complete answer is thus found in the above lines to the paper framed by the two Theosophists. Those who are now inclined to repudiate the hand that traced it & feel ready to turn their backs upon the whole Past & the original programme of the T.S. are at liberty to do so. The Theosophical body is neither a Church nor a Sect & every individual opinion is entitled to a hearing. A Theosophist may progress & develop, & his views may outgrow those of the Founders, grow larger & broader in every direction, without for all that abandoning the fundamental soil upon which they were born & nurtured. It is only he who changes diametrically his opinions from one day to another & shifts his devotional views from white to black — who can hardly be trusted in his remarks & actions. But surely this can never be the case of the two Theosophists who have just been answered...

Meanwhile, peace & fraternal good will to all.

Ostende. Oct. 3ᵈ   H.P. Blavatsky, Corres. Secy T.S.
          1886.

FACSIMILE No. 13

A reproduction of H. P. Blavatsky's writing. The last page of the manuscript known as the " Original Programme " of The Theosophical Society, dated October 3, 1886.

{without a parent}(8)

Commentary, on Stanza I.

[In order not to break the Stanzas by making the comments too long, the reader is referred for further explanations to the glossary in the Appendices attached to every chapter]

The Secret Doctrine postulates three propositions:—

(a) An Omnipresent, Eternal & boundless Principle, beyond the reach of words or thought, or in the words of Mandukya "unthinkable & unspeakable." In the Aitareya Upanishad this Principle is referred to as the Self, the only one — as just shown.

(b) The Eternity of the Universe as a fixed abstraction, with periodical appearances & disappearances of objective manifestation; like a regular tidal ebb of flux & reflux: coeval with, as being in one sense identical with the One Principle.

(c) The unity of all the Souls with the Over Soul or the unknown Root, & the continuous transmigration of each ray of the One infinite Light, in accordance with cyclic & Karmic Law, during the whole Cycle of Necessity: that is to say from the beginning of Manvantara to that of Pralaya, the Mayavi -Self"& starting as a pure Emanation [by the Chohan or angel] and returns as a purified Paramārthika — Self, merged in the One Being (or Non-Being) — the absolute "Paramārthika.

In its absolute abstraction, the One Principle though seemingly dual (Parabrahman & Mulaprakriti) is sexless, unconditioned, absolute. Its periodical radiation is, as a primal Emanation One, and androgynous & finite. When the "radiation radiates in its turn, all the secondary radiations are also androgynous to become male & female principles in their lower aspects. Pralaya whether the great or the minor, which leaves things status quo ‖ the first that reawakens

✱ The "Eye of Siva", the inner or spiritual Eye of the Seer or clairvoyant.
† Dogma - a purified [...]
[...] term given to the divine Ego of man, who labours under a delusion & he mistakes his Self, as separated from the One Self, the absolute. Nevertheless it is his own, individual & man personal Self throughout the Manvantaric eternities that returns into the absolute Self, like a drop of water into its Ocean, to reemerge from it at the following Manvantara.
‖ It is not the physical, organised body that remains status quo, not even the Soul of things during the great Cosmic or even Solar Pralayas, but only their idea or photograph. But during the planetary or minor pralayas, once overreached by the ✱ light, the planets remain intact though dead, "like a huge animal caught between the polar ice stands frozen for ages"

FACSIMILE No. 14

A reproduction of H. P. Blavatsky's writing. An early draft of the three Fundamental Propositions of *The Secret Doctrine*.

4. The calligraphy of the missive received no comment, other than it was signed by some Tibetan characters.

Had these items been noted by Mr. Sinnett, they would have greatly added to the value of his narrative; especially so had he but consulted H.P.B. regarding them. Since they are lacking, one must bypass the first three items and focus attention on the fourth. This item is indeed the most significant aspect of the missive, because the calligraphy is quite different from the handwriting usually associated with the Mahatma letters. In other words, the calligraphy is not that of the " K.H. script " and is totally different from the " M. script." If the assertion is made that the calligraphy resembles H.P.B.'s handwriting, then a comparison of this reproduction should be made with the facsimile of a page of *The Secret Doctrine*, * reproduced herewith— a typical example of H.P.B's writing.

After due comparison, if the statement is still made, then the mystery of how Madame Blavatsky could have reproduced the writing upon the blank piece of paper which was *not in her possession* is all the more remarkable. For Mrs. Sinnett testified to the fact that the blank pink paper had left her hands. Had she written the message on the paper before it left her hands, both Colonel Olcott and Mrs. Sinnett would have seen her do so. To declare that Mme. Blavatsky had written the message *before* leaving the residence for the outing is ridiculous, because Mme. Blavatsky had no knowledge that she would be asked " to leave a note here". The very words of the missive show that they were phrased by a person not present in the group; that it was a spontaneous message, not one which was penned with deliberation and forethought. If it is argued that an accomplice was involved in connection with H.P.B., who worded the note and

---

* The facsimile of H.P.B's handwriting was first published in the 6-volume edition of *The Secret Doctrine*, facing page 79 of Vol. I.

simulated her handwriting and then affixed the note on a twig of the tree situated on the hillside, then a rebuttal is at hand. Mme. Blavatsky and Col. Olcott had no knowledge of the terrain, and had had no previous information regarding the place or the route that would be followed for the day's outing; they did not select the route. As for searching for a pink note fastened on a twig of a tree: that would be the equivalent of looking for the proverbial needle in a haystack.

Because the calligraphy is different from the other scripts associated with the Mahatmas, it makes this epistle distinctive and of especial interest. It is, indeed, unique. That it was a genuine occult phenomenon may be determined from its calligraphy, from its content and from its transmission—the latter aspect having been so carefully described by Mr. Sinnett. It was definitely a precipitation.

Continuing now the theme under consideration, namely Classification (3): the ability to have an intermediary, or agent, fulfil the requirements of precipitation and transmission of messages. The principal point to bear in mind is this: when an intermediary is qualified to perform the requirements, the product—that is to say, the letter —is just as authentic as though coming from the hand of the Mahatma himself. For example: when a letter is received from a large business corporation, the recipient is fully aware of the fact that the document which was sent to him through the mail has not been typewritten by the person whose signature is appended to the epistle, whether it be the president, the vice-president, the secretary, or any one of the officials of the concern. In fact, this is usually made known to the recipient by means of the initials of the signatory, which are placed in the lower left-hand corner of the epistle and followed by the initials of the person to whom the letter was dictated, and who usually typewrites the missive. Even at times the signature is not actually signed by the one who dictated the letter, especially when the indication is given that the signature is being written by another person. Nevertheless, this does not invalidate the company's message. Consequently the validity of a message is not impaired because of being handled by an intermediary.

A similar situation arises in the case of the transmission of a message from a Mahatma by means of an intermediary. The intermediary is, of course, a chela under the training or tuition of the Teacher. To be sure, the Teacher is qualified to judge whether the pupil is prepared to fulfil the requirements.

Howsoever, it may be adduced that other chelas besides H. P. Blavatsky were available to act in the capacity indicated.

Reference to the functions performed by other chelas, shows that a person in such a position may act as an agent and fulfil the requirements of transmitting messages. This may be shown by means of an extract from a letter written by Damodar * to Mr. Sinnett:

> " Last year when Mme. B. was so much abused and when it was thought desirable that she should be out of this business as much as possible, *for her sake* I took it upon myself to be a medium of correspondence

---

* Damodar, as he is best known, although his full name was Damodar K. Mavalankar, held the official position of Joint Recording Secretary of the Theosophical Society, along with William Q. Judge. Col. Olcott records that he issued a diploma acknowledging Damodar's affiliation with the T.S. on August 3, 1879. A note appended by H.P.B. to an article in *The Theosophist* of December, 1883, entitled " A Psychological Phenomenon " provides the best possible description of this devoted worker in the T.S. :

" Mr. D.K.M. is a chela of hardly four years' standing, his remarkable psychic powers having received their development but lately. He is of a very delicate health and lives the life of a regular ascetic. Whenever the phenomenon of the separation of the astral from the physical body takes place, we are told, he falls invariably asleep or into a trance a few minutes before."

(Quoted in *H. P. Blavatsky Collected Writings*, Vol. VI, p. 71).

The phenomenon above mentioned refers to Damodar's travel from Moradabad, in the North West Province of India, to Adyar—a distance of 2,281 miles—in his Mâyâvi-rûpa and conversing with H.P.B. at the T.S. Headquarters.

between my MASTERS and the Simla Eclectic Theosophists." *

The following citation, which is appended as a postscript † to a letter addressed to Mr. Sinnett by one of the chelas of Mahatma K. H., clearly indicates that Damodar was qualified to act in the capacity of a transmitter:

" P. S. Should you desire to write to Him though unable to answer Himself, Master will receive your letters with pleasure; you can do so through D. K. Mavalankar." ‡

The commencement of the letter itself, to which the above postscript was added, also definitely shows that chelas may be given an assignment to act as transmitters:

" The Master has awaked and bids me write. To his great regret for certain reasons He will not be able until a fixed period has passed to expose Himself to the thought currents inflowing so strongly from beyond

---

In an article published in *The Theosophist*, Vol. V, Nos. 3-4, pp. 61-2, entitled " A Great Riddle Solved," Damodar tells of his going to an Âśrama with his Master (Mahatma Koot Hoomi) see *Collected Writings*, Vol. VI, pp. 39-40.

The successful completion of Damodar's probationary period may be recorded. In response to a summons, on February 23, 1885, Damodar left Adyar en route to Tibet. He left the Headquarters accompanied by Dr. Franz Hartmann, boarding the steamer *Clan Grant* bound for Calcutta. From there he travelled to Darjiling, arriving there on April 1st. He left Darjiling for Tibet on April 13th.

* *Letters of H. P. Blavatsky to A. P. Sinnett*, p. 355.

† The postscript is signed ' Dd.', an abbreviation for the signature of the letter itself, namely " The Disinherited ". From a paragraph in the letter the guess is hazarded that the letter was precipitated by Jual Khul. (His first name has been variously spelled as Djual, Gjual, and even Gywala; the last name Kool and Khool. Also frequently abbreviated by H.P.B. as simply D.K.).

‡ *The Mahatma Letters to A. P. Sinnett*, p. 250.

advance, you must humiliate the
Demon that obstructs your path —
Read Bulwer Lytton's Zanoni and
you will understand my allusion better.

These are the few words of advice
of a Friend and a Brother. Take heed in
time and let us see the opening of a
bright day for you. What more need
I say than what The Master says
in his letter. I have, however, to request that you will kindly return
to me, as soon as possible, My Master's
Letter to my address. You may keep
its enclosure, I mean your letter
and the Advice to you thereon. But
I should like to have the letter to
my address as it contains priceless
instructions to me, at least, who am
an implicit believer in "Upásiká"
and My Master. Yours fraternally,

Damodar K. Mavalankar

FACSIMILE No. 15

A reproduction of Damodar K. Mavalankar's writing. The third
page of a letter written to R. Keshava Pillai of Nellore, India;
dated October, 1882.

good of the Cause he represents. If he seems interested in it at all, it is because he is opposed and finds himself roused to combativeness. Thus the answer to Mr Terry's letter sent to him from Bombay ought to have been published in the January number. Will you kindly to see to it—Master asks? Master thinks you can do it as well as Mr Hume if you but tried, as the metaphysical faculty in you, is only dormant but would fully develop were you but to awake it to its full action by constant use. As to our reverenced M∴ he desires me to assure you, that the secret of Mr Hume's professed love for Humanity lies in and is based upon, the chance presence in that word of the first syllable; as for "mankind"—he has no sympathy for it.

Since Master will not be able to write to you himself for a month or two longer (tho' you will always hear of him)—He begs you to proceed for his sake with your metaphysical studies; and not to be giving up the task in despair whenever you meet with incomprehensible ideas in M∴ sahib's notes, the more so as M∴ sahib's only hatred in his life, is for writing.

In conclusion Master sends you His best wishes and praying you may not forget Him orders me to sign myself

P.S. Should you desire to (write to) Him tho' unable
to answer Himself Master will re-
ceive your letters with pleasure: you can
do so thro' D. K. Mavalankar. D∴

"Your obedient servant
the
"Desinherited"

FACSIMILE No. 16

A reproduction of Djual Khul's writing. The closing page of a letter received by A. P. Sinnett on January 3, 1882.

the Himavat. I am, therefore, commanded to be the hand to indite His message." *

Here is an instance of still another kind, in which a person possessing clairvoyant faculties may be employed as a transmitter. The citation which next follows is from a letter written by the Countess Wachtmeister, addressed to A. P. Sinnett, dated December 13 (1885):

"Yesterday evening a loud rap was suddenly heard and Jual Kool was with us. He signified his intention of writing through my hand. I saw him close to me indistinctly, felt the influence, heard the few words he said to me, and wrote. . . . . ." †

It scarcely seems necessary to furnish any further examples. Nevertheless, one more incident, described by H.P.B. herself will serve to illustrate the interaction as well as co-operation evoked in a precipitation, on occasions. The anecdote comes from a letter written to A. P. Sinnett while on board the ship *Clan Drummond*, off Algiers on her way to Adyar, India. It is simply dated Sunday, the 8th.‡ The *Clan Drummond* is unceremoniously dubbed "our Clan wash-tub"— referring to the rolling to which H.P.B. was subjected rather than to any water that was splashed on to her.

"Last night as we were hopelessly tossed about and pitched in our Clan wash-tub, Djual K. put in an appearance and asked in his Master's name if I would send you a chit. I said I would. He then asked me to prepare some paper—which I had not. He then said any would do. I then proceeded to ask some from a passenger not having Mrs. Holloway to furnish me with. Lo! I wish those passengers, who quarrel with us every day about the possibility of phenomena

---

* *The Mahatma Letters to A. P. Sinnett*, pp. 248-9.

† *The Letters of H. P. Blavatsky to A. P. Sinnett*, p. 265.

‡ Of November, 1884.

could see what was taking place in my cabin on the
foot of my berth! How D.K.'s hand, as real as life,
was impressing the letter at his Master's dictation,
which came out in relief between the wall and my
legs." *

How Precipitation is Accomplished

This concludes the consideration of the Classifications
into which the subject of Precipitation was divided.
However, thus far the presentation has covered what may
be regarded as the effects of the process, that is to say, the
utilization of the process which results in the materialization of a message. Attention has also been focussed
predominantly upon the transmission of a precipitation.
This was inevitable. Before leaving the subject, the
causative aspects of the process should certainly be
considered. Perhaps this may be expressed more clearly
by phrasing a question in this manner: How is precipitation accomplished? Or again: what is the method that
is employed for producing the materialization of a
message?

It should be understood at the outset that, as with so
many circumstances connected with H.P.B. and the
message which she brought, the full explanation is not
to be had—simply because it has not been provided.
Nevertheless, this should not deter one from seeking to
uncover as much as is possible on the subject. This
phase should be commenced by forming a basis for an
understanding of it. An excellent beginning may be
made towards this approach by directing attention to the
potencies which are available to man through the
processes of the brain. These powers remain unsuspected
by the vast majority. Yet, it should be understandable
that those who have probed into the mysteries of Nature
and discovered the means of developing man's inner
potencies may speak with authority.

---

* *The Mahatma Letters to A. P. Sinnett*, p. 467.

" The idea I wish to convey is that the result of the highest intellection in the scientifically occupied brain is the evolution of a sublimated form of spiritual energy, which, in the cosmic action, is productive of illimitable results; while the automatically acting brain holds, or stores up in itself, only a certain quantum of brute force that is unfruitful of benefit for the individual or humanity. The human brain is an exhaustless generator of the most refined quality of cosmic force out of the low, brute energy of Nature; and the complete adept has made himself a centre from which irradiate potentialities that beget correlations upon correlations through Æons of time to come. This is the key to the mystery of his being able to project into and materialize in the visible world the forms that his imagination has constructed out of inert cosmic matter in the invisible world. The adept does not create anything new, but only utilizes and manipulates materials which Nature has in store around him, and material which, throughout eternities, has passed through all the forms. He has but to choose the one he wants, and recall it into objective existence." *

---

* *The Occult World*, p. 129. This passage is from a very lengthy letter written to Mr. Alan O. Hume by the Mahatma K.H. Its opening paragraph gives the impression that it is one of the earliest —if not the very first epistle—sent to this correspondent. Although searched for, it was not found in the volume entitled *The Mahatma Letters to A. P. Sinnett*. Later on in the same letter another passage may be read with advantage:

" every thought of man upon being evolved passes into the inner world, and becomes an active entity by associating itself, coalescing we might term it, with an elemental—that is to say, with one of the semi-intelligent forces of the kingdoms. It survives as an active intelligence—a creature of the mind's begetting—for a longer or shorter period proportionate with the original intensity of the cerebral action which generated it. Thus, a good thought is perpetuated as an active, beneficent power, an evil one as a maleficent demon. And so man is continually peopling his current in space with a world of his own, crowded with the offsprings of his fancies, desires, impulses, and passions; a current which re-acts upon any sensitive or nervous organization which comes in contact

To say that Mr. Sinnett was elated with his letters and intrigued by the manner he received some of them, is putting it mildly, since he stated:

" In one or two cases I have got back answers from Koot Hoomi to my letters in my own envelopes, these remaining intact as addressed to him, but with the address changed, and my letter gone from the inside, his reply having taken its place. In two or three cases I have found short messages from Koot Hoomi written across the blank parts of letters from other persons, coming to me through the post. . . . ." *

He says he asked for information regarding the process of precipitation, phrasing his questions in this manner:

" Of course I wanted to know more about such precipitation; was it a process which followed thought more rapidly than any with which we were familiar? And as regards letters received, did the meaning of these penetrate the understanding of an occult recipient at once, or were they read in the ordinary way? "

" ' Of course I have to read every word you write,' Koot Hoomi replied, ' otherwise I would make a fine mess of it. And whether it be through my physical or spiritual eyes, the time required for it is practically the same. As much may be said of my replies; for whether I precipitate or dictate them or write my answers myself, the difference in time saved is very minute. I have to think it over, to photograph every word and sentence carefully in my brain, before it can be repeated by precipitation. As the fixing on chemically prepared surfaces of the images formed by the camera requires a

---

with it, in proportion to its dynamic intensity. The Buddhist calls this his ' Skandha '; the Hindu gives it the name of ' Karma.' The adept evolves these shapes consciously; other men throw them off unconsciously."—*The Occult World*, pp. 131-2.

* *The Occult World*, p. 143.

previous arrangement within the focus of the object to be represented, for otherwise—as often found in bad photographs—the legs of the sitter might appear out of all proportion with the head, and so on—so we have to first arrange our sentences and impress every letter to appear on paper in our minds before it becomes fit to be read. For the present it is *all* I can tell you. When science will have learned more about the mystery of the lithophyl (or litho-biblion), and how the impress of leaves comes originally to take place on stones, then I will be able to make you better understand the process. But you must know and remember one thing —we but follow and servilely copy Nature in her works.' " *

One might be justified in holding the thought that further insight into the process might be forthcoming. This actually proved to be correct. For in an article entitled " Precipitation," published a few years later, the citation from the letter was also quoted; then the article continued in this manner:

" Since the above was written, the Masters have been pleased to permit the veil to be drawn aside a little more, and the *modus operandi* can thus be explained now more fully to the outsider.

" Those having even a superficial knowledge of the science of mesmerism know how the thoughts of the mesmeriser, though silently formulated in his mind are instantly transferred to that of the subject. It is not necessary for the operator, if he is sufficiently powerful, to be present near the subject to produce the above result. Some celebrated practitioners in this Science are known to have been able to put their subjects to sleep even from a distance of several days' journey. This known fact will serve us as a guide in

---

* *The Occult World*, pp. 143-4. The answer to the queries appears in *The Mahatma Letters to A. P. Sinnett*, p. 22.

comprehending the comparatively unknown subject
now under discussion. The work of writing the letters
in question is carried on by a sort of psychological
telegraphy; the Mahatmas very rarely write their letters
in the ordinary way. An electro-magnetic connection,
so to say, exists on the psychological plane between a
Mahatma and his chelas, one of whom acts as his
amanuensis. When the Master wants a letter to be
written in this way, he draws the attention of the chela,
whom he selects for the task, by causing an astral bell
(heard by so many of our Fellows and others) to be
rung near him just as the despatching telegraph office
signals to the receiving office before wiring the message.
The thoughts arising in the mind of the Mahatma are
then clothed in word, pronounced mentally, and
forced along the astral currents he sends towards the
pupil to impinge on the brain of the latter. Thence
they are borne by the nerve-currents to the palms of
his hand and the tips of his finger, which rest on a
piece of magnetically prepared paper. As the thought-
waves are thus impressed on the tissue, materials are
drawn to it from the ocean of *âkâśa* (permeating every
atom of the sensuous universe), by an occult process,
out of place here to describe, and permanent marks
are left.

"From this it is abundantly clear that the success
of such writing as above described depends chiefly
upon these things: (1) The force and the clearness with
which the thoughts are propelled, and (2) the freedom
of the receiving brain from disturbance of every
description. The case with the ordinary electric
telegraph is exactly the same. If, for some reason or
other, the battery supplying the electric power falls
below the requisite strength on any telegraph line or
there is some derangement in the receiving apparatus,
the message transmitted becomes either mutilated or
otherwise imperfectly legible. The telegram sent to
England by Reuter's agent at Simla on the classification of the opinions of Local Governments on the
Criminal Procedure Amendment Bill, which excited so

much discussion, gives us a hint as to how inaccuracies
might arise in the process of precipitation. Such
inaccuracies, in fact, do very often arise as may be
gathered from what the Mahatma says in the above
extract: ' Bear in mind,' says He, ' that these my
letters are not written, but *impressed*, or precipitated,
and *then all mistakes corrected*.' To turn to the sources
of error in the precipitation. Remembering the circumstances under which blunders arise in telegrams,
we see that if a Mahatma somehow becomes exhausted
or allows his thoughts to wander off during the process
or fails to command the requisite intensity in the astral
currents along which his thoughts are projected, or the
distracted attention of the pupil produces disturbances
in his brain and nerve-centres, the success of the process
is very much interfered with." *

Further information in regard to the clarity of the message that is being transmitted from Mahatma to chela is
available in an article entitled " Helena Petrovna
Blavatsky ". Although published posthumously and
written entertainingly in the style of a reporter having
an interview with H.P.B., Charles Johnston (the author
of the article), certainly captured Mme. Blavatsky's
characteristic expressions. The citation also deals with
the ability of a Mahatma to send a precipitation to a
person, even though he does not know the language in
which the message is to be precipitated. An explanation
is presented indicating how this is done. The first
question in the interview is asked by the reporter, Charles
Johnston:

" What about the writing in the occult letters ? " . . .

" Let me explain it this way ," she answered.

---

* *The Theosophist*, Vol. V, p. 64; republished in *Five Years of Theosophy*, pp. 518-21; also *H. P. Blavatsky Collected Writings*, Vol. VI,
pp. 118-121.

" Have you ever made experiments in thought-transference? If you have, you must have noticed that the person who receives the mental picture very often colours it, or even changes it slightly, with his own thought, and this where perfectly genuine transference of thought takes place. Well, it is something like that with the precipitated letters. One of our Masters, who perhaps does not know English, and of course has no English handwriting, wishes to precipitate a letter in answer to a question sent mentally to him. Let us say he is in Tibet, while I am in Madras or London. He has the answering thought in his mind, but not in English words. He has first to impress that thought on my brain, or on the brain of someone else who knows English, and then to take the word-forms that rise up in that other brain to answer the thought. Then he must form a clear mind-picture of the words in writing, also drawing on my brain, or the brain of whoever it is, for the shapes. Then either through me or some Chela with whom he is magnetically connected, he has to precipitate these word-shapes on paper, first sending the shapes into the Chela's mind, and then driving them into the paper, using the magnetic force of the Chela to do the printing, and collecting the material, black or blue or red, as the case may be, from the astral light. As all things dissolve into the astral light, the will of the magician can draw them forth again. So he can draw forth colours of pigments to mark the figure in the letter, using the magnetic force of the Chela to stamp them in, and guiding the whole by his own much greater magnetic force, a current of powerful will."

" That sounds quite reasonable," I answered. " Won't you show me how it is done? "

" You would have to be clairvoyant," she answered, in a perfectly direct and matter-of-fact way, "in order to see and guide the currents. But this is the point: Suppose the letter precipitated through me; it would naturally show some traces of my expressions, and even of my writing; but all the same, it would be a perfectly genuine occult phenomenon, and a real message from that Mahatma." *

With regard to the synchronization of the two minds —the Mahatma's and the chela's—a śloka from the Yogasûtras is apropos:

" The nature of the mind of another person becomes known to the ascetic when he concentrates his own mind upon that other person." †

One more citation with regard to the processes involved in precipitation may be added. While in the main it would seem to reiterate much that has already been quoted, nevertheless, because additional features are mentioned it was thought better to reproduce the entire passage. Particular attention, therefore, is now directed to these statements, with especial regard to the activities of the chela: (1) both paper and envelope are materialized; (2) the process of transmittal; (3) the use of a particular stone in order to make certain of the transmittal, and that this will result in the formation of burnt ashes more minute than atoms would be; (4) that the transmitter need not be familiar with the language that is being transmitted.

" Suppose a chela receives an order from his Master to precipitate a letter to the . . . . family, only a general idea being given to him about what he has to write. Paper and envelope are *materialized* before him, and he has only to form and shape the ideas into *his* English, and precipitate them. What shall the result be? Why, *his* English, his ethics and philosophy —his style all round. . . ."

---

* Originally published in *The Theosophical Forum,* New York, Vol. V, No. 12 and Vol. VI, Nos. 1, 2, 3—1900. Republished in *H. P. Blavatsky Collected Writings,* Vol. VIII, pp. 397-8.

† *Yoga Aphorisms* of Patañjali (W. Q. Judge's recension) Book III, śloka 19.

"Now to *send on* a letter two or three processes are used: (1) To put the envelope sealed on my forehead, and then, warning the Master to be ready for a communication, have the contents reflected by my brain carried off of His perception by the *current formed* by Him. This, if the letter is in a language I know; otherwise, if an unknown tongue, (2) to unseal it, read it *physically* with my eyes, without understanding even the words, and *that which my eyes see* is carried off to Master's perception and reflected in it in His *own* language, after which to be sure no mistake is made, I have to burn the letter with a stone I have (matches and common fire would never do), and the ashes caught by the current become more minute than atoms would be, and are *re-materialized* at any distance where Master was. . . . ." *

"Two or three times, perhaps more, letters were precipitated in *my presence* by a Chela who could not speak English and who took ideas and expressions out of my head. The phenomena in *truth* and *solemn reality* were greater at those times than ever." †

Along the same line of thought, another letter is available on the subject of precipitation and trasmittal of documents. Although it does repeat some of the explanations of the process just given above, nevertheless, there are additional factors which make the citation well worthy of being dwelt on again. The letter was written by H. P. Blavatsky, bearing the date line "Adyar, March 17th, 1885," and addressed to Mr. Sinnett:

"I have never, before beginning the service for you and Mr. Hume, transmitted and received letters to, and from Masters except for myself. If you had any idea of the difficulties, or the *modus operandi* you would

---

* From a letter written by H. P. Blavatsky; published by W. Q. Judge in *The Path*, March, 1893, Vol. VII, No. 12, p. 384.

† *Ibid.*, p. 383.

not have consented to be in my place. And yet I
never refused. . . .

"I have often facilitated phenomena of letter-
transmission by easier but still occult means. Only
as none of the Theosophists, except occultists, know
anything of either difficult or easy means of occult
transmission nor are they acquainted with occult laws,
everything is suspicious to them. Take for instance
this illustration as an instance: transmission by *mechanical*
thought transference (in contradistinction with the
conscious). The former is produced by calling first
the attention of a chela or the Mahatma. The letter
must be open and every line of it passed over the forehead, holding the breath and never taking off the part
of the letter from the latter until bell notifies it is read
and noted. The other mode is to impress every
sentence of the letter (consciously of course) still
mechanically on the brain, and then send it phrase by
phrase to the other person on the other end of the
line. This of course if the sender permits you to read
it, and believes in your honesty that you read it mechanically, only reproducing the *form* of the words and
lines on your brain—and not the meaning. But in
both instances the letter must be open and then burnt
with what we call *virgin fire* (lit neither with matches,
brimstone nor any preparation but rubbed with a
resinous, transparent little stone, a ball that no naked
hand must touch). This is done for the ashes, which,
while the paper burns become immediately invisible,
which they should not, if the paper were lit otherwise;
because they would remain by their weight and gross-
ness in the surrounding atmosphere, instead of being
transferred instantaneously to the receiver. This
double process is done for double security: for the
words transmitted from one brain to another, or to
the *âkâśa* near the Mahatma or chela may, some of
them, be omitted, whole words slip out, etc., and the
ashes be not perfectly transmitted; and in this way one
corrects the other. I cannot do that, and therefore
speak of it only as an example how deception can be

21

easily fathered. Fancy A. giving a letter for the Mahatma to B. B. goes in the adjoining room and opening the letter—not one word of which will he remember if he is a true chela and an honest man— transmits it to his brain by one of the two methods, sending one sentence after the other on the current and then proceeds to burn the letter; perhaps—he has forgotten the 'virgin stone' in his room. Leaving inadvertently the opened letter on the table, he absents himself for a few minutes. During that time A. impatient and probably suspicious enters the room. He sees his letter opened on the table. He will either take it and make an EXPOSÉ (! !) or leave it and then ask B. after he has burnt it whether he sent his letter. Of course B. will answer he has. Then will come the *exposé* with consequences you may imagine, or A. will hold his tongue and do as many do: hold for ever B. for a fraud. This is one instance out of many and a real one, given to me as a caution by Master." *

One more illustration is appropriate here, even though it is of a different type of precipitation. It has special reference to the fixation of the product, and is from one of H.P.B.'s letters:

"I have often seen M. sit with a book of most elaborate Chinese characters that he wanted to copy, and a blank book before him and he would put a pinch of black lead dust before him and then rub it in slightly on the page; and then over it precipitate ink; and then, if the image of the characters was all right and correct in his mind the characters copied would be all right, and if he happened to be interrupted then there would be a blunder, and the work would be spoilt." †

---

* From Letter No. CXXXVIII: *The Mahatma Letters to A. P. Sinnett,* pp. 470-1.

† *The Letters of H. P. Blavatsky to A. P. Sinnett,* p. 32.

In concluding this chapter on Precipitation, a final citation should be added, for it is well worth remembering. To use an " Americanism," it comes straight from the shoulder:

" I tell you a profound truth in saying that if you (like your fabled Shloma) but choose wisdom all other things will be added unto it—in time. It adds no force to our metaphysical truths that our letters are dropped from space on to your lap or come under your pillow. If our philosophy is wrong a *wonder* will not set it right. Put that conviction into your consciousness. . . . ." *

---

* *The Mahatma Letters to A. P. Sinnett*, p. 262: a Letter by the Mahatma M., bearing the notation: received at Allahabad, Feb., 1882.

CHAPTER XIV

WRITING BY MEANS OF A PROCESS ANALOGOUS TO TULKU

There is no doubt about it: the process of writing by means of Precipitation has been difficult to describe; because of the field that it covers, as well as the fact that it takes cognizance of occult laws of nature. Furthermore, it deals with powers lying dormant within man— unsuspected though they may be. The present chapter continues the exploration of the subject in the same field. The task is still more difficult, however, in that what could have been given as demonstrable evidence on this subject is no longer available. In explanation of this statement: at the time that H. P. Blavatsky prepared her manuscripts for publication, they were all written by her own hand. Had we a handwritten manuscript before us, it could be pointed to and stated: here is evidence that *this* page, or *that* page, was prepared by a process analogous to Tulku.

In support of this contention, then, reference is made again to the documents known as the certificates concerning the writing of *The Secret Doctrine*, with specific reference to these portions:

" The certificate given last year saying that the Secret Doctrine would be when finished the triple production of Upasika, M.˙. and myself was and is correct. . . . And it may then be well to indicate to those wishing to know what portions in the Secret Doctrine have been copied by the pen of Upasika into its pages, though without quotation marks, from my own manuscript and perhaps from M.˙. though the last is more difficult from the rarity of his known writing and greater ignorance of his style." *

---

* From *The Path*, April, 1893, p. 2; also *Reminiscences*, etc. pp. 115-6.

Unfortunately, as the handwritten manuscript of H.P.B. was not preserved, this demonstrable evidence may not be brought forth here. Because of this lack, the theme must therefore be handled by means of a different approach. First, an attempt should be made to explain what is meant by "writing by means of a process analogous to Tulku".

To be sure, it involves knowledge of occult laws of nature, as well as arcane operations coming under the classification of the constitution of man, familiarly known in Theosophy as the seven principles of man. When an individual has acquired knowledge of such arcane operations and has become proficient in their use, he will have attained the ability of using a method (or one of the methods) of disengaging a certain portion of his inner self from the enmeshing bonds of his outer self. Of course, more is involved in the term "outer self" than simply the physical body, but just now it is not a matter of defining terms—this will be considered elsewhere; instead an effort is being made to explain what is meant. So, for the sake of clarity, in this description a division of three stages will be outlined. It is not asserted that the description which will be provided is definitive. It is given in this manner in an attempt to understand what takes place. Therefore, the division into three stages is made principally for purposes of study.

Having acquired such a faculty as mentioned above, an individual possesses the ability of withdrawing this specific portion of his inner self so that it may "stand aside" as an onlooker. This may be regarded as the first stage. When such an occurrence has taken place, the physical vehicle is observed as a casket, and an indescribable feeling of lightness is sensed by the freed portion—in which the "superior consciousness" is situated (in distinction to the "body consciousness").

The second stage may be described as the ability to project the freed portion of the inner self to any desired location. The third stage concerns the ability to enter a vehicle—such as a prepared receptacle. That is to say, a vehicle which has been made ready by means of the withdrawal of the analogous portion of the inner self (by one capable of doing so, to be sure). When this third stage of the process has occurred, the portion of the inner self that is projected may enlighten the assumed outer vehicle, enabling this sheath to express itself in any desired manner. Since writing is the category under consideration, therefore writing will be stressed here. Consequently it is asserted that the writing will reflect the capabilities of the entrant's inner self and take on characteristics pertaining thereto.

At this point it will be appropriate to cite a śloka.

" The inner self of the ascetic may be transferred to any other body and there have complete control, because he has ceased to be mentally attached to objects of sense, and through his acquisition of the knowledge of the manner in and means by which the mind and body are connected." *

In commenting upon this śloka, Mr. Judge gave the following explanation:

" As this philosophy holds that the mind, not being the result of brain, enters the body by a certain road and is connected with it in a particular manner, this aphorism declares that, when the ascetic acquires a knowledge of the exact process of connecting mind and body, he can connect his mind with any other body, and thus transfer the power to use the organs of the occupied frame in experiencing effects from the operations of the senses." †

H. P. Blavatsky hinted that she herself had the faculty referred to above. A letter is extant describing this condition. Since she was writing to her sister, naturally the narration was given in a non-technical manner, nevertheless, it is very clearly depicted:

---

* *Yoga Aphorisms* of Patañjali, Book III, śloka 39.

† *Yoga Aphorisms*, " An Interpretation by William Q. Judge assisted by James Henderson Connelly," Point Loma edition, pp. 52-3.

"Several times a day I feel that besides me there is someone else, quite separable from me, present in my body. I never lose the consciousness of my own personality; what I feel is as if I were keeping silent and the other one—the lodger who is in me—were speaking with my tongue. For instance, I know that I have never been in the places which are described by my ' other me,' but this other one—the second me —does not lie when he tells about places and things unknown to me, because he has actually seen them and knows them well." *

Realizing that her sister would be somewhat alarmed, to say the least, by what she had written, Helena gave this explanation to Vera:

"Do not be afraid that I am off my head. All that I can say is that someone positively *inspires me* . . . more than this: someone enters me. It is not I who talk and write: it is something within me, my higher and luminous Self, that thinks and writes for me. Do not ask me, my friend, what I experience, because I could not explain it to you clearly. I do not know myself! The one thing I know is that now, when I am about to reach old age, I have become a sort of storehouse of somebody else's knowledge. . . . ." †

Directing attention to the process of writing that would take place during such occasions as intimated by H.P.B., information is available on such occurrences. Because of the fact that during the time that H. P. Blavatsky was working on *Isis Unveiled*, Col. Olcott was her constant companion and acted as her assistant, he was careful

---

* " Letters from H. P. Blavatsky to Mme. Vera de Zhelihovsky," published in *The Path*, Dec. 1894, Vol. IX, pp. 269-70.

† *Op. cit.*, Vol. IX, No. 9, p. 266. The letters were written in Russian and translated by H.P.B.'s niece, Vera, who was married to Charles Johnston. The " Letters " ran serially in *The Path*, from December, 1894, to December, 1895.

in observing all that occurred. Since he was given all
the manuscript to look over, in order to correct punctua-
tion as well as to catch obvious errors, he soon became
aware of the fact that the handwriting of the manuscript
bore distinct changes. To be sure, *Isis Unveiled* was
written before the days of the typewriter. Consequently
all the manuscript was written by hand. Any changes
in the style of handwriting were immediately discernible.
Furthermore, Col. Olcott soon observed that when the
script was different there was a corresponding change in
the mood as well as characteristics and even a difference
in the features of the writer. As narrated by Col. Olcott:

". . . the H.P.B. manuscript varied at times, and
that there were several variants of the one prevailing
script; also that each change in the writing was
accompanied by the marked alteration in the manner,
motions, expression, and literary capacity of H.P.B.
. . . Now often things were, after a while, said to
me that would be more than hints that other intelligences than H.P.B.'s were at times using her body as
a writing machine; it was never expressly said, for
example, ' I am so and so,' or ' Now this is A or B.'
It did not need that after we ' twins ' had been working
together long enough for me to become familiar with
her every peculiarity of speech, moods, and impulses.
The change was as plain as day, and by and by after
she had been out of the room and returned, a brief
study of her features and actions enabled me to say to
myself, ' This is—, or—, or—' and presently my suspicion would be confirmed by what happened. One
of these *Alter Egos* of hers, one whom I have since
personally met, wears a full beard and long moustache
that are twisted, Rajput fashion, into his side whiskers.
. . . . . Then there was another Somebody, who
disliked English so much that he never willingly talked
with me in anything but French: he had a fine artistic
talent and a passionate fondness for mechanical invention. Another one would now and then sit there,
scrawling something with a pencil and reeling off for

me dozens of poetical stanzas, which embodied, now sublime, now humorous ideas. So each of the several Somebodies had his peculiarities distinctly marked, as recognisable as those of any of our ordinary acquaintances or friends. One was jovial, fond of good stories and witty to a degree; another, all dignity, reserve, and erudition. One would be calm, patient, and benevolently helpful, another testy and sometimes exasperating. One Somebody would always be willing to emphasize his philosophical or scientific explanations of the subjects I was to write upon, by doing phenomena for my edification, while to another Somebody I dared not even mention them . . .

"Now when either of these Somebodies was 'on guard,' as I used to term it, the H.P.B. manuscript would present the identical peculiarities that it had on the last occasion when he had taken his turn at the literary work. He would, by preference, write about the class of subjects that were to his taste, and instead of H.P.B. playing the part of an amanuensis, she would then have become for the time being that other person. If you had given me in those days any page of *Isis* manuscript, I could almost certainly have told you by which Somebody it had been written. . . ." *

Nevertheless, in spite of what Col. Olcott recorded, he still was obliged to draw this conclusion:

"Like as the daylight passing through cathedral windows becomes coloured to the tints of the stained glass, so the thoughts transmitted by them through H.P.B.'s peculiar brain would have to be modified into the literary style and habits of expression to which it had been by her developed." †

With this presentation of the writing of *Isis Unveiled*, the suggested manner of regarding the writing of the

---

* *Old Diary Leaves*, Vol. I, pp. 243-6.
† *Old Diary Leaves*, Vol. I, p. 256.

work as a process akin to Tulku certainly offers a solution to the problem. The assertion is made that the same condition prevailed during the writing of *The Secret Doctrine*, as was brought forth by means of the certificate which was cited. Furthermore, the condition is applicable to certain philosophical and scientific articles which have been gathered together in the series of volumes entitled *H. P. Blavatsky Collected Writings*.

Due to the nature of the subject under consideration, it hardly seems necessary to state that this outline carries the theme only to a certain point. Yet it is hoped that sufficient clues have been given, and that an explanation has been provided in regard to what this chapter has purported to cover. This should lead to a greater degree of appreciation for the labors of H.P.B. as manifested in her writings.

CHAPTER XV

ON TULKU AND ÂVEŚA

Writers on Tibetan subjects generally employ the word "Tulku" in connection with the succession of the Dalai Lamas and the Tashi Lamas, and therefore attach to it the significance of an Incarnation, popularly expressed as an Incarnation of a Living Buddha. It is also applied to other individuals who are believed to be able to maintain a similar series of incarnations. By extension of meaning the word is employed herein to include the *process* involved in the "Incarnation". This process is explainable by means of two other Tibetan terms, namely Phowa and Trongjug. Three reasons will be given for using a single word in place of three: (1) The terms Phowa and Trongjug are not familiar words in literary works on Tibet.* Furthermore, they are practically unknown in Theosophical literature. (2) It is easier to use one word with an amplified meaning, than to employ unfamiliar terms. (3) It will be shown that the word Tulku covers a large field of thought, as described in *A Tibetan-English Dictionary* by H. A. Jäschke.

Before giving this explanation, it is necessary to remark that Tulku (thus spelled) is not listed in this manner in the dictionary. The reason for this is that this spelling is intended to represent the "sound" of the word. As remarked previously: there are two schools of thought in regard to the spelling of Tibetan words. One school prefers the system of Anglicizing a Tibetan word by rendering it according to its sound. Translators of Tibetan texts are prone to favour the spelling by means of transliterating the Tibetan characters of the written alphabet. To illustrate the point: Devachan represents

---

* The writer has only met with them in W. Y. Evans-Wentz's works.

the spelling according to the first system; bDé-ba-can is representative of the second school.

Before proceeding with the transliteration of Tulku, it will doubtless be of interest to point out that the word is actually a compound, and that both portions of the compound word have different transliterations. Furthermore, it should be mentioned that basically the Tibetan language is monosyllabic in character. That is to say, a Tibetan word is said to be composed of but one syllable. These " one-syllabled words " are, however, variously compounded, and at times the component parts are not easily recognizable. Nevertheless, when writing grammatically, each syllable (or one-syllabled word) is indicated by means of a mark, termed a *t'seg*. This t'seg is indicated by a mark equivalent to a period, although this " full-stop " (as it is termed in England) is placed in a superior position. In other words, it is placed alongside the upper right-hand portion of a Tibetan letter. In transliterating into English (or Roman) letters, this t'seg is rendered by means of a hyphen. (This accounts for the hyphenations frequently used in Tibetan words.)

Tulku, then, is in reality two one-syllabled words. When transliterated from Tibetan characters it appears as *sprul-sku*. In the dictionary, sprul appears as sprul-pa. The final " pa " is a frequently used suffix. When used along with a noun the intent of " pa " is to represent a given root as a noun. When used in connection with a verb it indicates the infinitive form of the verb, or also a participial form. In the case of *sprul-pa* it indicates an infinitive and the word is rendered to appear, to change, to transform one's self. The second component, *sku*, signifies body. Hence the compound may be rendered: "to appear in a body," or the noun-form: " the appearance in a body." Again: " to change the body "; or " a changing of the body." Again: " to transform one's self in a body." All these literal renderings are thus actually connected with the ideas which are associated with the word Tulku, as will be shown.

After giving the three grammatical meanings, the lexicographer continues regarding *sprul-pa*: this,

"according to the doctrines of Buddhism is the highest acquisition of any man, that by his own holiness has assumed divine nature, viz., as long as he is capable of acting, not having yet been absorbed into the blessed state of nothingness." *

Here, the lexicographer's literal rendition of a term has caused him to construe the words into an erroneous concept. An obvious question points out the fallacy in the statement. How can a state of nothingness be blessed? A state of nothingness signifies neither blessedness nor sorrow, neither joy nor grief; nor does it represent any of the pairs of opposites. Furthermore, this concept of a state of nothingness is not at all in keeping with the next phrase of his rendering, which is:

"This power of transformation on the part of the Buddhist is the evidence of what he understands by divine omnipotence." †

Surely, divine omnipotence is not to be equated to a state of nothingness! Of course, it is quite apparent that the literal rendition of two Tibetan terms gives rise to misconceptions such as the above. The two terms are (1) Tong-pa-nyid; (2) Nipang.

(1) Tong-pa-nyid (also transliterated sTong-pa-nyid) translated literally means emptiness, vacuity, the void; it is equivalent to the Sanskrit term Śûnyatâ of the Northern Buddhists. This term is rendered by Orientalists as the Doctrine of the Void. The lexicographer adds this notation to Tong-pa-nyid:

"the chief product of the philosophical speculations of the Buddhists, and the aim and end of all their aspirations." ‡

---

* *A Tibetan-English Dictionary*, p. 336.

† *Ibid.*

‡ *Op. cit.*, p. 223.

In the Orient it is customary to refer to the most spiritual states by figures of speech. Instead of defining a state, then, it is preferably referred to by negatives: thus Absolute Darkness signifies Absolute Light; a state of nothingness stands for a fullness—in the sense of a complete knowledge of Reality. The idea being that as soon as the mind defines a superlative state it has limited the concept. Far better is it, then, to leave it undefined. To be sure, in so far as a person immersed in the material world is concerned, an exalted state would have no material thing in it, and contrariwise, to an individual in Tong-pa-nyid the material world would be entirely illusory.

In support of these statements reference is made to one of the letters sent to Mr. Sinnett by the Mahatma M., in which he refers to Mahatma K. H. going into the state of Tong-pa-nyid.* Upon returning from that state, Mr. Sinnett was apprised of that fact in this manner:

" My Brother—I have been on a long journey after supreme knowledge, I took a long time to rest. Then, upon coming back, I had to give all my time to duty, and all my thoughts to the Great Problem. It is all over now: the New Year's festivities are at an end and I am ' Self' once more. But what is *Self?* Only a passing guest, whose concerns are all like a mirage of the great desert. . . . . " †

" Nature has linked all parts of her Empire together by subtle threads of magnetic sympathy, and, there is a mutual correlation even between a star and a man; thought runs swifter than the electric fluid, and your thought *will find me* if projected by a pure impulse, as mine will find, has found, and often impressed your mind." ‡

---

* *The Mahatma Letters to A. P. Sinnett*, p. 375.

† *Op. cit.*, p. 264.

‡ *Op. cit.*, p. 267.

Here is another extract which states what Nirvâna is —from the standpoint of a Tibetan " Gelung of the Inner Temple—a disciple of Bas-pa Dharma, the Secret Doctrine: "

" Nirvâna is the ' unconscious whole.' He who becomes a Tong-pa-nyi—he who has attained the state of absolute freedom from any desire of living personally, the highest condition of a saint—exists in non-existence, and can benefit mortals no more. He is in ' Nipang,' for he has reached the end of ' Tharlam,' the path to deliverance. . . ." *

Nirvâna—Nipang in Tibetan—will be considered presently. Attention is directed to the manner in which a Gelung-pa refers to this state: not as equivalent to nothingness but as the " unconscious whole." This is the state attained when the Circle of Necessity is completed, by means of the path of deliverance therefrom. One who is unable to benefit mortals no longer has entered the Dharmakâya-state and " exists in non-existence " in Nirvâna.

(2) Nipang, or Nirvâna, is usually rendered extinction, or annihilation by Orientalists—which again is akin to a " state of nothingness." To be sure, the orthography of the word gives such a definition when the literal significance is alone considered. For *nir* is a prepositional prefix meaning " out," and *vâna* is the past participle of the verbal root *vâ*, to blow; hence *blown out*. And this is described by the following illustration: when a lighted candle is blown the flame is blown out. Even so, something remains when the flame is blown out—i.e., the candle. And yet, as the ancient śloka has recorded it: " e'en wasted smoke remains not traceless." † Withal, consideration should be given to ascertain which portion of the human constitution it is that is extinguished, since

---

* From " Tibetan Teachings " in *H. P. Blavatsky Collected Writings*, Vol. VI, p. 111.

† From *The Voice of the Silence*, p. 34 (or. ed.).

Nirvâna is a state that is entered by an exalted human being. Annihilation applies to the portion that is left behind after Tulku has been performed, not to the consciousness which has been withdrawn from the outer self. Since the component portions of the outer self are mortal, they no longer cohere; they fall apart. This is so because the inner self, which was responsible for bringing into being the outer vesture, is no longer present with the vehicle in order to maintain its coherence. In similar manner, when death occurs the physical body is no longer able to function in its normal manner, and commences to decompose. As an aggregate, the body is blown out. But this is not applicable to the inner self which is absent from its vehicle and which no longer causes the outer self to perform its accustomed pursuits.

Attention is directed to the fact that when pundits were translating the Sanskrit texts of the Mahâyâna School of Buddhism into Tibetan, Nirvâna was translated as Mya-ngán-las adáspa (which was abbreviated to myang-adas). This signifies "having been delivered from pain." But this pain is " mental pain," not " bodily pain," hence the Tibetan phrase is translated by some into English as " the sorrowless state." It is well to note what the lexicographer had to comment under this Tibetan term:

> " the usual, illiteral Tibetan version of Nirvâna, the absolute cessation of all motion and excitement both of body and mind, which is necessarily connected with personal existence; absolute rest, which by orientals is thought to be the highest degree of happiness, imagined by some as a perfect annihilation of existence, by others, more or less, only as a cessation of all that is unpleasant in human existence. *

Resuming the consideration of sPrul-pa. It is also to be translated by emanation; *yang-sprul*, emanation of the second degree, i.e., one emanation going forth from

---

* *A Tibetan-English Dictionary*, p. 420.

another; *nying-sprul*, an emanation of a third degree. Then *sPrul-pa mkyénpa* signifies an adept in the art of sPrul-pa. The word *mkyén-pa* is often used in connection with the Buddha, signifying the supernatural perception of the Buddha. When used in phrases the following may be noted: *mthoba bzhugs-pa sprul-nas*: changing himself into a high enthroned person; *dge-slóng zhig-tu*: transforming himself into a friar; *sprul-pai rguál-po*: a transformation into a royal person, such as a descent from Avalokiteśvara, or when some other divine person incarnates as a king; *gang-la-gang adúl-gyi sprul-pa*: the all-converting Avatâra —that is to say, the divine being that has converted himself into an appearance on this earth.

So much for the field covered by the association of words with sPrul-pa. It will be noted that the basic idea reverts to the concept of transforming oneself (considered to be the root meaning associated with the word). Obviously the transformation must be into something, —whether it be a person or a state. Furthermore, the query arises: What is it that is able to make the transformation possible? Here is where the explanation of the other two Tibetan terms mentioned in connection with Tulku will be of assistance in clarifying the theme.

Phowa, signifies projection, that is projection of the consciousness. Transliterated from Tibetan characters the word is: hPho-ba. Its grammatical meaning is to change place, to shift, to migrate; *śi-hPho-ba*, means to exchange life; to die. Thus, the term signifies the ability to project one's consciousness by withdrawing it from the physical body. To be sure, when the withdrawal is effected, the next stage is the ability of having the projected consciousness function as directed by the will of the transmitter. Trongjug is definitely associated with the latter phase.

Trongjug (also spelled Drongjug) means transference and animation, in the sense of vitalizing a body. Trongjug, therefore, deals with the science of animating a human form by means of the consciousness—which has been projected by Phowa. Thus, for instance, in the event that a human form has been vacated by the

22

death of an individual, the science of Trongjug would enable the projected consciousness to reanimate the abandoned human vehicle.

At this point, by supplying the cognate Sanskrit term, yet another factor is added towards the clarification of the theme. The word is Âveśa. Its significance is readily discernible. The prefix *â* in connection with verbs of motion means "in," "into." *Veśa* is derived from the verbal root, *viś*, signifying to enter, to possess. Hence the compound may be rendered: the entrance into, the taking possession of—a vehicle (an upâdhi).

CLASSICAL EXAMPLES OF ÂVEŚA AND TULKU

The classical example of the demonstration of the employment of the Sanskrit Âveśa is related in connection with the illumined Hindu teacher, Śankarâchârya. As the story runs: Śankarâchârya was one day holding a philosophical discourse with Mandana Misra—a renowned sage of the city of Mâhishmatî. For it was the custom of Śankarâchârya to expound the Vedas by means of dissertations held with sages as he travelled from place to place. Upon completing his discussion with Mandana Misra, the teacher continued it with the sage's wife. To every question that was put, an immediate reply was forthcoming. However, be it known, the wife of Mandana Misra was no common mortal, she was an embodiment of Sarasvatî herself, and the goddess of love determined she was not to be outdone, not even by the greatest of sages. Biding her time, at an appropriate pause, she quipped: "And what is the science of love?"

Śankarâchârya was, indeed, taken aback. He had no ready reply. Instead of the dissertation continuing like the flow of the Ganges, the discourse was marked by silence. Was the great sage to be outwitted by this clever opponent? Not so fast.

"Tarry a while, Sarasvatî—for she you must be, to have thought up such a query. Be patient! It will be necessary for me to interrupt our discussion for a while.

You shall have your answer as soon as I return to this very spot to continue the discourse."

Whereupon, gathering his disciples, Śankarâchârya left the city of Mâhishmatî and went into the forest. To his group he confided: "Guard ye well my mortal vehicle. I shall depart from it for a while, demonstrating for you the science of Âveśa. Sarasvatî's question is deserving of a response. And she shall certainly be answered— after I have learned the art of love."

Meanwhile, there in that very forest, under a tree lay the recumbent form of King Amaraka, for the monarch was dying. Around him his retinue had gathered, giving way to mourning, because of the impending departure of their sovereign. Grief-stricken, they knew not what to do. They watched as their beloved ruler breathed his last. He was no more. . . .

But their grief suddenly changed to wonder. They could not believe their senses. Their king was no longer prostrate. He raised himself. Nay, more, he stood up before the amazed group. His retinue could see that their sovereign's eyes were filled with the light of life. Before they could resume their accustomed demeanor they heard the voice of King Amaraka commanding them to cease weeping and make ready for the return to the palace.

Back at the royal mansion a change in the regal demesne was clearly evident. Instead of engaging in outdoor pursuits in the forest, magnificent festivities were instituted and kingly splendor exhibited as never before. Selected ministers were delegated to search the kingdom for the most beautiful damsels, who were invited to partake of the sovereign's hospitality. Along with the princely festivities the ministers marvelled still more at the superior intelligence displayed by their rejuvenated sovereign. They took counsel among themselves, the most sagacious opining that they must be witnessing the fabled demonstration of Âveśa—that some superior being had stepped into the body at the time that the former King Amaraka had swooned away in the forest.

Having come to this conclusion, the ministers reasoned: well, then, if such a superior being had indeed revivified the frame of the monarch, it would be just as simple a matter for him to leave as easily as he had come, and reassume his cast-off vehicle. Whereupon the chief minister issued a decree (without his sovereign's knowledge) commanding that all persons who had departed from life to take up their abode in the invisible realms, should forthwith have their bodies placed upon the funeral pyre. By thus cremating all vacated bodies, the ministers opined, they could thus prevent the new king from leaving his assumed vehicle.

Meanwhile, Śankarâchârya's disciples were become fearful, in their turn, lest their beloved master be too enamored in his new role and become too much absorbed in royal tasks thus continuing to reign in his borrowed vesture. "Let us go to the royal palace," said Padmapada, Śankarâchârya's first pupil. "Let us present ourselves before the monarch as singers. We can spin a tale around beautiful music, telling our gurudeva how we long for his return." And so they set out for the king's castle, leaving the vacant form of their master unguarded —not aware of the decree that had been issued.

Arriving at the palace, the festivities were in full swing: the ruler was surrounded by his courtiers, the vast hall was brilliantly lit and resounded with gaiety. The singers were ushered before the assemblage and marvelled greatly at what they beheld. Their singing, in very truth, was so melodious and so entrancing that all persons were carried along with it, seemingly spellbound by the strains.

The music had the desired effect upon Śankarâchârya. Before his attendants were aware of what was occurring, the king graciously dismissed the singers and left the hall. Entering his private chamber, Śankarâchârya released himself from the borrowed form and sought out his own. Barely in time was the exit performed. For his own unguarded body had in very truth been placed upon a pyre. In fact the funeral pile had already been lit and flames were commencing to mount to the skies. Entering his own form, Śankarâchârya stepped over the rising flames unscathed, shining with the illumination which streamed from his own being.

Rejoining his band of disciples, in a group they wended their way to the city of Mâhishmatî. Going to the dwelling of Mandana Misra, Śankarâchârya called to Sarasvatî to seat herself, so that the interrupted discourse might be continued. Forthwith, in response to her repeated question, the sage gave the required answer to the goddess concerning the science of love, embellished with wit and wisdom.

A fanciful story, say you? Perhaps. Nevertheless it is related by one of the biographers of Śankarâchârya, named Mâdhava, in his work called *Śankaravijaya* (a title which may be rendered " the Triumph of Śankara ".) It certainly illustrates the performance of Âveśa (or Tulku), albeit in dramatic manner.

When writing an article on Śankarâchârya for *The Theosophist*, Kashinath Trimbak Telang, M.A., LL.B., referred to the Âveśa performed by the great Sage, stating that he " caused his soul to enter the corpse " of King Amaraka. H. P. Blavatsky availed herself of her editorial prerogative to add an enlightening memorandum as a footnote:

" This incident is too important to pass by without editorial comment. The power of the Yogi to quit his own body and enter and animate that of another person, though affirmed by Patañjali and included among the Siddhis of Krishna, is discredited by Europeanized young Indians. Naturally enough, since, as Western biologists deny a soul to man, it is an unthinkable proposition to them that the Yogi's soul should be able to enter another's body. That such an unreasoning infidelity should prevail among the pupils of European schools, is quite reason enough why an effect should be made to revive in India those schools of Psychology in which the Âryan youth were theoretically and practically taught the occult laws of Man and Nature. We, who have at least some trifling acquaintance with modern science, do not hesitate to affirm our belief that this temporary transmigration of souls is possible. We may even go so far as to say that

the phenomenon has been experimentally proven to us
—in New York, among other places. And, since we
would be among the last to require so marvellous a
statement to be accepted upon any one's unsupported
testimony, we urge our readers to first study Âryan
literature, and then get from personal experience the
corroborative evidence. The result must inevitably
be to satisfy every honest inquirer, that Patañjali
and Śankarâchârya did, and Tyndall, Carpenter
and Huxley do not, know the secrets of our
being." *

Resuming the consideration of Âveśa by means of
another example in story form, there is one available in
a Tamil story-book entitled *Pésâmadandé Kathai*. This
title signifies The Vanquishing of Pésâmadandé. It
illustrates Âveśa of another type. While fanciful in
character, nevertheless it serves the purpose of imparting
knowledge—as fairy-stories often do.

Princess Pésâmadandé had made a vow that she would
maintain silence to all suitors that approached her, and
would give herself in marriage only to the prince who
would unseal her lips. To all comers, then, the princess
remained obdurate. She was determined not to be won
over from her solitude. And so it went on, until the
king-magician, Vikramâdityâ decided to try his hand in
the venture. Summoning his Râkshasa,† Bhetâla by
name, the magician ordered Bhetâla to bear him directly
into the princess's own chamber. Entreating the maiden
to respond to him, Vikramâdityâ received no replioo to
his advances. Whereupon the magician had recourse
to Mâyâ.

---

* Jan. 1880, Vol. I, p. 89; *The Complete Works of H. P. Blavatsky*,
II, 48.

† A Râkshasa is usually translated "demon." But there is no
cause for naming a fairy (or elemental) a demon, unless the being
is a wicked elemental. Here the Râkshasa certainly fulfilled the
commands of his master and is deserving of being called a good
fairy.

Commanding his Râkshasa, he had him enter into (Âveśa) each one of the ladies-in-waiting, so that all of them sang the praises of the king to their princess, and upbraided her for not responding to the king. This was too much for Pésâmadandé. She dismissed all her ladies and drew a curtain between herself and Vikramâdityâ. Not discomfited by this, the magician ordered Bhetâla to enter into the curtain and importune the damsel. She cast the curtain aside, only to find that her own sari was talking to her. Flinging that into a corner, her undergarment went on with the conversation. Tossed off, the four legs of the charpai (or lounge) continued addressing her, but even then the princess was not deflected from her purpose.

The magician had to resort to yet another type of magic. He turned his Râkshasa into a beautiful parrot—so beautiful that the princess beckoned the parrot to come to her. Forthwith the parrot went on to tell Pésâmadandé that she was obsessed by Śani, the deva of misfortune, and would be subjected to bad luck. The damsel could contain herself no longer. She knelt before the king and acknowledged that she had been vanquished.

While this story does not indicate an Âveśa of person to person, nevertheless it somewhat resembles the state or condition associated with the aspect of Tulku connected with H.P.B.—that is to say, an entrance into and departure as desired. This will be shown in the chapter dealing with that aspect.

Turning now to the land of Tibet for a story. One may be related which is even more direct to the point. In the land of Bod there lived a prince, who was a devoted follower of the precepts of the Buddha and who sought to exemplify the Noble Eightfold Path. As well as being versed in yoga, he had become accomplished in Tulku, particularly in the science of Trongjug (reanimation). One day he set forth on a mission accompanied by his friend, the prime minister's son, who also was a practitioner of the science of reanimation. On their way they spied a hawk winging its silent way above them. Suddenly the hawk swooped down upon an unsuspecting bird. It was a mother-bird, so intent upon bringing food to her fledgelings that she did not detect the danger lurking over her.

The prince's heart was moved by compassion, upon seeing the plight of the nestlings, pleading for nourishment and no mother-bird to still their shrill cries. The royal son frightened away the hawk, who dropped the lifeless form. Recovering the bird, the prince said to his companion: "Watch over my human frame, the while I practise the secret art. I will reanimate the mother-bird so that she may nourish her fledgelings; and then I shall return to my form."

And so it came to pass. With the reanimation of the feathered creature it resumed its motherly care of her nestlings. But mark the calamity that befell the prince! His companion, seeing the lifeless form of the royal son, was overcome by an iniquitous desire. He took advantage of the prince's absence therefrom and likewise practised the secret art. Withdrawing from his own frame, the prime minister's son transferred his consciousness to that of the motionless form of the prince. He reanimated the form and took possession of it. In fact, the prime minster's son refused to quit the usurped royal form. And the reason for it? It was later on proved that he had been secretly in love with the prince's wife.

As for the prince: perforce he was obliged to enter the body which the prime minister's son had vacated. And the story concludes by relating that it was only after several years that the prime minister's son was finally persuaded to leave the prince's frame and resume his own.

It is said that gurus are fond of narrating this story, especially to anyone seeking information on Tulku and the projection of the consciousness.

Another story in connection with Trongjug is centred around Marpa, the preceptor of Milarepa. Milarepa is regarded as the celebrated Tibetan Buddhist yogin who, it is said, attained Buddhahood in but one earthly incarnation. His guru, Marpa, so the story runs, was advised by his guru-preceptor, Naropa, to pass on the teaching relative to the transference of consciousness from one body to another, to his disciple Milarepa. Marpa bided his time, however, and did not hasten about doing so. Because of this, a misfortune befell his plans, consequently they were never fulfilled.

Marpa had a son, Doday-Bum, by name, and to him the guru imparted the teaching concerning Trongjug. But a mishap occurred to Doday-Bum. He met with death so suddenly and unexpectedly that no human frame in the vicinity was available to him for the performance of Tulku. There was no recourse for Doday-Bum other than to make use of a temporary vehicle and perform a transitional Trongjug. This he proceeded to do. Like a bird flying out of an open skylight, he vacated his human form. Then, following the method of transference in which he had been instructed, he projected his consciousness into the frame of a pigeon which had just died, and reanimated it.

Marpa, thereupon, by means of yoga, directed the pigeon to speed over the Himalayas, to the land of Hindusthan. There upon a funeral pyre lay the body of a boy of the Brâhmana caste. To it flew the pigeon. Approaching the vacated body, the pigeon cooed thrice and immediately fell down dead—to the amazement of the gathered group of relatives. But stranger still was their wonderment when they beheld their boy sit up, rise, and then descend from the funeral pyre. With great joy and acclamation was he greeted and escorted to the family home.

So much for stories about Tulku. Each one has its especial significance. When brought together they are representative of the teachings on the subject.

A Discourse on Yoga and the Siddhis

At this point an inclusion of a discussion with a Brahman on Yoga and the Siddhis, including particular reference to the science of Âveśa (regarded as one of the Siddhis), gives an insight into the subject from the point of view of the Hindu pundit. In order to indicate how the dissertation occurred, it will be introduced by means of a short biographical memorandum provided by Colonel H.S. Olcott, who was indeed responsible for framing the questions which were asked during the progress of the inquiry.

Before leaving America for India in December, 1878, Col. Olcott had been in correspondence with the Bombay branch of the Ârya Samâj, an organization in India then holding views similar to those of The Theosophical Society. On arrival at Bombay, the headquarters of The Theosophical Society was established in that city in February of 1879. After an extended trip of Ceylon, occupying the spring of 1880, in response to an invitation from the Sinnetts to visit them at Simla, H. P. Blavatsky and Col. Olcott set out in late summer for the north of India. On the 30th of August they arrived at Meerut and stayed there for several days. On their arrival they were met at the railway station by the entire local branch of the Ârya Samâj. A few days afterwards, Swâmi Dâyânand Saraswati,* the leader of the Ârya Samâj, called on the Theosophists.† One of the purposes of his

---

* H. P. B. described Swâmi Dâyânand Saraswati as a " first class scholar, a man who knows his Sanskrit as no one else here, a *Yogi* who has spent seven years in the *jungles* (a brush forest, a dense virgin growth, deserts covered with tropical vegetation where live but ferocious beasts and *Yogis* who have no fear of them), who is deeply versed in the occult science and the secrets of the pagodas, a Brahman himself . . ."—*The Complete Works of H. P. Blavatsky*, II, 46-47.

† Unfortunately, within two years of this meeting with the Theosophists, the Swâmi had altered the aims and purposes of his organization to such an extent that it became simply another Hindu sect, and not at all compatible with the Theosophical aims. Because of this, Col. Olcott realized that it was no longer possible to continue the amalgamation of the two organizations. Therefore a severance of the federation was accomplished in 1882. Writes Col. Olcott: " The Swâmi was undoubtedly a great man, a learned Sanskrit Pandit, with immense pluck, force of will and self-reliance— a leader of men. When we first met him, in 1879, he had recently recovered from an attack of cholera and his physique was more refined and delicate than usual. I thought him strikingly handsome; tall, dignified in carriage, and gracious in manner towards us, he made a very strong impression upon our imaginations."— *Old Diary Leaves*, I, 406-7 (2nd ed.).

visit was to arrange for the holding of a meeting, so that
as many members of the Ârya Samâj in the neighboring
localities might attend the gathering. Col. Olcott
welcomed the opportunity, inasmuch as the occasion
enabled him to prepare a series of questions and thus
have the Swâmi answer them publicly. Swâmi
Dâyânand responded capably to all the queries. Later,
the Colonel had these questions and answers published in
The Theosophist of December, 1880, from which magazine
the following are cited:

"The first question propounded to the Swami was
whether Yoga was a true science, or but a metaphysical
speculation; whether Patañjali described psychical
powers attainable by man, and whether they had
been attained, or not.

"The Swami's answer was that Yoga was true and
based upon a knowledge of the laws of Nature.

"It was then asked whether these powers could still
be acquired, or had the time passed by.

"The answer was that Nature's laws are unchange-
able and illimitable: what had been done once could
be done now. Not only can the man of today learn
to do all the things described by the ancient writers,
but he himself, the Swami, could teach the methods
to anyone who might sincerely wish to take up that
course of life. Many had come to him professing their
desire and asserting their ability to command success;
he had tried three, but all failed. One was a resident
of Agra. They began well, but soon grew impatient
of having to confine themselves to what they regarded
as trivial efforts, and, to their surprise, broke down
suddenly. Yoga is the most difficult science of all to
learn, and few men are capable of acquiring it now.

"He was asked if there are now living any real
Yogis who can at will produce the wonderful
phenomenon described in Aryan books.

"His reply was that there are such living men.
Their number is small. They live in retired places,
and in their proper persons seldom or never appear in

public. Their secrets are never communicated by
them to the profane, nor do they teach their secret
science (Vidyâ) except to such as upon trial they find
deserving.

" Colonel Olcott asked whether those great masters
(Mahatmas) are invariably dressed in the saffron
clothes of the ordinary sannyâsi or fakir we see every
day, or in common costume.

" The Swami answered, in either the one or the
other, as they may prefer, or circumstances require.

" In reply to the request that without suggestion he
would state what specific powers the proficient in
Yoga enjoys, he said that the true Yogi can do that
which the vulgar call miracles. It is needless to make
a list of his powers, for practically his power is limited
only by his desire and the strength of his will. Among
other things he can exchange thoughts with his brother
Yogis at any distance, even though they be as far apart
as one pole from the other, and have no visible external
means of communication, such as the telegraph or post.
He can read the thoughts of others. He can pass (in
his inner self) from one place to another, and so be
independent of the ordinary means of conveyance, and
that at a speed incalculably greater than that of the
railway engine. He can walk upon the water or in
the air above the surface of the ground. He can pass
his own soul (*Âtman*) from his own body into that of
another person, either for a short time or for years, as he
chooses. He can prolong the natural term of the life
of his own body by withdrawing his *Âtman* from it
during the hours of sleep, and so, by reducing the
activity of the vital processes to a minimum, avoid
the greater part of the natural wear and tear. The
time so occupied is so much time to be added to the
natural sum of the physical existence of the bodily
machine.

" *Question.* Up to what day, hour, or minute of his
own bodily life can the Yogi exercise this power of
transferring his *Âtman,* or inner self, to the body of
another?

" *Answer.* Until the last minute, or even second, of his natural term of life. He knows beforehand, to a second, when his body must die, and until that second strikes, he may project his soul into another person's body if one is ready for his occupancy. But, should he allow that instant to pass, then he can do no more. The cord is snapped for ever, and the Yogi, if not sufficiently purified and perfected to be enabled to obtain *Moksha*, must follow the common law of rebirth. The only difference between his case and that of other men is, that he, having become a far more intellectual, good, and wise being than they, is reborn under better conditions.

" *Q.* Can a Yogi prolong his life to the following extent; say the natural life of his own body is seventy years, can he, just before the death of that body, enter the body of a child of six years, live in that another term of seventy years, remove from that to another, and live in it a third seventy?

" *A.* He can, and can thus prolong his stay on earth to about the term of four hundred years.

" *Q.* Can a Yogi thus pass from his own body into that of a woman?

" *A.* With as much ease as a man can, if he chooses, put on himself the dress of a woman, so he can put over his own *Âtman* her physical form. Externally, he would then be in every physical aspect and relation a woman; internally himself.

" *Q.* I have met two such; that is to say, two persons who appeared women, but who were entirely masculine in everything but the body. One of them, you remember, we visited together at Benares, in a temple on the bank of the Ganges.

" *A.* Yes, ' Majji.' *

---

* In a previous chapter of *Old Diary Leaves*, Col. Olcott relates:

" we all drove to the retreat of Majji, a very well known female ascetic, learned in Vedânta, who occupied a *guhâ* (excavated cave) with buildings above ground, on the bank of the Ganges, a mile

"*Q*. How many kinds of Yoga practice are there?

"*A*. Two—*Hatha-Yoga* and *Râja-Yoga*. Under the former the student undergoes physical trials and hardships for the purpose of subjecting his physical body to the will. For example, the swinging of one's body from a tree, head downwards, at a little distance from five burning fires, etc. In *Râja-Yoga* nothing of the kind is required. It is a system of mental training by which the mind is made the servant of the will. The one—*Hatha-Yoga*—gives physical results; the other —*Râja-Yoga*—spiritual powers. He who would become perfect in *Râja* must have passed through the training in *Hatha*.

"*Q*. But are there not persons who possess the *Siddhis*, or powers, of the *Râja-Yoga*, without ever having passed through the terrible ordeal of the *Hatha*? I certainly have met three such in India, and they themselves told me they had never submitted their bodies to torture.

"*A*. Then they practised *Hatha* in their previous birth.

"*Q*. Explain, if you please, how we may distinguish between real and false phenomena when produced by one supposed to be a *Yogi*.

"*A*. Phenomena and phenomenal appearances are of three kinds: the lowest are produced by sleight-of-hand or dexterity; the second, by chemical or

---

or two below the city of Benares. , , , At that time Majji appeared about forty years of age, fair-skinned, with a calm dignity and grace of gesture that commanded respect. Her voice was tender in tone, face and body plump, eyes full of intelligence and fire." (ch. viii, pp. 120-1)

" A return visit paid by Majji to H.P.B. the next morning caused surprise, as we were told, it was a most unusual thing for her to call upon anybody save her Guru, and upon a European never . . . . she freely told Mrs. Gordon, Damodar, and myself, in H.P.B.'s absence, a marvellous tale about her. She said that H.P.B.'s body was occupied by a Yogi, who was working it so far as he could for the spread of Eastern philosophy. It was the third body he had so used, and his total age in the three bodies was about 150 years." (*Op. cit.*, pp. 123-4)

mechanical aids or appliances; the third and highest,
by the occult powers of man. Whenever anything
of a startling nature is exhibited by either of the first
two means, and it is falsely represented to have been
of an unnatural, or super-natural, or miraculous
character, that is properly called a *tamâsha*, or dishonest
deception. But if the true and current explanation
of such surprising effect is given, then it should be
classed as a simple exhibition of scientific or technical
skill, and is to be called *Vyavahâra-Vidyâ*. Effects
produced by the sole exercise of the trained human
will, without apparatus or mechanical aids, are
true *Yoga*.

"*Q*. Define the nature of the human *Âtman*.

"*A*. In the *Âtman* there are twenty-four powers.
Among these are will, passivity, action, determined
perception or knowledge, strong memory, etc. When
all these powers are brought to bear upon the external
world, the practitioner produces effects which are
properly classed under the head of Physical Science.
When he applies them to the internal world, that is
Spiritual Philosophy—*Yoga*—*Antaryoga*—or inner *Yoga*.
When two men talk to each other from far distant
places by means of the telegraph, that is *Vyavahâra-Vidyâ*;
when without any apparatus and by employing their
knowledge of natural forces and currents, it is *Yoga
Vidyâ*. It is also *Yoga Vidyâ* when an adept in the
science causes articles of any kind to be brought to him
from a distance, or sends them from himself to any distant place, in either case without visible means of transportation, such as railways, messengers, or what not.
The former is called *Âkarshana* (attraction), the latter
Preshana [repulsion]. The ancients thoroughly understood the laws of the attraction and repulsion of all
things in Nature, between each other, and the *Yoga*
phenomena are based upon that knowledge. The
Yogi changes or intensifies these attractions and
repulsions at will.

"*Q*. What are the prerequisites for one who wishes
to acquire these powers?

" *A*. These essentials are: (1) A desire to learn. Such a desire as the starving man has for food, or a thirsty one for water; an intense and eager yearning. (2) Perfect control over the passions and desires. (3) Chastity; pure companionship; pure food—that which brings into the body none but pure influences; the frequenting of a pure locality, one free from vicious taint of any kind; pure air; and seclusion. He must be endowed with intelligence—that he may comprehend the principles of Nature; concentrativeness—that his thoughts may be prevented from wandering; and self-control—that he may always be master over his passions and weaknesses. Five things he must relinquish—Ignorance, Egotism (conceit), Passion (sensual), Selfishness, and Fear of Death.

" *Q*. You do not believe, then, that the *Yogi* acts contrary to natural laws?

" *A*. Never; nothing happens contrary to the laws of Nature. By *Hatha-Yoga* one can accomplish a certain range of minor phenomena, as, for instance, to draw all his vitality into a single finger, or, when in Dhyâna (a state of mental quiescence), to know another's thoughts. By *Râja-Yoga* he becomes a *Siddha*: he can do whatever he wills, and know whatever he desires to know, even languages which he has never studied. But all these are in strict harmony with natural laws.

" *Q*. I have occasionally seen inanimate articles duplicated before my eyes, such as letters, coins, pencils, jewelry: how is this to be accounted for?

" *A*. In the atmosphere are the particles of every visible thing, in a highly diffused state. The *Yogi* knowing how to concentrate these, does so by the exercise of his will, and forms them into any shape of which he can picture to himself this model.

" Col. Olcott asked the Swami what he would call certain phenomena heretofore produced by Madame Blavatsky in the presence of witnesses—such as the causing of a shower of roses to fall in a room at Benares last year, the ringing of bells in the air, the causing of the flame of a lamp to gradually diminish until it

almost went out, and then at command to blaze up
again to the top of the chimney, without touching the
regulator in either instance, etc. The answer was that
these were phenomena of *Yoga*. Some of them might
be imitated by tricksters and then would be mere
tamâsha; but these were not of that class." *

The discourse on Yoga and the Siddhis between Colonel
Olcott and Swâmi Dayânand proved to be a lengthy one,
but since it dealt with so many of the phases associated
with H. P. Blavatsky and her writings, as well as with
her phenomena and other activities in connection with
her Teachers and with the Theosophical Society, it was
deemed advisable to reproduce the dissertation in full.
Attention is called to Col. Olcott's summation which
follows, with especial notice being paid to his comments
concerning Hatha-Yoga and Râja-Yoga.

"I think this one of the simplest, clearest, most
sententious and most suggestive digests of the Indian
view of the high science of Yoga in literature. My
respondent was one of the most distinctly Aryan
personages of the time, a man of large erudition, an
experienced ascetic, a powerful orator, and an intense
patriot. Attention should be paid to the Swami's
assertion that one *cannot* pass on to the practice of
Râja-Yoga without first having subjugated the physical
body by a course of Hatha-Yoga, or physiological
training, and that if one be found who is confining
himself with success to Râja-Yoga, this is *prima facie*
proof of his having done his Hatha-Yoga in the anterior
birth. This idea is shared by all orthodox educated
Hindus whom I have met, but my readers will decide
for themselves whether it is reasonable or not. We
may, at any rate, say that nothing is clearer than that
man's personal evolution towards the spiritual life is

---

* Reproduced in *Old Diary Leaves*, Vol. II, ch. xiv, pp. 215-222
(2nd ed.).

23

progressive, and that every stage of physical self-mastery must be passed before ' liberation ' can be attained. . . . . I think the will can be fortified even better without than with physical torture." *

On the Projection of the Consciousness

In the discourse one of the Siddhis mentioned indicated that a Yogi had the ability to project his consciousness to any desired distance. In an endeavor to obtain an understanding of the subject, particularly concerning the ability of an individual to make his projected consciousness visible to other persons, H. P. Blavatsky suggested that attention should be focused upon the occurrence known as the manifestation of the phenomenon of the " spirit hand " which may be witnessed at mediumistic seances. In writing on this theme, the projected consciousness is referred to as the appearance of the " astral body." It should be borne in mind that at the period of the writing of *Isis Unveiled*, the terminology for the exposition of the teachings being presented through the instrumentality of the Theosophical Society had not been formulated. Because of this, available terms were frequently used in more than one sense. " Astral body " is a case in point. The term was applied to three distinct rûpas, or vehicles, altogether different in character: (1) the Linga-śarîra, the model body, which is the vehicle of the Life-principle, Prâna; (2) the Kâma-rûpa, the eidolon, or shade, which comes into existence in the astral world for a certain time-period only after death occurs; (3) the Mâyâvi-rûpa, literally the " illusory form," or the body of projection. It is usually a replica of the individual's moral vehicle, although the consciousness has been projected into that form. Here is the citation on this theme:

" A familiar example of one phase of the power of the soul or astral body to manifest itself, is the phenomenon of the so-called spirit-hand. In the presence

---

* *Old Diary Leaves*, II, 222-3.

of certain mediums these seemingly detached members will gradually develop from a luminous nebula, pick up a pencil, write messages, and then dissolve before the eyes of the witnesses. Many such cases are recorded by perfectly competent and trustworthy persons. . . .

"Among those who have written most intelligently upon the subject of these luminous hands, may be reckoned Dr. Francis Gerry Fairfield, author of *Ten Years among the Mediums*, . . . A medium himself, he is yet a strong opponent of the spiritualistic theory. Discussing the subject of the ' phantom hand,' he testifies that ' this the writer has personally witnessed, under conditions of test provided by himself, in his own room, in full daylight, with the medium seated upon a sofa from six to eight feet from the table hovering upon which the apparition (the hand) appeared. The application of the poles of a horseshoe magnet to the hand caused it to waver perceptibly, and threw the medium into violent convulsions—pretty positive evidence that *the force concerned in the phenomenon was generated in his own nervous system*! '

"Dr. Fairfield's deduction that the fluttering phantom hand is an emanation from the medium is logical, and it is correct. The test of the horse-shoe magnet proves in a scientific way what every kabalist would affirm upon the authority of experience, no less than philosophy. The ' force concerned in the phenomenon ' is the will of the medium, exercised unconsciously to the outer man, which for the time is semi-paralyzed and cataleptic; the phantom hand an extrusion of the man's inner or astral member. . . .

"The same principle involved in the unconscious extrusion of a phantom limb by the cataleptic medium, applies to the projection of his entire ' double ' or astral body. This may be withdrawn by the will of the medium's own inner self, without his retaining in his physical brain any recollection of such an intent —that is one phase of man's dual capacity." *

---

* *Isis Unveiled*, Vol. II, pp. 594-5.

" The medium need not exercise any *will-power*. It suffices that she or he shall know what is expected by the investigators. The medium's ' spiritual ' entity, when not obsessed by other spirits, will act outside the will or consciousness of the physical being, as surely as it acts when within the body during a fit of somnambulism. Its perceptions, external and internal, will be acuter and far more developed, precisely as they are in the sleep-walker." *

On the other hand, one who has mastered the ability to perform consciously the withdrawal and projection of his consciousness, does exercise his will power. Moreover, he is able to demonstrate this ability at will. H. P. Blavatsky records the witnessing of such a withdrawal and projection. Following this she relates some instances culled from classical writers who mention individuals renowned for this accomplishment:

" An adept can not only project and make visible a hand, a foot, or any other portion of his body, but the whole of it. We have seen one do this, in full day, while his hands and feet were being held by a skeptical friend whom he wished to surprise. Little by little the whole astral body oozed out like a vapory cloud, until before us stood two forms, of which the second was an exact duplicate of the first, only slightly more shadowy." †

" Epimenides, the Orphikos, was renowned for his ' sacred and marvelous nature,' and for the faculty his soul possessed of quitting its body ' *as long and as often as it pleased.*' The ancient philosophers who have testified to this ability may be reckoned by dozens. Apollonius left his body at a moment's notice, but it must be remembered Apollonius was an adept—a ' magician.' Had he been simply a medium, he

---

* *Isis Unveiled*, Vol. II, p. 596.

† *Op. cit.*, II, 596.

could not have performed such feats *at will*.
Empedocles of Agrigentum, the Pythagorean thauma-
turgist, required no *conditions* to arrest a waterspout
which had broken over the city. Neither did he
need any to recall a woman to life, as he did.
Apollonius used no *darkened* room in which to perform
his aethrobatic feats. Vanishing suddenly in the air
before the eyes of Domitian and a whole crowd of
witnesses (many thousands), he appeared an hour
after in the grotto of Puteoli. But investigation would
have shown that his physical body having become
invisible by the concentration of Âkâśa about it, he
could walk off unperceived to some secure retreat in the
neighbourhood, and an hour after his astral form appear
at Puteoli to his friends, and seem to be the man himself.

" No more did Simon Magus wait to be entranced
to fly off in the air before the apostles and crowds of
witnesses. ' It requires no conjuration and ceremonies;
circle-making and incensing are mere nonsense and
juggling,' says Paracelsus. The human spirit ' is so
great a thing that no man can express it; . . . If
we rightly understood its power, nothing would be
impossible to us on earth." *

Since it has been stated that the chief purpose of this
work is to demonstrate by means of H. P. Blavatsky's
writings that she was familiar with the processes connected
with Tulku, and that her works may be employed for
an elucidation of these processes, citations are necessary to
demonstrate this—as should already be apparent to the
reader. Consequently, the theme may be continued by
means of additional extracts from that very informative
work, which she first named " The Veil of Isis, " but later
changed to *Isis Unveiled*. In writing upon a summary of
the principles of Magic she penned these paragraphs:

" One phase of magical skill is the voluntary and
conscious withdrawal of the inner man (astral form)

---

* *Isis Unveiled*, Vol. II, pp. 597-8.

from the outer man (physical body). In the cases of some mediums withdrawal occurs, but it is unconscious and involuntary. With the latter the body is more or less cataleptic at such times; but with the adept the absence of the astral form would not be noticed, for the physical senses are alert, and the individual appears only as though in a fit of abstraction—' a brown study', as some call it.

" To the movements of the wandering astral form neither time nor space offer obstacles. The thauma-turgist, thoroughly skilled in occult science, can cause himself (that is, his physical body) to *seem* to disappear, or to apparently take on any shape that he may choose. He may make his astral form visible, or he may give it protean appearances. In both cases these results will be achieved by a mesmeric hallucination of the senses of all witnesses, simultaneously brought on. This hallucination is so perfect that the subject of it would stake his life that he saw a reality, when it is but a picture in his own mind, impressed upon his con-sciousness by the irresistible will of the mesmerizer.

" But, while the astral form can go anywhere, pene-trate any obstacle, and be seen at any distance from the physical body, the latter is dependent upon ordinary methods of transportation. It may be levitated under prescribed magnetic conditions, but not pass from one locality to another except in the usual way. Hence we discredit all stories of the aerial flight of mediums in body, for such would be miracle, and miracle we repudiate. Inert matter may be, in certain cases and under certain conditions, disintegrated, passed through walls, and recombined, but living animal organisms cannot." *

An important point has just been mentioned in the last sentence of the above extract, namely the " disinte-gration " and " recombining " of " inert matter. "

---

* *Isis Unveiled*, II, 588-9.

This is the very method employed in the transmission of letters from the Mahatmas (the theme of Chapter 13). That the process was so clearly stated at the time of the writing of her first major work, demonstrates the fact that H.P.B. was familiar with the procedure. The term "astral form," as used in the two cited paragraphs, signifies the mâyâvi-rûpa, the conscious projection of which enables the thaumaturgist to transport himself wherever desired. As has been explained, this is one of the processes connected with Tulku. The next paragraph of the following quotation uses the same term, "astral form"—again indicating the mâyâvi-rûpa—and mentions what the "adept sorcerer" does in this performance of Tulku.

"Swedenborgians believe and arcane science teaches that the abandonment of the living body by the soul frequently occurs, and that we encounter every day, in every condition of life, such living corpses. Various causes, among them overpowering fright, grief, despair, a violent attack of sickness, or excessive sensuality may bring this about. The vacant carcass may be entered and inhabited by the astral form of an adept sorcerer, or an elementary (an earth-bound disembodied human soul), or, very rarely, an elemental. Of course, an adept of white magic has the same power, but unless some very exceptional and great object is to be accomplished, he will never consent to pollute himself by occupying the body of an impure person." *

Although some examples of exponents who had proficiency in accomplishing the projection of the consciousness, which was just referred to as the transference of the spirit from one body to another body, have been given in previous citations, additional examples are instanced by H. P. Blavatsky dealing with comparatively modern individuals. This would seem to indicate that the process

------

* *Isis Unveiled*, II, 588-9.

is not a power pertaining exclusively to the Orient. The first to be mentioned was Johann Tritheim (1462-1516), a learned Benedictine monk, who although abbot of Spanheim, was reputed to be a magician.

> " the famous author of *Steganographie* * could converse with his friends by the mere power of his will. ' I can make my thoughts known to the initiated,' he wrote, ' at a distance of many hundred miles, without word, writing, or cipher, by any messenger. The latter cannot betray me, for he knows nothing. If needs be, I can dispense with the messenger. If any correspondent should be buried in the deepest dungeon, I could still convey to him my thoughts as clearly and as frequently as I chose, and this quite simply, without superstition, without the aid of spirits.' " †

The next one to be instanced was Girolamo Cardan (1501-1576), who was renowned not only as an author but as a mathematician, physician and astrologer. One of his works, *De Varietate Rerum* (" On a variety of things "), is cited along with the reference to him in the brief but remarkable passage which follows. This work was published in 1557 as a supplement to his greatest book, entitled *De Subtilitate Rerum* (" On the subtility of things "), which appeared in 1551 during the height of his fame. Before that he had already gained distinction for his two works on mathematics (1539 and 1545) as well as for his treatise on astrology (1543).

---

* The authorship of this work is usually ascribed to Trithemius, which is the Latinized form of his name. Steganography (now an obsolete word) is defined as the art of writing in cipher, or in characters which are not intelligible except to the persons who correspond with each other. It is derived from two Greek compounds: *steganos*, covered, hidden away (from *stegô*, to keep secret, to hide); and *graphy*, writing (from *graphein*, to write).

† *Isis Unveiled*, I, 476-7.

" Cardanus * could also send his spirit, or any messages he chose. When he did so, he felt ' as if a door was opened, and I myself immediately passed through it, leaving the body behind me.' (*De Varietate Rerum*, v. iii, i; viii, c. 43.) †

The third exponent of the performance of the projection, Herr Wesermann, belonged to a much later period than the two preceding instances. He lived in 1820, as noted in the medical journal of that year.

---

* The career of Cardanus (to use the Latinized form of his name —in Italian Geronymo or Hieronimo Cardano) was a singularly dramatic one. Born at Pavia, the illegitimate son of Facio Cardano (1444-1524—a learned jurist of Milan) he was educated at Pavia and later at Padua, from the university of which city he graduated in medicine. But because of the stigma concerning his birth he was excluded from the Milan college of physicians. Cardanus therefore became an instructor of mathematics, teaching geometry at Milan; although at the same time acting as a physician to the Augustine Friars, the prior of which brotherhood he cured. However, following his cure of the child of the Milanese senator Sfondrato, Cardanus was actually admitted into the medical fraternity, later becoming rector of the physicians (in 1541). In 1544 he occupied the chair of medicine at the University of Pavia. So celebrated had Cardanus become, that he was requested to go to Scotland in order to attend the ailing Archbishop of St. Andrew, Abp. Hamilton. En route he stopped off at Paris so that he might be present at the conferences of the medical faculty being held there.

While at the height of his fame a karmic retribution overtook him. His son, Giovanni Batista, also a physician, had unwisely married Brandonia Seroni, who was unfaithful to her husband. The revengeful husband, under the cover of his practice, administered poison to his faithless spouse. However, this was detected and the physician was brought to trial and condemned to death (1560). The blow struck down the father as well: his reputation was sullied and his practice declined. In fact, Cardanus was banished from Milan, but the decree was rescinded and he was able to accept a professorship at Bologna (1562). But misfortune still pursued him. In 1570 he was arrested and deprived of his position. Cardanus retired to Rome and sustained himself by means of a pension from the Pope: he died six years later.

† *Isis Unveiled*, I, 477.

"The case of a high German official, a Counsellor Wesermann, was mentioned in a scientific paper.* He claimed to be able to cause any friend or acquaintance, at any distance, to dream of every subject he chose, or see any person he liked. His claims were proved good, and testified to on several occasions by skeptics and learned professional persons. He could also cause his double to appear wherever he liked; and be seen by several persons at one time. By whispering in their ears a sentence prepared and agreed upon beforehand by unbelievers, and for the purpose, his power to project the double was demonstrated beyond any cavil." †

With such instances available, it is not to be wondered at that a statement such as the following should have been made in *Isis Unveiled*:

"Some persons have the natural and some the acquired power of withdrawing the *inner* from the *outer* body, at will, and causing it to perform long journeys, and be seen by those whom it visits. Numerous are the instances recorded by unimpeachable witnesses of the 'doubles' of persons having been seen and conversed with, hundreds of miles from the places where the persons themselves were known to be. Hermotimus, if we may credit Pliny and Plutarch, ‡ could at will fall into a trance and then his *second* soul proceeded to any distant place he chose." §

Reverting to the Orient. Semedo, writing in his *Histoire de la Chine* ("History of China"), is cited in regard to one of the Chinese religious groups, which he

---

* Nasse: *Zeitschrift für Psychische Ärzte*, 1820 ("Journal for the Psychical Physician").

† *Isis Unveiled*, I, 477.

‡ Footnote added in I. U., I, 476: Pliny: *Natural History*, vii, c. 52; and Plutarch: "Discourse concerning Socrates' Daemon," 22.

§ *Isis Unveiled*, I, 476.

terms Taossé (probably signifying "followers of Tao "), in connection with their ability to perform the projection of the consciousness. This is followed by a comparison of that which occurs when one's image is reflected in a mirror; or when a photograph is taken (although, obviously, the taking of pictures in 1875 is completely out of date in so far as 1960 processes are concerned). It should be noted that two of the prerequisites in the process of projection are stated, namely, the intensified thought and the educated will. The concluding portion of the citation speculates upon the probability of electrically projecting the astral body which, indeed, is something upon which to ponder, especially in connection with the statement that " there is a higher form of electricity than the physical one known to experimenters."

"Numerous and varied are the sects in China, Siam, Tartary, Thibet, Kashmir, and British India, which devote their lives to the cultivation of 'supernatural powers,' so called. Discussing one of such sects, the *Taossé*, Semedo says: ' They pretend that by means of certain exercises and meditations one shall regain his youth, and others will attain to be *Shien-sien, i.e.,* " Terrestrial Beati," in whose state every desire is gratified, whilst they have the power to transport themselves from one place to another, *however distant* with speed and facility." * This faculty relates but to the *projection* of the *astral entity*, in a more or less corporealized form, and certainly not to bodily transportation. This phenomenon is no more a miracle than one's reflection in a looking-glass. No one can detect in such an image a particle of matter, and still there stands our double, faithfully representing, even to each single hair on our heads. If, by this simple law of reflection, our double can be seen in a mirror, how much more striking a proof of its existence is afforded in the art of photography! It is no reason, because

---

* Semedo: *Histoire de la Chine*, Vol. III, p. 114.

our physicists have not yet found the means of taking photographs, except at a short distance, that the acquirement should be impossible to those who have found these means in the power of the human will itself, freed from terrestrial concern. Our thoughts are *matter*, says science; every energy produces more or less of a disturbance in the atmospheric waves. Therefore, as every man—in common with every other living, and even inert object—has an *aura* of his own emanations surrounding him; and, moreover, is enabled, by a trifling effort, to transport himself in *imagination* wherever he likes, why is it scientifically impossible that his thought, regulated, intensified, and guided by that powerful magician, the educated WILL, may become corporealized for the time being, and appear to whom it likes, a faithful double of the original? Is the proposition, in the present state of science, any more unthinkable than the photograph or telegraph were less than forty years ago, or the telephone less than fourteen months ago? *

" If the sensitized plate can so accurately seize upon the *shadow* of our faces, then this shadow or reflection, although we are unable to perceive it, must be something substantial. And, if we can, with the help of optical instruments, project our *semblances* upon a white wall, at several hundred feet distance, sometimes, then there is no reason why the adepts, the alchemists, the savants of the secret art, should not have already found out that which scientists deny today, but may discover true tomorrow, *i.e.,* how to project electrically their astral bodies, in an instant, through thousands of miles of space, leaving their material shells with a certain amount of animal vital principle to keep the physical life going, and acting within their spiritual, ethereal bodies as safely and intelligently as when clothed with the covering of flesh? There is a higher form of electricity than the physical one known to

---

* This was written in 1876.

experimenters; a thousand correlations of the latter are as yet veiled to the eye of the modern physicist, and none can tell where end its possibilities." *

During the time that *Isis Unveiled* was being written, in which Colonel Olcott nightly assisted Madame Blavatsky in her work, he was given a testimonial of the projection of the Mâyâvi-rûpa (which he calls the "astral body"). He relates that he penned a memorandum of a conversation which he had with a Hungarian Mahatma † in New York concerning this topic, which reads:

" He shades his eyes and turns down the gas in the standing burner on the table. Ask him why. Says that light is a physical force, and entering the eye of an unoccupied body, encounters—*i.e.*, strikes against, the astral soul of the temporary occupant, gives it a shock and such a push that the occupant might be pushed out. Paralysis of the occupied body is even possible. Extreme caution must be used in entering a body, and one cannot thoroughly fit oneself to it throughout until the automatic movements of the circulation, breathing, etc., adjust themselves to the automatism of the occupier's own body—with which however far distant, his projected astral body is most intimately related. I then lit a burner of the chandelier overhead, but the occupier at once held a newspaper so as to shade the crown of the head from the light. Surprised, I asked for an explanation, and was told that it was even more dangerous to have a strong top

---

* *Isis Unveiled*, II, 618-20.

† In the " Introductory " to *The Secret Doctrine* H.P.B. refers to the Hungarian Mahatma as one of Colonel Olcott's teachers:

" Of the three teachers the latter gentleman [Colonel Olcott] has had, the first was a Hungarian Initiate, the second an Egyptian, the third a Hindu." (S.D. Vol. I, p. xix; I, 42, 6-vol. ed.; I, 3, 3rd ed.)

light strike upon the crown of the head than to have light shine into the eyes." *

PHASES OF TULKU IN THE ERA OF GNOSTICISM AND THE MODERN ERA

Directing attention to the period regarded as the founding era of Christianity: it would certainly come as a surprise to most Christians to be told that the early followers of their religion held that Jesus was a Tulku —of course, they would have used the equivalent term in Gnostic terminology. Yet, early Christians did hold such a view. To be sure, it may be contended that the Gnostics were regarded as heretics by some *later* Christians. In spite of that view, however, it may be pointed out that the earlier Christians were entitled to their religious views—for the simple reason that the Gnostics flourished before the formularization of present-day Christianity. For that matter, dogmas and creeds had not yet been established. On the testimony of the avowed champion of orthodox Christianity, none other than Irenaeus, he declares that the Gnostic views of the Basilidean † system held that:

" ' When the uncreated, *unnamed* Father saw the corruption of mankind, he sent his first-born *Nous*,

---

* *Old Diary Leaves*, Vol. 1, p. 275 (2nd ed.).

† Clement of Alexandria said of the Gnostic Basilides that he was a " philosopher devoted to the contemplation of divine things." (*Isis Unveiled*, II, 123) In fact, Basilides was regarded as the bright sun of Gnosticism, " for all the founders of other Gnostic sects group round him, like a cluster of stars borrowing light from their sun." (I. U., II, 155) According to Eusebius, the early Christian chronicler, Basilides had published 24 volumes of " Commentaries upon the Gospels," all of which were burned (*Ecclesiastical History*, IV, vii), " a fact which makes us suppose that they contained more truthful matter than the school of Irenaeus was prepared to deny." (I. U., II, 155).

into the world, in the form of Christ, for the redemption of all who believe in him, out of the power of those who fabricated the world (the Demiurgus, and his six sons, the planetary genii). He appeared amongst men as the man, Jesus, and wrought miracles. This Christ did *not die* in person, but Simon the Cyrenian suffered in his stead, *to whom he lent his bodily form*; . . . for the Divine Power, the Nous of the Eternal Father, *is not corporeal*, and *cannot die*. . . . Whoso, therefore, maintains that Christ has died, is still the bondsman of ignorance; whoso denies the same, he is free, and hath understood the purpose of the Father.' " *

The loaning of his bodily form is equivalent in meaning to one of the phases connected with the performance of Tulku. Of course, the *philosophical* aspect connected with the teaching of the Gnostics was not presented by Irenaeus—for the simple reason that he was not fully aware of the esoteric teaching of the Gnostics.

In the third century the Manicheans arose under the leadership of Mani, who proclaimed himself as an Ambassador of Light. Basing their teachings partly on Christian tenets and partly on the Zoroastrian dualistic scheme, the followers of Mani declared that Jesus was a permutation of Gautama the Buddha, and furthermore that Buddha, Christ and Mani were one and the same person.†

This idea of interchanging from person to person, or permutation, conveys the same conception that is present in Tulku, although expressed in an easily understood manner, rather than philosophically phrased. This is the basic idea that is present in the lamaistic succession of the Dalai Lamas and Tashi Lamas.

---

* *Isis Unveiled*, II, 157, quoting Irenaeus: *Against Heresies*, I, xxiv, 4.

† *Isis Unveiled*, II, 286 based on Neander's *General History of Christian Religion and Church*, sect. IV (appx. under Manichaeans).

In more recent times an instance illustrative of a phase of Tulku is given by H. P. Blavatsky as occurring in medieval Europe:

" some medieval Kabalists cite a well-known personage of the fifteenth century Cardinal de Cusa; Karma, due to his wonderful devotion to Esoteric study and the *Kabalah*, led the suffering Adept to seek intellectual recuperation and rest from ecclesiastical tyranny in the body of Copernicus. *Se non e vero e ben trovato* [If it is not true it is cleverly invented]; and the perusal of the lives of the two men might easily lead a believer in such powers to a ready acceptance of the alleged fact. The reader having at his command the means to do so is asked to turn to the formidable folio in Latin of the fifteenth century, called *De Docta Ignorantia*, written by the Cardinal de Cusa, in which all the theories and hypotheses—all the ideas—of Copernicus are found as the key-notes to the discoveries of the great astronomer." *

The above example was instanced in explanation of three types of Aveśa, illustrating the application of this ability of transference. The passage was introduced by supplying a comparison of that which takes place in the normal process when death occurs, to that ability which the Adept employs enabling him to alter these processes. The example just cited had reference to the first of the three types to be explained. In this instance, because of being compared to the other two types, it is regarded as the lowest of the three degrees of development.

" there are cases—rare, yet more frequent than one would be disposed to expect—which are the voluntary and conscious reincarnations of Adepts, on their trial. Every man has an inner, a ' Higher Self,' and also an Astral Body. But few are those who, outside the

---

* *The Secret Doctrine*, Vol. V, p. 355.

higher degrees of Adeptship, can guide the latter, or any of the principles that animate it, when once death has closed their short terrestrial life. Yet such guidance, or their transference from the dead to a living body, is not only possible, but is of frequent occurrence, according to Occult and Kabalistic teachings. The degrees of such power of course vary greatly. To mention but three: the lowest of these degrees would allow an Adept, who has been greatly trammelled during life in his study and in the use of his powers, to choose after death another body in which he could go on with his interrupted studies, though ordinarily he would lose in it every remembrance of his previous incarnation. The next degree permits him, in addition to this, to transfer the memory of his past life to his new body; while the highest has hardly any limits in the exercise of that wonderful faculty." *

The second example mentioned above, i.e., " the next degree " closely resembles the Tulku of the Dalai Lamas and Tashi Lamas.

Returning to the era of the present Theosophical Movement, for a final example of Âveśa. It has already been recorded herein that Damodar—one of the chelas associated with H.P.B. at the headquarters of the Society in India—had demonstrated the performance of the projection of his consciousness while he was absent from Adyar. He was fulfilling an assignment at Moradabad, which is in the United Provinces of India. Damodar performed the projection to Adyar and then the return to Moradabad. Another noteworthy example of Damodar's, concerning Âveśa, is related by him in his own words. It was recorded by him in the form of a letter written to William Q. Judge, with whom he corresponded on subjects of mutual interest. After Damodar's departure into Tibet, Mr. Judge published portions of this correspondence in his magazine, The Path, under the significant title: " A Hindu Chela's Diary." The account

* The Secret Doctrine, Vol. V, pp. 354-5.

24

is of exceptional interest, bearing directly upon Âveśa, and especially because of the manner in which it is presented.

"X. came to see us. He never speaks of himself, but as ' this body'. He told me that he had first been in the body of a Fakir, who, upon having his hand disabled by a shot he received while he passed the fortress of Bhurtpore, had to change his body and choose another, the one he was now in. A child of about seven years of age was dying at that time, and so, before the complete physical death, this Fakir had entered the body and afterwards used it as his own. He is, therefore, doubly not what he seems to be. As a Fakir he had studied Yoga science for 65 years; but that study having been arrested at the time he was disabled, leaving him unequal to the task he had to perform, he had to choose this other one. In his present body he is 53 years old, and consequently the inner X. is 118 years old. . . . In the night I heard him talking with Kunâla, and found that each had the same Guru, who himself is a very great Adept, whose age is 300 years, although in appearance he seems to be only 40. . . .

"After I had finished my work and was preparing to return here, a wandering Fakir met me and asked if he could find from me the proper road to Karli. I directed him, and he then put to me some questions that looked as if he knew what had been my business; he also had a very significant look upon his face, and several of his questions were apparently directed to getting me to tell him a few things Kunâla had told me just before leaving Benares, with an injunction of secrecy. . . . . He then left me saying: ' You do not know me, but we may see each other.' . . . I got back last night and saw only X., to whom I related the incident with the fakir, and he said that, ' it was none other than Kunâla himself using the fakir's body who said those things, and if I were to see that fakir again he would not remember me and would not be able to repeat his questions, as he was for the time being taken possession of for the purpose, by Kunâla, who often performs such things.' I then asked him if in that case Kunâla had really entered the fakir's body. . . . and X. replied that, if I meant to ask if he had really and in fact entered the fakir's person, the answer was no; but that if I meant to ask if Kunâla had overcome that fakir's senses, substituting his own, the answer was, yes; leaving me to make my own conclusions. . . .

"I was fortunate enough yesterday to be shown the process pursued in either entering an empty body, or in using one which has its own occupant. I found that in both cases it was the same. . . . With any person but Kunâla I would not have allowed my own body to have been made use of for the experiment. But I felt perfectly safe, that he would not only let me in again, but also that he would not permit any stranger, man or gandharva, to come in after him. We went to——and he . . . . The feeling was that I had suddenly stepped out into freedom. He was beside me, and at first I thought that he had but begun. But he directed me to look, and there on the mat I saw my body, apparently unconscious. As I looked, the body of myself opened its eyes and arose. It was then superior to me, for Kunâla's informing power moved and directed it. It seemed even to speak to me. Around it, attracted to it by those magnetic influences, wavered and moved astral shapes, that vainly tried to whisper in the ear or to enter by the same road. In vain! They seemed to be pressed away by the air or surroundings of Kunâla. Turning to look at him, and expecting to see him in a state of samâdhi, he was smiling as if nothing, or at the very most, but a part of his power, had been taken away. . . Another instant and I was again myself, the mat felt cool to my touch, the *bhūtas* were gone, and Kunâla bade me rise." *

---

* *The Path*, Vol. I, No. 3, June, 1886 (New York).

In rare instances some people who have been anaesthetized have had the experience of "viewing their own physical bodies" at a distance. This was made possible because of the effect of the anaesthesia (a word literally meaning "without pain"), which usually dissociates the "sense of feeling" of being *in* the body. An anaesthetic acts on the brain and spinal cord, and produces unconsciousness and an insensibility to pain, so that to all intents and purposes a person is "asleep". Of course, because of the anaesthetic, the pain is not registered by the brain, and hence the cutting of the body for surgery is not "felt" by the sleeper, who is really dissociated from the body temporarily and is unconscious to external impressions. On rare occasions the disassociation may be effected and the consciousness retained, so that it closely approximates or resembles the state of a projection of the consciousness.

THREE TYPES OF ÂVEŚA DESIGNATED

The chela writing the letter clearly illustrates three types of Âveśa, as they may be referred to for the sake of clarity. In the first paragraph of the citation the first type (Type I) is mentioned, namely, the entrance into the body of a seven-year-old child by a fakir. In this instance, the physical vehicle of the practitioner of yoga who had been wounded was vacated, and of course that body perished. By means of the projection of consciousness the vehicle of the seven-year-old boy was entered and reanimated. Therefore, the fakir continued existence, or life on earth, in the new body.

This, to be sure, illustrates the conscious employment of Âveśa, although it is somewhat different from the Tulku performed by the Dalai Lamas of Tibet, in that the Âveśa is employed immediately without any intervening period.

In the second paragraph of the citation, the illustration provided is that of Type II, and is made explicit by means of the question: Did Kunâla really enter the fakir's body? Observe the reply given, which may be clarified by means of direct speech. No, Kunâla did not really in fact enter the fakir's body. In further explanation of what has been here termed Type II of Âveśa, the answer continued: Kunâla was able to " over- come the fakir's senses," and for the time being, temporarily substituted his own senses.

Type III, as specified here, in the third paragraph of the citation, indicates a conscious performance of Âveśa of a temporary nature, employed by a guru to demonstrate to the chela what takes place. The chela was enabled to see the process accomplished, by viewing it (as he himself states) enacted on his own physical vehicle. Could any method be superior to this as a means of imparting knowledge? The chela remarks the sense of freedom experienced for a time upon being no longer in the body, the while he retains consciousness of external impressions (not possible during anaesthesia, as noted above). The chela is also able to communicate with his guru—by thought-transference. Thus, even though the Tulku was but a temporary one, nevertheless it illustrates the same method that was employed in Type I of Âveśa.

The clue is here provided for understanding the processes involved in connection with H.P.B. Both Types II and III were unquestionably employed—as will be shown in the next chapter, entitled " H.P.B. and Tulku."

CHAPTER XVI

H. P. B. AND TULKU

Now that Âveśa and Tulku have been presented; the next stage in the development of the theme is to show H.P.B.'s connection with Tulku.

A commencement may be made by referring to an episode in H. P. Blavatsky's career not often associated with her. An account of this was written by her sister, and included in Mr. A. P. Sinnett's book entitled *Incidents in the Life of Mme. Blavatsky* under the section " Mme. de Zhelihovsky's Narrative." In order to cover all the points intended, it is necessary to make a lengthy citation. Reference is made to what is termed a " strange illness," although in all likelihood it concerned a particular stage in the development of Mme. Blavatsky, marking the period when she became able to exercise conscious control over herself and her condition which had existed from childhood. The portion of the citation that is given in the first person is taken from a letter written by H.P.B.* to her sister:

> " Mme. Blavatsky resided at Tiflis less than two years, and not more than three in the Caucasus. The last year she passed roaming about in Imeretia, Georgia, and Mingrelia. . . .† The native *Koodiani* (magicians, sorcerers), Persian thaumaturgists, and old Armenian hags—healers and fortune-tellers—were the first she generally sought out and took under her protection. . . . .
>
> " Her occult powers all this while, instead of weakening, became every day stronger, and she seemed

---

* Particular attention is directed to H. P. B.'s statement: " I became somebody else "—that is to say, a status equivalent to Tulku.

† *Op. cit.*, p. 112.

finally to subject to her direct will every kind of manifestation. . . . Meanwhile sporadic phenomena were gradually dying away in her presence. They still occurred, but very rarely, though they were always very remarkable. . . . . . .

" It must, however, be explained that, some months previous . . . Mme. Blavatsky was taken very ill. From the verbal statements of her relatives, recorded under their dictation, we learn that no doctor could understand her illness. It was one of those mysterious nervous diseases that baffle science, and elude the grasp of everyone but a very expert psychologist. Soon after the commencement of that illness, she began—as she repeatedly told her friends—'to lead a double life.' What she meant by it, no one of the good people of Mingrelia could understand, of course. But this is how she herself describes that state:

" ' Whenever I was called by name, I opened my eyes upon hearing it, and was myself, my own personality in every particular. As soon as I was left alone, however, I relapsed into my usual, half-dreamy condition, and become *somebody else* (who, namely, Mme. B. will not tell). I had simply a mild fever that consumed me slowly but surely, day after day, with entire loss of appetite, and finally of hunger, as I would feel none for days, and often went a week without touching any food whatever, except a little water, so that in four months I was reduced to a living skeleton. In cases when I was interrupted, when in my other *self*, by the sound of my present name being pronounced, and while I was conversing in my dream life—say at half a sentence either spoken by me or those who were with my second *me* at the time—and opened my eyes to answer the call, I used to answer very rationally, and understood all, for I was never delirious. But no sooner had I closed my eyes again than the sentence which had been interrupted was completed by my other self, continued from the word, or even half the word, it had stopped at. When awake, and *myself*, I remembered well *who I was* in my second capacity, and what I had been and was doing. When *somebody else, i.e.*, the personage I had become, I know I had no idea of who was H. P. Blavatsky! I was in another far-off country, a totally different individuality from myself, and had no connection at all with my actual life.'

" Such is Mme. Blavatsky's analysis of her state at that time. She was residing then at Ozoorgetty, a military settlement in Mingrelia, where she had bought a house. It is a little town, lost among the old forests and woods, which, in those days, had neither roads nor conveyances, save of the most primitive kind, and which, to the very time of the last Russo-Turkish war, was unknown outside of Caucasus. The only physician of the place, the army surgeon, could make nothing of her symptoms; but as she was visibly and rapidly declining, he packed her off to Tiflis to her friends. Unable to go on horseback, owing to her great weakness, and a journey in a cart being deemed dangerous, she was sent off in a large native boat along the river —a journey of four days to Kutais—with four native servants only to take care of her.

" What took place during that journey we are unable to state precisely; nor is Mme. Blavatsky herself certain of it, since her weakness was so great that she lay like one apparently dead until her arrival. In that solitary boat, on a narrow river, hedged on both sides by centenarian forests, her position must have been precarious.

" The little stream they were sailing along was, though navigable, rarely, if ever, used as a means of transit, at any rate not before the war. Hence the information we have got came solely from her servants and was very confused. It appears, however, that as they were gliding slowly along the narrow stream, cutting its way between two steep and woody banks, the servants were several times during three consecutive nights frightened out of their senses by seeing, *what they swore was their mistress*, gliding off from the boat, and across the water in the direction of the forests, while the body of that same mistress was lying prostrate on her bed at the bottom of the boat. Twice the man who towed the canoe, upon seeing the 'form,' ran away shrieking, and in great terror. Had it not been for a faithful old servant who was taking care of her, the boat and the patient would have been abandoned in the middle of the stream. On the last evening, the servant swore he saw two figures, while the third —his mistress, in flesh and bone—was sleeping before his eyes. No sooner had they arrived at Kutais, where Mme. Blavatsky had a distant relative residing, than all the servants, with the exception of the old butler, left her, and returned no more.

"It was with great difficulty that she was transported to Tiflis. A carriage and a friend of the family were sent to meet her; and she was brought into the house of her friends apparently dying.

"She never talked upon that subject with anyone. But, as soon as she was restored to life and health, she left the Caucasus, and went to Italy. Yet it was before her departure from the country in 1863 that the nature of her powers seems to have entirely changed." *

The portion of the citation in which the narrative was given in the words of H.P.B. herself is indicative of a state very similar to one of the types of Âveśa described in the preceding chapter. Since it was never referred to by Mme. Blavatsky, and because, as her sister already remarked, Helena never mentioned this "strange illness" (as it was called) to Vera, no explanation was ever offered concerning it. The reason for bringing it forward at this point is to show that testimony may be submitted regarding the fact that this withdrawal of H.P.B.'s inner self was possible of accomplishment. There is no doubt whatsoever that the servants on the boat could see the recumbent form of their mistress at the same time that they

* *Incidents in the Life of Madame Blavatsky*, pp. 114-18.

viewed her projected self gliding off from the boat. Such a striking incident was indeed something to relate! The significant factor is this: If this projection of the self were accomplished unconsciously, it gave evidence of the fact that H.P.B. was so constituted that the withdrawal of the inner self was possible of execution. Moreover, as brought forward previously, this represents the first stage in the performance of Tulku (to make use of the classification into which the process was divided).

The specific point, then, to be noted is, that because of having aptitude for using powers normally dormant within man, one of which was this faculty of being able to leave the physical body, even though accomplished unconsciously at first, H.P.B. was selected as one best suited for the role that she did fill—later on in her career. Here is an extract from one of the Mahatma letters indicating this factor:

"After nearly a century of fruitless search, our chiefs had to avail themselves of the only opportunity to send out a European *body* upon European soil to serve as a connecting link between that country and our own." *

Next in the line of presentation is an extract from a letter written by Stainton Moses, dated December 22, 1877, and addressed:

"My dear Sphinx":

"Lying, as I sadly fear, under the ban of your wrath, I sit down with some awe to write to the Co-operative Society that are running the Blavatsky machine. If I err it is thro' ignorance. Lighten my darkness! If I fail to understand the complicated . . . problem you set me last time you deigned to address me, and I verily believe (tho' I should be sorry to assert such a paradox positively) that I have succeeded in understanding you! I seem to see that you mean me to gather that I have

---

* *The Mahatma Letters to A. P. Sinnett*, p. 203.

not been in correspondence with you—H.P.B.—but with a Brother who has used the B. shell as a vehicle of his lucubration for my benefit: that I shall meet him in the future, but 'know him not'; and that as to 'the Blavatsky' I shall never know anything more. . . . ." *

Significantly enough, Dr. Archibald Keightley's † conclusions in regard to H. P. Blavatsky, were similar in character as may be seen by reference to his narration entitled " Reminiscences of H. P. Blavatsky ":

---

* Portion of a letter of which a photographic reproduction was published in *Old Diary Leaves*, by Col. Olcott, Vol. I, facing p. 352.

† Archibald Keightley will go down in Theosophical annals because of the assistance given to H.P.B. in the preparation and publication of *The Secret Doctrine*. A practising physician, Dr. Keightley first met Mme. Blavatsky in 1884 in London, while she was on a short visit from Paris. In 1886 he spent some days with H.P.B. in Ostend, Belgium; and then in May, 1887, supervised the moving of H.P.B. across the Channel to Maycot. This was the name of a house situated in Norwood, a southern residential area of London, although " a long way out of London proper " (in those days of the horse and buggy). Not only the moving but the packing as well. " The main difficulty," wrote Dr. Keightley " was to get her papers and books packed up. No sooner was one packed than it was wanted for reference; if part of the MSS. were put in a box it was certain to be that part which already contained some information which had to be cut out and placed elsewhere: and as H.P.B. continued to write until the very day before her departure, such was her unflagging industry, it was not an easy matter to get her belongings packed.

" When she arrived at Norwood the reverse process went on, but the difficulty was to get unpacked quickly enough. . . . All through the summer of 1887 every day found her at work from six to six, with intervals for meals only." (From an article written by Dr. Keightley and published in *Reminiscences of H. P. Blavatsky and The Secret Doctrine*, by Countess Wachtmeister, pp. 97-8. The other citations in this footnote are from the same source.)

In October, 1887, the household was moved from Maycot to larger quarters at 17 Landsdowne Road, Notting Hill, London west; and again to 19 Avenue Road, St. John's Wood, London north-west, where H.P.B. died on May 8, 1891.

It is to Dr. Keightley and his uncle, Bertram, that we are indebted for the arrangement of *The Secret Doctrine* as published, for

" Some people have advanced as a theory to account for these changes, that Mme. Blavatsky was the scene of mediumistic oscillations or that, at least, she was the scene of action of not merely double but of multiple personality. These suggestions are really the wildest of hypotheses—much less, working hypotheses. To those who know the laws which govern the relation of the physical instrument to the subtle astral and spiritual forces which dominate it, the explanation is simple. But I will put forward my own theory. For the purpose of the theosophical work that body was an instrument used by one of the Masters, known to us as H.P.B. When he had to attend to other business, the instrument was left in charge of one of his pupils

---

when the manuscript was placed in his hands to prepare for the printer it " was a mass of MSS. with no definite arrangement." (p 97)

" All through that summer [of 1887] Bertram Keightley and I were engaged in reading, re-reading, copying and correcting. Many of the quotations had to be verified. . . . .

" Much of the MSS. was typewritten at this period. This was H.P.B.'s opportunity. The spaces were large and much could be inserted. Needless to say, it was. The thick type-MSS. were cut, pasted, recut and pasted several times over, until several of them were twice the size of the original MSS. But in it all was apparent that no work and no trouble, no suffering or pain could daunt her from her task. Crippled with rheumatism, suffering from a disease which had several times nearly proved fatal, she still worked on unflaggingly, writing at her desk the moment her eyes and fingers could guide the pen

". . . Certain requirements as to size of page and margin were particular points with H.P.B., as also were the thickness and quality of paper. Some of her critics had disliked the thickness of *Isis Unveiled*, so the paper had to be thinner so as to reduce the size. These points decided, the book began to go to press. It so happened that I was called into the country and so did not see the first half or more of the first volume as it passed. But it went through three or four other hands besides H.P.B.'s in galley proof, as well as in revise. She was her own most severe corrector, and was liable to treat revise as MSS., with alarming results in the correction item in the bill. Then came the writing of the preface, and finally the book was out. . . ." (pp. 98-100)

or friends, who ran the body as an engineer directs his machine when taking duty for another. But the substitute engineer has not the same sympathy with his machine or instrument as the regular man and is ' outside the machine.' " *

Even more clearly put than the above citations is H.P.B.'s own description of what occurred to herself. This leaves no room for doubt that Tulku was performed:

" *Someone* comes and envelops me as a misty cloud and all at once pushes me out of myself, and then I am not ' I ' any more—Helena Petrovna Blavatsky— but someone else. Someone strong and powerful, born in a totally different region of the world; and as to myself it is almost as if I were asleep, or lying by not quite conscious,—not in my own body but close by, held only by a thread which ties me to it. However, at times I see and hear everything quite clearly: I am perfectly conscious of what my body is saying and doing—or at least its new possessor. I even understand and remember it all so well that afterwards I can repeat it and even write down *his* words. . . . At such a time I see awe and fear on the faces of Olcott and others, and follow with interest the way in which *he* half-pityingly regards them out of my own eyes and teaches them with my physical tongue. Yet not with my mind but his own, which enwraps my brain like a cloud. . . . Ah, but really I cannot explain everything." †

---

* This article by Dr. Keightley was first published in a magazine entitled *Theosophical Quarterly*, New York, Vol. VII, October, 1910. Republished in *Theosophia*, Los Angeles, Vol. XVI, No. 1, p. 20.

† From a letter written by H.P.B. to her sister, Vera, and translated from the Russian by her niece, Mrs. Charles Johnston. This letter was one of a series published by William Q. Judge in his magazine, *The Path*, December, 1894, Vol. IX, No. 9, p. 266.

Having this narration of H.P.B.'s clearly in mind, one is able to understand one of Colonel Olcott's anecdotes, which bears directly on the process under consideration:

" She and I were in our literary work-room in New York one summer day after dinner. It was early twilight, and the gas had not been lighted. She sat over by the South front window, I stood on the rug before the mantel-piece, thinking. I heard her say: ' Look and learn '; and glancing that way, saw a mist rising from her head and shoulders. Presently it defined itself into the likeness of one of the Mahatmas, the one who, later, gave me the historical turban, but the astral double of which he now wore on his mist-born head. Absorbed in watching the phenomenon, I stood silent and motionless. The shadowy shape only formed for itself the upper half of the torso, and then faded away and was gone; whether re-absorbed into H.P.B.'s body or not, I do not know. She sat statue-like for two or three minutes, after which she sighed, came to herself, and asked me if I had seen anything. When I asked her to explain the pheno-menon she refused, saying that it was for me to develop my intuition so as to understand the phenomena of the world I lived in." *

In order to strengthen the point he is striving to impress upon the minds of his readers, Col. Olcott draws atten-tion to photographs showing locks of hair cut from H.P.B.'s head on different occasions:

" Numerous witnesses can testify to another pheno-menon which may or may not go towards proving that other entities were sometimes occupying the H.P.B. body. On five different occasions—once to please Miss Emily Kislingbury, and once my sister, Mrs. Mitchell, I remember—she gathered up a lock of her fine, wavy auburn hair, and either pulled it

---

* *Old Diary Leaves*, Vol. I, pp. 266-7.

out by the roots or cut it off with scissors, and gave it
to one of us. But the lock would be *coarse, jet black,
straight* and without the least curliness or waviness in
it; in other words, Hindu or other Asiatic human hair,
and not in the least like her own flossy, baby-like,
light-brown locks. My Diary for 1878 shows that other
two occasions were on July 9th, when she did the thing
for Hon. J. L. O'Sullivan, ex-U.S. Minister to Portugal,
and on November 19th, when she did it for Miss Rosa
Bates in the presence of six other witnesses besides
Miss Bates and H.P.B. and myself. The enemy may
suggest that this was but a trick of simple ' palming,'
but that is met by the statement that in the case of the
lock given to Miss Kislingbury or my sister—I forget
which—the recipient was allowed to take the scissors
and cut out the lock herself. I have two locks taken
from her head, both black as jet and far coarser than
hers, but one distinctly coarser than the other. The
former is Egyptian, and the latter Hindu hair. What
better explanation of this phenomenon is there than
that of supposing that the men to whom these black
locks had belonged were actually occupying the
mâyâvic H.P.B. body when they were removed from
the head ? " *

There is one more aspect to be considered along with
the theme of H.P.B. and Tulku. While at first sight it
may be thought that there is no connection—in that the
subject deals with the sevenfold constitution of man, or
the seven principles—nevertheless, it is asserted that there
is a connection. Attention is drawn, then, to an
enlightening comment, which was precipitated by
Mahatma M. upon a letter written by Allan O. Hume at
Simla, India, dated January 4, 1881, and addressed to

---

* *Old Diary Leaves*, pp. 267-9. Col. Olcott adds: " This occupancy by living persons of another living person's body, though so
outside our Western experience that we have no word for it is, like
all else in psychological science, known and defined in India."
(p. 269). The term for it is Âveśa.

H. P. Blavatsky. In order to understand the comment, however, it becomes necessary to reproduce the extract, sarcastic though it be, which brought forth the message. Immediately after the first phrase of nine words, a marginal comment was interjected reading: " He is mistaken—*he does not.*" This signifies that all the statements made in the extract are erroneous. Here are Mr. Hume's words:

" Now I know all about the Brothers' supposed explanation,* that you are a psychological cripple, one of your seven principles being in pawn in Tibet —if so more shame to them keeping other people's property to the great detriment of the owner. But grant it so, then I ask my friends the Brothers to ' préciscz ' as the French say—which principle have you got old chaps?

" It ain't the Hoola sariram, the body—that's clear for you might truly say with Hamlet ' Oh that this too solid flesh would melt! '

" And it can't be the linga sariram, as that can't part from the body, and it ain't the kama rupa and if it were, its loss would not account for your symptoms.

" Neither assuredly is it the Jivatma, *you* have plenty of life in you. Neither is it the fifth principle or mind, for without this you would be ' quo ad ' the external world, an idiot. Neither is it the sixth principle for without this you would be a devil, intellect without conscience, while as for the seventh that is universal and can be captured by no Brother and no Buddha, but exists for each precisely to the degree that the eyes of the sixth principle are open.

" Therefore to me this explanation is not only not satisfactory—but its having been offered—throws suspicion on the whole thing." †

---

* Here supply the six words precipitated by Mahatma M.: " *He is mistaken—he does not.*" The correct transliteration of the seven principles in Sanskrit follows: Sthûla-śarîra; Linga-śarîra; Prâna (or Jîva); Kâma; Manas; Buddhi; Âtman. The French word " précisez " signifies: " Be precise! " (from the verb " préciser ").

† *The Letters of H. P. Blavatsky to A. P. Sinnett,* p. 307.

Amazing deduction! Because a thing is not understood it is to be regarded with suspicion! One is reminded of the fond mother viewing a company of soldiers on the parade ground, in which her son was taking part. " Do you know," was her comment, " it was a fine spectacle; but the only one who was in step was my son, John." Mark the Mahatma's precipitated comment:

> " Very clever—but suppose it is neither *one of the seven* particularly but all? Every one of them a ' cripple ' and forbidden the exercise of its full powers? And suppose such is the wise law of a far foreseeing power!" *

This apocalyptic answer is somewhat mystifying—in view of the manner in which the first letter on the subject was presented.† It only goes to show that one must be careful not to jump to conclusions, unless there is sure footing—both on the spot from which one takes off for the jump, as well as for the landing. Be that as it may, there must be a solution—else the answer would have been given in a different manner. Pondering upon this problem, a suggestion is offered:

A " principle " may be regarded in a dual manner: (1) the principle *per se*; (2) the development aspect of the principle; especially in regard to its development in the human constitution. To make this intended meaning clear, let us regard two human beings: Plato, and an illiterate individual. Intrinsically the Manas-principle is of the same essential quality in both individuals. But Plato represents the Manas-principle functioning in the capacity of a Fifth Rounder; whereas the illiterate individual represents the Manas-principle only partially functioning (if at all) in the capacity of an unenlightened Fourth Rounder. Ah, comes the rejoinder, but one is a developed individual, the other is not. Exactly so. A person such as Plato gives evidence of the *developmental aspect of a principle.*

---

* *Op. cit.*, p. 307.

† This letter was quoted in a previous Chapter.

25

The writer does not hesitate to state that no two human individuals demonstrate the identic developmental status of the seven principles as functioning aspects in the human constitution. Unfortunately, Theosophists have become so accustomed to consider the seven principles as seven distinct blocks, one on top of another, and separable (as so often depicted in words—in diagrammatic manner) that seldom, if ever, is the idea dwelt upon that has just been expressed. The seven principles are interblended, or interpenetrate each other. Consequently, as a human being develops himself, he also develops the quality of his principles. One citation should be sufficient at this point.

" The principles do not stand one above the other, and thus cannot be taken in numerical sequence; their order depends upon the superiority and predominance of one or another principle, and therefore differs in every man." *

Then, too, a principle should be regarded from the standpoint of its sevenfold aspect. The significance of this viewpoint is that it clearly indicates the reason for following the Circle of Necessity, or accomplishing the Seven Rounds: it is for the purpose of awakening the " 49 Fires." Thus, at the conclusion of the seven-Round cycle, each one of the principles in its sevenfold aspect will have become illumined and the 49 Fires will have become fully awakened: $7 \times 7 = 49$.

There is yet another manner in which a principle may be regarded: that is, by using the clue given in the " loka-tala twins." In explanation: a principle may be regarded from the " spirit-side," representing its loka aspect, and also from the " matter-side," the latter standing for its tala aspect. In the final analysis, the same conclusion will be reached, whether regarded from this point of view, or from the standpoint of the former explanation.

Reverting to the Mahatma's explanation regarding the " retained principles ": there is, then, what may be

---

* *The Secret Doctrine*, Vol. V, p. 440.

termed a bi-polar phase in regard to the principles. In
H.P.B.'s case, the "retained aspect" of the principles
acted in the capacity of a wire of transmission, or formed
a link of communication between the Mahatmas and
H.P.B., and their projection of consciousness was rendered
more facile. Thus, either one of the Types of Tulku
(which have been described) was made possible of
achievement. Therefore, because of the retained aspect
of the principles, in the instance of H.P.B., she manifested in the world in a particular role (so to phrase it,
for lack of an appropriate term), and it may be stated
that she demonstrated an aspect of Tulku.

At this point it is appropriate to add a pertinent passage,
which was previously quoted, but may be repeated with
advantage:

"Acting in accordance with my wishes, my brother
M. made to you through her a certain offer, if you
remember. You had but to accept it, and at any time
you liked, you would have had for an hour or more,
the real *baitchooly* to converse with, instead of the
psychological cripple you generally have to deal with
now." *

The "psychological cripple," of course, had reference
to H.P.B. minus the "retained principles".

This is unquestionably what H.P.B. had in mind
when she penned this unique inscription in her own
copy of *The Voice of the Silence*:

"H.P.B. to H. P. Blavatsky with *no* kind regards".

One more illustration of what has been termed "the
real baitchooly" in the foregoing citation, will prove
helpful in understanding the situation in connection
with H.P.B. In this instance she herself is referring to
the matter (although in her own words) in one of her

---

* *The Mahatma Letters to A. P. Sinnett*, p. 204.

letters, dated simply March 17th (of the year 1882). She is giving Mr. Sinnett an opportunity to fathom (if he could) the mystery in which she was involved. In characteristic fashion H.P.B. has been berating herself and writing rather caustically about affairs in connection with the Theosophical Society, and she breaks out in the midst of it in this fashion:

"Why, such an extravagant, seemingly useless *tirade* as contained in this letter? Because, the hour is near; and that after having proved what I have to, I will bow myself out from the refined Western Society and —be no more. You may all whistle then for the Brothers—GOSPEL.

"Of course *it was* a joke. No; you *do not hate me*; you only feel a friendly, indulgent, a kind of *benevolent contempt for H.P.B.* You are right there, so far *as you know her* the one who is ready to fall into pieces. Perchance you may find out yet your mistake concerning the other—the well hidden party. . . . .*

"Now, do you really think that you know ME, my dear Mr. Sinnett? Do you believe that, because you have fathomed—as you think—my physical crust and brain; that shrewd analyst of *human* nature though you be—you have ever penetrated even beneath the first cuticles of my *Real Self*? You would gravely err, if you did. I am held by all of you as *untruthful* because hitherto I have shown the world only the true *exterior* Mme. Blavatsky. It is just as if you complained of the *falseness* of a moss and weed covered, and mud-covered, stony and rugged rock for writing outside ' I am not moss covered and mud-plastered; your eyes deceive you for you are unable to see beneath the crust,' etc. You must understand the allegory. It is not *boasting* for I do not say whether *inside* that unprepossessing rock there is a palatial residence or an humble hut. What I say is this: you *do not know* me;

---

* *The Mahatma Letters to A. P. Sinnett,* p. 466; p. 459 (3rd ed.).

for whatever there is *inside* it, is *not what you think* it is; and—to judge of me therefore, as of one *untruthful* is the greatest mistake in the world besides being a flagrant injustice. *I*, (the inner real ' I ') am in prison and cannot show myself as I am with all the desire I may have to. Why then, should I, because speaking for myself *as I am* and feel myself to be, why should I be held responsible for the *outward* jail-door and *its* appearance, when I have neither built nor yet decorated it? " *

In view of that which has been presented thus far, the following citation from a letter written by H. P. Blavatsky to her aunt, Nadyezhda de Fadeyev, from America dated simply October 29 (most likely 1877) clearly indicates the accomplishment of one of the aspects of Tulku, although it is not explained in technical language —because of being written to her aunt in Odessa:

" It seems strange to you that a Hindu Sahib comes like an intruder and a ' host ' into my house. Do admit at last that the human soul, his ' perispirit,' is a completely separate entity in man, that it is not attached by some paste-gum to the miserable physical frame, and that it is just the same perispirit as that which exists also in every animal, from the elephant to infusoria, being different from the animal double only by the fact that it is more or less overshadowed by the immortal spirit, and is also capable of acting independently—in the ordinary (not initiated) man during his sleep—and in the initiated Adept at all times; and you will understand everything I wrote, and it will become quite clear to you. This fact has been known and believed since very ancient times. Hierophants and adepts of the Orphic mysteries were initiated into these secrets. St. Paul, who was the

---

* *Op. cit.*, pp. 465-6.

only one among all the Apostles who was an Adept
of the Greek mysteries, was hinting at this rather
openly when he tells about a certain young man who
' in his body or out of it, that is known only to God,'
was taken up to the third heaven." *

Later on, in the same letter, the theme is continued
in this manner:

"When his double, or the real Sahib leaves temporarily his vehicle, the body is left in a similar state
to that we can observe in a calm idiot. He orders it
either to sleep or it is guarded by his men. At first it
seemed to me that he pushed me out of my body, but

---

* *H.P.B. Speaks*, Vol. I, pp. 219-220. Writing on the *perisprit* in
Isis Unveiled: it appears that the term was borrowed from the
Kardecists: "The philosophers, and especially those who were
initiated into the Mysteries, held that the astral soul is the impal-
pable duplicate of the gross external form which we call body. It
is the *perisprit* of the Kardecists and the *spirit-form* of the spiritualists.
Above this internal duplicate, and illuminating it as the warm ray
of the sun illuminates the earth, fructifying the germ and calling
out to spiritual vivification the latent qualities dormant in it, hovers
the divine spirit. The astral *perisprit* is contained and confined within
the physical body as ether in a bottle, or magnetism in magnetized
iron. It is a centre and engine of force, fed from the universal supply
of force, and moved by the same general laws which pervade all
nature and produce all cosmical phenomena. Its inherent activity
causes the incessant physical operations of the animal organism and
ultimately results in the destruction of the latter by overuse and
its own escape. It is the prisoner, not the voluntary tenant, of the
body. It has an attraction so powerful to the external universal
force, that after wearing out its casing it finally escapes to it. The
stronger, grosser, more material its encasing body, the longer is the
term of its imprisonment. Some persons are born with organizations so exceptional, that the door which shuts other people in
from communication with the world of the astral light, can be
easily unbarred and opened, and their souls can look into, or even
pass into that world, and return again. Those who do this consciously, and at will, are termed magicians, hierophants, seers,
adepts; those who are made to do it, either through the fluid of the
mesmerizer or of ' spirits ', are ' mediums.' " (Vol. 1, pp. 197-8)

soon I seemed to become accustomed to it, and now during the moments of his presence *in* me, it only seems (to me) that I am *living* a *double* life. . . . .

"I am learning only now to leave my body; to do it alone I am afraid, but with him I am afraid of nothing.

"I shall try it with you. Only be kind enough to not resist and do not cry. And—do not forget." *

---

* *H.P.B. Speaks*, Vol. I, pp. 224-225. See also under Facsimile No. 15 in Appendix I.

CHAPTER XVII

AN EXPOSITION OF TULKU

Having presented the narrative aspect of Tulku, there yet remains for consideration the exposition—using this term in its dictionary definition, as referring to that portion of writing which explains, in contrast to that which narrates or describes. Therefore it is necessary to become technical: to employ terms which are not familiar to English-speaking persons, for the simple reason that terminology is lacking in this field of study. This should not be a hindrance, inasmuch as when these terms are used they will be defined.

At the same time a difficulty is encountered which is not easily remedied. In order to understand a subject one must apply one's mind towards that subject with attention, resolving not to permit oneself to be distracted from its consideration. Here one of the quirks of the human mind is discovered. As soon as one decides that one must apply one's attention upon a fixed subject, it seems that the mind delights in darting away from it— like a butterfly, hovering over this bloom or that blossom, flitting to another plant which has the same kind of flowers, then off and away again. So when something " new " is presented to the mind, immediately the " darting-off process " automatically commences to function at top performance. Wouldn't it be much more satisfactory to give the mind something with which it is familiar; or perhaps tell a story?

That's just it: why does a person like to follow a story rather than pursue a recitation of statistics? Isn't it because the mind is permitted to follow this trend of " flitting "; because it does not have to work; because it is not subjected to being still?

So it comes to this: in order to learn something, one must find out how to overcome the " darting-off process "

and acquire the ability to concentrate—which signifies
the process of holding the mind steadily upon a desired
subject.

And what has this to do with an exposition of Tulku?
It points to the fact that a dual process of the mind has
been demonstrated. And since this has been undeniably
shown to be a fact on a subject which is readily understandable—which anyone can prove to oneself, at any
time and at any place; it should follow, then, as a natural
deduction that there are other powers pertaining to the
human constitution, even though these are unsuspected by
humanity at large, which have been studied by persons
interested in this field. Therefore, it is asserted that
there are individuals who have been able to demonstrate
the process that has been described in this work as Tulku.

In order to present this exposition, then, it is necessary
at the outset to review the septenary constitution of man,
since this bears directly upon the theme. It is customary
to enumerate the seven principles in tabular form, but
for clarity a division will now be made: a grouping into
immortal components and mortal constituents.

THE HIGHER TRIAD—THE IMMORTAL COMPONENTS

Âtman—The Divine Spark (The Monadic Essence)
Buddhi—The Discriminating Principle
Manas—The Mind Principle

THE LOWER QUATERNARY—THE MORTAL CONSTITUENTS

Kâma—The Desire Principle
Prâna—The Life-Principle
Linga-Sarîra—The Model Body
Sthûla-Sarîra—The Physical Body

While asserting that familiarity with these terms is
required for an understanding of the exposition of Tulku,
nevertheless, a seeming contradiction will confront the
reader. The writer has discovered that it is easier to
approach the subject of Tulku by means of another
classification of man's constitution!

May this seeming contradiction be resolved? Yes, indeed. In this solution lies the key to an understanding of the subject of Tulku.

First of all, then, it is affirmed that the septenary classification of man's constitution (familiarly known as the seven principles of man) gives the esoteric composition of man and may be used to explain *why* man is the being that he is. For that matter, the sevenfold constitution is as applicable in its essential nature and composition to the Animal Kingdom, to the Plant Kingdom and to the Mineral Kingdom, albeit it does not go into the matter of how these three Kingdoms *function*.

The above statements lead to this deduction. It supplies the clue to the " learned dissertation " which took place between H.P.B. and Subba Rao. H.P.B. was dealing with the essential components of a human being (in the sevenfold enumeration). Subba Rao was concerned with the *functional aspect* of a human being in his fourfold classification. (Perhaps it would be more correctly phrased by stating that he was considering a highly evolved human being.)

Now, it is the functional aspect that supplies the clue to an understanding of the performance of Tulku. Thus, we find it stated in *The Secret Doctrine*:

" Though there are seven principles in man, there are but three distinct Upâdhis (bases), in each of which his Âtman may work independently of the rest. These three Upâdhis can be separated by an Adept without killing himself. He cannot separate the seven principles from each other without destroying his constitution." (I, 158 *)

The Sanskrit word *upâdhi* is generally translated *base*, or *vehicle*, since it is compounded of *upa*, a prepositional prefix signifying direction towards, near, upon; and *âdhâ*, to place on, or even to deposit upon. It may also

---

* *S.D.* Vol. I, p. 182, 3rd and revised ed.; I, 213, 6 vol. ed.

be rendered " substitute," or " veil of spirit "—that
through which the spirit may act, the " spirit " here
referring to Âtman. Âtman is defined as a universal
principle, not a " personal principle." In the familiar
Theosophical exposition, Âtman is unable to function on
the lower planes of the cosmos, such as the physical plane.
It requires an upâdhi, through which it may shed its
radiance. Buddhi acts as the upâdhi for Âtman, the
union forming the Monad. As for the three upâdhis
referred to in the citation, with Âtman they compose the
fourfold classification of man according to the Târaka
Râja-Yoga system of philosophy. Enumerating the three
upâdhis, in descending order, they are:

Kârana-upâdhi—(which may be compounded as:
                                    Kâranopâdhi)

Sûkshma-upâdhi   ,,   Sûkshmopâdhi

Sthûla-upâdhi   ,,   Sthûlopâdhi

However, in order to understand the functioning of
the Tryopâdhis (three upâdhis) a key is required.
Because a mere statement of upâdhis does not provide the
clue to the *functioning of the upâdhis*. Mark this singular
feature. The key to the functioning of the upâdhis is
supplied by the sevenfold classification! Hence, because
of the data supplied by the two great exponents of Occult
philosophy, we may gain an understanding of the
operation of Tulku.

Thus, the Sthûlopâdhi (meaning the " physical veil of
spirit ") does not function by means of the physical body
(Sthûla-śarîra) alone. Both Prâna and Linga-śarîra (the
Life-principle and the Model Body) are required for its
upkeep. This is so because the physical body would be
incapable of sustaining life without Prâna. Furthermore,
Prâna courses through the physical body by means of
the Linga-śarîra, since the latter is the vehicle (or upâdhi)
for Prâna.

The intermediate upâdhi is termed Sûkshma-upâdhi—
the fine or subtile (sûkshma) veil of spirit. It should not

be equated to Kâma (the Desire-principle) alone, nor yet
to Manas (the Mind-principle) alone. Here a difficulty
is encountered, inasmuch as it is not simply a matter of
making the usual division of Manas into Higher Manas
and Lower Manas. Such a division (without qualifications) does not accurately correspond to the two higher
upâdhis of the Târaka system. In order to explain this
aspect, another classification may be utilized—that of
the Vedântic system, termed the Pañcha-kośas, or the
fivefold sheaths (*pañcha*, five; *kośas*, sheaths). Enumerated
in descending order:

> Ânandamaya-kośa
> Vijñânamaya-kośa
> Manomaya-kośa
> Prânamaya-kośa
> Annamaya-kośa

The lowest sheath or vesture, representing the physical
body is termed the Annamaya-kośa—literally the sheath
builded of food (*maya*, builded of; *anna*, food). Prâna-
maya-kośa is the sheath builded of the Life-principle
(Prâna) plus its carrier (as previously explained under
the Sthûlopadhi).

The next two sheaths explain the Sûkshmopadhi (of
the Târaka system): Manomaya-kośa—the sheath builded
by Manas; Vijñânamaya-kośa—the sheath builded by
intellection. Here again the sevenfold classification
provides the clue towards the understanding of these two
vestures (kośas). The Manas-principle is dual in manifestation—or rather in its functioning capacity—not a
"single-functioning" principle. It coalesces on the
one hand with Kâma—the Desire-principle—and on the
other hand with Buddhi, the discriminating principle.
Thus Kâma and Manas—commonly termed "Lower
Manas"—jointly form the Manomaya-kośa. This very
well describes the personality (plus the two lower kośas,
of course, since the personality does not function on
earth without its vehicles). Then Manas and Buddhi—
forming the union commonly termed "Higher Manas"—

with the Manas-aspect predominating (*not* Buddhi plus Manas, please note) represent the Vijñânamaya-kośa.

To all intents and purposes the topmost kośa may be equated to the highest upâdhi—the Kâranopadhi. For Ânandamaya-kośa (literally the sheath of bliss) stands for Buddhi. Yet the experiencing of the bliss of Buddhi may only be accomplished by means of an upâdhi—for Buddhi is not able to function on the lower planes without its vehicles, which is Higher Manas. This is the reason that the highest upâdhi is termed the Kâranopâdhi—the " operative veil of spirit," or the " motivating vehicle " for Âtman. It is also called " the Causal Vehicle". In this upâdhi reside the causes producing embodiments upon earth. Hence the Reincarnating Ego (which represents Higher Manas to the exclusion of Lower Manas) is also represented as pertaining to the Kârano-padhi. It is responsible for bringing about another incarnation on earth following the death of the physical body.

In the case of the ordinary person, when the lowest upâdhi is dropped—which occurs at death—because of the inability of Buddhi to function consciously on the physical plane, there is no longer a coherence between the upâdhis. Consequently the intermediate upâdhi, the Sûkshmopadhi, must also be left in the sphere or region appropriate to its subtile condition—namely, the Kâma-loka. Whereupon the Kâranopadhi (with Âtman) continues to sojourn in its appropriate loka. Its *state* is known under the Tibetan term " Devachan," a state of bliss. This condition lasts until another incarnation takes place on earth.

When Tulku is to be performed, the Adept separates the required upâdhis, since he can function in each one separately. The two higher upâdhis (with Âtman, of course) are then transferred, independently of the Sthûlo-padhi, the lowest vesture, into another upâdhi. The transference is, of course, effected without the processes of physical birth.

As to how the Âveśa is performed: one can safely assert that this will remain one of the secrets of Occultism.

H. P. Blavatsky gave a hint concerning its performance
when she associated it with the functioning of a certain
principle in the constitution of man. And there is no
doubt that this is the principle *par excellence*: the goal
and endeavour of man being to activate it; one word, in
fact, representing the height of its attainment—Buddhahood. Because the Buddhi principle is at present dormant
within man, it is needless to mention that the knowledge
of being able to activate it and use it, is not generally
known. In offering the explanation regarding this
constituent in the human constitution, Mme. Blavatsky
found it advisable to consider it in connection with the
highest principle of man's constitution, Âtman, which is
defined as a universal principle, rather than an indivi-
dualized principle. As this principle, Âtman,

" can neither be located nor limited in philosophy,
being simply that which IS in Eternity, and which
cannot be absent from even the tiniest geometrical or
mathematical point of the universe of matter or substance,
it ought not to be called, in truth, a ' human ' principle
at all. Rather, and at best, it is in Metaphysics, that
point in space which the human Monad and its vehicle
man occupy for the period of every life. Now that
point is as imaginary as man himself, and in reality
is an illusion, a *mâyâ*; but then for ourselves, as for
other personal Egos, we are a reality during that fit
of illusion called life, and we have to take ourselves into
account, in our own fancy at any rate, if no one else
does. To make it more conceivable to the human
intellect, when first attempting the study of Occultism,
and to solve the A B C of the mystery of man, Occultism
calls this *seventh* principle the synthesis of the sixth, and
gives it for vehicle the *Spiritual* Soul, *Buddhi*. Now the
latter conceals a mystery, which is never given to any
one, with the exception of irrevocably pledged *chelas*,
or those, at any rate, who can be safely trusted. Of
course, there would be less confusion, could it only
be told; but, as this is directly concerned with the
power of projecting one's double consciously and at

will, and as this gift, like the 'ring of Gyges,' would prove very fatal to man at large and to the possessor of that faculty in particular, it is carefully guarded." *

So be it. And so, since further information on this theme is not to be provided, and since the ring of Gyges is similarly unavailable—and there is little likelihood that it will be obtained, because the possession of that ring conveys to its wearer the magical power of becoming invisible—it is advisable to practise a little concentration upon some Yoga sûtras. From these one learns that:

"The ascetic acquires complete control over the elements by concentrating his mind upon the five classes of properties in the manifested universe; as, first, those of gross or phenomenal character; second, those of form; third, those of subtile quality; fourth, those susceptible of distinction as to light, action, and inertia; fifth, those having influence in their various degrees for the production of fruits through their effects upon the mind." †

Here we are back again on the all-important need for controlling the mind!—in a word, *Concentration*. To what purpose does such exercise in concentration lead? It is recorded:

"From the acquirement of such power over the elements there results to the ascetic various perfections, to wit, the power to project his inner-self into the smallest atom, to expand his inner-self to the size of the largest body, to render his material body light or heavy at will, to give indefinite extension to his astral body or its separate members, to exercise an irresistible will upon the minds of others, to obtain the highest excellence of the material body, and the ability to preserve such excellence when obtained.

---

* *The Key to Theosophy*, pp. 119-20 (or. ed.).

† *Yoga Aphorisms of Patañjali*, Book III, śloka 45.

"Excellence of the material body consists in color, loveliness of form, strength, and density." *

The śloka indicates the preliminary phases in the performance of Âveśa. Its projection is described by means of two more ślokas:

"The ascetic acquires complete control over the organs of sense from having performed concentration (Samyama) in regard to perception, the nature of the organs, egoism, the quality of the organs as being in action or at rest, and their power to produce merit or demerit from the connection of the mind with them.

Therefrom spring up in the ascetic the powers: to move his body from one place to another with the quickness of thought, to extend the operations of his senses beyond the trammels of place or the obstructions of matter, and to alter any natural object from one form to another." †

Types of Tulku

Several illustrations or examples of the performance of Tulku have been provided throughout this work. For purposes of identification these are now enumerated as illustrative examples:

1. The Tulku performed by the Dalai Lamas and Tashi Lamas.
2. The Tulku performed by Shaberons.
3. The Tulku performed by Śankarâchârya.
4. The Tulku performed by a Fakir.
5. The Tulku performed by Kunâla and the Fakir.
6. The Tulku performed by Kunâla and Damodar.
7. The Tulku performed in connection with H.P.B.

Other performances of Tulku were also mentioned in the chapter on Âveśa and Tulku, but they need not be

---

* *Yoga Aphorisms of Patañjali*, Book III, ślokas 46-47.
† *Op. cit.*, ślokas 48-49.

included in the above enumeration since they were referred to sufficiently when mentioned.

1. In the Tulku of the Dalai Lamas and Tashi Lamas there is a continuance in the "stream of consciousness" in the "Incarnations". This is so because the transference from one vehicle, in which a Lama had formerly operated, into a new vehicle has been effected. This is described as usually taking place after a short lapse of years. Expressed technically: the Kâranopâdhi and the Sûkshmopâdhi (with Âtman) are transferred to a new vehicle, a new Sthûlopâdhi.

2. The Tulku of the Shaberon clearly indicates the conscious transference from one vehicle to another, the size of the vehicle offering no impediment. Following the projection and withdrawal process, the Shaberon resumed his own Sthûlopâdhi, the babe being unaffected by the processes. This gives rise to the question: What becomes of the upâdhis "belonging" (for lack of a better word) to the four-month-old infant?

Because the baby does not "die" there is, of course, a difference to be noted. First, it should be stated that there is no difficulty and no impediment to be encountered. Since the Tulku is not a permanent one, only temporary, it is therefore accomplished for a desired interval of time. In explanation: the highest upâdhi, the Kâranopâdhi, is not actually incarnated *in* the physical body; it may be described as "over-enlightening" the Sthûlopâdhi. Of course, from the esoteric standpoint, it might be said that the Sthûlopâdhi is appended to the Kâranopâdhi, since the causal aspects of an incarnation on earth are actually the resultants of the causes which have been "stored" in the Kâranopâdhi during the life last lived on earth and work out as effects upon the Sûkshmopâdhi and Sthûlopâdhi during an incarnation on earth. However, as the case under consideration is that of a four-month-old infant, the Kâranopâdhi is not actually functioning in the Sthûlopâdhi. In further explanation of this statement: Higher Manas, which is technically the Reincarnating Ego, normally does not commence to function before the seventh year of a child's

26

life. Moreover, in an infant the Sûkshmopâdhi is functioning but little, if at all. Therefore, the Shaberon had no difficulty in performing the projection and withdrawal in connection with this type of Tulku.

3. Śankarâchârya represents the classical example of Âveśa, illustrating the projection, the entrance and the reanimation of a body. As it was performed for a specific purpose, when that had been fulfilled the Tulku was terminated. It could, of course, have been continued longer, if desired. Nevertheless, it poses this question: What becomes of the upâdhis belonging to King Amaraka?

With the death of the king, the sovereign's Sûkshmopâdhi and Kâranopâdhi had withdrawn from the Sthûlopâdhi, entering the appropriate after-death states, just the same as normally occurs when a person dies. The two upâdhis had ceased to function on the physical plane when King Amaraka's lowest upâdhi, the Sthûlopâdhi, was laid aside. In due time, pursuing the pattern followed by every individual when death takes place, the Kâranopâdhi of the deceased monarch will bring about a rebirth on earth. It will cause two "new" lower upâdhis to come into manifestation along with the birth of the physical body.

4. The Tulku performed by the Fakir (as narrated by Damodar). This is the same type of Âveśa as Śankarâchârya's. Because of sustaining an injury the Fakir decided to make use of another physical vehicle. Therefore, he performed the Tulku by transferring his Kâranopâdhi and Sûkshmopâdhi into the seven-year old's Sthûlopâdhi, which was in process of "dying," thus revivifying that vehicle.

5. The Tulku performed by Kunâla—upon a fakir. This does not refer to the Fakir of No. 4. It is definitely a different type of Tulku. In this case the complete transference of upâdhis was not effected—there is a type of projection, but no reanimation is involved. A Yogasûtra at this point will assist in the clarification:

"by performing Samyama (concentration) in regard to any particular organ of sense—such as that of hearing, or of feeling, or of tasting, or of smelling—the ascetic acquires the power to cause cessation of the functions of any of the organs of another or of himself, at will." *

The query that was raised at the time of the narration of the incident is worthy of repetition here: The question was asked: Did Kunâla really enter the body of the second fakir? And the reply was: No. Kunâla had temporarily overcome the fakir's senses and substituted his own.

6. The Tulku performed by Kunâla and Damodar. While the narrative that was cited is not very explicit upon the subject, one may assume that Damodar assisted in the performance of the Tulku. Elsewhere it was shown that Damodar had acquired the faculty of projecting his consciousness—a necessary step in the performance of Tulku. Because of the co-operation of the two persons there was no difficulty in connection with the appropriate upâdhis. Attention is again directed to this extract:

"I was fortunate enough yesterday to be shown the process pursued in either entering an empty body, or in using one which has its own occupant. I found that in both cases it was the same." †

7. The Tulku in connection with H.P.B. Pursuant to the description given under No. 5 (above), it would be possible that this type of Tulku could be performed in connection with H.P.B.—when desired. From the testimony provided, however, it would seem to be more likely that the type of Âveśa performed was that similar to the one just instanced in No. 6. Two Tulkus are involved: one partially accomplished (especially in regard to its

---

* *Yoga Aphorisms of Patañjali*, Book III, śloka 22.

† From "A Hindu Chela's Diary," *The Path*, Vol. I, No. 3 (June, 1886).

first stage), and the other, completely so. The first, by H.P.B. herself, who " stepped aside " for the time being, in order that the second Tulku might be accomplished. Co-operation of two individuls is, of course, required in such cases: that of the transmitter and that of the one in whom the transmittal is effected.

On the Origin of the Science of Âveśa or Tulku

The origin of the science of Âveśa is made known in a passage which refers to the early history of the human race on this globe. First it is presented in allegorical manner: by reference to Nârada, the divine Rishi, who is regarded as the representative of the race of " fruitless ascetics." The meaning of this is that Nârada " is said, as soon as he dies in one body, to be reborn in another." *
The esoteric significance of this is thus summed up:

" Happily for the human race the ' Elect Race ' had already become the vehicle of incarnation of the (intellectually and spiritually) highest Dhyânis before Humanity had become quite material. When the last sub-races—save some lowest—of the Third Race had perished with the great Lemurian Continent, ' the seeds of *the Trinity of Wisdom*,' had already acquired the secret of immortality on Earth, that gift which allows the same great personality to step *ad libitum* from one worn-out body into another." †

With regard to the " Elect Race ": it is also known by other names, such as the Sons of the Fire-Mist, the Sons of Ad, the Hierarchy of the Elect. More frequently it is called the Sons of Will and Yoga, because of the fact

---

* *The Secret Doctrine*, Vol. II, p. 275; III, 277, 6 vol. ed., II, 288, 3rd ed.

† *Op. cit.*, Vol. II, p. 276; III, 278, 6 vol. ed.; II, 288, 3rd ed.

that this Elect Race was produced by Kriyâ-śakti, that is through the performance of will and yoga, during the early portion of the Third Root-Race, when that race was still in its state of purity, before the separation of the sexes. These Sons of Will and Yoga

" were a conscious production, as a portion of the race was already animated with the divine spark of spiritual, superior intelligence. It was not a Race, this progeny. It was at first a wondrous Being, called the ' Initiator,' and after him a group of semi-divine and semi-human beings. ' Set apart ' in Archaic genesis for certain purposes, they are those in whom are said to have incarnated the highest Dhyânis, ' Munis and Rishis from previous Manvantaras '—to form the nursery for future human adepts, on this earth and during the present cycle. These ' Sons of Will and Yoga ' born, so to speak, in an immaculate way, remained, it is explained, entirely apart from the rest of mankind." *

Thus the knowledge of this secret science was perpetuated, because the Elect Race was set apart. That there have been exponents of this art from time to time has been made manifest herein. In Tibet and China, in addition to the Dalai Lamas and the Tashi Lamas, those who are proficient in this science are known as Byang-tsiubs and Chang-chubs—

" the Brothers who pass from the body of one great Lama to that of another. . . . . The Tchang-chub (an adept who has, by the power of his knowledge and soul enlightenment, become exempt from the curse of UNCONSCIOUS transmigration)—may, at his will and desire, and instead of reincarnating himself only after bodily death, do so, and repeatedly—during his life if he chooses. He holds the power of choosing for himself

---

* The Secret Doctrine, Vol. I, p. 207; I, 255-6, 6 vol. ed.; I, 288, 3rd ed.

new bodies—whether on this or any other planet—
while in possession of his old form, that he generally
preserves for purposes of his own." *

Chang-chub, or Byang-tsiub is analagous in meaning to
the Mongolian word Kubilkhan, or Kubilgan. It is also
used as an equivalent for the Sanskrit term Bodhisattva,
although the latter term signifies, as well, one who
renounces Nirvâna in order that he might yet remain in
the world of men as a Nirmânakâya.

One who has attained the Path of Deliverance only to
renounce it, is regarded as a Saviour. Truly so. Yet,
another difference is to be noted between one who has
renounced Nirvâna and one who enters the Path of
Deliverance. The one who relinquishes the goal is
acclaimed as a Buddha of Compassion—he who follows
the Secret Path; while he who treads the Open
Path is known as a Pratyeka-Buddha, "the Solitary
One."

Of him who has made the choice of the Open Path
it is written:

"Having reached the Path of Deliverance (Thar-
lam) from transmigration, one cannot perform Tulpa
any longer, for to become a Paranirvânî is to close
the circle of the Septenary Ku-Sum. He has merged
his borrowed Dorjesempa (Varjasattva) into the
Universal and become one with it." †

Thar-lam is a Tibetan term, derived from thar-ha, to
become free, to be saved. Thar-(pai)-lam, meaning the
road to happiness is a common expression in Tibet.
Tulpa is equivalent in meaning to Tulku. The spelling
follows the "phonetic rendering" of the Tibetan word,
which more accurately should read sPrul-pa, although
pronounced Tul-pa). A Paranirvânî (or Paranirvânin)

---

* *The Mahatma Letters to A. P. Sinnett*, p. 285.
† *The Secret Doctrine*, Vol. V, p. 374.

is one who has entered the highest Nirvâna and who is beyond the reach of the Seven-Round cycles. Nipang is the Tibetan word for Nirvâna.

The Path of Deliverance from transmigration signifies freedom from the cyclic Rounds, that is to say, of passing (transmigrating) from globe to globe of the Earth planetary chain for seven complete circuits (accomplishing seven Races on each Globe of the Chain).

The statement is made that one cannot perform Tulku any longer, and the next phrase explains why this is so, namely, because once that Paranirvâna is entered, freedom from the cycle of rebirths has been attained. The circuit of the seven globes is no longer necessary and vehicles for pursuing the transmigrations are no longer required. A footnote explains that

> "Ku-sum is the triple form of the Nirvâna state and its respective duration in the 'cycle of Non-Being'. The number seven here refers to the seven Rounds of our septenary System." *

Dorjesempa is rendered "Diamond Soul" by H. P. Blavatsky. Literally Dorje (or rDorje) signifies jewel, also a diamond; sempa, from sems—spirit. Hence the Nirvânin's individual spirit—"individual," that is, for purposes of manifesting with a vehicle during the period of the seven-round cycle of activity, therefore " borrowed " —has become united with the Universal Spirit or Chang, " the Supreme Unmanifested and Universal Wisdom that has no name." Such a one is a Nirvânin, or one who has become a Tong pa-nyi.

> "He who becomes a Tong-pa-nyi—he who has attained the state of absolute freedom from any desire of living personally, the highest condition of a saint— exists in non-existence and can benefit mortals no more. He is in ' Nipang,' for he has reached the end of ' Tharlam,' the path to deliverance, or salvation from

---

* *The Secret Doctrine*, Vol. V, p. 374.

transmigrations. He cannot perform Trul-pa—voluntary incarnation, whether temporary or life-long—in the body of a living human being; for he is a 'Dangma,' an absolutely purified soul. Henceforth he is free from the danger of ' Dal-jor,' human rebirth; for the seven forms of existence—only six are given out to the uninitiated—subject to transmigration have been safely crossed by him. ' He gazes with indifference in every sphere of upward transmigration on the whole period of time which covers the shorter periods of personal existence,' says the *Book of Khiu-ti*." *

It should be quite apparent that the above citation is very similar to, if not identical with, the śloka from the Commentary which was quoted by H. P. Blavatsky—except that this second citation contains more explanatory phrases. This passage was penned by a Tibetan Gelung of the Inner Temple in answer to questions submitted by H. P. Blavatsky concerning Tibetan teachings. This portion of the citation was written in order to explain mistaken notions published by an Orientalist concerning the Chang-chubs. It therefore has a direct bearing upon the theme under consideration. At the same time it presents an excellent opportunity for calling attention to certain salient points of paramount importance.

1. A Tibetan of the Yellow Cap Order is quoting a passage from the Book of Khiu-ti,† which is available to him. It is virtually the same as a citation made by H. P. Blavatsky from the Commentaries on the Book of Dzyan, to which she had access.

---

* From an article entitled " Tibetan Teachings," first published in *Lucifer*, Vol. XV, pp. 97-104; re-published in *H. P. Blavatsky Collected Writings*, Vol. VI, pp. 111-112.

† H.P.B.'s notation regarding the Book of Dzyan and the Khiu-ti (also spelled Kiu-te) is worthy of repetition here:

" The Book of Dzyan—from the Sanskrit word ' Dhyâna ' (mystic meditation)—is the first volume of the Commentaries

2. It shows that those who are familiar with the Archaic Esoteric Doctrines also have access to its folios.

3. The charge made by critics that H.P.B. invented the Stanzas of Dzyan and the Commentaries as given in *The Secret Doctrine* is hereby shown to be groundless.

4. Therefore, the only alternative left to such critics is that of admitting that the statements made by H.P.B. were true.

5. The secret folios are available to those who are entitled to use them.

THE CULMINATING ACHIEVEMENT OF TULKU

There is but one more phase in the exposition of Tulku, and it may fittingly be regarded as the culminating achievement in the science of Tulku. It especially concerns one who has become proficient in the art of performing Tulku, with specific reference to what has been termed the first phase of the process. Expressed technically, it relates to the ability of accomplishing Pho-wa, or the projection of the consciousness. Likewise, experience has been gained concerning the entrance into the state known as Tong-pa-nyid.* The same procedure is involved in entering this beatific state as in performing the first stage of Tulku, namely, it is accomplished by the projection of the consciousness. That which is now termed the final state, or the

---

upon the seven secret folios of *Kiu-te*, and a Glossary of the public works of the same name. Thirty-five volumes of *Kiu-te* for exoteric purposes and the use of the laymen may be found in the possession of the Tibetan Gelugpa Lamas, in the library of any monastery; and also fourteen books of Commentaries and Annotations on the same by the initiated Teachers."—*The Secret Doctrine*, Vol. V, p. 389.

* It will be recalled that reference was made to the fact that the Mahatma K.H. had entered into the state of Tong-pa-nyid, and also that he had relinquished it.

culmination of achievement in this stage of effort, is encountered when the choice is to be made between entering the Open Path or the Secret Path.*

Irrespective of the choice that is made, whether that of the Open Path, or that of the Secret Path, the resultant robe that is donned (to make use of symbolic language) is made use of by means of Tulku.

The three Robes, or Vestures (as H.P.B. expressed them—the "Shangna Robes") are known in Tibetan as the *s*Ku-*g*sum: *sku*, body, an equivalent of the Sanskrit *kâya*; *g*sum, three; hence literally the Tri-kâya (in Sanskrit).

The first of the Robes sublime, the thrice glorious Shangna Robe, attained by the choice of the Open Path is named chhós-kyi-sku: the Dharmakâya: *chhós*, a word with a great many meanings, such as doctrine, religion, religious books, etc.—in philosophy, absolute existence ("non-existence" from the standpoint of the material world; which may be rendered "Be-ness," the equivalent of the Sanskrit Sat), hence called by Orientalists "the absolute body"; *kyi*, a suffix signifying the genitive case; and *sku*, body.

The second Robe: longs-spyód-kyi-sku. This is equivalent to the Sambhogakâya: generally rendered by Orientalists as the body of enjoyment, which also literally translates the Tibetan words: *longs*, enjoyment; *spyód*, accomplishment; *sku*, body. This second state is described, exoterically, as the body of happiness or glory in which a Buddha experiences the perfection of a conscious and active life of bliss in the second world, or heaven. This second state, nevertheless, still enables the Initiate to return to the third of the *s*Ku-*g*sum; or conversely, enter the first state and attain Nirvâna.

---

* Here use is made of the terms made familiar in *The Voice of the Silence*, where the exposition of the Open and the Secret Path is given (Fragment II—The Two Paths, p. 33 *et seq.*).

The third Vesture: sPrul-pai-sku: * the Nirmânakâya, generally translated by Orientalists as the " transformation body". But as *sprul-pai* signifies " to change," " to appear," the term may well be rendered " the Body of Change," in other words, the body into which a Changchub has changed himself. Some Orientalists also render the term " the emanation body," thus signifying the vehicle which the Nirmânakâya projects.

Such are the names by which the Three Vestures are known in Tibet.

The choice of the Open Path leads to Thar-lam, the Path of Deliverance, the height of attainment, culminating in " donning the Robe sublime," the Dharmakâya. But this Vesture inexorably leads away from spheres of activity, into the heights of Tong-pa-nyid (non-existence from the standpoint of the material world)—at one with All-Being, the while becoming a Pratyeka-Buddha. On the other hand, the choice of the Secret Path achieves the sublimest expression of the Law of Compassion: to remain in the sphere of suffering for others' sake—as a Nirmânakâya: the while still holding the possibility of experiencing the state of Tong-pa-nyid when desired.

But while reciting the glorious achievements and sublime attainments of the Trikâya, there is, nevertheless, the lurking query: *How* does one proceed to enter the sKu-gsum—any one of the three: the Nirmânakâya, the Sambhogakâya, the Dharmakâya?

True, it is said, forsooth, that the Robes sublime are woven by the Pilgrim himself, as he advances up the stream. He himself fashions the Shangna Vestures. But how and of what?

Are not these Robes his " principles "? How could they be aught else? After all, the Pilgrim is still living in the world of men while preparing the Vestures—whether dwelling in verdant forest or on icy mountain. Since

---

* On page 92 of *The Voice of the Silence* (or. ed.) the term *Prulpai Ku* appears which, of course, is sPrulpai sKu without the unpronounced " s's ". It is also given as an equivalent for Nirmânakâya.

the aspirant must of necessity don one of the three Shangna Vestures, how is this accomplished?

He accomplishes this by means of Tulku: by withdrawing himself from the enmeshing bonds of his outer self, and projecting himself within his finer vesture—albeit wrapped in his Robe Sublime—projected into the *state of Being* of his choice and into the arûpa. Cosmic Planes.

Should the choice be made of entering Nipang (Nirvâna), then the Pratyeka-Buddha has attained Tharlam—the Path of Deliverance. Then, of a certitude his physical sheath is "blown out," since it has been abandoned in the sphere of activity, the while his Kâranopâdhi (the Causal Vehicle) has been rendered inoperative, because the Septenary Rounds have been terminated. For such a one Tulku is no longer required to be performed on the material spheres. And in very truth the Kâranopâdhi is "wrapped up" in a Sublime Robe—sublime because no longer pertaining to the world of form, having become at one with "All-Consciousness".

As for the Nirmânakâya: by the śakti pertaining to the Buddhi principle, now fully vitalized because no longer impeded by the shrouding vestures of the lower sheaths, a temporary vehicle may be fashioned to remain in the non-physical plane so long as desired. Since this vehicle is not of physical stuff it does not deteriorate and can remain as the "Continuance Vehicle" as long as the Nirmânakâya wills it so to endure.

"Om! I believe it is not all the Arhats that get of the Nirvânic Path the sweet fruition."

"Om! I believe that the Nirvâna-Dharma is entered not by all the Buddhas." *

---

* Quoted in *The Voice of the Silence*, page 70, and credited to "*Thegpa Chenpoido*, ' Mahâyâna Sûtra,' ' Invocations to the Buddhas of Compassion,' Part I, iv."

" But, as ' there is more courage to accept being than non-being, life than death,' there are those among the Bodhisattvas and the Lha—' and as rare as the flower of udambara are they to meet with '—who voluntarily relinquish the blessing of the attainment of perfect freedom, and remain in their personal selves, whether in forms visible or invisible to mortal sight—to teach and help their weaker brothers." *

Om Vajrapâni Hum!

---

* Quoted from an article entitled " Tibetan Teachings," written for *The Theosophist* by the Chohan-Lama of Rin-cha-tze (Tibet), the Chief of the Archive-registrars of the secret libraries of the Dalai Lama and the Tashi Lama at Tashi-Lhünpo, published in *H. P. Blavatsky Collected Writings*, Vol. VI, p. 112. First published in *Lucifer*, Vol. XV, October, 1894, pp. 97-104.

APPENDIX

I

EXPLANATIONS REGARDING THE FACSIMILES

The purpose of this Appendix is to supply detailed information in connection with the facsimiles which have been included in this work. Grateful appreciation is extended to N. Sri Ram, President of The Theosophical Society, who permitted the inclusion of these reproductions from earlier Theosophical publications.* These examples of calligraphy have added greatly to the historical value, as well as providing authenticity to the documentary evidence, which is so essential in a work of this nature.

As observed in Chapter XIII, where the greatest number of the facsimiles are reproduced, the recipients of these remarkable letters did not give sufficient detailed information concerning them. Notwithstanding this, however, these reproductions are unique and are deserving of the greatest consideration and attention. Primarily the first facsimile: there is no question but that it is an outstanding document. If there had been no other epistle, this in itself would be corroborative evidence that supra-normal powers had been present both in connection with its message and its delivery. Nor should mention be omitted in regard to the paper on which the letter is written. How could anyone possibly have formed the opinion that Mme. Blavatsky might have written this first document, in view of the following considerations:

1. The letter was enclosed in an envelope simply addressed *Odessa*. There is no street address and no name of a country. Certainly the postal authorities would not have accepted such an envelope for delivery, without postage. Had Mme. Blavatsky written the letter and envelope she certainly would have put the street address and " Russia " on the envelope.

2. The letter and address were written in French. Had Helena been writing to her aunt, without thinking of it she would have used Russian.

---

*Most of the reproductions have appeared in the work prepared by C. Jinarājadāsa entitled *Did Madame Blavatsky Forge The Mahatma Letters?* Two were published in the *H. P. Blavatsky Collected Writings* series.

3. The letter was written on what is known as "rice paper". In that era (1870) such paper would have been unprocurable in Russia or in Europe. It was available only in Tibet or in northern India.

4. Regarding the assertion that an accomplice was involved in writing the Mahatma letters: What would be the purpose of arranging to have an accomplice write to her aunt? Then, too, there would have been the necessity of providing some one else to deliver the letter in person—requiring a travel of hundreds of miles, simply to deliver a letter!

5. What would be the purpose of having an accomplice write to her aunt that she would be home in 18 moons? Two or three, perhaps, but why 18? In any event, certainly not a phrase that Helena would have used.

6. Another ridiculous assertion was made: Dâmodar was responsible for "writing" the Mahatma letters. Dâmodar first contacted Mme. Blavatsky in India during July 1879— nine years *after* the receipt of the first Mahatma letter. Furthermore, Dâmodar had no knowledge of French when he first contacted H. P. Blavatsky.

FACSIMILE No. 1

The circumstances regarding the receipt of the first Mahatma letter in 1870 have already been related in Chapter VI, but they will bear repetition in connection with the explanation regarding the first facsimile, which is reproduced on the inserted page facing page 140.* It was fortunate that the recipient of the letter, H. P. Blavatsky's aunt, placed a notation upon the envelope indicating when the letter was received. Not only was the date of the delivery indicated, but the date on which the notation was made was also included, thus giving added certification. This notation is reproduced along with the facsimile of the address on the envelope, appearing in the upper portion of the reproduction. Below the address, which is written in French, is the pencilled notation in Russian made by Nadyejda de Fadeyev. It reads, in translation:

"Received at Odessa November 7, about Lelinka— probably from Tibet—November 11, 1870, Nadyejda F."

---

* Reproduced from *Did Madame Blavatsky Forge The Mahatma Letters?*, p. 7. Published by The Theosophical Publishing House, Adyar, Madras 20, India, 1934 (55 pp.). Also published in *H. P. Blavatsky Collected Writings*, Vol. VI, p. 276.

The transcription of the address on the envelope and the letter in French is here given, followed by its translation:

" À l'Honorable,
    Très Honorable Dame—
      Nadyéjda Andréewna
        Fadeew.
        Odessa.

" Les nobles parents de Mad. H. Blavatsky n'ont aucune cause de se désoler. Leur fille et nièce n'a point quitté ce monde. Elle vit et désire faire savoir à ceux qu'elle aime, qu'elle se porte bien et se sent fort heureuse dans la retraite lointaine et inconnue qu'elle s'est choisie. Elle a été bien malade, mais ne l'est plus: car gràce à la protection du Seigneur Sang-gyas elle a trouvé des amis dévoués qui en prennent soin physiquement et spirituellement. Que les dames de sa maison se tranquillisent donc. Avant que 18 lunes nouvelles se lèvent—elle sera revenue dans sa famille.
                            [symbol] "

" To the Honourable,
    Most Honourable Lady—
      Nadyéjda Andréewna
        Fadeew.
        Odessa.

" The noble relatives of Mad. H. Blavatsky have no cause whatsoever for grief. Their daughter and niece has not left this world at all. She is living and desires to make known to those whom she loves that she is well and feels very happy in the distant and unknown retreat she has selected for herself. She has been very ill, but is so no longer; for owing to the protection of the Lord Sang-gyas she has found devoted friends who take care of her physically and spiritually. Let the ladies of her house, therefore, remain calm. Before 18 new moons shall have risen—she will have returned to her family.
                            [symbol] "

As well as considering the general tenor of the letter, there are seven factors deserving particular attention:

1. The document is a facsimile reproduction of *the first known* " Mahatma letter," written in 1870, before H. P. Blavatsky had made her appearance in the western world.

2. It is an excellent example of what is known as the **K. H.** script—the script used in the bulk of the letters incorporated in the volume entitled *The Mahatma Letters to A. P. Sinnett.*

3. The letter was written and addressed to H. P. Blavatsky's aunt, Nadyejda de Fadeyev, giving information about her niece at a time when her family believed that she was dead. The writer was aware of this.

4. The letter establishes the fact that H. P. Blavatsky was in Tibet in the year 1870—long before she had ever mentioned to anyone that she had been in that land.

5. The letter was delivered in person. As described by Mlle. de Fadeyev, it " was brought to me in the most incomprehensible and mysterious manner, in my house by a messenger of Asiatic appearance, *who then disappeared before my very eyes.*" *

6. The letter uses a Tibetan word for Gautama the Buddha, namely " Sang-gyas " (in Tibetan script *saṅs-rgyas*), which no European of that period would have used.

7. The letter was written five years before the founding of The Theosophical Society. It was therefore written several years before the knowledge of Mahatmas was made known to the Western world.

The size of the envelope is 15 cm. by 12½ cm. The writing on it as well as on the letter appears to be in ink.

Facsimile No. 2

The second facsimile, which is printed on the page facing page 141, is a reproduction of the first page of a handwritten letter from H. S. Olcott,† orginating from the Editor's office of *The Theosophist*, Adyar, Madras, dated the 5th of August, 1888, addressed to Charles W. Leadbeater. The latter was informed that he was placed in charge of the journal during the editor's absence. It was written at a time when H. P. Blavatsky was no longer in India.

The purpose of including this example of Col. Olcott's calligraphy is to enable the reader to compare his handwriting with the other facsimiles included herein. The transcript of the facsimile reads:

---

* From a document published in 1885 by the General Council of The Theosophical Society at Adyar, entitled *Report of the Result of an Investigation into the Charges against Madame Blavatsky*, p. 94.

† Reproduced from *Did Madame Blavatsky Forge The Mahatma Letters?*, page 55.

" My dear Leadbeater:

" I give over into your exclusive charge the *Theosophist* until my return. You will be the sole judge as to the admission of matter and its sequential order. The only limitation I impose is that you shall not admit anything of a personally aggravating nature (anything calculated to provoke unpleasant controversy); or any announcements of resignations of membership, with or without reasons given, unless they are first submitted to me."

In connection with H. S. Olcott's handwriting, the Colonel related that the precipitation of an official document had been accomplished in a truly unique manner: a message was precipitated on the document in *his own* handwriting, although as he stated " if I had not known the contrary, I should have been ready to swear that I had myself written it." *

FACSIMILE No. 3

The third facsimile, printed on the insertion facing page 240, is a very interesting reproduction of a letter,† because of the incidents connected with it and the manner in which it was received. The script is that which is associated with the Mahatma K. H., and as may be seen by means of the notation penned by Colonel Olcott in the lower righthand corner, below the signature, it was " Received and opened by me this 7th June, 1886," and signed: " H. S. Olcott."

First, explaining the reason for the writing of this singular document. It concerns the individual referred to in the first three words of the facsimile as " the poor boy," namely Dâmodar K. Mâvalankar, a young Mahratta Brahman. He was so called because he had not attained majority—that is, from the standpoint of " chelaship ". Shortly after attaining manhood, Dâmodar (as he was known at Adyar) came to visit Mme. Blavatsky and Col. Olcott in July, 1879, within half a year of their arrival in India, and immediately joined The Theosophical Society. He rendered invaluable service at Headquarters, first at Bombay, then at Adyar. In fact, he held the position of Recording Secretary.

---

* *Old Diary Leaves*, II, p. 237. The narration of the episode in connection with the document is given in Chapter XIII, pp. 243-4.

† Reproduced from *Did Madame Blavatsky Forge The Mahatma Letters?*, page 23.

Writing to Mr. Sinnett from Adyar, India, on November 26, 1883, H.P.B. stated that Dâmodar " is hardly four years " a chela.* However, on June 21, 1885, from Torre del Greco, Italy, she commented: " dear Dâmodar is in Tibet." †

It was on February 23, 1885, that Dâmodar left Adyar via steamer to Calcutta, then travelling from there to Darjiling. On April 13 he left Darjiling for Tibet and his Hindu friends heard no more from him. It was rumored that he had died. About a year later, a devoted Theosophist in Bombay, when writing to Col. Olcott in connection with T. S. affairs added a closing paragraph requesting information concerning Dâmodar. The letter, written by Tookaram Tatya, was dated June 5, 1886, and posted in Bombay on the same date. It should be borne in mind that H.P.B. was in Elberfeld, Germany, at that time, staying with the Gebhards, and that Col. Olcott was in Adyar. Neither of them had any word from Dâmodar since the Hindu chela's departure from Darjiling. Imagine the colonel's surprise, therefore, when he opened the envelope which had been delivered at Headquarters, Adyar, by postal service on the 7th of June, to find a message to him in response to the question regarding Dâmodar, which was asked in the letter addressed to him, and, moreover, which he could not have answered.

Tookaram Tatya's letter was written on very thin paper, customarily in use in India, because postal rates were one-half anna for one-half tola (the equivalent of one-fifth of an ounce, or less than six grams). It was handwritten in black ink. Here is his letter:

" Bombay, 5th June, 1886.
" My respected Brother and Sir,

" I have received yours of the 1st inst. There is no doubt that these constant references to you for improving matters must have tired your patience. You have enough to do and I hope in a few months more, we shall find ourselves in a very satisfactory position.

" I am not sufficient learned, neither have I the time to prepare a hand-book which would be universally approved. But I am trying to collect some materials, and after arranging them I shall forward them to you.

---

* *The Letters of H. P. Blavatsky to A. P. Sinnett*, p. 72.
† *Op. cit.*, p. 100.

" In regard to the verses for the Oriental Library I wish you kindly to let me know, what should be the substance of the verses you want the Goozrathi poet to write. We shall have to assure him that there are satisfactory reasons to show that the Society has the means of raising up such a grand and universally useful library as you expect it to be.

" Our respected Brother, Mr. Shri Niwas Rao, was living with me for two days and I had some interesting conversation with him.

" I am sorry to say that I am unable at present to go to Madras. How long will you be staying at Adyar? I have received a letter from Pandit Gopinath of Lahore saying if you were again to visit Panjaub many good branches could be opened there.

" I have certainly been thinking of poor brother Damodar. It is nearly a year and a half since he left and we have hitherto had no authentic news about him. If you have any recent information about him please communicate it to me.

" Yours sincerely,
TOOKARAM TATYA." *

On one of the blank pages of the thin sheet of paper, written diagonally across the sheet in what appears to be blue pencil, in the script associated with Mahatma K. H., the following message had been precipitated, while the sealed envelope was in the custody of the postal authorities:

" The poor boy has had his fall. Before he could stand in the presence of the ' Masters ' he had to undergo the severest trials that a neophyte ever passed through, to atone for the many questionable doings in which he had overzealously taken part, bringing disgrace upon the sacred sciences and its adepts. The mental and physical suffering was too much for his weak frame, which has been quite prostrated; but he will recover in course of time. This ought to be a warning to you all. You have believed ' not wisely but too well.' To unlock the gates of the mystery you must not only lead a life of the strictest probity but learn to discriminate truth from falsehood. You have talked a great deal about Karma but have hardly realized the true significance of that doctrine.

---

* Reproduced from *Did Madame Blavatsky Forge The Mahatma Letters?*, p. 21.

The time is come when you must lay the foundation of that strict conduct—in the individual as in the collective body— which, ever wakeful, guards against conscious as well as unconscious deception.

K. H."

That very day Col. Olcott showed the two letters to the staff at Headquarters, three of whom placed their signatures on another corner of the document indicating by their endorsement that it had been
" Seen
June 7th, 1886
T. Subba Rao
A. J. C-O.
J. N. C."
The letters A. J. C-O. are the initials of A. J. Cooper-Oakley; J.N.C.—Dr. J. Nield Cook.

Testimony is also available that Tookaram Tatya was also shown the message which had been precipitated upon the inside of his folded sheet of paper, giving a direct reply to his question about Dâmodar. For on the 14th of June he addressed a second letter to Col. Olcott, from Bombay. The pertinent paragraph from his epistle is alone cited:

" I feel extremely obliged to you for your kind letter of the 8th inst. handing me my own letter with the remarks of our Gooroo Dewa. I look upon this as a beginning of a new era in connection with our Society's movement. We must all heartily follow the invaluable instructions of our revered Master to place the Society on the firm rock of truth and never at any moment do or say anything that may bring discredit upon our Masters and their teaching. Really this new circumstance has put a fresh life into me to work without any fear of bad results hereafter. I quite agree with you that we are all imperfect and our zeal may sometimes unconsciously lead us to do things that may not be consistent with the strict rules of uprightness. I have one request to make to you: not to show the letter with Master's remarks to any one except those who can be safely relied upon, for I find that even the best of men discredit such phenomena for one reason or other." *

---

* Op. cit., pp. 24-25. These documents are on file in the archives of The Theosophical Society at Adyar. " Gooroo dewa " (in the last cited paragraph) is usually spelled " Gurudeva "; the Sanskrit compound signifies " divine Teacher ".

FACSIMILE No. 4

The fourth facsimile, appearing on the insertion facing page 241, is another example of the K. H. script. Its chief interest lies in the fact that it conclusively negates the charge which had been made, that it was either Dâmodar or H. P. Blavatsky who were responsible for the handwriting of the Mahatma letters. This was the theory put forward by the envoy who had been selected by the Psychic Research Society and sent from England to Adyar to investigate the phenomena which had been taking place at the Headquarters.

Here is an instance in which a forthright action could have altered the history of The Theosophical Society and saved H. P. Blavatsky from experiencing intense agony and suffering. When the Researcher's envoy, Richard Hodgson, arrived at Adyar from London, Dâmodar was interrogated concerning the letters which had been phenomenally received. However, the letter reproduced as Facsimile No. 4 was not shown to the investigator; doubtless because Dâmodar considered it to be too precious—too sacred to show to prying eyes. Had he shown this letter to Dr. Hodgson, the charge would not have been formulated against Dâmodar, accusing him of fabricating the handwriting of his revered Guru.

Observe the notation in the top left-hand corner of the facsimile: it was placed there by Dâmodar, reading: " Rd. 5 A.M. 27-2-84," indicating that it was received at 5:00 in the morning of February 27, 1884. Certain it is that the letter was not delivered by postal service at that hour in the morning!

With regard to the charge that Dâmodar was collaborating with H.P.B. in producing letters: it may be refuted, because of the fact that at the time this letter was received neither Mme. Blavatsky nor Col. Olcott were present at Adyar. In fact they had left the Headquarters twenty days before the receipt of the letter—on February 7th. Furthermore, they had sailed from Bombay on February 20th en route to Europe, leaving Dâmodar in charge of affairs at Adyar—a great responsibility. This was the reason that he was so dejected.

The reproduction* shows the exact size of the front page of the letter. The back page contained twelve more words, concluding with the initialed signature. The letter gives the

---

* Reproduced from *Did Madame Blavatsky Forge The Mahatma Letters?*, pp. 19-20.

appearance of having been written in blue pencil, and is on very thin paper. On reading it one can well understand why Dâmodar cherished the epistle so dearly. The transcription of the complete letter is given below:

"Do not feel so dejected, my poor boy, no need for that. As Mr. Sinnett rightly says in his *Esoteric Buddhism*, the higher spiritual progress must be accompanied by intellectual development on a parallel line. You have now the best opportunities for doing that where you are working. For your devotion and unselfish labour, you *are* receiving help, silent tho' it be. Your time is not yet come. When it does, it shall be communicated to you. Till then make the best of the present favourable opportunity to improve yourself intellectually, while developing your intuitions. Remember that no effort is ever lost, and that for an occultist there is no past, present, or future, but ever an *Eternal Now*. Blessings.

K. H."

FACSIMILE No. 5

The fifth facsimile, which is reproduced on the insertion facing page 242, is a portion of a letter which was received by Dr. Franz Hartmann,* to which he assigned the date of January 12, 1885. The letter was received during the time that the doctor was residing at Adyar and assisting in the activities at the Headquarters.

Dr. Hartmann joined The Theosophical Society in 1882 while residing in Colorado, and in response to an invitation made in 1883 by Col. Olcott to come to Adyar, the doctor arrived there on December 4th, after having travelled from California to Hong Kong and other parts of China and Japan.

During the catastrophic period of 1884-85, Dr. Hartmann was at Adyar, leaving the Headquarters on March 31, 1885. While there, however, he was the recipient of ten Mahatma letters: seven from Mahatma M., three from Mahatma K.H. He received his first letter on December 25, 1883, three weeks

---

* Reproduced from *H. P. Blavatsky Collected Writings*, Vol. VIII, p. 449, which in turn was reproduced from a microfilm copy of the original letter, which was filmed when in possession of Hugo Vollrath, of Leipzig, Germany.

after his arrival at Adyar, in response to a letter which the doctor had placed " in the Shrine".

The facsimile is a portion of the tenth letter and is an example of the script associated with the Mahatma M. The transcription of the reproduction is as follows:

" The fool is making capital against Society out of your letter (about discovery). He quotes from, reads it to all, reviles the entire Theosophical household on its strength. You ought to stop him. Again. In such a great work as this Movement no one should expect to find his associates all congenial, intuitive, prudent or courageous. One of the first proofs of self-mastery is when one shows that he can be kind and forbearing and genial with companions of the most dissimilar characters and temperaments. One of the strongest signs of retrogression [is] when one shows that he expects others to like what he likes and act as he acts. You know whom of you the cap fits. Be a help to us and act accordingly. You are too many here. With more or less bits of too much self-personality.

" You have earned much good karma during past year, friend and brother, though, of course mistakes and small sins of commission and omission have now and then been made. It is not best for you that I should specify exactly what you should do, or where you should go. Do not quit this place at any rate before K. 's pamphlet has been revised and corrected thoroughly.' It must be *very strong*. There are still black clouds over Headquarters and rumblings of dangerous thunder. The woman has the malice of a *dugpa* in her and the ' one Eyed ' is good help in her infernal concoctions. The young man from London cool and prepared for anything as he is, was stunned by her the other day—her *lie* [*facsimile* ends abruptly here]."

The letter refers to the very trying period that was being experienced at the Theosophical Society's Headquarters. The investigation pursued by Richard Hodgson for the Society for Psychic Research was under way—he had arrived at Adyar in December, 1884. The Coulombs were already involved in their malicious schemes. " The woman " who has " the malice of a dugpa " mentioned in the second paragraph is Mme. Emma Coulomb. She was also described as a medium in the 4th letter which Dr Hartmann received. " Dugpa " is a Tibetan word, derived from a root *gdug*, meaning poison; hence *g*Dug-pa signifies generally anything hurtful, any injury; it is also applied to a person who makes mischief or does harm. The " one Eyed " individual, acting as a collaborator with Mme. Coulomb, is her husband, M. Alexis Coulomb. Richard Hodgson is referred to as " the young man from London, cool and prepared for anything."

The closing sentences of an additional portion of the letter should be included:

". . . An infinite field of activity lies before you; the whole world is open to you. . . . Great obstacles are to be overcome; the greater is the power required to overcome them, the greater is the growth that comes from it. A constant restraint of passions, a sleepless watch over, and patient forbearance of, human weaknesses, will help towards victory.

M." *

FACSIMILE No. 6

The sixth facsimile, which is printed on the insertion facing page 243, is another example of the script associated with the Mahatma M. It is a reproduction of a letter † which was not sent to an individual; instead it was addressed to a group. It was folded in a triangular manner and came fluttering down through the air, as though it were a winged message, bearing the notation: on the envelope: " To all those whom this may concern—to the honourable and doubting company". The incident took place in the city of Bhavnagar, situated in the then Western India States Agency, on the Gulf of Cambay, on the occasion when Mme. Blavatsky and Col. Olcott were at Wadhwan (another city not far from Bhavnagar) in Kathiawar, on June 22-23, 1882. They had received an invitation to visit the ruler, Daji Raj, the Thakore Sahib of Wadhwan, because the monarch was a cousin of Prince Harisinghji. Prince Harisinghji Rupsinghji had joined The Theosophical Society in 1882; he remained a devoted Theosophist until his death. He is remembered by a trilithon which he had erected in the name of his wife on the estate of Adyar, just west of the Headquarters Hall.

---

* *Op cit.*, pp. 449-451. For an account of where one of Dr. Hartmann's letters originated, see Chapter VI, pages 135-9.

† Reproduced from *Did Madame Blavatsky Forge The Mahatma Letters?*, p. 27—the exact size of the letter.

Three members of the gathering were known to be present: Professor J. N. Unwala, who had joined The Theosophical Society, along with Prince Harisinghji in 1882, and who had possession of the letter for many years; a doctor on the staff of the Bhavnagar Railway, who was considered to be an excellent disputant as well as being an atheist; Murad Ali Beg, an Englishman who was born in India but had become a Mohammedan and who was the chief cavalry officer of the Maharajah of Bhavnagar. Before his acceptance of Mohammedanism he had been a Theosophist and had written for *The Theosophist* a splendid article entitled " The Elixir of Life " under the name of Godolphin Mitford, F.T.S. He passed away in 1884.

On the evening that the group had gathered together they were discussing whether or not there were such individuals as the Mahatmas. Some had expressed doubt in regard to their existence, and while they continued their consideration of the subject their attention converged on the note which came fluttering into their midst. It read:

" Foolish are the hearts, who doubt of our existence! or of the powers our community is in possession of for ages and ages. Would that you would open your hearts to the reception of the blessed truth, and obtain the fruits of the Arhatship if not in this then in another and better rebirth.

" Who is for us—answer! "

M. ∴ "

In connection with this facsimile, another short message addressed to and received by R. S. (usually known as S. Ramaswamier, F.T.S.—a chela of Mahatma M.) is appropriate. It reads:

" In the name of M——, R. S. is ordered to take the enclosed to Subba Row. R. Swami has my blessings, and is commanded not to reveal this to any one. He may, however, say that he received this letter—a new proof of our reality *independently* of *Upasika*.

M. ∴ " *

---

* Quoted from *Letters from The Masters of the Wisdom*, Second Series, Letter No. 53, pp. 100-1. *Upasika* signifies H. P. Blavatsky.

Facsimile No. 7

Facsimile No. 7, which is reproduced on the page inserted facing page 246 is representative of an earlier era than the preceding five facsimiles, in fact it antedates the founding of The Theosophical Society. The letter was addressed to "Brother Henry" and is written in black ink on white parchment paper. The date on which it was received was placed in the lower left-hand corner of the page by Henry S. Olcott: June 11, 1875.

The reproduction* is an example of the script associated with the Master Serapis, who designated himself as a member of the Brotherhood of Luxor—which is often referred to by Col. Olcott as the Egyptian Branch of the Brotherhood. It was this Brotherhood which acted in a supervisory capacity in connection with the founding of The Theosophical Society in New York, in September, 1875. The letter is one of a series of about twenty letters. As well as giving Col. Olcott personal advice, the messages dealt with the furtherance of the Cause which he had espoused. Of even greater significance is the fact that a number of the letters dealt with problems concerning Mme. Blavatsky and assistance that was being provided to her without her knowledge. The writer enjoined Col. Olcott to maintain secrecy with respect to the instructions he was receiving and that he should not mention the fact to H. P. Blavatsky. At the same period it would seem that Mme. Blavatsky was undergoing a certain phase in her occult development.

In his autobiographical account, Col. Olcott narrated that most of the letters were delivered to him at his New York residence by the mail-man and some in Boston. The envelopes, bearing postage, had been mailed in Philadelphia; one in Albany. This is indeed a remarkable fact, because the writer of the letter was certainly not stationed in the city where the letters were posted. Seven of the letters of the series were written on green paper with what appears to be black ink.

In this facsimile, instead of the signature "Serapis" (as in Facsimile No. 8) a symbol has been used: a letter "S" superimposed upon a triangle. In some of the letters both the symbol and "Serapis" appear, indicating that whether the symbol or the signature are used, they come from the same source. The transcription of the facsimile is as follows:

---

* Reproduced from *Did Madame Blavatsky Forge The Mahatma Letters?*, p. 39.

"Brother Henry—Greeting!

". . . ' *Be courageous and hopeful* '. . . Blessed words! The divine, ever working Law of Compensation, whose humble ministry we are, has not overlooked the tiny seed, cast by the charitable hand of our brother on the soil of the future harvests—of Good and Evil. The above words *will* come back to thee, brother. Thou hast created—happiness—and happiness must be created unto thee. The seed will grow and thrive, and under the beneficent shade of the heavenly shrub planted by thine own hands wilt thou one day seat thyself with thy beloved boys—and may be find rest for thy weary head.

"Brother—wise beginnings ought to grow in size as in beauty. Advise thy youngest brother of the city of Boston ' to try ' and increase his paper to XVI pages.

[Symbol] "

The phrase " thy beloved boys," had reference to Col. Olcott's two sons: Morgan Olcott (born 1861) and William Topping Olcott (born 1862). " Thy younger brother of the city of Boston " signified Elbridge Gerry Brown, who was the editor of the *Spiritual Scientist* of that city. The letter also referred to this magazine and its editor, when the Colonel was petitioned: " ' to try ' and increase his paper to XVI pages."

In regard to E. G. Brown, the comment made by H.P.B. in her Theosophical " Scrap-Book No. I " explains the outcome of her efforts:

"Between Col. Olcott and myself, H.P.B., we have spent over a 1,000 dollars given him to pay his debts and support his paper. Six months later he became our *mortal* enemy because only we declared our unbelief in *Spirits*. Oh grateful mankind! "

"A constant shower of abuse and sneering in *his* paper against us, and in other papers too, and bankruptcy to end the whole without a single line of acknowledgment, excuse or regret. Such is Gerry Elbridge Brown the Spiritualist! " *

However, because of the failure of this effort we find this encouraging memorandum:

"*Orders* received from India direct to establish a philo-sophico-religious society and choose a name for it, also to choose Olcott. July, 1875." †

---

* Quoted from *Letters from the Masters of the Wisdom*, Series, II, p. 15.
† *Op. cit.*, p. 15.

FACSIMILE No. 8

The eighth facsimile, which is reproduced* on the insertion facing page 247, is another example of the script associated with the Master Serapis. It is one of the latest in the series of letters received from this Master—if not the very last one of the lot. Although Col. Olcott did not supply the date of its receipt, the context favours the assumption just made, because the first sentence requests a postponement of " the meeting "— almost certainly referring to a meeting of The Theosophical Society, which had been scheduled. A meeting of the T.S. was actually held on Saturday, the 16th of October, 1875, while the previous meeting had taken place on the 13th of September. Here is the transcription of the letter:

" I pray thee, Brother mine, to take necessary steps to adjourn the meeting until Saturday which will be. Sister has a labour to perform. Be *friendly* to the English seer, Emma, for she is a noble woman and her soul hath many gems hidden within it. Begin not without our Sister.—Unto the regions of Light I send for thee my prayer.

SERAPIS "

The word " Sister," which is twice used, signifies H.P.B., while " the English seer, Emma," has reference to the spiritualist author of *Art Magic*, Emma Hardinge Britten. She and her husband, Dr. Britten, were among the sixteen persons present at the founding of The Theosophical Society in New York, on September 8, 1875. In compliance with the request made in the letter, Col. Olcott so arranged it that the meeting which was convoked for Saturday, was held at No. 206 West 38th Street, New York, which was the residence of the Brittens.

On the reverse side of the facsimile (which is not reproduced here) is an interesting item. It is a sentence in Latin, closing with three words in Greek:

" Sub pretextu juris summum jus saepe summa injuria, Frater; suaviter in modo, fortiter in re. Tantaene animis coelestibus aut vere adepti IRAE?

" In Nomine

ΑΒΛΑΝΑΘΑΛΒΑ

ΣΕΜΕΣ ΕΙΛΑΜ."

---

* Reproduced from *Did Madame Blavatsky Forge The Mahatma Letters?*, p. 41.

Translation: "Under pretext of justice, a strict application of law is often the gravest injury, Brother. Be gentle in manner though resolute in execution. Can such Wrath towards divine souls befit one fully proficient? In the Name of Ablanathalba Semes Eilam." *

The three Greek words are Gnostic terms. The first word "Ablanathalba" is a word which reads the same from left to right, or from right to left, because the "th" represents the single Greek character *theta*—when rendered in Roman letters· About this Gnostic word H.P.B. writes:

" A term similar to ' Abracadabra ". It is said by C. W. King to have meant ' thou art a father to us '; it reads the same from either end and was used as a charm in Egypt. †
Abracadabra is explained in this manner:
" The word ' Abracadabra ' is a later corruption of the sacred Gnostic term ' Abrasax', the latter itself being a still earlier corruption of a sacred and ancient Coptic or Egyptian word: a magic formula which meant in its symbolism ' Hurt me not,' and addressed the deity in its hieroglyphics as ' Father'. It was generally attached to an amulet or charm and worn as a *Tat*, on the breast under the garments." ‡

FACSIMILE No. 9

The ninth facsimile, appearing on the insertion facing page 272 reproduces the script § associated with the Master Hilarion, in a letter received by Col. Olcott, on which he placed the date of its receipt (on page 2 of the letter—Facsimile No. 10) as June 11, 1883. The epistle is written in French in what appears to be green ink, on both sides of a letter-size sheet of white paper. As the account of its receipt was fully covered on the page facing the facsimile, as well as the inclusion of the translation into

---

* Quoted from *Letters from the Masters of the Wisdom*, Second Series, p. 44. A note is added suggesting that *Semes Eilam* signifies " Eternal Sun "—which is usually referred to in *The Secret Doctrine*, as the Central Spiritual Sun.

† *The Theosophical Glossary*, pp. 3-4.

‡ *Op. cit.*, p. 4. The *Tat* is equivalent to the Egyptian Tau, or *ankh*, which is represented in the center of the T. S. Seal.

§ Reproduced from *Did Madame Blavatsky Forge The Mahatma Letters?*, p. 45, the exact size of the letter. The date placed on the letter by Col. Olcott (11th of June, 1883) does not tally with his diary entry (of June 6). An explanation may be offered: June 11th was very likely the date he made the entry on the letter: it was placed in the archives of the T. S. at Adyar.

English of Hilarion's letter, these need not be repeated here.
The transcription of the French text follows:

" Maha Sahib avec qui je suis pour le moment, m'ordonne
de dire que le plan le plus raison[n]able serait de faire un
tour des pays adjacents—pour un mois. De Tinnevelly ou
bien le Malabar, le Col. pourrait se rendre pour quelques
jours à Colombo—mais *seulement pour quelques jours*—pour les
encourager et les remplir de son *Akasa personnel*—ce qui ne
pourrait que leur faire du bien. Les Sociétés du Midi ont
besoin de sa présence vivifiante. Cerclant tout autour dans
la Présidence—il pourrait être ainsi rappelé à tout moment
au *headquarter* si besoin il y avait. Le 17 Juillet serait le vrai
temps d'aller aux provinces du Nord, visitant toutes les
Sociétés sur son chemin,—depuis Bellary jusqu'au Poona, etc.
"Maha Sahib prie le Col. de ne pas risquer trop sa santée.
Son avis serait de donner d'une tuile magnétique sur la têt,
de trois quatre personnes ici et tâcher d'entrer en relation
avec Venkategiri et le Vizionagrom. Il y a assez de temps
pour cela jusqu'au Juin 17. Qu'il fasse un plan et le dise."

Some notes may be added in regard to the Master Hilarion.
H.P.B. first met him in 1860.* Some years later he visited her
in Egypt, where he gave her certain warnings.† When *The
Theosophist* had been established in Bombay, during the first
year of its publication it contained a story entitled " The
Ensouled Violin " ‡ and it carried the signature: Hilarion
Smerdis, F.T.S., Cyprus, October 1, 1879.

In a letter to Miss Francesca Arundale from the Mahatma
K. H., reference is made to " the adept who writes stories with
H.P.B.", § thereby signifying Hilarion. Unquestionably this
adds to the interest in connection with the story just mentioned.
However, no information is available as to the processes or
methods involved in this collaboration. Furthermore, in a
letter which Mr. Sinnett received from the Mahatma K. H.,
most likely Hilarion is referred to in the passage: " one of ours,
who is passing through Bombay from Cyprus, on his way to

---

* *H. P. Blavatsky Collected Writings*, Vol. VI, pp. 291-2.

† *The Letters of H. P. Blavatsky to A. P. Sinnett*, p. 189. In her letter to Sinnett
the name is spelled " Illarion."

‡ Volume I, January, 1880.

§ *Letters from the Masters of the Wisdom*, First Series, p. 57 (4th ed. 1948).

Tibet. . ." * Especially so, as H.P.B. mentions in an article that this Eastern adept visited her in Bombay, while en route to Tibet.† Col. Olcott was a little more specific. In his Diary, under date of February 19, 1881, he made this entry: " Hilarion is here en route for Tibet, and has been looking over, in and through the situation." ‡

FACSIMILE No. 10

The tenth facsimile, appearing on the insertion which faces page 273 is a reproduction § of the concluding portion of the letter which was reprinted as Facsimile No. 9. The notation in the lower left-hand corner was added by Col. Olcott, reading: " Rec'd. 11/6/83 instantaneously formed in Shrine, Madras." The circumstances connected with this note were fully covered in the explanation provided alongside the facsimile. Nevertheless, a further testimonial as to the efficacy of the Shrine, as a means of communication, may be presented. Especially so, as the anecdote to be recounted deals with an incident which occurred during H.P.B.'s *absence from Adyar*. Its inclusion at this point is well worthy of narration, in spite of the lengthy nature of the anecdote. Moreover, it likewise records the receipt of a precipitation of a message upon a note between two ladies, again not in connection with Mme. Blavatsky. The testimonial is entitled: " Testimony to Phenomena." ‖

" In the month of August last having occasion to come to Madras in the absence of Col. Olcott and Madame Blavatsky, I visited the Head-Quarters of the Theosophical Society to see a wonderful painting of the Mahatma K. H. kept there in a shrine and daily attended to by the chelas. On arrival at the house I was told that the lady, Madame C., who had charge of the keys of the shrine, was absent, so I awaited her return. She came home in about an hour, and we proceeded

---

* *The Mahatma Letters to A. P. Sinnett*, p. 36.

† *H. P. Blavatsky Collected Writings*, Vol. VI, p. 271.

‡ *Op. cit.*, Vol. VI, p. 280.

§ Reproduced from *Did Madame Blavatsky Forge The Mahatma Letters?*, p. 46.

‖ Reprinted from *The Theosophist*, Supplement to December, 1883, Vol. V. No. 3, p. 31. The testimonial was supplied by Major-General Henry Rhodes Morgan, who with his wife joined the T. S. in Sept., 1883. The Morgans made their home in Ootacamund, in the Nilgiri Hills, and Mme. Blavatsky visited them there.

upstairs to open the shrine and inspect the picture. Madame
C. advanced quickly to unlock the double doors of the hanging
cupboard, and hurriedly threw them open. In so doing she
had failed to observe that a china tray inside was on the edge
of the shrine and leaning against one of the doors, and when
they were opened, down fell the China tray, smashed to
pieces on the hard chunam floor. Whilst Madame C. was
wringing her hands and lamenting this unfortunate accident
to a valuable article of Madame B—'s, and her husband was
on his knees collecting the *debris*, I remarked it would be
necessary to obtain some China cement and thus try to
restore the fragments. Thereupon Monsieur C. was des-
patched for the same. The broken pieces were carefully
collected and placed, tied in a cloth, within the shrine, and
the doors locked. Mr. Dâmodar K. Mâvalankar, the Joint
Recording Secretary of the Society, was opposite the shrine,
seated on a chair, about ten feet away from it, when after
some conversation an idea occurred to me to which I
immediately gave expression. I remarked that if the Brothers
considered it of sufficient importance, they would easily
restore the broken article, if not, they would leave it to the
culprits to do so, the best way they could. Five minutes had
scarcely elapsed after this remark when Dâmodar, who during
this time seemed wrapped in a reverie—exclaimed, ' I think
there is an answer.' The doors were opened, and sure
enough, a small note was found on the shelf of the shrine—on
opening which we read ' To the small audience present.
Madame C. has occasion to assure herself that the Devil is
neither so black nor so wicked as he is generally represented;
the mischief is easily repaired.'

" On opening the cloth the China tray was found to be
whole and perfect; not a trace of the breakage to be found
on it! I at once wrote across the note, stating that I was
present when the tray was broken and immediately restored,
dated and signed it, so there should be no mistake in the
matter. It may be here observed that Madame C. believes
that the many things of a wonderful nature that occur at the
Head-Quarters, may be the work of the Devil—hence the
playful remark of the Mahatma who came to her rescue. The
matter took place in the middle of the day in the presence
of four people. I may here remark that a few days before, I
came into the room in my house just as Madame B— had
duplicated a ring of a lady in a high position, in the presence
of my wife and daughter in broad day-light. The ring was

a sapphire and a valuable one—and the lady has preserved it.* On another occasion a note came from the above lady to my wife and was handed into the drawing-room in the presence of several people. On opening it a message was found written across the note in the well known characters of the Adept. The question is how the message got into the note? The lady who wrote it was perfectly astounded when she saw it—and could only imagine it was done at her own table with her own blue pencil.

" Whilst on the subject of the shrine I may mention that it is a small cabinet attached to the wall with shelves and double doors. The picture of the Mahatma that I came to see, lately given to the Founders of the Society, is a most marvellous work of art. Not all the R.A.'s put together could equal such a production. The coloring is simply indescribable. Whether it has been produced by a brush or photographed, entirely passes my comprehension. It is simply superb.

H. R. MORGAN, F.T.S.,

" Ootacamund,   *Major-General."*
" 2nd November, 1883." †

FACSIMILE No. 11

The eleventh facsimile, which appears on the insertion facing page 280, is a reproduction ‡ of a missive which has come to be known as " the pink note." It is the first known Mahatma

---

* Reference is here made by Maj.-Gen. Morgan to the ring which was duplicated by Mme. Blavatsky for Mrs. Sarah M. Carmichael—during the latter's visit to the Morgans. Two months later, when in Madras, Mrs. Carmichael took the ring to Orr & Sons, jewellers, who appraised the sapphire which had been duplicated at 150 rupees (Cf. *Incidents in the Life of Mme. Blavatsky*, p. 204, 2nd ed.) Mme. C., mentioned previously, has reference to Mme. Emma Coulomb, who was at the time employed as a housekeeper at the T. S. Headquarters at Adyar.

† Also published in *H. P. Blavatsky Collected Writings*, Vol. VI, pp. 418-9, following an article entitled " My Justification " (pp. 414-7), in which H. P. B. refers to the construction of " the Shrine " by M. Coulomb, as well as to Major-General Morgan's anecdote as here reprinted.

‡ The reproduction portrayed as Facsimile No. 11 was especially prepared at Adyar for publication in this volume. So far as is known, this is the first time that this celebrated note has been reproduced. Although included in the collection of the Mahatma letters filed in the British Museum, it was not included in the volume entitled *The Mahatma Letters to A. P. Sinnett*. The anecdote covering the receipt of " the pink note " is fully covered in Chapter XIII, pp. 279-284, therefore not repeated here.

letter which was received in India and was transmitted in response to a request which was specifically made by Mrs. Patience Sinnett. She herself also decided where she would like to have the missive placed, namely on a twig of a tree. Her wish was indeed fulfilled. A blank piece of pink paper was transmitted by H. P. Blavatsky to the Mahatma, and the same pink paper was returned, in the manner specified, bearing this message: " I have been asked to leave a note here for you. What can I do for you? " It was signed by some Tibetan characters.

FACSIMILE No. 12

The twelfth facsimile, printed on the insertion which faces page 281, reproduces a letter * which was received by Col. Olcott some time in 1875, while he and Mme. Blavatsky were residing in New York. From the context one may assume that it was written before the founding of The Theosophical Society. Col. Olcott left no notation regarding this letter, nor any memorandum concerning the occurrence mentioned in the letter, because it is not referred to in his autobiographical account, published under the title of *Old Diary Leaves*. It unquestionably deals with a personal incident. Thus, although the letter is a personal one, its reproduction is worthy of note because of its singular characteristics. It is the only available letter in this script, which is an entirely different style of writing from any of the others portrayed. Here is the transcription:

" You may—and ought to be—kind to and lenient with an insane person. But not even for the sake of such a kindness have you the right to keep back your religion and allow him even for one twinkling of the eye to believe *you are* a Christian or that you may be one. You have to make once for ever your choice—either your duty to the Lodge or your own personal ideas.

[Signature]
" (the old gentleman, your Narayan) "

The letter is written in what appears to be red pencil on a large sheet of paper, about 12 by 15 inches. The signature is undecipherable, as it is probably in some Hindu script (?). Below it are five words, which were added by H.P.B. in blue

---

* Reproduced from *Did Madame Blavatsky Forge The Mahatma Letters?*, p. 43.

pencil: "the old gentleman, your Narayan." Subba Row refers to this Mahatma in a pamphlet which he issued in 1884, as one "who resides in Southern India." *. Col. Olcott in writing to Miss Francesca Arundale, under date of February 9, 1885, mentions a certain Yogi who came to see him, and then states: "He had been sent by the Mahatma at Tirivellum (the one who dictated to H.P.B. the 'Replies to an English F.T.S.') to assure me that I should *not* be left alone." †

In the June Supplement to *The Theosophist*, 1882, there is printed a letter from the writer of the facsimile bearing the caption: "Tirivellum Hills, May 17." It is signed: "One of the Hindu Founders of the Parent Theos. Soc." ‡

FACSIMILE No. 13

The thirteenth facsimile, which appears on the insertion facing page 282, is a reproduction of H.P.B.'s handwriting. It reproduces her signature and gives her official position in the T.S., that of Corresponding Secretary. It is dated: Ostende, October 3, 1888. The facsimile is the 25th page of the original handwritten manuscript of a lengthy article from which the title is missing, although a typewritten copy preserves the opening page minus the title. It has been named "The Original Programme of The Theosophical Society." The reproduced page of the manuscript reads:

"... Do not indulge in unbrotherly comparisons between the task accomplished by yourself and the work left undone by your neighbour or brother, in the field of Theosophy, *as none is held to weed out a larger plot of ground than his strength and capacity will permit him.* ... Do not be too severe on the merits or demerits of one who seeks admission among your ranks,

---

* Cf. *H. P. Blavatsky Collected Writings*, Vol. V, p. 135.

† *The Theosophist*, Vol. LIII, p. 733; September, 1932.

‡ *Op. cit.*, pp. 6-8.

§ Reproduced from *H. P. Blavatsky Collected Writings*, Vol. VII, p. 172. The complete "Original Programme" manuscript is on file in the archives of the T. S. at Adyar. It is printed in the volume mentioned, pp. 145-171, and is preceded by a lengthy explanatory note prepared by the compiler of the volume (pp. 135-145). The "Programme" is deserving of careful reading, followed as it is by the complete text of the Letter from a Master of Wisdom, the closing paragraph of which was quoted in the facsimile reproduction. The Letter is entitled "Some Words on Daily Life," first published in *Lucifer*, Vol. I, pp. 344-6, January 1888.

as the truth about the actual state of the inner man can only be known to, and dealt with justly by KARMA alone. Even the simple presence amidst you of a well-intentioned and sympathising individual may help you magnetically. . . . . You are the Free-workers on the Domain of Truth, and as such, must leave no obstructions on the paths leading to it."
. . . The letter closes with the following lines which have now become quite plain, as they give the key to the whole situation . . . ' *The degrees of success or failure are the landmark we shall have to follow, as they will constitute the barriers placed with your own hands between yourselves and those whom you have asked to be your teachers. The nearer your approach to the goal contemplated—the shorter the distance between the student and the Master. . . .*'

"A complete answer is thus found in the above lines to the paper framed by the two Theosophists. Those who are now inclined to repudiate the Hand that traced it and feel ready to turn their backs upon the whole Past and the original programme of the T.S. are at liberty to do so. The Theosophical body is neither a Church nor a Sect and every individual opinion is entitled to a hearing. A Theosophist may progress and develop, and his views may outgrow those of the Founders, grow larger and broader in every direction, without for all that abandoning the fundamental soil upon which they were born and nurtured. It is only he who changes diametrically his opinions from one day to another and shifts his devotional views from white to black—who can be hardly trusted in his remarks and actions. But surely, this can never be the case of the two Theosophists who have now been answered. . . .

"Meanwhile, peace and fraternal good-will to all."

"*Ostende,* Oct. 3rd., 1886."

II. P. Blavatsky,
Corres. Secty. T.S.

Facsimile No. 14

The fourteenth facsimile, printed on the insertion facing page 283, is a characteristic example of H. P. Blavatsky's writing.* It is a photographic reproduction of an early draft

---

* Reproduced from Volume I, facing page 79 of the six-volume Adyar edition of *The Secret Doctrine,* first published in 1938.

of the three fundamental propositions intended for *The Secret Doctrine*. It bears the heading "Commentary on Stanza I". However, in the final draft, appearing in the printed volume, the three propositions are placed in the " Proem," which is positioned prior to the consideration of Stanza I of the Stanzas of Dzyan. The ideas in connection with the three propositions were greatly expanded from this early draft as may readily be seen by turning to pages 79-83 * of the Proem in the printed volume. The facsimile reads:

" COMMENTARY ON STANZA I

" (In order not to break the *Stanzas* by making the comments too long, the reader is referred for further explanations to the glossary in the Appendices attached to every chapter.)

" The Secret Doctrine postulates three propositions:

" (*a*) An Omnipresent, Eternal and boundless Principle, beyond the reach of words or thought, or in the words of *Mandukya* " unthinkable and unspeakable." In the *Aitareya Upanishad* this Principle is referred to as the SELF, the only one—as just shown.

" (*b*) The Eternity of the Universe as a fixed abstraction, with periodical appearances and disappearances of objective manifestation; like a regular tidal ebb of flux and reflux; coeval with, as being in one sense identical with, the One Principle.

" (*c*) The unity of all the souls with the OVER SOUL or the unknown *Root*, and the continuous transmigration of each ray of the One Infinite Light, in accordance with cyclic and *Karmic* Law, during the whole Cycle of Necessity, that is to say from the beginning of Manvantara to that of Pralaya, [*undecipherable* word: ** since (?)†] the " *Mayava*-Self" ‡ starts

---

* Of the 6-volume edition of Volume I; I, pp. 14-18 of the original edition (1888); I, pp. 42-46 of the 3rd edition (1893).

** The ' Eye of Śiva,' the inner or spiritual Eye of the Seer or clairvoyant.

† *Dangma*—a purified Soul, the highest adept.

‡ *Māyava*-Self, is the term given to the Divine *Ego* of man, who labours under a delusion if he mistakes his *Self*, as separated from the ONE SELF, the Absolute. Nevertheless, it is his own *individual and man's* personal Self throughout the Manvantaric eternities that returns into the Absolute Self, like a drop of water into its Ocean, to re-emerge from it at the following Manvantara.

as a pure Emanation and returns as a purified *Pâramârthika-*
Self, merged in the One-Being (or *non*-Being)—the absolute
Paramârthika.

" In its absolute abstraction, the One Principle though
seemingly dual (Parabrahman and Mûlaprakriti) is sexless,
unconditioned, absolute. Its periodical radiation is as a
primal emanation, one and androgynous and finite. When
the radiation radiates in its turn, all the secondary radiations
are also androgynous to become male and female principles
in their lower aspects. Pralaya—whether the great or the
minor—which leaves things *in statu quo**—the first that
reawakens."

FACSIMILE No. 15

The fifteenth facsimile, which is printed on the insertion
facing page 286, is a reproduction of Dâmodar K. Mâvalankar's
handwriting.† It represents the third page of a handwritten
letter, addressed to R. Keshava Pillai of Nellore—a town and
district of India, 109 miles north of Madras and situated on the
Bay of Bengal. The letter-head carrying the address of the
T.S., indicates that it was written prior to the transference of
the headquarters from Bombay to Adyar, Madras. The
departure from Bombay took place on December 17, 1882.
The date of the letter is October 26, 1882. It was written on
very thin paper—the quality of paper that was used in India
at the time.

In regard to Dâmodar's correspondent: R. Keshava Pillai
was an Inspector of Police in Nellore. In the Spring of 1882,
the Founders visited Nellore and a Lodge (called a Branch in
those days) was established, with Pillai as Secretary. Because
of his interest in the T.S., he was the recipient of a letter from
Dâmodar's Guru, the Mahatma K. H. In fact, Pillai received

---

* It is not the physical, organized body that remains *in status quo,* not even the
Soul of things during the great Cosmic or even Solar Pralayas, but only their ākāśic
ideal or photograph. But during the *planetary* or minor pralayas, one overreached
by the Night, the planets remain intact though dead, ' like a huge animal caught
between the polar ices stands frozen for ages' ".

† Reproduced from *Did Madame Blavatsky Forge The Mahatma Letters?*, page 17.

a second letter * in which he was given the opportunity of becoming a lay chela—a preparatory step towards becoming a fully accepted chela. Evidently doubts assailed his mind, hence the reason for Dâmodar's letter, who relates in the document how he was prompted to write to Pillai. In his letter Dâmodar refers to Mme. Blavatsky as " Upâsikâ " (signifying a woman lay-disciple in Buddhism) and refers to Mme. Emma Coulomb (the wife of M. Alexis Coulomb) as Mme. C.

In order to understand the significance of the first four lines of the facsimile—which are the concluding portion of a sentence —it is necessary to read the whole sentence. For that matter the whole letter gives an insight into Dâmodar's position at the T.S. headquarters, hence the whole letter is published. The facsimile begins with the 21st word—i.e., " advance "—before the conclusion of the lengthy first paragraph. The letter commences in this manner:

" *Thursday evening*, 7-25 P.M.

" My dear Brother:
    " You know very well with what feelings I look upon you. I have always regarded you as a Brother and counted upon you as the most useful member who could give life to our Nellore Branch. Whatever, therefore, I may say, believe me, it is as a Brother who has your good at heart and of the CAUSE. And this letter I write in that spirit. I will first narrate what happened to me just now, as commanded by my MOST REVERED MASTER. I had just returned from the Printing Office, and, after taking my dinner in the dining-room below, was seated on the balcony opposite our Library Room. This balcony, I have told you, is the very place where the MASTERS had many times shown themselves. Only two of us were there—Mr. Coulomb and myself. He was on my right. Mme. C was also there when I first came. I had made a cigarette and was lighting it. Mme. C, feeling very cold, went in to get her shawl. No servants were there, and not a soul besides myself and Mr. Coulomb. I first gave him the light and was afterwards lighting my cigarette when I just heard quite near my foot (opposite which was a teapoy with the box of tobacco and nothing else on it) some noise as of something falling on the ground. Mr. Coulomb

---

* This letter from Mahatma K. H. is preserved in the archives of the T. S. at Adyar. It was published, together with three others, in the work entitled *Letters from the Masters of the Wisdom*, Second Series, Letters 64-67.

heard the noise but saw nothing; and, being surprised, remarked what had fallen on the ground? I immediately looked near my foot, whence the sound had come, and at once saw the enclosed letter between my foot and the teapoy, and recognized at once my MASTER's handwriting, this being a very bright moonlight night. When the letter fell, Mme. C was in her room, as I saw her just then coming out of her room which is at the other end of the Dining Room. And not a soul, besides Mr. Coulomb and myself was there. We were face to face with one another as I was giving him the light and then lighting my own cigarette. I brought the letter up at once and read it. As COMMANDED therein, I now send it on to you, together with the outer envelope also, and the letter to my address. I am exceedingly grieved to find that you doubt ' Upasika.' Remember that she is the only one in this visible world, through whom we have had the good fortune of having our eyes opened to *the* TRUTH. And is it possible that we Hindus should be so ungrateful to our benefactors by doubting them! My dear Friend, I do hope that you will at least believe my word when I tell you how I received the enclosed, and still if you like, you may write *independently* to Mr. Coulomb, and then compare notes as to whether what I have here said about the enclosure is the exact truth or not. We may doubt ' Upasika ' now, and when she is no more, then, perhaps, we may regret our ingratitude, and our having lost the only chance that was ever conceded to us degenerate Hindus by the OCCULT WORLD. We may, however, do well to remember the proverb that ' Repentance is too late.' Take time by the fore-lock and don't let us lose this golden opportunity. ' A penny saved is a penny gained '—so ' A moment saved is a moment gained.' Having given to you the necessary advice and the details COMMANDED by my MOST REVERED MASTER, I now leave it to your sense of justice and to your intuition, if it still lingers in you, as I believe it does, how you would act and whether you would not successfully combat this ' evil genius ' of yours—*viz.*, doubt and suspicion. Each and every one of us has to conquer the Dweller of our Threshold, and if you would advance, you must humiliate the Demon that obstructs your path. Read Bulwer Lytton's *Zanoni*, and you will understand my allusion better.

"These are the few words of advice of a friend and a Brother. Take heed in time, and let us see the opening of a bright day for you. What more need I say than what the

MASTER says in his letter. I have, however, to request that you will kindly return to me, as soon as possible, *my* MASTER's letter *to my address*. You may keep its enclosure, I mean your letter and the ADVICE to you thereon. But I should like to have the letter to my address as it contains priceless instructions *to me*, at least, who am an implicit believer in ' Upasika ' and MY MASTER.

> " Ever yours sincerely and fraternally,
> " DĀMODAR K. MĀVALANKAR." *

Along with the consideration of this letter to Keshava Pillai, an appropriate place presents itself to include some documents concerning Damodar himself. These indicate stages in the development of the Siddhis, which Damodar achieved in connection with certain occult processes, during his association with Mme. Blavatsky at the T.S. headquarters. These are of especial significance, in that the ability to project the mâyâvi-rûpa is indicated.† An instance of Damodar's ability to function in the mâyâvi-rûpa is attested to by Col. Olcott, who narrates the incident in this manner—terming it an " astral flight ":

> " Between the two stations [i.e., Meerut and Lahore] Damodar made another astral flight which was capable of verification. Three of us—he, I, and T. Narainswamy Naidu—were in the same railway carriage, Damodar apparently moving uneasily. as if in sleep, on one of the berths: I was reading a book by the lamp-light. Damodar suddenly came over to me and asked the time, which by my watch was some minutes before 6 p.m. He told me that he had just come from Adyar, where H.P.B. had met with an accident; whether a serious one or not, he could not tell me, but he thought she had tripped her foot in the carpet and fallen heavily on her right knee. . . .
> " For my own satisfaction I did two things on hearing his story. I wrote a certificate of the occurrence and got Narainswamy to sign it with me, noting the time; and from the next station, Saharanpore, telegraphed H.P.B. a question as to ' what accident happened at headquarters at about 6 o'clock? ' We reached Lahore the next morning at 9. . . . [Later]

---

* From *The Theosophist*, Vol. XXIX, p. 945, Part II, July, 1908.

† This is the theme considered in Chapters XVI and XVII.

while I was sitting under the shadow of my tent with Mr. R. C. Bary, Editor of the *Ārya* magazine, a Government telegraph peon was seen coming toward us with a brown-covered telegram in his hand. I made Mr. Ruttan Chand take it into his own hands and keep it unopened until the return of our party, in whose presence it should be opened and read. This was done at 12 noon by Mr. R. C. Bary, and the nine present signed on the back to attest the circumstances. The contents were these: ' Nearly broke right leg, tumbling from Bishop's chair, dragging Coulomb, frightening Morgans. Damodar startled us.' My Saharanpore despatch was received by H.P.B. late at night on the 17th: her reply was dated at Adyar at 7-55 a.m. on the 18th, and I got it at Lahore at noon." *

The second instance is even more outstanding than the first, because the projection of the mâyâvi-rûpa was performed both by H.P.B. and by Dâmodar between Adyar and London. This remarkable achievement is presented here by means of a letter, which Dâmodar addressed to H.P.B. and dated:

Adyar, Madras, 16th August, 1884.

" Respected Upasika,

"I could not make out what you wanted here when you came here on the morning of the 15th at about two or three of Madras time. So in the night I attempted to come and ask you. It was between 10 and 11 in the night here; so it must be between five and six in the evening of London time. Who was that gentleman sitting near you under a big looking-glass and what was that short old lady about? I think there were several others in the room at the time; but I could not make out how many or who they were. If I had known that at that time you would be amidst so many people I would not have attempted to come. I might have seen you later, when you were alone. And why was it that you asked me to make myself visible to all? You know I am too much of a beginner yet, in this line. It was only because you asked me to do so, I attempted. Whether I succeeded or failed, I do not know. And in all this affair, the main object I came for was not quite accomplished. I wanted to know exactly

---

* *Old Diary Leaves*, III, pp. 33-35. The certificates mentioned in Col. Olcott's account have been published in the book entitled *Dâmodar*, pp. 348-9.

what you had come here for? I heard something about a trunk; but whether you wanted me to take care of something you had sent or whether you wanted me to send you something I do not quite remember. However, I have sent you a parcel and I believe it is that which you mean. Did you find in your pocket that Tibetan order from the MASTER to come here, to notify you about which he sent me to you again? I hope yourself, nor the friends who were there, will not speak about this to anyone and not make a public talk of it in the Society for Psychical Research and such other places. I am sure Mr. Ewen and others would have done it, if I had not asked you privately to prevent the publication of the fact of Mr. Ewen having seen me when I came to see you and Colonel Olcott and committed a blunder. I hope I have not committed a mistake in sending you the parcel.

> "Ever yours respectfully and sincerely,
> "DĀMODAR K. MĀVALANKAR." *

In view of this description of Dâmodar's account of his visit to H.P.B. in London—made in his mâyâvi-rûpa—it would be most appropriate to add a citation concerning the Sthûla-śarîra (the physical body) during the absence of the " projected consciousness "—or as the Tibetans express it, when the Phowa is performed. The explanation is provided by H.P.B. in a letter to her sister, which was published in *The Path*—one of a series of letters written to Mme. Vera de Zhelihovsky. Because of being written to her sister it is not couched in technical or philosophical language and is, therefore, all the clearer. The date of the letter is not given—presumably written in the 1870's. The citation is introduced in this manner:

" H.P.B. wrote to Madame Zhelihovsky (date unknown) that she was learning to get out of her body, and offering to pay her a visit in Tiflis ' in the flash of an eye.' This both frightened and amused Madame Zhelihovsky, who replied that she would not trouble her so unnecessarily. H.P.B. answered:

---

* *Dâmodar and the Pioneers of the Theosophical Movement*, pp. 482-3; by Sven Eek. Published by The Theosophical Publishing House, Adyar, Madras 20, India, 1965; 720 pp. with index. This letter is here quoted by permission of the author. The document had not been published prior to its inclusion in this cited work. The letter is in the archives of the T.S., Adyar.

" ' What is there to be afraid of? As if you had never heard about apparitions of doubles. I, that is to say, my body, will be quietly asleep in my bed, and it would not even matter if it were to await my return in a waking condition—it would be in the state of a harmless idiot. And no wonder: God's light would be absent from it, flying to you; and then it would fly back and once more the temple would get illuminated by the presence of the Deity. But this, needless to say, only in case the thread between the two were not broken. If you shriek like mad it may get torn; then Amen to my existence: I should die instantly. . . . .' " *

An additional paragraph from another letter, this time written to her aunt, Nadyezhda A. de Fadeyev, in Odessa, Russia, likewise tells of H.P.B.'s preliminary efforts at mastering the accomplishment of Phowa: The letter is dated New York, October 28-29, 1877:

" I am learning just now to leave my body; to do it alone I am afraid, but with him [Master M.] I am afraid of nothing. I shall try it with you. Only be kind enough not to resist and do not scream. And—do not forget." †

These citations serve to explain an incident narrated by Countess Wachtmeister, which occurred during the period she was staying with H.P.B. at Würzburg, at the time that *The Secret Doctrine* was being written. The anecdote is well worthy of being included in full at this point:

" There was one occurrence, continuously repeated over a long period, which impressed me very strongly with the conviction that she was watched and cared for by unseen guardians. From the first night that I passed in her room, until the last that preceded our departure from Würzburg, I heard a regularly intermittent series of raps on the table by her bedside. They would begin at ten o'clock each evening, and would continue, at intervals of ten minutes, until six o'clock in the morning. They were sharp, clear raps, such

---

* From " Letters from H. P. Blavatsky to Mme. Vera de Zhelihovsky ", published in *The Path*, Vol. IX, p. 299. These " Letters " were written in Russian and translated by H. P. B.'s niece, Vera Johnston.

† From a microfilmed copy of a letter (from the archives of the T. S., Adyar), written in Russian and translated by Boris de Zirkoff.

as I never heard at any other time. Sometimes I held my watch in my hand for an hour at a stretch, and always as the ten minute interval ticked itself out, the rap would come with the utmost regularity. Whether H.P.B. was awake or asleep mattered nothing to the occurrence of the phenomenon, nor to its uniformity.

" When I asked for an explanation of these raps I was told that it was an effect of what might be called a sort of psychic telegraph, which placed her in communication with her teachers, and that the chelas might watch her body while her astral left it.

" In this connection I may mention another incident that proved to me that there were agencies at work in her neighbourhood whose nature and action were inexplicable on generally accepted theories of the constitution and laws of matter.

" H.P.B. was accustomed to read her Russian newspapers at night after retiring, and it was rarely that she extinguished her lamp before midnight. There was a screen between my bed and this lamp, but, nevertheless, its powerful rays, reflected from ceiling and walls, often disturbed my rest. One night this lamp was burning after the clock had struck one. I could not sleep, and, as I heard by H.P.B.'s regular breathing that she slept, I rose, gently walked round to the lamp, and turned it out. There was always a dim light pervading the bedroom, which came from a night-light burning in the study, the door between that room and the bedroom being kept open. I had extinguished the lamp, and was going back, when it flamed up again, and the room was brightly illuminated. I thought to myself—what a strange lamp, I suppose the spring does not act, so I put my hand again on the spring, and watched until every vestige of flame was extinct, and, even then, held down the spring for a minute. Then I released it and stood for a moment longer watching, when, to my surprise, the flame reappeared and the lamp was burning as brightly as ever. This puzzled me considerably, and I determined to stand there by that lamp and put it out all through the night, if necessary, until I discovered the why and wherefore of its eccentricities. For the third time I pressed the spring and turned it down until the lamp was quite out, and then released it, watching eagerly to see what would take place. For the third time the lamp burned up, and this time I saw a brown hand slowly and gently turning the knob of the lamp. Familiar as I was with

29

the action of astral forces and astral entities on the physical plane, I had no difficulty in coming to the conclusion that it was the hand of a chela, and, surmising that there was some reason why the lamp should remain alight, I returned to my couch. But a spirit of perversity and curiosity dwelt within me that night. I wanted to know more, so I called out, 'Madame Blavatsky!' then, louder, 'Madame Blavatsky!' and again 'Madame Blavatsky!' Suddenly I heard an answering cry—'Oh, my heart! my heart! Countess, you have nearly killed me;' and then again, 'My heart! my heart!' I flew to H.P.B.'s bedside. 'I was with Master,' she murmured, 'why did you call me back?' I was thoroughly alarmed, for her heart fluttered under my hand with wild palpitation.

"I gave her a dose of digitalis, and sat beside her until the symptoms had abated and she had become calmer. Then she told me how Col. Olcott had once nearly killed her in the same way, by calling her back suddenly when her astral form was absent from her body. She made me promise that I would never try experiments with her again, and this promise I readily gave, out of the fulness of my grief and contrition for having caused her such suffering." *

Because of the foregoing citations, the following cryptic remark, made by H.P.B. in connection with a real chela and his reflection, should be comprehensible:

"I too was made a *reflection* several times and during months; but I never abused of it, to try and palm off my *personal* schemes on those who mistook H.P.B. of Russia, for the high Initiate of xxx whose telephone she was at times."†

Facsimile No. 16

The sixteenth facsimile, appearing on the insertion which faces page 287, reproduces the concluding portion of a letter received by Mr. Sinnett ‡ "at Allahabad in January, 1882,"

---

* *Reminiscences of H. P. Blavatsky and " The Secret Doctrine "*, pp. 43-45.

† *The Letters of H. P. Blavatsky to A. P. Sinnett*, p. 174.

‡ Reproduced from *Did Madame Blavatsky Forge The Mahatma Letters?*, p. 49. The complete letter is printed in *The Mahatma Letters to A. P. Sinnett*, as Letter No. 37; pp. 248-250 (2nd ed.); pp. 245-7 (3rd ed.). The name " Djual Khul " has been variously spelled as Gjual Khool, Jual Kul, etc., with initials D.K., J.K. The variant forms intend to indicate the pronounciation of the Tibetan word-forms.

as he himself made the notation. It is in the handwriting of Djual Khul, a chela of the Mahatma K. H. In the opening sentences of the letter, the writer introduces himself and explains why he was designated to convey the message to A. P. Sinnett. The conclusion indicates that the writer's Guru " orders me to sign myself, your obedient servant, The ' Disinherited.' " The name " Disinherited " was adopted by Djual Khul because the Mahatma's chela actually had undergone such an experience. Reference was made to it when the Mahatma mentioned to Mr. Sinnett that he was out of writing paper and his chela promised to supply him with " a few stray sheets, memento relics of his grandfather's will, by which he disinherited him and thus made his ' fortune.' " *

Prior to the writing of the letter (the portion of which is here reproduced) one of the methods in which " the Disinherited " assisted his Guru was explained to Mr. Sinnett in this manner:

" Another of our customs, when corresponding with the outside world, is to entrust a chela with the task of delivering the letter or any other message; and if not absolutely necessary —to never give it a thought. Very often our very letters— unless something very important and secret—are written in our handwritings by our chelas. Thus, last year, some of my letters to you were *precipitated*, and when sweet and easy precipitation was stopped—well I had but to compose my mind, assume an easy position, and—think, and my faithful ' Disinherited ' had but to copy my thoughts. . . ." †

Directing attention now to the facsimile. The first three sentences opening the letter read:

" The Master has awaked and bids me write. To his great regret, for certain reasons He will not be able until a fixed period has passed to expose Himself to the thought-currents inflowing so strongly from beyond the Himavat. I am therefore, commanded to be the hand to indite His message. I am to tell you. . . ." ‡

Instead of copying the entire document, attention is directed to the reproduced portion of the facsimile. The complete

* *The Mahatma Letters to A. P. Sinnett*, Letter No. 8, p. 33.
† *Op. cit.*, Letter No. 53, p. 296 (2nd ed.); p. 291 (3rd ed.).
‡ *Op. cit.*, Letter No. 37, pp. 248-9 (2nd ed.); p. 245 (3rd ed.).

sentence, preceding the five closing words of the printed facsimile, reads:

" Master regrets to find in him [Allan O. Hume] the same spirit of utter, unconscious selfishness with no view to the good of the Cause [of Theosophy] he represents. If he seems interested in it at all, it is because he is opposed and finds himself roused to combativeness. Thus the answer to Mr. Terry's letter sent to him from Bombay ought to have been published in the January number. Will you kindly to see to it—Master asks? Master thinks you can do it as well as Mr. Hume if you but tried, as the metaphysical faculty in you, is only dormant but would fully develop were you but to awake it to its full action by constant use. As to our reverenced M.·.: he desires me to assure you that the secret of Mr. Hume's professed love for Humanity lies in, and is based upon, the chance presence in that word of the first syllable; as for ' mankind '—he has no sympathy for it.

" Since Master will not be able to write to you himself for a month or two longer (though you will always hear of him) —He begs you to proceed for his sake with your metaphysical studies; and not to be giving up the task in despair whenever you meet with incomprehensible ideas in M.·. Sahib's notes, the more so, as M.·. Sahib's only hatred in his life, is for writing.

" In conclusion Master sends you His best wishes and praying you may not forget Him, orders me to sign myself, your obedient servant,

THE ' DISINHERITED.'

" P.S. Should you desire to write to Him though unable to answer Himself Master will receive your letters with pleasure; you can do so through D. K. Mavalankar.

DD." *

With regard to the reference concerning Mr. Terry's letter. William H. Terry was the editor of *The Harbinger of Light*, Melbourne, Australia's famous Spiritualistic journal, which he founded in 1870. His journal carried all the doings of what may be termed the Spiritualist movement in America in the eighteen-seventies, as well as the founding of The Theosophical Society and its activities in America. When H. P. Blavatsky

---

* *Op.* cit., p. 250 (2nd ed.); pp. 246-7 (3rd ed.).

established *The Theosophist* in India in 1879, Mr. Terry opened correspondence with her. Shortly thereafter he joined the Society. Already in October, 1880, he signed his articles by including F.T.S. after his name, thus signifying his Fellowship in the Society.

When the series of articles entitled " Fragments of Occult Truth " were published in *The Theosophist*, the first one of the series appearing in October 1881, William H. Terry wrote to Allan O. Hume, the author of the first three "Fragments," challenging some of the statements in his articles. This is referred to in the first two lines of the facsimile: " If he seems interested in it at all, it is because he is opposed and finds himself roused to combativeness." Evidently Mr. Hume's interest waned, because, as the next sentence of the letter states: " the answer to Mr. Terry's letter sent to him from Bombay ought to have been published in the January number " of *The Theosophist*. Because of this negligence, Mr. Sinnett's assistance was enlisted by means of D.K.'s letter, and he was requested " to see to it " that Mr. Terry be answered. In a sentence prior to the printed facsimile he is entreated not to feel " such an exaggerated delicacy " about taking up the work which Mr. Hume had left undone.

Since A. P. Sinnett actually did take on the writing of " Fragments of Occult Truth," the purpose of D.K.'s letter was indeed accomplished.

Attention is called to the post-script, in which Mr. Sinnett is directed to utilize the services of Dâmodar for forwarding his letters to the Mahatma K.H. This indicates that Dâmodar was able to function in the capacity of an intermediary—as outlined in Chapter XIII.

THE TIBETAN ALPHABET

The Tibetan alphabet, as now written, was devised by Thonmi Sambhota, the minister of the Tibetan monarch, Srongtsangampo. This king sent his minister to India during the first half of the seventh century A.D., for the specific purpose of studying Sanskrit. Thonmi Sambhota was so fascinated with Devanâgarî—the manner of writing the Sanskrit alphabet—that he determined to adapt the Devanâgarî characters to Tibetan. This was not a simple matter, for the reason that the Tibetan language is monosyllabic in structure, like Chinese; whereas Sanskrit is not. Furthermore, the Tibetan language contains consonantal sounds which are not present in Sanskrit, just as there are some Sanskrit sounds not found in Tibetan.

Thus the Tibetan alphabet is patterned after the Sanskrit. It follows the same order of its consonants. It starts with the sounds which are produced in the throat, working forward to lip-sounds in this sequence: gutturals, palatals, dentals, labials. Five consonants are placed following the labials—regarded as palatal sibilants—which are not present in the Sanskrit alphabet. The sequence continues with the semivowels and concludes with the sibilants and aspirates.

Vowels

In the Sanskrit alphabet the vowels precede the consonants. There are 16 in number. In the Tibetan alphabet the vowels are placed after the consonants. The alphabetical order of the five vowels is: a, i, u, e, o. The vowel *a* is implied as following every consonant character, or sign, except when one of the four vowel signs is placed above or below the consonant. Thus a single letter, or character, may form a Tibetan word. For example, *ba* (cow); *sa* (earth). The vowel signs for *i, e, o* are placed above the consonants; the sign for *u* is placed below. The five vowels are short in sound except for some particular indicated cases. Two vowels coming together are not elided; each one is pronounced separately.

There are no initial vowel characters, other than an " a-sound." This is altered by the same vowel signs as used on the consonants to suit the four other vowels. There is also a character which may be termed a " smooth breathing," equivalent to the character so used in the Greek alphabet. It is also modified by the vowel signs. When a vowel commences a word, the vowel " a-sound " is used as a base for indicating the required vowel sound. The following are examples of initial vowels: 'ama—mother; 'i—the number 60; 'u—the number 90; 'ema—hey! indeed!; 'ogma—throat. The vowels are pronounced in this manner (using English equivalent vowel-sounds) (pronounced):

a   as in part
i   as in pin
u   as in pull
e   as in pet
o   as in pot

Final n alters the vowel sounds preceding it in this manner:

gan   —pronounced gän (ä like the e in den)
bon   —pronounced bön (ö like the u in burn)
kun   —pronounced kün (ü as in dune)

The vowels i and e when followed by n remain unchanged.

CONSONANTS

Every consonant character implies that an a follows it, as in Sanskrit, except when a vowel sign indicates otherwise. The alphabetical order of the consonants also follows that of the Sanskrit alphabet, commencing with the gutturals and concluding with the sibilants. In the following tabulation the sequence of the letters should be read from left to right, each line at a time, instead of in columnar manner. (For example: cha follows nga.)

	Surd	Aspirate	Sonant	Nasal
Gutturals	ka	kha	ga	ña or nga
Palatals	cha	chha	ja	ña or nya
Dentals	ta	tha	da	na
Labials	pa	pha	ba	ma
Palatal Sibilants	tsa	tsha	dsa	
	wa	zha	za	a
Semivowels	ya	ra	la	
Sibilants	sha	sa		
Aspirate		ha	'a (Smooth breathing)	

Listed below are the consonants in Tibetan alphabetical order, giving an example as used in a Tibetan word, followed by its meaning, as well as the manner of pronouncing the character by means of an English word.

Tibetan character	Tibetan word	Meaning	Pronunciation as in English
ka	ka-ra	sugar	cart
kha	ka-kha	alphabet	inkhorn
ga	ga-da	club	gander
ña or nga	ganga-bu	pod	gang
cha	cha-ga	hem, edge	chug
chha	chhos (pr. chhö)	doctrine	witch-hazel
ja	jus (pr. jü)	strategy	jew
ña or nya	nyi-ma	the sun	new
ta	ta-ku	crutch	tack
tha	thub-pa	sage	cart-horse
da	da-kha	horse-shoe	Dakota
na	na-ma	praise	name
pa	pa-wa-sangs	planet Venus	planet
pha	phur-bu	planet Jupiter	uphill
ba	bod (pr. bhö)	Tibet	abhor
ma	mig-dmar (migmar)	planet Mars	meager
tsa	tsong-kha-pa	Tsongkhapa	parts
tsha	tshag-tshe	bruised barley	harts-horn
dza	dzam-bu	rose apple-tree	adze
wa	wa	water-channel	wan
zha	zha-ba	lame	azure
za	za-zi	trouble, noise	ozone
a	a-chog	we	ah!

(the pure vowel sound without any consonantal sound; performed with an open glottis)

ya	ya-tra	festivity	yacht
ra	ra-ma	goat	ram
la	la	mountain-pass	lamb
sha	sha-ba	hart, stag	shabby
sa	sa	earth	sap
ha	ha-ha	laughter	lha-ha
lha	lhag-pa	planet Mercury	all-hail
a	'ajo; 'ochhe	Mr.; Mrs.	ajar, achieve

(the smooth breathing—produced by the opening of the glottis)

PRONUNCIATION OF TIBETAN WORDS

Because of the fact that the pronunciation of Tibetan words differs from the written characters, this becomes perplexing. As an instance, sprulsku is pronounced *tulku*. Assistance in the pronunciation of Tibetan words, with specific regard to the transliteration of the written characters in connection with their pronunciation, may be obtained by means of the following classification:

1. Non-pronunciation of certain initial consonants, which may therefore be regarded as "silent letters," or "mute consonants."

2. Alteration of certain consonants when combined with other consonants, thus changing their pronunciation.

3. Non-pronunciation of certain final consonants, thereby causing modification of vowels.

With regard to accentuation. The accent in Tibetan words is placed on the first syllable, because this first syllable contains the root of the word.

1. Tibetan words which commence with more than one consonant character sometimes signify that the first consonant is not pronounced. This applies specifically to the following letters: b, d, g, m' (smooth breathing—which in some systems of transliteration is rendered as ḥ); l, r, s. The last three consonants (l, r, s) in addition to not being pronounced when commencing a word, remain unpronounced when occurring between two consonants. Examples:

> bdebachan, pronounced dewachan (chan as in chant); signifying * the blissful after-death state
>
> dgu, pr. gu (u as oo in good); sig. nine
>
> gsang-bai-chhos, pr. sang-bai-chhö (bai as in bye; chh as in witch-hazel; ö as in churn); sig. esoteric doctrine
>
> mkha, pr. kha (kh as in ink-horn); sig. the 5th element— âkâśa 'khor-lo, pr. khor-lo; sig. circle
>
> lche, pr. che; sig. tongue
>
> lha: when l precedes h both are pronounced—as in valhalla; sig. a divine being
>
> rgyal, pr. gyal; (gy as in ghyll); sig. victory
>
> sgo-lo, pr. go-lo; sig. face

When two of the consonants specified above precede another consonant, both are not pronounced. Ex.:

> brda, pr. da; sig. sign

---

* Please note the abbreviations which follow: sig.=signifying; pr.=pronounced; Ex.=Examples.

bstan-pa, pr. tämpa (as in tempo); sig. doctrine

brling-ba, pr. ling-wa (Note. When ba does not occur initially it is often pronounced va or wa); sig. sure

mchhod-rten, pr. chhörten (chh as in witch-hazel; ö as in church); sig. dagoba (a Buddhist monument)

2. When the following consonants: b, d, g, k, kh, p, ph are followed by *r*, the consonants are pronounced as though changed into the cerebrals: ṭ, ṭh, ḍ. The cerebrals are pronounced by placing the tip of the tongue against the roof of the mouth. Examples:

br becomes ḍ; dr becomes ḍ; gr becomes ḍ

kr becomes ṭ; pr becomes ṭ

khr becomes ṭh; phr becomes ṭh (as in nut-hatch; not as in nothing)

brag, pr. ḍag, or even ḍa; sig. rock

drilbu, pr. ḍilbu; sig. bell

grub-pa, pr. ḍuppa; sig. perfect (i.e., one who has attained)

krad-pa, pr. ṭad-pa; sig. leather half-boot, or shoe

sprul-ba, pr. ṭul-ba; sig. to transform oneself

khrag, pr. ṭhag (as in nut-hatch) sig. blood

phra, pr. ṭha; sig. ornament, jewel

When the following consonants: b, m, p, ph are followed by *y*, the following changes in pronunciation take place:

by becomes j; becomes ñ (as in canyon); py becomes ch (as in chant); phy becomes ch-h (as in witch-hazel). Examples:

byang, pr. jang—as in byang-chub; sig. enlightenment; byang-chub-sems-dpa', pr. jang-chup-sempa, sig. a being filled with enlightenment-consciousness—i.e. a Bodhisattva

myu-gu, pr. nyugu (ny as in canyon); sig. a reed, a rush; dmyal-ba, pr. nyal-wa; sig. hell

dpyid, pr. chi (as in chin; sig. spring

phyag, pr. chhag (as in witch-hazel); sig. hand; phyag-rgya, pr. chag-gya; sig. gesture

spyan, pr. chen; sig. eye. The Tibetan equivalent of Avalokiteśvara is written spyan-ras-gzigs, pr. chen-re-zi.

Additional modifications. In certain instances gy is pronounced ja. Thus the famous Tibetan scriptures, Kanjur and Tanjur—generally so spelled according to their manner of pronunciation—are written in Tibetan characters: bka-'gyur, sig. the translated word (of the Buddha): it consists of 100 volumes and represents the oral tradition. The word is pronounced Kanjur (a as in far; u as in adjure). The second scripture:

bstan-'gyur, sig. the translated teaching (of the Buddha), consists
of 225 volumes: it contains comments on the Kanjur; the word
is pronounced Tanjur (a as in ten; u as in adjure).

3. Final Consonants. Three consonants become silent, that
is unpronounced, when appearing as final consonants, namely
d. l. s. But in so doing they alter the vowel sounds of a, o, u;
but *not* of e and i. Thus when the vowel a precedes final d, l, s,
it is pronounced as ä or as the e in tend. When the vowel o
precedes final d, l, s, it is pronounced as ö, or as the u in burn.
When the vowel u precedes final d, l, s, it is pronounced as ü,
or as the u in duty. Examples:

> skad, pr. kä (as in kettle); sig. voice; in compounds, language
> bod, pr. bhö (as in burn); sig. Tibet
> bod-skad, pr. bhö-ske; sig. the Tibetan language
> dud-pa, pr. dhü-pa (as in d'ew); sig. smoke
> ngal, pr. ngä (ng as in song; ä as in ten); sig. weary, tired
> rol-mo, pr. rö-mo; sig. music
> dngul, pr. nü (in Tsang); nul (in Ü); sig. silver
> ti-bril, pr. ti-bri; sig. tea-pot
> tshil, pr. tshi (tsh—as in harts-horn); sig. fat
> khas, pr. khe; sig. weak, poor
> sangs-rgyas, pr. sang-gye; sig. Buddha
> chhos, pr. chhö (as in church); sig. doctrine
> bka-chhos, pr. ka-chhö; sig. the doctrine of Buddha
> gus, pr. ghü (as in hue); sig. respect, devout
> des, pr. dhe: des-pa, pr. dhe-pa; sig, fine, brave, noble
> phebs, pr. pheb (ph as in up-hill); sig. to go
> chhibs, pr. chhib (chh as in witch-hazel); sig. horse
> ris, pr. rî (as in reel); sig. figure, form, design

Note. When g precedes s, it too remains unpronounced. **Ex:**
> legs, pr. lê (as in lay); sig. good
> rigs, pr. rî; sig. family, birth

When n is the final consonant, it is pronounced; however,
the preceding vowels a, o, u are altered. When the n is followed
by *pa*, it is pronounced as m. **Ex.:**
> sman, pr. men; sig. medicine, remedy
> gyon-pa, pr. ghyöm-pa; sig. to put on, to wear
> bdun, pr. dün (as in dune); sig. seven
> bden-pa, pr. dem-pa; sig. truth
> mchhin-pa, pr. chhim-pa (chh as in witch-hazel); sig. the liver

When words terminate in ba or bo, they are generally
pronounced as wa or wo. Especially is this the case when ba
or bo follow the vowels, and the consonants ng, r and l.

za-ba, pr. za-wa; sig. to eat

zhi-ba, pr. zhi-wa (zhi as in azure); sig. to become quiet, calm

zhu-ba; pr. zhu-wa; sig. to request

jo-bo, pr. jho-wo (jh as in hedgehog); sig. elder brother

dar-ba, pr. dhar-wa (dh as in adhere); sig. buttermilk

It should be mentioned that the pronunciation of Tibetan words here supplied is that which is in use at Lhasa and by the best educated classes. It is also applicable to the districts of Tibet which are termed the Central Provinces—known as Spiti, Tsang and Ü. In the Western Provinces of Ladak and Lahoul there are variants in the pronunciation, as well as in the Eastern Province of Khams. These are the six principal districts. But there are many more dialects than these. Each small district, in fact, has its own variances in the pronunciation of the spoken language.

At first sight the rules given for the pronunciation of Tibetan words appear to be difficult. Nevertheless, they do not present as many perplexities as do English words, where there are silent vowels and consonants, as well as vowel and consonant changes without any apparent rhyme or reason. English words also have initial unpronounced (or silent, or mute) letters: for example, czar; gnome; knit, knob; write, wrong. Mute letters are present within words and at their conclusion. As an instance, there are three unpronounced letters in the word *though*, and four in *acknowledgement* (k, w, d, e).

To indicate all the different pronounciations of the same letters with different consonantal combinations that occur in English spelling would be too extensive an undertaking. Yet examples will now be given of English words having the same pronunciation but spelled differently:

airy, aerie; bosun, boatswain; Chile, chili, chilly; doe, dough; eight, ate; for, fore, four; genes, jeans; hew, hue, Hugh; idle, idol; jail, goal; know, no; links, lynx; main, mane, Maine; nay, neigh; oar, o'er, or, ore; pair, pare, pear; queue, cue; rough, ruff; sear, seer, sere; tail, tale, tael; uhlan, ulan; vain, vane, vein; write, right, rite; excite, example; yew, ewe, you; zincky, zinky.

Unless a Tibetan word has been anglicized, the key to mastering its pronunciation, when viewing its spelling, is to remember the silent letters and the modifications caused by combining consonants.

BIBLIOGRAPHY

WORKS BY H. P. BLAVATSKY

(ARRANGED IN ORDER OF PUBLICATION)

Isis Unveiled: A Master-Key to the Mysteries of Ancient and Modern Science and Theology. Vol. I—Science, 628 pp.: Vol. II—Theology, 692 pp. with index. Originally published by J. W. Bouton, 10 West 28th Street, New York; Bernard Quaritch, London: 1877.

Iz pescher i debrey Indostana (From the Caves and Jungles of Hindostan), in Russian: by Radda-Bai (the author's penname), 508 pp. Produced by the University Printing House, Moscow, 1883: Part I only. Another edition published by A. S. Suvorin, St. Petersburg, 1912: 438 pp., profusely illustrated. Originally published serially in the *Moskovskiya Vedomosti* from Nov. 30, 1879, through Dec. 16, 1882. Reprinted in *Russkiy Vestnik*, Vols. 163-166, Jan. through Aug., 1883, approximately to the point where *Moskovskiya Vedomosti* left off: then continued in Vol. 180, Nov., 1885, running through Vol. 184, Aug., 1886.

Five Years of Theosophy: Mystical, Philosophical, Theosophical, Historical and Scientific Essays, Selected from *The Theosophist*; 575 pp. with index. Published by Reeves & Turner, 196 Strand, London, W.C., 1885.

The Secret Doctrine: The Synthesis of Science, Religion, and Philosophy. Vol. I—Cosmogenesis, 676 pp.; Vol. II—Anthropogenesis, 798 pp., with index of xxx pp. Originally published by The Theosophical Publishing Co., Ltd., 7 Duke Street, Adelphi, London, W.C.; William Q. Judge, 117 Nassau Street, New York; The Manager of *The Theosophist*, Adyar, Madras, India: 1888.

The Key to Theosophy, being a Clear Exposition, in the Form of Question and Answer, of the Ethics, Science, and Philosophy, for the Study of which The Theosophical Society has been founded; 307 pp. Published by The Theosophical Publishing

438   H. P. BLAVATSKY, TIBET AND TULKU

Society, 7 Duke Street, Adelphi, London, W.C.; William
Q. Judge, 144 Madison Ave., New York: 1889. 2nd ed.
added a Glossary of 61 pp.

The Voice of the Silence, being Chosen Fragments from the
" Book of the Golden Precepts ", for the daily use of Lanoos
(Disciples); 97 pp. Published by The Theosophical Pub-
lishing Society, 1889.

Gems from the East: A Birthday Book of Precepts and Axioms.
Published by The Theosophical Publishing Society, 1890.

Transactions of the Blavatsky Lodge. Published by The Theo
sophical Publishing Society—in two parts: Part I, 1890;
Part II, 1891.

POSTHUMOUS WORKS

Nightmare Tales. A collection of seven occult stories, published
by The Theosophical Publishing Society, London, New York,
Madras, 1892.

The Theosophical Glossary; 389 pp. Published by The Theosophical Publishing Society, London, New York, Madras:
1892.

From the Caves and Jungles of Hindostan. Translated from the
Russian of Helena Petrovna Blavatsky by Mrs. Charles
Johnston. (A portion of Part I only). Published by The
Theosophical Publishing Society, London, 1892.

Zagadochniya plemena na Golubih Gorah (The Enigmatical Tribes
on the Azure-Blue Hills) in Russian: by Radda-Bai. 309 pp.
Published by V. I. Gubinsky at St. Petersburg (passed by the
Censor February 18, 1893—but with no publication date).
Originally published serially in *Russkiy Vestnik,* Vol. 174,
Dec., 1884; Vol. 175, Jan. and Feb., 1885; and Vol. 176,
March and April, 1885.

Durbar v Lahore (The Durbâr in Lahore) in Russian; by
Radda-Bai. Published as Part II of the above work.
Originally published serially in *Russkiy Vestnik,* Vol. 153,
May and June, 1881, and Vol. 154, July, 1881.

Zagadochniya plemena was translated into French under the
title: *Au Pays des Montagnes Bleues,* by Marc Semenoff: with
Preface written by Albert de Pouvourville (well-known scholar
and author). Published in 1926.

A Modern Panarion: A Collection of Fugitive Fragments from the pen of H. P. Blavatsky, 504 pp. Published by The Theosophical Publishing Society, London, New York and Madras, 1895. A selection of articles which were published in Spiritualistic journals (1874-1879) and some articles from early issues of *The Theosophist* (1879-1882).

Letters from H. P. Blavatsky to the American Conventions. Reprinted in pamphlet form; as for instance: *Five Messages from H. P. Blavatsky to the American Theosophists*; Theosophy Company, Los Angeles, 1922.

The Letters of H. P. Blavatsky to A. P. Sinnett and other miscellaneous Letters; Transcribed, Compiled, and with an Introduction by A. T. Barker; 404 pp. with index. Published by T. Fisher Unwin Ltd., Adelphi Terrace, London, and F. A. Stokes Co., New York, N.Y., 1925.

Some Unpublished Letters of Helena Petrovna Blavatsky, by Eugene Rollin Corson, B.S., M.D. Published by Rider & Co., Paternoster House, London [1929].

The Complete Works of H. P. Blavatsky, Edited by A. Trevor Barker. Published by Rider & Co., Paternoster House, London, E. C.

Volume I, 358 pp. with index. 1874-1879. Articles from Spiritualistic journals and from *The Theosophist*. Published 1933.

Volume II, 342 pp. with index. December 1879-May 1881. Articles from *The Theosophist*. Published 1933.

Volume III, 345 pp. with index. June 1881-June 1882. Articles from *The Theosophist*. Published 1935.

Volume IV, 367 pp. with index. June 1882-July 1883. Articles from *The Theosophist*. Published 1936.

H. P. Blavatsky Collected Writings, Edited by Boris de Zirkoff. Volume V, 416 pp. with Bibliography and index; preface, etc. xxxii pp., May 1883-November 1883. Published by the Philosophical Research Society, Inc., Los Angeles, 1950.

Volume VI, 481 pp. with Bibliography and index; preface, etc. liv pp. December 1883-November 1885. Published by the Blavatsky Writings Publication Fund, Los Angeles, 1954.

Volume VII, 433 pp. with Bibliography and index; preface, etc. xxxiv pp. January 1886-August 1887. Published by The Theosophical Publishing House, Adyar, 1958.

Volume VIII, 507 pp. with Bibliography and index; preface, etc. xxviii pp. September 1887-December 1887. Articles principally from *Lucifer*. Published at Adyar, 1960.

Volume IX, 487 pp. with Bibliography and index; preface, etc. xxx pp. January 1888-June 1888. Articles principally from *Lucifer*. Published at Adyar, 1962.

Volume X, 461 pp. with Bibliography and index; preface, etc. xxxiv pp. July 1888-January 1889. Articles principally from *Lucifer*, with the inclusion of *Transactions of the Blavatsky Lodge*, Parts I and II. Published at Adyar, 1964.

BOOKS ON OR ABOUT HELENA PETROVNA BLAVATSKY

(or in which she is mentioned)

Art of Life and How to Conquer Old Age, The: by William Kingsland. With an autobiographical appendix. C. W. Daniel Co., London, 1934; 102 pp.

Autobiography: by Princess Helene von Racowitza. Translated from the German by Cecil Marr, and published by Constables, London, 1910.

Blavatskaya, Yelena Petrovna, Biografichesky ocherk (Biographical Sketch): in Russian: by Helena Fyodorovna Pissarev. First published in an anthology called "Theosophical Problems" by the Russian Theosophical Society, about 1911.

H. P. Blavatsky and the Masters of Wisdom, by Annie Besant: 1907 and 1922.

H. P. Blavatsky and The Secret Doctrine, by Max Heindel. Introduction by Manly P. Hall. Phoenix Press, Los Angeles, 1933, 133 pp. index.

H. P. Blavatsky and the Theosophical Movement: A Brief Historical Sketch: by Charles J. Ryan: Theosophical University Press, Point Loma, California: 1937. 369 pp. index.

H. P. Blavatsky, as I Knew Her: by Alice L. Cleather. Thacker Spink & Co., Calcutta, 1923.

H. P. B., Concerning: by G. R. S Mead. The Theosophical Publishing House, Adyar. Pamphlets, iii. 1920.

H. P. Blavatsky, Her Life and Work for Humanity, by Alice L. Cleather: Thacker Spink & Co., 1922.

H. P. Blavatsky, In Memory of: by Some of Her Pupils. The Theosophical Publishing House, London, 1891 (in pamphlet form). Also The Blavatsky Association, London, 1931 (in book form).

H. P. B. Speaks: A Collection of Letters written by H. P. Blavatsky. Published by The Theosophical Publishing House, Adyar, India; 1951. Vol. I, viii, 248 pp.; Vol. II, xvi, 181 pp.

Madame Blavatsky; by G. Baseden Butt. Rider & Co., London, 1926.

Madame H. P. Blavatsky: *Her Occult Phenomena and the Society for Psychical Research*: by K. F. Vania. Sat Publishing Co., Bombay, 1951. 488 pp.

Madame Blavatsky, Defence of: by Beatrice Hastings. Vols. I and II. Published by the author, Worthing, Sussex, England. 1937. 60 and 105 pp.

" The Brothers " of H. P. Blavatsky: by Mary K. Neff. The Theosophical Publishing House, Adyar, 1932.

Contribution à l'Histoire de la Société Théosophique en France: by Charles Blech. Editions Adyar, Paris, France, 1933. 215 pp.

Dâmodar and the Pioneers of the Theosophical Movement. Compiled and Annotated by Sven Eek. Published by The Theosophical Publishing House, Adyar, India, 1965. 720 pp. with index and glossary.

Did Madame Blavatsky Forge the Mahatma Letters?: by C. Jinarâjadâsa. The Theosophical Publishing House, Adyar, 1934. 55 pp.

Early Teachings of the Masters: 1881-1883, *The*: Edited by C. Jinarâjadâsa, The Theosophical Press, Chicago, 1923. 245 pp.

Episodes from an Unwritten History: by Claude Bragdon; 2nd enl. ed., Rochester, The Manas Press, 1910. 109 pp.

Golden Book of the Theosophical Society, The: by C. Jinarâjadâsa. The Theosophical Publishing House, Adyar, 1925.

How Theosophy Came to Australia and New Zealand: by Mary K. Neff. Australian Section T.S., Sydney, 1943. 99 pp., Ill.

How Theosophy Came to Me: by C. W. Leadbeater. Theosophical Publishing House, Adyar, 1930.

Incidents in the Life of Madame Blavatsky: Compiled from Information Supplied by her Relatives and Friends, and Edited by A. P. Sinnett. George Redway, London, and J. W. Bouton, New York, 1886. 324 pp. 2nd ed. The Theosophical Publishing Society, London, 1913.

Letters from the Masters of the Wisdom: Transcribed and Annotated by C. Jinarâjadâsa. With a Foreword by Annie Besant. 1st Series: Theosophical Publishing House, Adyar, 1919: 124 pp.; 4th ed., 1948. 2nd Series: Theosophical Publishing House, Adyar, 1925; 191 pp.

Mahatma Letters to A. P. Sinnett, The: from the Mahatmas M. and K. H. transcribed, compiled, and with an Introduction by A. T. Barker. T. Fisher Unwin, London, 1923, 492 pp.; 3rd ed., The Theosophical Publishing House, Adyar, 1962, 524 pp. with index.

My Guest—H. P. Blavatsky: by Francesca Arundale. The Theosophical Publishing House, London, 1932.

Memorabilia. Reminiscences of a Woman Artist and Writer: by Isabel de Steiger. With a Preface by A. E. Waite, Rider & Co., London, 310 pp.

Moyo otrochestvo (My Adolescence), in Russian: by Vera Petrovna de Zhelihovsky (H.P.B.'s sister). Portions were included by A. P. Sinnett in his *Incidents, etc.*, under the title " Juvenile Recollections compiled for my Children."

Memories: by Count Axel Raoul Wachtmeister. John M. Watkins, London, 1936, 55 pp.

Obituary. The " Hodgson Report " on Madame Blavatsky: 1885-1960. By Adlai E. Waterman. Preface by N. Sri Ram. Published by The Theosophical Publishing House, Adyar, 1963. xx, 92 pp., folding diagrams.

Occult World, The: by Alfred Percy Sinnett. Trübner & Co., 1881. 172 pp.

" Occult World Phenomena " and the Society for Psychical Research, The: by A. P. Sinnett. George Redway, London, 1886. 60 pp.

Old Diary Leaves: The True History of The Theosophical Society: by Henry Steel Olcott. Vol. I: G. P. Putnam's Sons, New

York and London, *The Theosophist*, Madras: 1895. 491 pp. with index. Vols. II—VI, published by The Theosophical Publishing House, Adyar, 1900-1935.

People from the Other World: by Henry Steel Olcott. The American Publishing Co., Hartford, Connecticut, 1875. 492 pp.

Personal Memoirs of H. P. Blavatsky: Compiled by Mary K. Neff. With 12 illustrations. E. P. Dutton & Co., Inc., New York, 1937. 323 pp. with index.

Personality of H. P. Blavatsky, The: by C. Jinarâjadâsa. The Theosophical Publishing House, Adyar, 1930.

Real H. P. Blavatsky, The: A Study in Theosophy, and a Memoir of a Great Soul: by William Kingsland. Watkins, London, 1928. 322 pp.

Reminiscences of H. P. Blavatsky: by Bertram Keightley. Virile Sketches of H.P.B. at work. The Theosophical Publishing House, Adyar, 1931.

Reminiscences of H. P. Blavatsky and " The Secret Doctrine ": by the Countess Constance Wachtmeister and others. The Theosophical Publishing Society, London, 1893. 162 pp.

Report of Observations Made during a Nine Months Stay at the Head-quarters of The Theosophical Society at Adyar (Madras) India: by Dr. Franz Hartmann. Printed at the Scottish Press, by Graves, Cookson & Co., Madras, 1884. 60 pp.

Short History of The Theosophical Society, A: Compiled by Josephine Ransom, with a Preface by G. S. Arundale. The Theosophical Publishing House, Adyar, 1938. 591 pp. with Bibliography and Index.

Some Experiences in India: by W. T. Brown. The Theosophical Society, London, 1884. 19 pp.

Studies in Occult Philosophy: by G. de Purucker. Containing several articles on H. P. Blavatsky. The Theosophical University Press, Covina, California, 1945. 754 pp. with index.

The Theosophical Movement—1875-1925: A History and a Survey. Prepared by the United Lodge of Theosophists, Los Angeles. Published by E. P. Dutton & Co., New York, 1925. 705 pp.

The Theosophical Movement—1875-1950. Prepared by the United
Lodge of Theosophists. Published by The Cunningham
Press, Los Angeles, 1951. 351 pp. with index.

Tradition of Silence: by Arthur Gebhard. 1940.

Truth about H. P. Blavatsky, The (in Russian: " Pravda o Yelene
Petrovne Blavatskoy "): by Vera Petrovna de Zhelihovsky.
Issued as a pamphlet. Originally published in *Rebus,* Vol.
II, Nos. 40, 41, 43, 46, 47, 48; 1883.

Voice of the Soul, The: by Katherine Tingley. Contains a chapter
on H. P. Blavatsky. Published by the Woman's International
Theosophical League, Point Loma, California, 1928. 308 pp.

Wie ich mein Selbst fand (in German): by Princess Helene von
Racowitza; published by C. H. Schwetschke, Berlin, 1901;
2nd edition, Leipzig, 1911.

Wind of the Spirit: A Selection of Talks on Theosophy as related
primarily to Human Life and Human Problems: by G. de
Purucker. (Contains a chapter on " The Exoteric and
Esoteric H.P.B."). Theosophical University Press, Covina,
California, 1944. 254 pp.

THEOSOPHICAL PERIODICALS

(in which references are made to H. P. Blavatsky)

Arena, The: article " Madame Blavatsky in India," by W. Q.
Judge. March, 1892.

Canadian Theosophist, The. Monthly Organ of the Theosophical
Society in Canada. First issue, March 15, 1920. (Later
bi-monthly). In progress.

Journal of The Theosophical Society, Madras, India. Title for the
Supplement to *The Theosophist,* from January to December, 1884.
12 issues, pp. 1-168.

Lotus, Le. Revue de Hautes Études Théosophiques. Sous
l'inspiration de H. P. Blavatsky. Organ of the Isis Branch
of the Theosophical Society. Published from March, 1887
to March, 1889.

Lucifer. Monthly. Edited by H. P. Blavatsky (and Mabel
Collins until October, 1888): London, September, 1887 to

May, 1891. Thereafter edited by Annie Besant and G. R. S. Mead until August, 1897. Superseded by *The Theosophical Review*.

New Century, The. Weekly, New York. Editor, Katherine Tingley. First issue: September 30, 1897. With Vol. III, No. 47, October 6, 1900 issued from Point Loma, California, until Vol. VI, No. 20, March 29, 1903. Continued as:

New Century Path, The. Weekly, Vol. VI, No. 21, April 5, 1903 to Vol. X, No. 8. Continued as *The Century Path*, Vol. X, No. 9, Jan. 6, 1907, to Vol. XIV, No. 32, June 11, 1911. Superseded by *The Theosophical Path*.

Occult World, The. Monthly, Rochester, New York. Edited by Josephine W. Cables and W. T. Brown. Vols. I-III, April 1884 to March 1888.

Path, The. Monthly. A Magazine devoted to the Brotherhood of Humanity, Theosophy in America, and the Study of Occult Science, Philosophy, and Aryan Literature. Published and Edited at New York by William Q. Judge. Vols. I-X, April, 1886 to March, 1896. Superseded by *Theosophy*, April, 1896 to October, 1897. Continued as *Universal Brotherhood*, November, 1897 to March, 1899. Continued as *Universal Brotherhood Path*, April, 1899 to March, 1903.

Theosophia. Bi-monthly; later quarterly: Los Angeles, California. Started May-June, 1944: in progress. Sponsored by an international group of Theosophists.

Theosophical Forum, The. Monthly. New Series. Published under the authority of The Theosophical Society, Point Loma, California. Editor, G. de Purucker: September, 1929 to September 1942. (Editor: Arthur L. Conger at Covina. California: 1945-March 1951.) Vol. J, September, 1929 to Vol. XXIX, March, 1951.

Theosophical Path, The. Monthly. Published under the authority of The Theosophical Society, Point Loma, California, Editor, Katherine Tingley: July, 1911 to July, 1929. Editor, G. de Purucker: August, 1929 to December, 1935. Issued a serial under the title "H. P. Blavatsky, the Mystery": Vol. XXXVI, April, 1929 to Vol. XXXIX, January, 1931,

Theosophist, The. A Monthly Journal Devoted to Oriental Philosophy, Literature and Occultism. Conducted by H. P. Blavatsky: October, 1879 to 1885, under the auspices of The Theosophical Society. Bombay, 1879 to December, 1882; published at Adyar, Madras, January, 1883—in progress. Volumes run from October to September inclusive.

Theosophy. Monthly, published by The Theosophy Co., Los Angeles, California. Established November, 1912, by Robert Crosbie. In progress. Issues reprints of articles by H. P. Blavatsky and W. Q. Judge.

Word, The—A Monthly Magazine devoted to Philosophy, Science, Religion, Eastern Thought, Occultism, Theosophy, and the Brotherhood of Humanity. Edited by H. W. Percival, New York: The Theosophical Publishing Co. Vols. I-XXV, October, 1904 to September, 1917.

INDEX

INDEX

This index is intended to serve a dual purpose: that of a glossary as well as an index. Thus, when a term has been defined on the page where it has been used, it is so indicated in the index by means of the abbreviation *def.*, and this is placed first.

References to H. P. Blavatsky's major works are italicized and listed under book-titles, instead of under BLAVATSKY. Her lesser known books, and posthumous works, are listed under BLAVATSKY. Attention is called to this distinction: the work is listed under two categories: (1) " on the writing of " (2) citations from—abbreviated to " cited ". For example:

Isis Unveiled—on the writing of, 33 (et seq.)

Isis Unveiled—cited: on musical sand in California, 25 fn., (et seq.). Works by other authors, which are cited or referred to, are italicized and listed under book-titles.

ABBREVIATIONS

biog.	brief biographical sketch of
def.	defined (or definition supplied)
et seq.	et sequens (meaning " and the following " pages)
expl.	explanation of
fn.	footnote
i.e.	id est (meaning " that is ")
lit.	literally (or the literal meaning)
Mong.	Mongolian
pron.	pronounced
publ.	published or publication of
q.v.	quod vide (meaning " which see ")
re	regarding
Sans.	Sanskrit
Tib.	Tibetan

INDEX

A

ABLANATHALBA (Gnostic) def. 409; Greek letters of, 408

ABRACADABRA (Gnostic) def. 409

ABRASAX (Gnostic) def. 409

ADEPT, does not create anything new, 289; utilizes and manipulates materials which Nature has in store, 289; evolves shapes consciously, 290 fn.; can project any limb or the whole astral body, 332; demonstration of projection performed by an, 332; may enter a vacant carcass, 335; can project the astral body through thousands of miles of space, 340; is able to alter the normal processes when death occurs, 344; voluntary and conscious reincarnation of an, 344; three degrees of power of an, described, 345; of the Orphic Mysteries was initiated, 365; the three upâdhis can be separated by an, without killing himself, 370; Tulku is performed when an, separates and transfers the appropriate upâdhis, 373

ADEPTSHIP, is the crown of spiritual self-evolution, 261

ADHYÂYA (Sans.) def. 130 fn.

Aitareya Upanishad, refers to the Omnipresent Principle as the SELF, 417

ÂKARSHANA (Sans.), attraction (laws of) 327

ÂKÂSA, images of events are retained in, 135 fn.; matter may be defined as condensed, 261; permeates every atom of the sensuous universe, 292; concentration of, around physical body renders it invisible, 333

ÂKÂSIC RECORDS, H. P. B. was able to read the, 212

AKSAKOFF, N. ALEXANDER, extract from H. P. B.'s letter to, cited, 150-1; an eminent St. Petersburg publisher, 151 fn.

AMARAKA, the story of, and the Âvesa of Śankarâchârya, 315-7; clarification of the upâdhis of, in connection with Tulku, 378

AMITÂBHA, def. 88; or Ö-pa-me, 86; or Amita-Buddha or Amita-pho, 87-8; is

Chinese perversion of Sanskrit Amrita Buddha, 88

AMITA-BUDDHA, def. 87-8

AMRITA (Sans.) def. 88 fn.

ANAESTHESIA, of animals, 119-20 fn.; known and practised by Tibetan shepherds, 119-20

ANAESTHETIC, an, occasionally produces a state resembling the projection of the consciousness, 348

ANÂGARIKA (Sans. lit. houseless, i.e. an ascetic), Dharmapala becomes an, 65

ÂNANDAMAYA-KOSA (Sans.) def. 373; functioning of the, 373

ANNA (Sans.) def. 372

ANNAMAYA-KOSA (Sans.) def. 372; functioning of the, 372

ANI (Tib. 'a-ne—equivalent to a Bhikshunî or nun), H. P. B.'s experience with an, 127

ANIMA MUNDI (Latin—Soul of the World), or Astral Light, 135 fn.

ANTAR-YOGA (Sans.) def. 327

APOLLONIUS, an adept and magician, 332-3; his aethrobatic feats, 333

ARHATS (Sans. lit. worthy ones), it is not all, that get the fruition of the Nirvânic Path, 388

ARUNDALE, FRANCESCA, receives letter from Mahatma K. H., 410; Olcott writes memo to, re Narayan, 415

ÂRYA SAMÂJ a Hindu organization which was affiliated with the T. S. for a while, 322-3; Swâmi Dayânand Saraswati was leader of the, 322

Asia (magazine) cited: on Dharmapala's association with the T. S. and his Buddhist work, 61-5

ASOKA (Dharm-Asoka) biog. note, 124 fn.

ASTRAL BODY, a term used for three vehicles, 330; power of the, to manifest itself, 330 et seq.; on the projection of the, 331, 339-40; or Mâyâvi-rûpa may go anywhere and penetrate any obstacle, 334; Olcott's testimonial on the projection of the, 341; every man has a Higher Self and also an, 344

ASTRAL FLIGHT, Olcott's testimonial re Dâmodar's, 421-2

ASTRAL JOURNEY, performed by a Shaman, 113-5; of H. P. B., 120; or

transmission of, by agents, 276-99;
receipt of the first, in India by Mrs.
Sinnett—the "pink note incident",
279-84; transmission of, by Damodar,
285-6; by Djual Khul, 286-8; how
precipitation of, and transmission of,
are accomplished, 288-99; the first,
sent to A. O. Hume, 289-90; writing
of, is carried on by a sort of psychological telegraphy or an electro-
magnetic connection, 292; success of
writing of, depends on two factors, 292;
are not written, but impressed or
precipitated, 293; may be precipitated
in a language not known by sender,
293-4; how the color of, is prepared
and utilized, 294; paper of, may be
materialized, 295; processes in sending
on of, 296-8; receipt of, by Damodar,
401-2; receipt of, by a group of
doubters, 404-5; before the founding
of the T.S. Olcott received several,
without H. P. B.'s knowledge, 406 et
seq.; receipt of, by S. Ramaswamier,
405; Maj.-Gen. Morgan testifies to
receipt of, 412-3; Damodar writes to
Pillai re receipt of, 419-20
——Facsimiles, reproductions of (for
complete listing see under Facsimiles)
——Precipitation of, 222-99; materialization of the, 223-57; quality of the,
230-7; color of the, 237-42; caligraphy
of the, 242-54; permanence or
impermanence of the, 255-6; ability
to erase the, 256; by means of an
intermediate agent, 276-98; how, is
accomplished, 288-98; H. P. B.
describes processes she used in, 296-8;
how one process of, is done by
Mahatma M., 298
——Delivery of, 257-99; and extract-
ing from sealed envelopes, 258-62; by
normal procedures, 262-5; at any
specified spot, 265-73; to and from
Adyar, 268-73; by Mahatmas in
person, 273-5; by chelas in person,
275-6
——By Intermediate Agents—precipitation of and delivery of accomplished:
H. P. B.'s qualifications and abilities,
276-85, 296-8; Damodar's qualifications and abilities, 285-6; Djual
Khul's qualifications and abilities,
286-8
Mahatma Letters to A. P. Sinnett, The,
publ. in 1923, 160;—cited: on M.'s
visits to N. de Fadeyev, 18-19, 142;
on the two who were selected to
found the T.S., 58; on a century of

fruitless search, 59; on the Forlorn
Hope, 59; on Theosophy—no new
candidate, 59; on the Chiefs want a
Brotherhood of Humanity, 60; on the
greater work of the T.S., 60; on
H. P. B. in Tibet with the Masters,
133-5; on the retention of H. P. B.'s
principle and "the psychological
cripple," 143-4; on conversing and
teaching through astral light, 191; on
communicating by occult means,
192-3; on communicating through
sound and colors, 194-5; on the
writing of Isis Unveiled, 197, 210 fn.;
on correcting a passage in Isis Unveiled,
210 fn.; on a receipt for blue ink, 240;
on erased and re-precipitated portions
in a letter, 256; on the precipitation
and correction of letters, 256; re
sending of a telegram in K. H.'s own
handwriting, 263-4; on delivery and
sending of letters, 263-5, 267-8, 275-6;
on H. P. B.'s ability to produce
phenomena, 277; on the transmission
of letters by Djual Khul, 286-8; on
transmission of letters by Damodar,
286, 428; on transmission cf letters
by H. P. B., 296-8; on metaphysical
truths, 299; on returning from the
state of Tong-pa-nyi, 310; on thought
runs swifter than the electric fluid,
310; on H. P. B. as the "connecting
link," 354; on the real baitchooly (re
H. P. B.), 363; on H. P. B.'s real Self,
364-5; on the Chang-chubs who pass
from the body of one lama to another,
381-2; on having chelas attend to
correspondence, 427; on Djual Khul's
letter, 427-8
Maitreya Buddha (Sans.—in Tib.:
byams-pa mgon po—the Buddha of
the future period of the world), the
expected Buddha, 94-5; re the "Secret
Book" of, 186
Majji, a well-known female ascetic,
325-6 fn.; visited H. P. B., 326 fn.;
her remarks concerning H. P. B.,
326 fn.
Man, continually peoples his current in
space with a world of his own, 289
fn.; there is a mutual correlation
between a star and a, 310; how to
solve the A B C of the mystery of, 374
Manas (Sans.) def. 176; Higher and
Lower, 177, 372-3; Universal, in the
animal has begun and in man completed its differentiation into individual entities, 261; is dual in its
functioning, 372; with Kâma forms

second vol. towards end of year), 41;
re writing of, 156, 165, 179-88; re
publ. posthumous " third volume,"
159-60, 188; Countess Wachtmeister
on writing of, 179-83, 203; supervision
exercised over writing of, 182-4, 186;
H. P. B. on writing of, 184-7, 198-9,
219-20; the " Archaic Doctrine " of,
184; the " Preamble " to (although
written is not present in published
vols.), 186-8; *Champai chhos Nga* in
re, 186-7; H. P. B.'s plan for vols. I,
II and III, of, 187-8; H. Coryn on
the third vol. of, 188; re writing of,
by clairaudient dictation, 198; writing
of, by Directive Clairvoyance, 203-5;
Dr. Hübbe-Schleiden's narrative re
writing of, 208-9, 242; " will be the
triple production of M, Upasika and
K. H.", 247; " I certify that, is dictated
to Upasika partly by myself and
partly by my Brother K. H.—M.,"
248; " The certificate that, would be
the triple production of Upasika, M.
and myself is correct—K. H.," 249,
300; facsimile of a page of the MSS.
of, facing 283; writing of, by means
of a process analogous to Tulku, 306;
Archibald Keightley and Bertram
Keightley assist in preparation and
typewriting of the MSS. of, 355-6 fn.
——cited: on the: Books of *Kiu-te* and
the Book of Dzyan, 79-80, 384-5 fn.;
Yamabûshi, 117; machines depicting
celestial spheres and planets, 117 fn.;
Senzar and Sanskrit alphabets, 134
fn.; evanescent personalities and the
immortal Monad, 175-6; Astral Light
—the picture-gallery, 212; 3 teachers
that Col. Olcott had, 341 fn.; Cardinal
Cusa who sought recuperation in the
body of Copernicus, 344; voluntary
and conscious reincarnations of
Adepts, 344-5; three degrees of power
of transference, 345; superiority and
predominance of one principle, 362;
3 upâdhis which an adept may
separate, 370; Elect Race, 380; secret
of immortality on Earth, 380; nursery
for future human adepts, 381; Sons
of Will and Yoga, 381; Tharlam—
the Path of Deliverance from transmigration, 382; Ku-sum, 383
——termed the *Third Volume*: on the
posthumous publ. 159-60, 188
SEDMICHKA (Russian) def. 175 fn.;
H. P. B.'s nickname when a child, 175
SEERESS OF PREVORST, a precocious
person born out of time, 200

SELF, what is, 310
SEMEDO, author of *Histoire de la Chine*,
338; is cited on the supernatural
powers of the Taossé, 339
SEMPA (Tib. sems-pa, pron. sempa, lit.
to think), def. 383
SEMS (Tib. pron. sem: kun-gzhíi sems—
the eternal spirit), def. 383
SENSES, the sixth and seventh, 200
SENZAR, def. 134 fn.; re the alphabet and
language of, 134 fn.
SERAPIS, facsimiles of script associated
with the Master, facing 246, 247;
sends letter to Col. Olcott through
Hilarion, 272-3; designated himself a
member of the Brotherhood of Luxor,
406; sent several letters to Olcott
independently of H. P. B. before the
founding of the T.S., 406; text of
letters from, received by Olcott, 407,
408
SETH, significance of, 219-220
SEVEN PRINCIPLES OF MAN (see under
PRINCIPLES)
SEVENTH SENSE, may be developed by
occult methods, 200
SHABERON(s), the performance of the
Incarnation of a Living Buddha by a
Superior or, 101-5; demonstrates the
ability to project the individuality-
consciousness, 105; H. P. B.'s rescue
by a, 115; Tsong-Kha-pa is called a,
125; rendered " reincarnations " or
Khubilhans, 126; the Tulku performed
by the, clarified, 377-8
SHAKANG (Tib. mchod-khang, pron.
shakhang) def. 137 fn.
SHAMAN (Mong.) def. 102; account of
an astral journey by a, 113-5
SHANGNA ROBES or VESTURES, the three,
def. 386-7; what are the, 387
SHIEN-SIEN (Chinese: " a state of bliss
and soul-freedom, during which a
man can travel in spirit where he
likes." *Th. Gloss.* 297), 339
SHRINE, THE, a means of communication to and from the Mahatmas and
Adyar, 269-73; Mrs. Sinnett tests use
of, 269; description of, 269-70, 413;
Kingsland's description of, 270; Hartmann testifies to use of, 270-1; Olcott
tests use of, 272-3; Maj.-Gen.
Morgan's testimonial re efficacy of,
411-3
SIDDHA (Sans. lit. one endowed with
supernatural faculties), by practice of
Râja—Yoga one becomes a, 328
SIDDHI(s) (Sans.) def. 3, 189; H. P. B.'s
use of, 2-3; Khechara is one of the

appropriate upâdhis, 373; 7 types of,
enumerated, 376: (1) of the Dalai and
Tashi Lamas clarified, 377; (2) cf the
Shaberon clarified, 377-8; (3) of
Sankarâchârya—classical example of
Âvesa, 378; (4) of the Fakir clarified;
378; (5) of Kunâla upon a fakir
clarified, 378-9; (6) of Kunâla and
Damodar clarified, 379; (7) in connection with H. P. B., 379-80; on the
origin of the science of, 380-5; having
reached Tharlam one cannot perform,
382-3; freed from transmigration one
cannot perform, 383-4; Trul-pa (Tib.
sPrul-pa) equivalent to, 384; the
culminating achievement of, 385-9;
in connection with Tong-pa-nyid,
385, 387-8; in connection with the
Shangna Robes or the Trikâya, 386-8;
when, is no longer required, 388

TULPA (Tib. sprul-pa, pron. tulpa, lit.
to appear in a body), 308

TURNER, SAMUEL, CAPTAIN, the second
emissary to the court of the Tashi
Lama, 91, 106-7; author of *An Account
of an Embassy to the Court of the Teshoo
Lama in Tibet*, 106-7

T'SEG (Tib.) def. 75, 308

U

UDAMBARA (Sans. *udumbara*: the *ficus
glomerata* or the *nîla udumbara*), the
rarity of the flower of the, 389

United, a novel by A. P. Sinnett, 184 fn.;
re review of, by H. P. B., 184-5; 2
pages of review of, were dictated, 185

Unseen Universe, The (by B. Stewart and
P. G. Tait), cited on magnetic effluvia,
220; re the authors of, 220 fn.

UNWALA, PROFESSOR J. N., joined the
T.S. in 1882, 405; was one of a group
who received a message from Mahatma
M., 405

UPADESA (Sans.) def. 119 fn.

UPÂDHI(s) (Sans.) def. 370; there are
three distinct, in man, 370; enumeration of the three, 371; the key to the
functioning of the, is supplied by the
sevenfold classification, 371; exposition of the, 371-3; Tulku is performed
by means of the separation of, and
transference of, 373

UPÂSAKA (Sans.: masc. upâsaka; fem.
upâsikâ) def. 124 fn.

UPÂSIKÂ (Sans.) def. 248; a term applied
to H. P. B. by her Teachers, 248;
"*The Secret Doctrine* is the triple
prcduction of, M and myself—K. H.",
249

V

VAJRADHARA (Sans. lit. Holder of the
Thunderbclt), a title bestowed on the
Dalai Lama, 81

VAJRAPÂNI (Sans. lit. Thunderbolt-
wielder), 389

VAJRASATTVA (Sans. lit. diamond-heart
or diamond-essence), equivalent to
Dorjesempa, 382

VAKIL (Anglo-Indian) def. 263 fn.

VIHÂRA (Sans.) def. 126 fn.; Dharmapala erects a, 65

VIJÑÂNA (Sans.) def. 372

VIJÑÂNAMAYA-KOSA (Sans.) def. 372;
functioning of the, 372-3

VÎNÂ-DEVAS (Sans. vînâ—lute; devas—
gods; devîs—goddesses), 174

VIRGIN FIRE, def. 297

VIRGIN STONE, use of the, 297-8

Voice of the Silence, The, (written in
Fontainebleau) publ. 41, 157; belongs
to the same series as that from which
the Stanzas of Dzyan were taken, 79;
H. P. B.'s inscription in her own ccpy
of, 363

——cited on the: Iddhis and Siddhis, 3;
Kundalinî, 129-30; Khechara (sky-
walker), 130; Open and Secret Paths,
386-7; Nirvânic Path and Nirvâna-
Dharma, 388

VOID, DOCTRINE OF THE, of Northern
Buddhists, 309; equivalent to Tong-
pa-nyid (q. v.), 309-10

VYAVAHÂRA-VIDYÂ (Sans.) is an exhibition of scientific or technical
skill, 327

W

WACHTMEISTER, CONSTANCE—COUNTESS,
author of *Remi uscences of H. P. Blavatsky and " The Secret Doctrine,"* 20, 181;
narrates the account of H. P. B.'s
meeting with Master Morya, 17-23;
with H. P. B. at Würzburg, 19, 40,
181; in England, 20, 41; why she
joined the T.S., 20; biog. 181 fn.;